Managing Human Resources in Central and Eastern Europe

Against the backdrop of ancient cultures, a communist legacy and eventual institutional atrophy, many of the societies of Central and Eastern Europe have pursued aggressive development trajectories since the early 1990s. This part of Europe is now characterized by a rising economic heterogeneity and a rapidly changing socio-cultural context, underscored by waves of restructuring, privatization, increasing foreign direct investment and an emerging individualism. While there has been a growing interest in the transition economies in the past number of years, the contemporary nature of human resource management in these societies is not well documented.

This long-awaited text seeks to chart the contemporary landscape of HRM in this region. In doing this, it describes key aspects of the transition process as experienced in each of the economies under consideration, as well as describing key legislative and labour market developments and reforms. Finally, it discusses key trends in HRM policy and practice.

Michael J. Morley is Professor of Management and Head of the Department of Management and Marketing at the Kemmy Business School, University of Limerick, Ireland.

Noreen Heraty is Assistant Dean for Academic Affairs and Senior Lecturer in Human Resource Management at the Kemmy Business School, University of Limerick, Ireland.

Snejina Michailova is Professor of International Business at the University of Auckland Business School, New Zealand.

Routledge Global Human Resource Management Series

Edited by Randall S. Schuler, Susan E. Jackson, Paul Sparrow, and Michael Poole

Routledge Global Human Resource Management is an important new series that examines human resources in its global context. The series is organized into three strands: content and issues in global human resource management (HRM); specific HR functions in a global context; and comparative HRM. Authored by some of the world's leading authorities on HRM, each book in the series aims to give readers comprehensive, in-depth, and accessible texts that combine essential theory and best practice. Topics covered include cross-border alliances, global leadership, global legal systems, HRM in Asia, Africa and the Americas, industrial relations, and global staffing.

Managing Human Resources in Cross Border Alliances
Randall S. Schuler, Susan E. Jackson, and Yadong Luo

Managing Human Resources in Africa
Edited by Ken N. Kamoche, Yaw A. Debrah, Frank M. Horwitz, and Gerry Nkombo Muuka

Globalizing Human Resource Management
Paul Sparrow, Chris Brewster, and Hilary Harris

Managing Human Resources in Asia-Pacific
Edited by Pawan S. Budhwar

International Human Resource Management (second edition)
Policy and practice for the global enterprises
Dennis R. Briscoe and Randall S. Schuler

Managing Human Resources in Latin America
An agenda for international leaders
Edited by Marta M. Elvira and Anabella Davila

Global Staffing
Edited by Hugh Scullion and David G. Collings

Managing Human Resources in Europe
A thematic approach
Edited by Henrik Holt Larsen and Wolfgang Mayrhofer

Managing Human Resources in the Middle East
Edited by Pawan S. Budhwar and Kamel Mellahi

Managing Global Legal Systems
International employment regulation and competitive advantage
Gary W. Florkowski

Global Industrial Relations
Edited by Michael J. Morley, Patrick Gunnigle, and David G. Collings

Managing Human Resources in North America
Current issues and perspectives
Edited by Steve Werner

Global Leadership
Research, Practice, Development
Edited by Mark E. Mendenhall, Gary Oddou, Allan Bird and Martha L. Maznevski

Global Compensation
Foundations and Perspectives
Edited by Luis Gomez-Mejia and Steve Werner

Global Performance Management
Edited by Arup Varma, Pawan S. Budhwar and Angelo DeNisi

Managing Human Resources in Central and Eastern Europe
Edited by Michael J. Morley, Noreen Heraty and Snejina Michailova

Forthcoming:

Global Careers
Michael Dickman and Yehuda Baruch

Managing Human Resources in Central and Eastern Europe

Edited by Michael J. Morley,
Noreen Heraty and Snejina Michailova

Routledge
Taylor & Francis Group

LONDON AND NEW YORK

First published 2009
by Routledge
2 Park Square, Milton Park, Abingdon, Oxon OX14 4RN

Simultaneously published in the USA and Canada
by Routledge
270 Madison Avenue, New York, NY 10016

Routledge is an imprint of the Taylor & Francis Group, an informa business

© 2009 Michael J. Morley, Noreen Heraty and Snejina Michailova

Typeset in Times New Roman by
Florence Production Ltd, Stoodleigh, Devon
Printed and bound in Great Britain by
TJ International Ltd, Padstow, Cornwall

British Library Cataloguing in Publication Data
A catalogue record for this book is available from the British Library

Library of Congress Cataloging in Publication Data
Managing human resources in Central and Eastern Europe /
edited by Michael J. Morley, Noreen Heraty and Snejina Michailova
    p. cm.
  Includes bibliographical references and index
1. Personnel management–Europe, Eastern.   2. Personnel management–Europe,
Central.   3. Personnel management–Former Soviet republics.   I. Morley,
Michael.   II. Heraty, Noreen.   III. Michailova, Snejina, 1965–
HF5549.2.E92M36 2009
658.300943–dc22   2008024911

ISBN10: 0–415–40560–2 (hbk)
ISBN10: 0–415–40561–0 (pbk)
ISBN10: 0–203–88633–x (ebk)

ISBN13: 978–0–415–40560–7 (hbk)
ISBN13: 978–0–415–40561–4 (pbk)
ISBN13: 978–0–203–88633–5 (ebk)

Contents

List of illustrations

FIGURES

TABLES

Foreword

Global HRM is a series of books edited and authored by some of the best and most well-known researchers in the field of human resource management. This series is aimed at offering students and practitioners accessible, coordinated and comprehensive books in global HRM. To be used individually or together, these books cover the main bases of comparative and international HRM. Taking an expert look at an increasingly important and complex area of global business, this is a groundbreaking new series that answers a real need for serious textbooks on global HRM.

Several books in this series, **Global HRM**, are devoted to human resource management policies and practices in multinational enterprises. For example, some books focus on specific areas of global HRM policies and practices, such as global leadership development, global staffing and global labour relations. Other books address special topics that arise in multinational enterprises across the globe, such as managing HR in cross-border alliances, developing strategies and structures, and managing legal systems for multinational enterprises. In addition to books on various HRM topics in multinational enterprises, several other books in the series adopt a comparative, and within region, approach to understanding global human resource management. These books on comparative human resource management can adopt two major approaches. One approach is to describe the HRM policies and practices found at the local level in selected countries in several regions of the world. This approach utilizes a common framework that makes it easier for the reader to systematically understand the rationale for the existence of various human resource management activities in different countries and easier to compare these activities across countries within a region. The second approach is to describe the HRM issues and topics that are most relevant to the companies in the countries of the region.

This book, *Managing Human Resources in Central and Eastern Europe,* takes the first approach as a comparative human resource management book in describing the human resource policies and practices in nine Central and Eastern European nations. Michael Morley, Noreen Heraty and Snejina Michailova serve as editors of this book and authors of the opening chapter that provides an excellent overview of the state of the art and state of the practice of HRM in several Central and Eastern Europe nations today. In the following nine chapters the expertise of almost twenty country-based authors is represented. The countries described include: Estonia, Lithuania, Poland, the Czech Republic, Slovakia, Hungry, Slovenia, Bulgaria, and Russia. Each chapter follows a similar framework and offers the reader a complete set of very useful references for each country. We are convinced that readers will find this book an invaluable one in the **Global HRM** Series.

This Routledge series, **Global HRM**, is intended to serve the growing market of global scholars and professionals who are seeking a deeper and broader understanding of the role and importance of human resource management in companies as they operate throughout the world. With this in mind, all books in the series provide a thorough review of existing research and numerous examples of companies around the world. In addition, many of the books in the series include at least one detailed case description that serves as convenient practical illustrations of topics discussed in the book.

Because a significant number of scholars and professionals throughout the world are involved in researching and practicing the topics examined in this series of books, the authorship of the books and the experiences of companies cited in the books reflect a vast global representation. The authors in the series bring with them exceptional knowledge of the human resource management topics they address, and in many cases the authors have been the pioneers for their topics. So we feel fortunate to have the involvement of such a distinguished group of academics in this series.

The publisher and editor also have played a major role in making this series possible. Routledge has provided its global production, marketing and reputation to make this series feasible and affordable to academics and practitioners throughout the world. In addition, Routledge has provided its own highly qualified professionals to make this series a reality. In particular we want to indicate our deep appreciation for the work of our series editor, Francesca Heslop. She has been behind the series from the very beginning and has been invaluable in providing the needed support and encouragement to us and to the many authors in the series. She, along with her production editor Antonia Edwards, has helped make the process of completing this book an enjoyable one. We would also like to thank John Szilagyi, Simon Whitmore, Russell George and Lisa Williams. For everything they have done, we thank them all.

Randall S. Schuler, Rutgers University and GSBA Zurich
Paul Sparrow, Lancaster University
Susan E. Jackson, Rutgers University and GSBA Zurich
Michael Poole, Cardiff University

Contributors

EDITORS

Michael J. Morley [michael.morley@ul.ie] is Professor of Management and Head of the Department of Management and Marketing at the Kemmy Business School, University of Limerick, Ireland, where he teaches international management. He has co-authored/edited some 17 books and more than 100 book chapters and refereed journal articles. Among his recent books are *Global Industrial Relations* (Routledge, 2006), *International Human Resource Management and International Assignments* (Palgrave 2006), *New Directions in Expatriate Research* (Palgrave 2006), *Human Resource Management in Europe: Evidence of Convergence* (Butterworth-Heinemann, 2004) and *New Challenges for European Human Resource Management* (Palgrave Macmillan, 2000). His refereed journal articles have appeared in sources such as the *Journal of World Business*, *Advances in International Management*, *International Journal of Human Resource Management*, *Human Resource Management Journal* and *Human Resource Management Review*. Associate Editor of the *Journal of Managerial Psychology* and Regional Editor of the *European Journal of International Management*, his Editorial Board memberships include *International Journal of Cross Cultural Management*, *Leadership and Organization Development Journal*, the *International Journal of Employment Studies* and the *International Journal of Strategic Change Management*.

Noreen Heraty [noreen.heraty@ul.ie] is Assistant Dean for Academic Affairs at the Kemmy Business School, University of Limerick, Ireland. She has co-authored/co-edited five books, guest edited several journal special issues and has produced numerous book chapters and refereed journal articles in sources such as *International Studies of Management and Organization*, *International Journal of Manpower*, *Journal of Managerial Psychology* and *Personnel Review*. Her research interests include the creation and development of learning environments at the organizational level; competency development of HR practitioners and the nature of multinational HR operations across countries.

Snejina Michailova (s.michailova@auckland.ac.nz) is Professor of International Business at The University of Auckland Business School. She is a graduate of Copenhagen Business School, Denmark (PhD in 1997) and the University of National and World Economy, Sofia, Bulgaria (MSc in 1989). Her main research areas are international management and knowledge management. She has co-edited the books *Fieldwork in Transforming Societies: Understanding Methodology from Experience* (Palgrave Macmillan, 2004) and *Knowledge Governance: Processes and Perspectives* (Oxford University Press, 2008). Her academic work has been published in, among others, *Business Strategy Review, California Management Review, Employee Relations, European Management Journal, European Journal of International Management, Journal of Knowledge Management, Journal of Management Studies, Journal of World Business, Long Range Planning, Management International Review, Management Learning, Organizational Dynamics,* and *The Academy of Management Executive.* She was Editor Europe for *Journal of World Business* from 2001 to 2007.

CONTRIBUTORS

Ruth Alas [ruth.alas@ebs.ee] is Professor of Management at the Estonian Business School. She has a PhD in economics and a PhD in business administration. She has written 17 books in the Estonian language, including: *Fundamentals of Management, Human Resource Management, Organizational Change and Learning* and *Strategic Management.* Her research focuses on behavioural and institutional factors influencing changes in organizations. She has written chapters for the books *HRM in Europe: Evidence of Convergence?* (Elsevier, 2004) and *HRM in Europe: A Thematic Approach* (Routledge, 2006). She has published in international journals such as: *Human Resource Development International* and *Women in Management Review.*

Jana Blštáková [j.blstak@euba.sk] is an Assistant Professor at the Department of Management, Faculty of Business Management, University of Economics in Bratislava. After graduating from the University of Economics in Bratislava (2003) specializing in Personnel Management she became an internal doctoral student at the Management Department at the University of Economics under the supervision of associate professor Anna Kachaňáková, PhD, the leader of the team of Personnel Management at the Management Department. In her doctoral studies she focuses on HRM in the context of Business Process Modelling. After one year of internal doctoral studies she became the professor's assistant and continued her studies externally. She is a member of the course team for Human Resource Management and the course Employee Compensation System and Benefits. She is the co-author of two textbooks for the course and many papers at international conferences and articles in professional journals. She's been active in projects focusing on the area of HRM. She is also the contact person for the Slovak team within the CRANET project on international HRM.

Ilona Bučiūnienė [ilobuc@ism.lt] is a Professor at the University of Management and Economics (ISM) in Lithuania, where she directs the HRM Programme in the Master of Management Studies Degree. Her PhD dissertation focused on changes in employee motivation in Lithuanian industrial companies during the transition to a market economy period (1996). Her research and publications area is HRM, especially employee motivation, job satisfaction and commitment to organizations in the business and health care sectors in the context of a changing environment.

Igor Gurkov [igor_gurkov@yahoo.com] graduated with distinction from the Economics Faculty of Moscow State University and subsequently received a PhD in organizational economics from Moscow State University. Between 1992 and 1993 he was a Post-doctoral Fellow of the Faculty of Industrial Engineering and Management of Technion – Israel Institute of Technology. Between 1994 and 1997, he was a research fellow at Erasmus University, Rotterdam. Since 1997, Igor has been Professor of Management at the State University – Higher School of Economics, Moscow, taking visiting and adjunct positions in such places as the University of Michigan, Maastricht School of Management and the Academy of the National Economy of the Russian Government. He has published some seven books, including *Management Development in Russia* (Geneva, ILO, 1997), and more than 80 academic articles in such journals as *European Management Journal, Post-Communist Economies, Journal for East European Management Studies* and *Thunderbird International Business Review.*

Zuzana Joniakova [joniakov@euba.sk] is a graduate of the University of Economics in Bratislava, where she is currently employed as Assistant Professor at the Department of Management. She is a member of the Personnel Management team at the Department of Management, where she focuses on the area of human resources management, in particular on employees' compensation and reward systems. She is the co-author of several textbooks and monographs in this area. Her research interest is currently focused on applying key functions of HRM in the conditions of the present business environment in Slovakia. She is also a member of the team for the CRANET project on international HRM in Slovakia.

Tõnu Kaarelson [tonu.kaarelson@ebs.ee] received the MBA degree from Tallinn University of Technology. At the beginning of the 1990s he was a co-founder and consultant in Estonian leading consultancies dealing with executive training, management consultation and recruitment services. Since 1999 he has been the Director of the Management Institute and a lecturer at the Estonian Business School. His research is focused on strategic and international issues in HRM. He is the author of several papers on comparative HRM published in international journals and has presented at several conferences. He has carried out numerous consultancy assignments focused on organization and human resource development in Estonian companies and public sector organizations.

Anna Kachaňáková [kachanak@euba.sk] is an Associate Professor in the Management Faculty at the University of Economics in Bratislava, where she leads the HRM team of academics. Her research, pedagogical and publishing interests focus on the issues of human resources management and corporate culture. She has been an author and co-author of numerous monographs, university textbooks and published papers within the area of her professional orientation. Among her most significant publications are *Human Resources Management* (2003) and *Corporate Culture* (2003). She has been leading three funded projects for the Ministry of Education of the Slovak Republic. The most recent project which she is leading seeks to solve the issue of human resources management in Slovak enterprises in the context of the latest European trends. She is also a leader of a Slovak team involved in research within the CRANET project on International Human Resource Management. Anna is also a member of three scholarly committees, a lecturer of doctoral students in the area of Company Management and a member of the editorial committee of the journal *The Personnel and Wage Advisor*.

Josef Koubek [koubek@vse.cz] is Professor Emiretus at the Department of Personnel Management, University of Economics, Prague, Czech Republic. He has authored around 350 publications, including more than 80 in international publications. His most important publications include: *Řízení lidských zdrojů. Základy moderní personalistiky* (Human resource management. Principles of modern personnel management) (Praha, Management Press, 1995), *Personální práce v malých podnicích* (Personnel management in small business) (Praha, Grada, 1996), *ABC praktické personalistiky* (ABC of personnel practice) (Praha, Linde, 2000), *Anglicko-český výkladový slovník personalistiky* (English–Czech glossary of HRM terms) (Praha, Management Press, 2003), *Řízení pracovního výkonu* (Performance management) (Praha, Management Press, 2004), *Německo český výkladový slovník personalistiky* (German–Czech glossary of HRM terms) (Praha, Management Press, 2005).

Tadeusz Listwan [tadeusz.listwan@ae.wroc.pl] is a Professor and Head of the HRM Department at Wroclaw University of Economics and Vice-Rector of the Higher School of Management and Banking in Poznan. He holds Master of Economy and Doctor of Economy degrees and is a full Professor of HRM from Wroclaw University of Economics. He has published over a dozen books, several of which have attained significant awards, and more than 100 other publications. He's a member of the Management Committee at the Polish Academy of Sciences.

Olga Nachtmannova [nachtman@euba.sk] is an Assistant Professor at the Management Department, Faculty of Business Management, University of Economics in Bratislava. She teaches Human Resources Management and Work Organization. She has co-authored an HR textbook and presented many papers at international conferences. She's been active in projects focusing on the area of HRM. She is also a member of the Slovak team within the CRANET project on international HRM. She is also active in Slovak politics. She has been a member of the Slovak Parliament since 2006.

Aleksy Pocztowski [pocztowa@janek.ae.krakow.pl] is Professor, Head of the Department of Personnel Management and Dean of the Faculty of Economics and International Relations at the Krakow University of Economics. An academic teacher and researcher in the field of Strategic and International Human Resources Management, he is the author and editor of more than 100 publications. His recent books include *Human Resources Management: Strategies-Processes-Methods* (2003), *International HRM* (2002), *HRM in M&A* (2004), *Best Practices in HRM in Poland* (2002–4). During his research career he has held scholarships and grants from, among others, the DAAD (German Academic Exchange Service) and Volkswagen Foundation (Germany).

József Poór [poor@ktk.pte.hu] is Professor of Management at the University of Pecs (Hungary), where he currently teaches International Management, Human Resource Management and International Human Resource Management in English and in Hungarian. Dr Poór earned his PhD from the Hungarian Academy of Sciences. He has taught International Management and International Human Resource Management at different American (CSU-Cleveland, PAMI-Honolulu, Bellarmine-Louisville, EKU-Richmond, SU-Saginaw) and European (CU-Lyon) business schools. He has been a management consultant and senior manager in different professional service firms.

Asta Pundziene [astpun@ism.lt] is a Professor of Human Resource Development and Change Management at the University of Management and Economics (ISM) in Lithuania, having earlier in her career worked at Vytautas Magnus University, Kaunas, Lithuania. Asta has also served as a National Seconded Expert (END) at the European Training Foundation (ETF) in Turin, Italy. Since 2004 she has worked as Head of the Research Unit and Director of the Change Management Programme at ISM. Since 1997 she has been an academic visitor at, among others, the Free University of Amsterdam, Uppsala University, Heidelberg University and Sheffield University.

Zuzana Roby [zuzanaroby@euba.sk] is a University teacher at the University of Economics in Bratislava, Faculty of Business Management – Department of Management (Teacher and Coordinator for the subject Management Simulations), teaching Management Simulations in English (for international students) (teacher of the subject International Management and Business). She works part time as a methodologist in the Methodology Centre of Pedagogy in Bratislava and teaches English part time at the Ministry of Economy.

Marzena Stor [marzena.stor@wp.pl] is Associate Professor at the Department of Human Resources Management, Wroclaw University of Economics (WUE), Poland. She received her doctorate in Management Economics from the Faculty of Management and Computer Science at WUE. Her major scientific interests cover strategic and cross-cultural aspects of HRM, interpersonal business communication and managing international teams. She has published around 30 scientific articles as well as chapters in scholarly books. She is the co-author of two well-recognized books in Poland: *Human Resources Management* and *Dictionary of HRM*.

Ivan Svetlik [ivan.svetlik@fdv.uni-lj.si] is Professor of HRM, labour market and employment policy at Ljubljana University. He chairs the Organizations and Human Resources (OHRRC) Research Centre. His research is focused on employment, knowledge, education and training. He co-edited *HRM's Contribution to Hard Work*

(Peter Lang, 2005); contributed to CRANET publications such as *Human Resource Management in Europe* (Elsevier, 2004); to *Europe's New State of Welfare: Unemployment, employment policies and citizenship* (Policy Press, 2002), and to the *European Journal of Vocational Training*.

Elizabeth Vatchkova [evatchkova@cablebg.net] is a Professor at the International University, Sofia, and President of the International Business School Transbusiness – E, also based in Sofia. She lectures primarily in strategic HRM and strategic management. She is the Bulgarian partner in the CRANET project on international HRM and has authored more than 80 publications in Bulgaria and abroad, including *HRM – European Comparative Research* and a *Practical Handbook on HRM*. She is a founding member of the Bulgarian Human Resource Management and Development Association and served as its Vice-President between 2000 and 2003.

Olga Zelenova [ozelenova@hse.ru] is Associate Professor of the Department of HRM at the State University – Higher School of Economics, Moscow. She also teaches in ANBA-accredited MBA programmes at the Academy of National Economy and other Moscow business schools. She is author of 36 publications, including the *Handbook in HRM of the Russian Center for Distance Learning* (International Labour Organization). She has been involved in various research and consulting projects and currently participates in the Russian part of the CRANET project on international HRM.

Darina Zubrikova [dzubrik@euba.sk] is an Assistant Professor in the Management Department at the Faculty of Business Management, University of Economics, in Bratislava. She graduated from the University of Economics in Bratislava specializing in Personnel Management. In 2003 she became a professor's assistant and started her external doctoral studies at the Management Department at the University of Economics under the supervision of associate professor Anna Kachaňáková, PhD. She is a member of the course team for Human Resources Management and the course Job Organization. She is a co-author of the textbook for the course and many papers at international conferences and articles in professional journals. She's been active in projects focusing on the area of HRM. She is also a member of the Slovak team within the project on international HRM.

Studying human resource management in the international context

The case of Central and Eastern Europe

SNEJINA MICHAILOVA, NOREEN HERATY
AND MICHAEL J. MORLEY

INTRODUCTION

Like all edited books, this volume is a result of the collective efforts over a long
period of time of a number of individual researchers and research teams with whom
we have had the pleasure of working. Many trade-offs have had to be made in terms
of the range and depth of the material presented in the text, but our guiding principle
was always to ensure an appropriate treatment of subject and of a geographic territory
not historically well documented. With this in mind, and drawing upon the expertise
of local authors/author teams in each country, we set ourselves the task of charting
the landscape of human resource management (HRM) in the complex terrain that is
contemporary Central and Eastern Europe and to do so in a way that would provide a
broad account of commonalities and differences apparent in the range of economies
examined. We openly acknowledge that each of the countries under investigation
here is deserving of further in-depth analyses in its own right. That, however, is a
task for others and for another day and one which will no doubt excavate in a much
deeper way than we have attempted here in this broader regional comparative
volume. Dedicated country-specific volumes on HRM in Central and Eastern
Europe in this genre are beginning to emerge (see, for example, the edited
volume by Domsch and Lidokhover (2007) on *Human Resource Management
in Russia*).

Arguing that there are significant structural/institutional and configurational
differences, along with significant practice differences, in HRM in Central and
Eastern Europe (CEE) in contrast to Western Europe, *Managing Human Resources in
Central and Eastern Europe* provides country derived, comparative, accounts of

HRM in Estonia, Lithuania, Poland, the Czech Republic, Slovakia, Hungary, Slovenia, Bulgaria and Russia. It details key aspects of the transition process as experienced in each of these economies under consideration, describes key legislative and labour market developments and reforms and discusses key trends in HRM policy and practice which are evident at organizational level.

In this introductory chapter, we explain the origin, the motivation and the purpose of the book. We then outline a number of main themes and issues that are of significance when studying human resource management in an international and comparative context and, in this instance, the context of Central and Eastern Europe. Finally, we introduce the contributions.

THE ORIGIN OF THE BOOK

Against the backdrop of ancient cultures, a communist legacy and eventual institutional atrophy, many of the societies of CEE have pursued aggressive development trajectories since the early 1990s. This part of Europe is now characterized by a rising economic heterogeneity and a rapidly changing socio-cultural context, underscored by waves of restructuring, privatization, increasing foreign direct investment and an emerging individualism. However, while there has been a growing interest in the transition economies in the past number of years, the contemporary nature of HRM in these societies is not well documented.

This volume in the Routledge Global HRM series represents one attempt to address this lacuna. The Global HRM Series has dedicated itself to providing accessible, coordinated, comprehensive texts on a diverse range of topics in global HRM. The texts to date have taken different approaches, some dedicated to providing comparative accounts of HRM in particular regions, including Africa, Asia-Pacific, Europe, Latin America, the Middle East and North America, others taking a particular global HRM practice as their point of departure, including, for example, global leadership, global careers, global industrial relations, global legal systems, global staffing and global compensation. This volume is designed to complement the earlier geographic regions covered in the series and to contribute to the emerging understanding of people management practices in this underdocumented region.

Several of the chapter contributors are members of the Cranfield Network on Comparative Human Resource Management (CRANET) and draw upon HRM data gathered under the auspices of this Network to detail the situation in their respective countries. The Network is a collaboration between 42 universities and business schools which

● carries out a regular international comparative survey of organizational policies and practices in comparative HRM across Europe; and

● provides benchmarks for comparing Europe with developments elsewhere in
the world.

The data is collected through a standardized postal questionnaire addressed to the
most senior HR/personnel specialist. Questions are focused at organizational level and
cover major areas of HRM policies and practices. The standardized questionnaire is
translated into all relevant languages and then adapted to the different national
contexts (taking into consideration such factors as legislation, labour markets,
culture). The results of the survey can only be understood in this context. During each
round of the survey, amendments are made to capture new developments but on the
whole, the questionnaire stays unchanged in order to be able to observe developments
over time.

STUDYING HRM IN THE INTERNATIONAL CONTEXT

The traditional notion of HRM, which has for long been embedded in, and influenced
by thinking in the United States of America, has been increasingly crowded out by
the term 'international human resource management' (IHRM) as, for example, simply
indicated by the growth in volume, range and diversity of contributions to this
emerging literature.

The notion of IHRM has evolved to accommodate the needs associated with
increasing globalization (Warner, 2005). IHRM comprises the world management of
human resources (Schuler and Tarique, 2007; but see also Brewster, 2002; Brewster
and Suutari, 2005; Briscoe and Schuler, 2004; Harris and Brewster, 1999; Poole,
1999), including issues related to enabling the multinational corporation (MNC) to be
globally successful. Nonetheless, despite emerging evidence on its value to the
international firm, and its increased visibility within academic quarters, confirming its
own unique kind of legitimacy, defining and delimiting the nature of IHRM and all its
constituent parts poses something of a challenge. This is perhaps hardly surprising.
Determining the anatomy and impact of HRM and its associated activities in a
domestic context has proven somewhat elusive. It was always going to be more so in
an international one. The inevitable consequence is that there are many ongoing
questions surrounding its pedigree and legitimacy (Morley *et al.*, 2006a).

One of the fundamental questions in this regard is what is the most appropriate
paradigm for enquiry in the field. Mayrhofer *et al.* (2000), among others, argue that
there are essentially two paradigms for researching HRM in an international and/or
comparative way, namely a *universalist* paradigm and a *contextual* paradigm. They
highlight that it is to some degree the difference between these paradigms which has
led to the conceptual confusion of what is the appropriate scope of the subject matter
often obvious in the literature. The *universalist paradigm*, Mayerhofer *et al.* (2000)
argue, which is dominant in the United States of America but is widely used in many
other countries, is essentially a nomothetic social science approach: using evidence to
test generalizations of an abstract and law-like character. The strength of this

approach, they argue, is that good research based upon it tends to have a clear potential for theoretical development, it can lead to carefully drawn research questions, the research tends to be easily replicable and research methodologies sophisticated, and there is a coherence of criteria for judging the research. The *contextual paradigm*, by contrast, according to Mayrhofer *et al.* (2000) is idiographic, searching for an overall understanding of what is contextually unique and why. In the IHRM field it often involves a focus on understanding what is different between and within HRM in various contexts and what the antecedents of those differences are. As a contributor to explanation, this paradigm emphasizes external factors as well as the actions of the management within an organization and the approach acknowledges the importance of context.

Thus this approach to researching HRM explores the importance of such factors as culture, ownership structures, labour markets, the role of the state and trade union organization as aspects of the subject rather than external influences upon it. The scope of HRM goes beyond the organization: to reflect the reality of the role of many HR departments.

Beyond the paradigmatic question, distinct lines of enquiry are evident in the field. Morley (2007) describes three distinct, but overlapping, research trajectories that provide important lenses through which to explore HRM in an international context, namely an *international*, a *comparative* and a *cross-cultural* trajectory. The concept of 'trajectory' is used here in order to denote the existence of a distinctive line of enquiry, a distinctiveness which may be observed both in terms of differing points of departure in the original research effort and consequently unique developmental paths in terms of the major themes investigated.

Thus, it is suggested that an *'international' trajectory in the study of HRM* can be conceptualized as an area of enquiry dedicated to charting the anatomy of HRM in the MNC and the unearthing of the HRM strategies, systems and practices pursued in the context of internationalization. In this trajectory, it is recognized that the ever-increasing complexity and uncertainty in which MNCs operate creates a unique set of organizational, co-ordination and managerial issues for the managers of these MNCs. Central among these is the management of employees on a global scale. In this international trajectory, HRM is concerned with identifying and understanding how MNCs manage their geographically dispersed workforces in order to leverage their HR resources for both local and global competitive advantage (Schuler *et al.*, 2002).

The body of work arising from this trajectory has several unique features. A good deal of the theoretical and empirical effort in this trajectory has focused on expatriation and the international assignment cycle, where much evidence has now been accumulated. There is evidence too in this trajectory of a focus on the dominant coalition of the firm as the human capital base deserving of our research attention. Furthermore, given the MNC as a unit of analysis, much of the work has sought to examine headquarter–subsidiary relations and the diffusion of managerial practices and systems throughout firm subsidiaries.

The overlapping '*comparative*' trajectory in the study of HRM shows a preference for exploring the landscape, contours and national patterns of HRM as a result of the distinctive developmental paths of different countries and their subsequently idiosyncratic institutional and economic regimes. A long-established tradition, it is based on the premise that many relevant insights into organization processes and systems in a global era will come from studying them in a comparative context (Evans *et al.*, 2002). Morley and Collings (2004) point to an increasing interest in comparative studies in a broadening range of countries, most especially CEE, China and India. This, they suggest, can be explained in part by the changing contours of foreign direct investment (FDI) location decisions in the global economy. While traditionally FDI flows have been concentrated in developed countries, recent years have heralded a shift in investment locations toward new destinations, on many of which there is a dearth of knowledge. Such new locations are now proving fertile ground for generating insights in this comparative tradition. Within this comparative trajectory, there is a focus on national systems elements as a basis for legitimate comparison and, as indicated above, the focus until relatively recently has largely been on economically successful and developed economies, with a growing emphasis in recent years on emerging economies.

The third trajectory, here labelled '*cross-cultural*', may be conceived of as a research tradition dedicated to explicating tenets of national culture as the dominant paradigm for conditioning what is acceptable organizational practice in that socio-cultural context. In this genre, significant explanatory power is accorded to tenets of societal culture in accounting for similarities and differences in the conceptualization of, and in the practice of, HRM. Much of the empirical effort in this trajectory has been focused on the issue of dimensionalizing these cultural tenets and replicating enquiry in an array of contexts. And, as with the other trajectories outlined above, the range of contexts is continuously expanding.

An alternative approach to generating insight in the field is to take a 'levels of analysis' approach. The notion of studying HRM in the international context has been broadly related to two levels of analysis: macro (societal) and micro (organizational). The macro level is associated with how HRM and IHRM are developed, viewed and practised in different parts of the world, as summarized in a recent special issue on 'Globalizing International Human Resource Management' (Rowley and Warner, 2007). This analysis is predicated on the understanding that operating across national boundaries brings with it a bewildering variety of cultural and institutional specificities that make managing in this context especially complex (Morley *et al.*, 2006b). Reflecting this complexity, studies conceptualized and pursued at the macro level of analysis typically examine the influence of national origin, institutions and culture on the respective country's employment legislation, industrial relations, trade unions, consultation, patterns of company ownership, etc. and how specific company-related HRM practices are impacted by these macro conditions. All these contextual differences have led to different perspectives on the concept of HRM from the outset at the strategic and functional level in different regions: Asia (e.g. Wu and Chiang, 2007; Zhu *et al.*, 2007), Europe (e.g. Brewster, 1995; 2007; Brewster and Bournois,

1991; Sparrow and Hiltrop, 1997; Larsen and Mayrhofer, 2006), Central America (Osland and Osland, 2005). Comparisons across countries (Hendry, 1991; Kopp, 1994; Templer *et al.*, 1997; Suda, 2007) in relation to HRM also belong to this macro stream of research. The micro actors under this umbrella tend to be domestic firms rooted in these regions and MNCs originating from or operating there.

Although the universality of the US-rooted HRM theories and practices have been tested in firms located in other countries such as Russia (e.g. Welch, 1994; Michailova, 2002) and China (e.g. Law *et al.*, 2003), it is the latter group, MNCs, that has been most frequently examined in the IHRM literature. While the expatriate approach to IHRM with a particular focus on international assignment and expatriation issues (e.g. Maisonrouge, 1983; Ondrack, 1985; Bird and Mukuda, 1989; Stephens and Black, 1991; Welch, 1994; Brett and Stroh, 1995; Caligiuri *et al.*, 1998; Porter and Tansky, 1999; Bennett *et al.*, 2000; Mendenhall and Stahl, 2000; Black and Gregersen, 2000; Carpenter *et al.*, 2000, 2001; Bauer and Taylor, 2001; Toh and Denisi, 2003; Stahl and Caligiuri, 2005; Morley *et al.*, 2006c) was regarded as unsatisfactory (Duane, 2001), a number of other HRM-related issues have been discussed in relation to MNCs. These include the impact of national culture on HRM practices in general (Laurent, 1986; Schuler and Rogovsky, 1998; Miah and Bird, 2007), HRM issues in international joint ventures (IJV) (e.g. Shenkar *and* Zeira, 1987; Cyr and Schneider, 1996; As-Saber *et al.*, 1998; Bjorkman and Lu, 2001; Yan, 2003; Kabst, 2004; Gong *et al.*, 2005; Yan *et al.*, 2007), the balancing between global and local HRM practices (e.g. Martinez and Ricks, 1989; Rosenzweig and Nohria, 1994; Kamoche, 1996; Tregaskis *et al.*, 2001; Wocke *et al.*, 2007), the functional realignment to do with recruitment, staffing, management development and careers, and rewards within MNCs (e.g. Kim and Gray, 2005; Sparrow, 2007), the design of strategic international human resource management (SIHM) for MNCs (Milliman *et al*, 1991; Schuler *et al.*, 1993; Caligiuri and Stroh, 1995; Paik and Teagarden, 1995; Taylor *et al.*, 1996; Fenwick, 2005; Som, 2007), the so-called best practices across countries (Mroczkowski and Hanaoka, 1997; Von Glinow *et al.*, 2002; Huo *et al.*, 2002; Geringer *et al.*, 2002; Lowe *et al.*, 2002) and MNC knowledge transfer (e.g. Minbaeva *et al.*, 2003; Minbaeva and Michailova, 2004).

Apart from the particular research focus on the MNCs' IHRM at the micro level, the broad categorization of the perspectives on HRM and IHRM in terms of North America, Asia and Europe (Rowley and Warner, 2007) is contestable too. The naming of 'Europe', for instance, is acknowledged as only one possible means of analysis, as the regional cultural clusters approach involves substantial generalization about European approaches to HRM (Brewster, 2007). Even the so-called 'European approaches' to HRM are literally Western Europe oriented (e.g. Camuffo and Costa, 1993; Hiltrop, 1996; Tyson, 1995; Guest, 1997; Paauwe, 1996; Boxall and Purcell, 2000; Boselie *et al.*, 2001; Camelo *et al.*, 2004; Cabral-Cardoso, 2004; Brewster, 2007). However, as Zupan and Kase (2005) asserted, there is still an important region of Europe about which researchers know very little in terms of HRM, namely Central and Eastern European (CEE) countries. These countries underwent a fundamental transition from centrally planned to market economies in the late 1980s and early

1990s, which, in combination with several other macro factors, has provided firms with very specific external and internal conditions for HRM practices. Even within the category of CEE region, the relative size, importance and performance of the CEE states differs widely (McCann and Schwartz, 2007), which could impact the nature of HRM differently in every single state. In this sense, CEE countries since 1989 have represented a form of test laboratory for HRM, which is central to the strategic directions and competitive advantage of the firms operating there (Taylor and Walley, 2002). Hence, the questions of to what extent the US and Western Europe-dominated HRM theories and practices can be applied to the CEE countries and whether there is evidence of a unique approach to HRM emerging in this region deserve serious research attention.

THE CASE OF HRM IN CENTRAL AND EASTERN EUROPE

While accepting the importance of knowing the nature of HRM in these European transition economies, a review of journal publications and books reveals that there has been very limited specialized and systematic research dedicated to HRM in the CEE region. Although some CEE countries (e.g. Bulgaria, Czech Republic, Estonia, Hungary, Poland, Slovenia and Russia) were included in the CRANET research comparative studies of European HRM and received attention in the latest CRANET publications (Brewster *et al.*, 2004), a closer review of the literature reveals most studies to be rather general, fragmented and subordinate to the Western European studies, in most cases under the umbrella of European Union (EU) membership (e.g. Mako *et al.*, 2003; Brewster *et al.*, 2004; Communal and Brewster, 2004; Larsen and Mayrhofer, 2006; Brewster, 2007). There has been one full special issue on 'Issues in Human Resource Management in Central Europe' (Jankowicz, 1998), which focused on a limited number of countries (e.g. Mills, 1998; Garavan *et al.*, 1998; Crow, 1998; Letiche, 1998). A more recent issue of *Human Resource Management*, the journal of the Polish Academy of Sciences Labour and Social Policy Scientific Committee, presented a themed section on the state of HRM in a number of countries of CEE, with a particular emphasis on two interconnected aspects, namely international comparative HRM and HRM in international corporations. While not explicitly dealing with the convergence/divergence debate, the papers did provide a platform for further explication of this thesis in the context of providing new insights into contemporary developments in HRM in CEE (see Pocztowski, 2008). Valuable as these thematic special issues have been in further advancing our understanding of HRM in CEE, we propose that if the notion of 'European HRM' was developed arguably in reaction to the hegemony of US conceptions of HRM (e.g. Brewster, 1994, 1995, 2007; Sparrow and Hiltrop, 1994; Brewster *et al.*, 2000), further independent and systematic analyses into the HRM issues in CEE countries is now needed. This is especially important in light of the transitions experienced by many of the economies of CEE in the past decade. All areas of business management from financing through distributing to human resource management had to be newly defined according to market economy criteria during the transitional period (Domsch and Lidokhover, 2007: 15)

Prior research on HRM in CEE countries can be seen to have a few characteristic features. First of all, the HRM issues in the CEE region that have been examined appear to be inevitably associated with the context of economic transition and the phenomenal transformations that have taken place in the region (e.g. Koubek and Brewster, 1995; Meardi, 2006; Tung and Lazarova, 2006). For example, in his book on policies and practices in global human resource systems, Duane (2001) included Eastern Europe in the comparative discussion by region, and provided a brief but objective overview of the transition consequences in relation to HR issues. He concluded that, although the labour market context in Eastern Europe has been improving especially in countries like the Czech Republic, Hungry and Russia, through the processes of privatization and economic restructuring, unemployment problems persist. There is evidence of some movement away from centrally controlled human resource planning and employment is no longer guaranteed the way it was in the socialist past. Human resource development in this region appears to be delivered through a combination of private school education programmes, and training provision by Western countries is commonplace. Another significant development relates to the introduction of some employment equality legislation and provisions such as anti-discrimination laws and child labour laws in some countries; however, the degree of actual enforcement has varied somewhat. There have been profound changes with respect to the funding and delivery of welfare services and, with respect to managing labour relations, unions have been formed to adapt to the demands of a market economy and to deal with collective bargaining issues.

Recent research effort in serving the needs of CEE economic transition is evident too. For example, in terms of obtaining human capital as a source of competitive advantage (Porter, 1990; Tung, 1988), the study by Tung and Lazarova (2006) sought to examine the experiences and challenges encountered by 'ex-host nationals' in CEE countries upon their return home after having studied and lived abroad for a long period of time. The study was concerned with the desire of these CEE countries to reverse the brain drain and facilitate the transition from socialist to market economies. With regard to managing employment in the transitional context, Soulsby and Clark (2006) developed an alternative theoretical framework to the dominant 'top-down' macroeconomic and institutional views to explain unemployment dynamics in the Czech Republic as outcomes of everyday real decision-making practices and processes of socially embedded enterprise managers. Martin (2006) even segmented the capitalism in CEE countries into managerial capitalism, entrepreneurial capitalism and international capitalism, each of which represents respective characteristic pattern of employment relations. However, similar to the Western European concept of HRM, most of those studies mentioned above have been at a conceptual and 'macro' level of analysis (McCann and Schwartz, 2007), emphasizing the firm-external perspective rather than firm-internal perspective, and rarely touching on the core tasks and basic functions of HRM (Zupan and Kase, 2005; Mayrhofer and Larsen, 2006).

In addition and, arising from the diversity of geographical and cultural coverage in CEE countries, much of the prior research has extensively utilized case studies and has drawn conclusions from relatively small and unrepresentative samples (Zupan and Kase, 2005). A number of studies present general descriptions of HRM in specific CEE countries like Slovenia (Zupan, 1998), Bulgaria (Gorcheva, 2005), Croatia (Taylor and Walley, 2002), Poland (Tung and Havlovic, 1996; Crow, 1998; Mroczkowski *et al.*, 2005), Czech Republic (Koubek and Brewster, 1995; Tung and Havlovic, 1996; Mills, 1998), Estonia (Mia and Suutari, 2004), Hungary (Pearce, 1991; Bangert and Poor, 1993; Karoliny, 2003; Sousa and Richet, 2003; Simonyi, 2003) and Russia (Fey *et al.*, 1999; May *et al.*, 1998; Shekshnia, 1998). Some of them made comparisons between countries such as Bulgaria and the Czech Republic (Koubek and Vatchkova, 2004), Estonia and Slovenia (Alas and Svetlik, 2004), and Hungry and Poland (Ishikawa, 2003). At the functional level, there have been studies concerned with specific HR practices like training and development, motivation, selection and recruitment, downsizing, performance management, compensation issues (Cakrt, 1993; Puffer, 1993; Vikhanski and Puffer, 1993; Kiriazov *et al.*, 2000; Szalkowski and Jankowicz, 2004; Zupan and Kase, 2005). Some also explored HRM issues at the strategic level (Garavan *et al.*, 1998; Jankowicz, 1998; Letiche, 1998; Fey *et al.*, 2000; Fey and Bjorkman, 2001; Weinstein and Obloj, 2002; Zupan and Ograjensek, 2004, Zupan and Kase, 2005). Other studies have probed into both HRM strategies and functions (Duane, 2001; Koubek and Vatchkova, 2004; Alas and Svetlik, 2004). However, a unified analysis of HRM in CEE region is missing, despite recent attempts to delimit HRM convergence in Europe (Tregaskis and Brewster, 2006; Mayrhofer *et al.*, 2000).

The idea of HRM convergence in Europe became closely related to the EU enlargement with a number of CEE countries joining the Union. The enlargement process has initiated a cluster of studies examining the processes of transfer of 'better practices' from Western to Eastern Europe through, among others, MNCs' foreign direct investment activities (e.g. Warhurst *et al.*, 2003). An implicit underlying assumption of the majority of these studies has been the emerging need to move away from mostly administrative and towards more strategic and business-oriented HRM in CEE. Unsurprisingly, the diffusion of employment practices and HRM policies in the CEE region was most frequently examined in the case of East–West joint ventures, drawing implications on how Western MNCs can successfully manage HRM in subsidiaries in CEE countries (Cyr and Schneider, 1996; Karoliny, 2003; Mia and Suutari, 2004; Kahancová and van der Meer; 2006). In MNC foreign subsidiaries, the reform of selection procedures, compensation and performance management systems has resulted in Western HR models being quickly disseminated to the domestic sector in CEE countries (Zupan and Kase, 2005). This dissemination has been variously received on a continuum ranging from blind acceptance through misuse to strong resistance resulting from the general lack of HR traditions prior to transition in this region (Taylor and Walley, 2002). This has resulted in differences in how HR practices are adopted both between and within industries in CEE countries, making the HRM issues in the CEE region even more variable.

INTRODUCING THE CONTRIBUTIONS TO THIS VOLUME

Each of the nine chapters that follow is presented as a contextual account that may be read individually in order to provide insights into developments in the country under study. In each case, the transition process is described, followed by an account of the context for HRM. Here the key stakeholders in the employment relationship are described, key labour market developments are set down, legislative provisions are established and the impact of the move to EU membership is presented. This context description is followed by a presentation of trends and developments in HRM practice. Here, the nature of the HR function is set down and core aspects of practice, including recruitment and selection, reward management, performance management and training and development, are discussed. Each chapter culminates in a discussion of the future of HRM and an illustrative case vignette.

Chapter 2 provides the account of HRM in *Estonia*. Many of the critical developments in HRM in Estonia emerged as a result of significant social changes that occurred towards the end of the 1980s. Following independence in 1991, the transition to a market economy was facilitated by the formation of a competitive business sector that was based on private ownership and which replaced the strong state regulatory system that had been in existence. A period of market liberalization, significant tax reforms and privatization preceded membership of the EU in 2004 and the country has experienced strong GDP growth since then. The population of Estonia has declined by 10 per cent, employment has increased and overall educational levels have increased since 1993. Regulation governing the employment relationship is contained in the Constitution and Estonia is a member of the Inernational Labour Organization.

Social dialogue between the various social partners is a characteristic feature of the labour landscape. Regional employment councils are being established to feed into national tripartite and bipartite negotiations. The Estonian Employers' Confederation represents employer concerns at such events, while trade unions are similarly recognized for bargaining and negotiation purposes. Although union membership and the right to strike are enshrined in the Constitution, union density overall has fallen dramatically in recent years and currently stands at 15 per cent – one of the lowest density figures in Europe.

Estonia's business base is largely characterized by micro and small enterprises that do not usually have a dedicated HR specialist employed to manage human resources. However, there is a growing number of MNC and larger organizations based in Estonia and the HRM practices here tend to be more formalized. The professionalization of HRM has been accelerated by the establishment of the HRM Association PARE in the 1990s and the concomitant development of a range of educational and qualification programmes in the field of HRM.

Moving from a largely administrative function in the 1950s, today HRM in Estonia shows evidence of considerable convergence to a more central role. HR specialists have been to the forefront in managing many of the change initiatives in medium-sized and larger organizations. Line managers play a central role in aspects of recruitment/retention and pay/benefits. There is a considerable focus on training and development to meet demands of the transition to the market economy and for retention and career development purposes. Direct relations between management and employees remain a central feature of HRM and are predicted to remain such for the foreseeable future.

Chapter 3 presents the landscape of HRM in *Lithuania*. The development of the modern conception of HRM in Lithuania can be traced to the broader development of the market economy around the mid-1990s. During this time, the country witnessed considerable foreign investment that brought with it a new approach to labour management thought appropriate to the new economy. This was especially apparent at the management level, where it became clear that the type of managerial skills and competencies required for competing in this post-Soviet era were in short supply.

Industrial relations in Lithuania are today characterized by social partnership and social dialogue, another development of recent vintage. Although trade unions have a long history in Lithuania, their experience with social partnership is new. Tripartite councils, encompassing representatives of trade unions, employer organizations and national government, regulate aspects of the labour code and collective agreements are concluded that deal with broad aspects of remuneration, working time, diversity, job security and training and development.

One of the key labour market developments has been the move to privatization and the beginnings of the growth of a knowledge economy since the 1990s. This period was marked by considerable recruitment and retention difficulties for employers, as the supply of appropriate skills was insufficient to meet demand. This was further exacerbated by outward migration to other EU states. This trend is putting more pressures on the government to initiate national economic and industry-specific reforms to increase competitiveness and help to offset the 'brain drain' of the young and most educated to other countries.

Developing out of an administrative 'cadre' department, the HRM function in Lithuania is today considered an important functional role within organizations. That said, there is general agreement that more attention needs to be focused on HRM matters, most especially in indigenous and capital industries. In an effort to respond to changing market demands, increased attention is being paid to recruitment and selection, performance management and training and development, particularly competence development. It is envisaged that a stronger focus on education and training should help to meet strategic goals and facilitate innovations in the Lithuanian economy.

Chapter 4 provides an account of HRM in *Poland*, a country that has been undergoing significant economic reforms towards a market economy since 1989 and one culturally viewed as a bridge between East and West and between socialism and capitalism. Four major waves of economic reform dedicated to stabilization and liberalization have resulted in major progress on privatization, on the transition from a manufacturing-dominated to a service-led economy, on the emergence of an entrepreneurial class and on membership of the EU. Poland is the largest economy among the new member states of the EU. The latter move has proven to be the wellspring for much reform on the HRM front in Poland in order to ensure a cadre of able and committed employees, appropriately managed.

On the industrial relations front, while trade union membership has suffered a dramatic decline, employer organizations are on the rise and social partnership and tripartism dedicated to wage certainty and minimum wage provision are now legislatively provided for.

Conventionally viewed as a highly centralized, politically influenced, middle-level administrative function with few underpinning systems, the recent transition years have witnessed the emergence of an HRM function with a strong awareness of the importance of having a strategic orientation, but struggling to develop this orientation. Indigenous and foreign owned companies operating in Poland are notably different on the HRM front, with foreign owned appearing more systematic and innovative.

On the HR practice front, several important observations are made in this chapter. While a more systematic approach to recruitment and selection, in light of pressing labour market dynamics, is evident, it is still somewhat dominated by short-term thinking and an underutilization of sophisticated selection tools. The filling of key managerial posts is more systematically handled. While reward systems vary widely, depending on several contextual factors, including ownership, sector, size and firm location, a flat rate system, established through job evaluation, is the norm, with variable pay and incentive schemes being less common. However, the war for talent in competitive, fast-growing sectors is evident, with some companies paying above the norm in order to attract and retain key skill sets. Finally, in the HR practice domain, a growing emphasis on training and development and on career management systems is in evidence, most especially again among foreign owned companies operating in Poland. Also, there is an important divide between larger and smaller enterprises, with micro enterprises demonstrating a lack of awareness of the value of human resource development (HRD) activity to business development and success. Where such interventions are provided for, there is a marked preference for on-the-job training and externally sourced training.

As to the future of HRM in Poland, several challenges are outlined. Alternative and flexible forms of employment are set to grow and the war for talent set to intensify as the talent pool shrinks. The institutionalization and normalization of lifelong learning as an important dimension of success in the labour market is also identified as a challenge, as is the capacity to operate in the international arena. Above all, the authors argue that the capacity of the HRM function in Poland to add real value will become the benchmark against which it will be judged.

Chapter 5 details the situation in the *Czech Republic*, which, prior to World War II, was one of the most prosperous and developed regions in Europe. During this time personnel management was a well-established and respected profession, but with the imposition of communism after the war, much decision making became centralized and personnel practice took an administrative turn, something which was to last until the 1989 revolution, which culminated in the commencement of a period of significant economic transformation. This transformation has been underpinned by an emphasis on human capital and on appropriate labour market and social policy interventions.

Recent years have witnessed a steady increase in the role and visibility of HRM as a field of academic enquiry and, in terms of professional practice, as a field facilitating change and economic transition and in bringing about a new situation at the organizational level. These years have also resulted in an altered institutional environment for HRM practice and brought with them mixed fortunes for the trade union movement. The transition period saw the emergence of independent trade unions, but there has been a steady decline in membership of these unions in the past 12 years.

The HR function has been in a state of flux in the Czech Republic throughout the 1990s and the early part of this century. The head of the HR function was likely to be a Board Member, but the extent to which they and their function were taken seriously was often in question. In situations where such functions grew, it was often in a decentralized fashion, with increasing involvement of line management in HR activity domain areas.

On the activity front, recruitment and selection activity has emerged as a shared responsibility between the HR function and line managers where it is handled internally, or in many instances is handled by external agencies. With respect to appraisal, the proportion of organizations with formal appraisal systems has been increasing and in the area of remuneration data points to an increase in the use of variable and performance based pay systems.

Overall it is argued in the chapter that there have been several positive changes in HRM in the Czech Republic in recent years as a result if which it is possible to observe some convergence towards 'Western' practices, but there are several ongoing challenges in this transition, not least among them securing top management support for HRM as a valuable contributor to sustainable competitive advantage.

Chapter 6 presents the case of *Slovakia*, a country that has undergone enormous change in the past several decades. During the communist era, it was dominated by agriculture, with the consequence that its expanding industrial base is of relatively recent vintage. While the personnel function with a completely administrative focus characterized the communist era, recent waves of transformation have resulted in a new situation with a gradual rise in the status of HR within the organizational hierarchy and a growing professionalism among managers. The institutional and legislative framework for HRM in Slovakia has also altered significantly as part of the transformation process. Labour law reform has taken place, resulting in the implementation of collective agreements. However, despite the emergence of a more positive environment for the trade union movement, in common with trends evident in several of the other countries examined in this text, trade union membership has been declining, many perceiving the unions to be a barrier to the development of an enterprise culture.

Despite the significant reforms that have characterized Slovakia's transformation, HRM remains somewhat more operational than strategic and often relatively unsystematic. With respect to recruitment and selection, the internal labour market is typically preferred for filling managerial positions and a variety of recruitment and selection techniques are employed. The one-on-one interview remains the most common selection technique for most vacancies. On the remuneration front, a mix of flat rate and incentive systems is in evidence, the latter incentives having either an individual or a team element. Non-financial incentives have grown in popularity according to recent survey evidence. Finally, training and development activity remains relatively modest, organizations spending on average 2.1 per cent of their annual wage bill on such activity, somewhat behind the average for developed EU economies.

Chapter 7 details the case of *Hungary*. Prior to the changes which occurred in the late 1980s, Hungary had approximately 20 years of what is termed 'market socialism'. The period since then has been characterized by a gradual, incremental process of convergence toward international norms as a result of waves of privatization and structural change and significant FDI inflows. Significant developments include increased competition, improved economic performance, integration with the global free market economy, coupled with EU membership, which occurred in 2004. The industrial relations institutional environment has as a central operating plank the National Interest Reconciliation Council, a tripartite body establishing wage rates in the public sector and, under the Hungarian Labour Code introduced originally in 1992, trade unions have the right to organize and bargain collectively.

In the HR practices domain, several important observations are made in this chapter. First, the significance of the FDI sector is noted and the potential of the spillover effect of practices common in this sector to other sectors of the economy is noted. Second, the basic HR architecture common in Hungary points to a function which is striving to institutionalize a more systematic and strategic approach. Third, on the practice front, while several strides have been made, Hungary still has significant progress to make here. Thus, further progress needs to be made on the training and development front in order to enhance national competitiveness, and fears of a 'brain drain' as a result of the lagging behind of wage rates in certain sectors of the economy remain as a real concern for policy makers and practitioners alike.

Slovenia forms the subject of Chapter 8. Its recent economic transformation has commenced from a relatively positive trajectory, when compared with several of the other countries explored in this text, and HRM practice was relatively well established in the socialist period. The consequence of this is that its transition can be considered relatively 'soft' and economically and socially successful. The transition to EU membership has not brought radical change.

In the industrial relations sphere, trade unions are a common feature of the landscape, with approximately 40 per cent of the employed labour force in membership, and the relative influence of trade unions in the society is said to be increasing. Social partnership-type agreements between government, employers and trade unions are the preferred approach to wage negotiation and wage setting in Slovenia. At organizational level there is an increasing strategic approach to HRM, along with an emerging devolution of HR responsibilities to line managers. In recruiting to fill senior positions, there is an expressed preference for the internal labour market. Performance appraisal in both the public and private sector is commonplace and there is an increasing trend toward share ownership and financial participation in company performance.

In Chapter 9 we present the case of *Bulgaria*, whose transition process has been marked by a desire to establish a competitive, knowledge based economy. Inward foreign direct investment is on an upward trajectory and the economic situation has stabilized on several fronts. EU membership was achieved in January 2007, something which is proving a major catalyst for reform in the social and labour environment. Institutionally, industrial relations is regulated through a Labour Code which provides for tripartite cooperation between stakeholders in the employment process. Unionization is high in Bulgaria relative to other European countries, but, in common with other states, trade union recognition is declining, as is perceived trade union influence.

Turning to the nature of the HR function, the level of involvement of HR at the strategic level has increased in recent years, as has the sharing of responsibility for HR activity between the specialist function and line managers. Flexible working practices, many forms in response to the emerging service sector in the economy, are on the increase. A majority of Bulgarian organizations recognize the importance of training and development to business success, but many face difficulties in funding this activity, with the consequence that in many instances engaging in training and development is viewed as a matter for the individual. The relative lack of emphasis on human resource development has prompted the establishment of a National Social Network for Vocational Training designed to increase the skill set in the human capital base. This was accompanied by the launching of an EU-supported Human Resource Development Operational Programme in 2007 designed to facilitate Bulgaria's successful integration in the European labour market.

Our final chapter focuses on *Russia*. With respect to the transformation process of the past 20 years, the authors argue that Russia is set apart somewhat from its East European neighbours discussed in this volume. Russian exceptionalism in this regard is accounted for by the fact that there was no clearly identified destination underpinning the transformation process, there was a protracted period of forced labour camps and there was a longer period of communism with the result that private-enterprise 'know-how' was lost in a more complete way.

The industrial relations environment in Russia is characterized by a significant degree of state involvement and unions are relatively weak. The 2002 Labour Code has underscored this position, continuing as it does to restrict the rights of trade unions on many fronts. Official unemployment is running at approximately 8 per cent of the economically active labour force, but many regard the true figure to be significantly higher and labour market inefficiencies are a significant barrier to sustainable economic and social progress.

During the communist era, the HR function was structured as a decentralized activity, with responsibility for HR matters being divided between the local Communist Party, the personnel department, the representative trade union, the salary department and the engineering function, which took responsibility for work design and health and safety matters. The consequence of this distribution of responsibility for various HR matters was that there was no clear articulation of a centralized HR role and how it could strategically support the organization.

In the present situation, HR activity has become more centralized, but the functions level of strategic involvement is minimal. Skill shortages in certain sectors of the economy have emerged, with the consequence that recruitment and selection activities constitute a major component of the function's activities and a boarder range of techniques are employed to create a pool of applicants. Performance based variable pay, derived from the paying of monthly premiums, is commonplace and for senior managerial posts in some sectors financial participation and stock-related rewards are practised. Training and development activity, especially for managerial employees, has become relatively extensive, with a strong underlying value being attached to professional education and development.

As to the future of HRM in Russia, the authors argue that there are several unique contextual factors at play in the Russian socio-economic environment which will shape the nature of likely future development. Chief among these are the likely performance of the energy sector, which is hugely significant in the Russian context, the launching of a significant infrastructural development plan and a renewed emphasis on the armaments sector. Developments in these and related sectors will create new pressures for the HR-related activities, including newer and more sophisticated approaches to selection, an emphasis on performance management and more innovative approaches to rewards in order to attract specialist skills in relatively short supply.

CONCLUSION

Overall, the chapters in this volume provide important contextual insights into the development and the practice of HRM in countries that have been undergoing a unique social experiment over the past twenty years or so.

While it might be legitimately argued that a 20 year timeline of transition and transformation is far too short a period of change against which to look at national socio-economic and firm level developments, nevertheless it does provide a benchmark timeframe against which to examine the unfolding landscape of HR and to set this in the context of the significant development trajectory that these countries have been on. Of particular note is the fact that several of the countries selected for inclusion in this volume rarely feature in the English-language literature. Their inclusion here is occasioned by the significant journey they have been on in recent years and what we might all learn from this experience.

Taken together, and read in a comparative way, the chapters point to core challenges which all of these transition economies are facing. On the other hand, each of the accounts, read individually, highlights the unique political, socio-cultural and economic features of each country, draws attention to the development path and presents the basic architecture of HRM, past and present. The country-specific illustrative case presented at the end of each chapter serves to provide further insights into the unique contextual landscape within which HRM is institutionalized and practised and which is demanding our time and attention in order that we might better understand the importance of context as a determinant of the likelihood of, and limits to, transition and transformation. Theoretically, several have argued for the critical role played by the context and the necessity to give expression to this in conceiving our intercultural research models and in explaining differences in HRM practices in comparative HRM. These countries provide a particularly interesting location in which to explore this issue because of what has been referred to as 'the contextual uniqueness of the landscape of European HRM' (Morley, 2004) derived from a rather unique 'mixture of unifying and dividing elements' (Mayrhofer *et al.*, 2000). There are fewer places where this is truer than in the transition economies of CEE.

REFERENCES AND FURTHER READING

Alas, R. and Svetlik, I. (2004). 'Estonia and Slovenia: Building Modern HRM Using a Dualist Approach', in Brewster, C., Mayrhofer, W. and Morley, M. *Human Resource Management in Europe: Evidence of Convergence?* Oxford: Elsevier Butterworth-Heinemann, pp. 353–84.

As-Saber, S. N., Dowling, P. J. and Liesch, P. W. (1998). 'The Role of Human Resource Management in International Joint Ventures: A Study of Australian–Indian Joint Ventures. *International Journal of Human Resource Management*, 9, 5: 751–66.

Bangert, D. and Poor, J. (1993). 'Foreign Involvement in the Hungarian Economy: Its Impact on Human Resource Management'. *International Journal of Human Resource Management*, 4, 4: 817–40.

Bauer, T. N. and Taylor, S. (2001). 'When Managing Expatriate Adjustment, Don't Forget the Spouse'. *Academy of Management Executive*, 15, 4: 135–7.

Bennett, R., Aston, A. and Colquhoun, T. (2000). 'Cross-cultural Training: A Critical Step in Ensuring the Success of International Assignments'. *Human Resource Management*, 39, 2, 3: 239–50.

Bird, A. and Mukuda, M. (1989). 'Expatriates in Their Own Home: A New Twist in the Human Resource Management Strategies of Japanese MNCs'. *Human Resource Management*, 28, 4: 437–53.

Bjorkman, I. and Lu, Y. (2001). 'Institutionalization and Bargaining Power Explanations of HRM practices in International Joint Ventures – the case of Chinese–Western joint ventures', *Organization Studies*, 22, 3: 491–512.

Black, J. S. and Gregersen, H. B. (2000). 'High Impact Training: Forging Leaders for the Global Frontier'. *Human Resource Management*, 39, 2, 3: 173–84.

Boselie, P., Paauwe, J. and Jensen, P. (2001). 'Human Resource Management and Performance: Lessons from the Netherlands'. *International Journal of Human Resource Management*, 12, 7: 1107–25.

Boxall, P. and Purcell, J. (2000). 'Strategic Human Resource Management: Where Have We Come From and Where Should We Be Going?' *International Journal of Management Reviews*, 2, 2: 183–203.

Brett, J. M. and Stroh, L. K. (1995). 'Willingness to Relocate Internationally'. *Human Resource Management*, 34, 3: 405–24.

Brewster, C. (1994). 'European HRM: Reflection of, or Challenge to, the American Concept?', in Kirkbride, P. S. (ed.) *Human Resource Management in Europe*. London: Routledge, pp. 56–89.

Brewster, C. (1995). 'Towards a "European" model of human resource management'. *Journal of International Business Studies*, 26, 1: 1–21.

Brewster, C. (2002). 'Human Resource Practices in Multinational Companies', in Gannon, M. and Newman, K. (eds) *Handbook of Cross-cultural Management*. London: Blackwell.

Brewster, C. (2007). 'Comparative HRM: European Views and Perspectives'. *International Journal of Human Resource Management*, 18, 5: 769–87.

Brewster, C. and Bournois, F. (1991). 'Human Resource Management: A European Perspective'. *Personnel Review*, 20, 6: 4–13.

Brewster, C. and Suutari, V. (2005). 'Global HRM: Aspects of a Research Agenda'. *Personnel Review*, 34: 5–21.

Brewster, C., Mayrhofer, W. and Morley, M. (2004). *Human Resource Management in Europe: Evidence of Convergence?* Oxford: Elsevier Butterworth-Heinemann.

Briscoe, D. and Schuler, R. (2004). *International Human Resource Management: Policies and Practices for Global Enterprise*, 2nd edn. New York: Routledge.

Cabral-Cardoso, C. (2004). 'The evolving Portuguese Model of HRM'. *International Journal of Human Resource Management*, 15, 6: 959–78.

Cakrt, M. (1993). 'Management Training in Eastern Europe: Toward Mutual Understanding'. *Academy of Management Executive*, 7, 4: 63–67.

Caligiuri, P. M. and Stroh, L. K. (1995). 'Multinational Corporation Management Strategies and International Human Resources Practices: Bringing IHRM to the Bottom Line'. *International Journal of Human Resource Management*, 6, 3: 494–507.

Caligiuri, P. M. and Hyland, M. A. M., Joshi, A. and Bross, A. S. (1998). 'Testing a Theoretical Model for Examining the Relationship Between Family Adjustment and Expatriates' Work Adjustment'. *Journal of Applied Psychology*, 83, 4: 598.

Camelo, C., Martin, F., Romero, P. M. and Valle, R. (2004). 'Human Resources Management in Spain: Is It Possible to Speak of a Typical Model?' *International Journal of Human Resource Management*, 15, 6: 935–59.

Camuffo, A. and Costa, G. (1993). 'Strategic Human Resource Management – Italian Style'. *Sloan Management Review*, 34: 59–67.

Carpenter, M. A., Sanders, W. G. and Gregersen, H. B. (2000). 'International Assignment Experience at the Top Can Make a Bottom-line Difference'. *Human Resource Management*, 39, 2, 3: 277.

Carpenter, M. A., Sanders, W. G. and Gregersen, H. B. (2001). 'Bundling Human Capital with Organizational Context: The Impact of International Assignment Experience on Multinational Firm Performance and CEO Pay'. *Academy of Management Journal*, 44, 3: 493–511.

Communal, C. and Brewster, C. (2004). 'HRM in Europe', in A. Harzing and J. Van Ruysseveldt (eds) *International Human Resource Management*. Sage: London, 167–94.

Crow, M. (1998). 'Personnel in Transition: The Case of Polish Women Personnel Managers'. *Personnel Review*, 27, 3: 243.

Cyr, D. J. and Schneider, S. C. (1996). 'Implications for Learning: Human Resource Management in East–West Joint Ventures'. *Organization Studies*, 17, 2: 207–26.

Domsch, M. and Lidokhover, T. (eds) (2007). *Human Resource Management in Russia*. Aldershot: Ashgate.

Duane, M. J. (2001). *Policies and Practices in Global Human Resource Systems*. London: Quorum Books.

Evans, P., Pucik, V. and Barsoux, J. L. (2002). *The Global Challenge: Frameworks for International Human Resource Management*. New York: McGraw Hill-Irwin.

Fenwick, M. (2005). 'Extending Strategic International Human Resource Management Research and Pedagogy to the Non-profit Multinational'. *International Journal of Human Resource Management*, 16, 4: 497–512.

Fey, C. F. and Bjorkman, I. (2001). 'The Effect of Human Resource Management Practices on MNC Subsidiary Performance in Russia'. *Journal of International Business Studies* 32, 1: 59–75.

Fey, C. F., Engstrom, P. and Bjorkman, I. (1999). 'Doing Business in Russia: Effective Human Resource Management Practices for Foreign Firms in Russia'. *Organizational Dynamics*, 28, 2: 69–81.

Fey, C. C., Bjorkman, I. and Pavlovskaya, A. (2000). 'The Effect of Human Resource Management Practices on Firm Performance in Russia'. *International Journal of Human Resource Management*, 11, 1: 1–18.

Garavan, T., Morley, M., Heraty, N., Lucewicz, J. and Suchodolski, A. (1998). 'Managing Human Resources in a Post-command Economy: Personnel Administration or Strategic HRM'. *Personnel Review*, 27, 3: 200.

Geringer, J. M., Frayne, C. A. and Milliman, J. F. (2002). 'In Search of "Best Practices" in International Human Resource Management: Research Design and Methodology'. *Human Resource Management*, 41, 1: 5–30.

Gong, Y., Shenkar, O., Luo, Y. and Nyaw, M. K. (2005). 'Human Resources and International Joint Venture Performance: A System Perspective'. *Journal of International Business Studies*, 36, 5: 505–18.

Gorcheva, T. (2005). 'The Differences in the Interactive Modification of Interaction Between Target Groups and Personnel Management Tools'. *Journal for East European Management Studies*, 10, 1: 75–91.

Guest, D. E. (1997). 'Human Resource Management and Performance: A Review and Research Agenda. *International Journal of Human Resource Management*, 8, 3: 263–76.

Harris, H. and Brewster, C. (1999). 'International Human Resource Management: the European Contribution', in Brewster, C. and Harris, H. (eds) *International HR*. London and New York: Routledge.

Hendry, C. (1991). 'International Comparisons of Human Resource Management: Putting the Firm in the Frame'. *International Journal of Human Resource Management*, 2, 3: 415–40.

Hiltrop, J. M. (1996). 'The Impact of Human Resource Management on Organizational Performance: Theory and Research'. *European Management Journal*, 14, 6: 28–637.

Huo, Y. P., Huang, H. J. and Napier, N. K. (2002). 'Divergence or Convergence: A Cross-national Comparison of Personnel Selection Practices'. *Human Resource Management*, 41, 1: 31–44.

Ishikawa, A. (2003). 'Employee Representation and Alienation in the Transition Economies: The Case of Hungary and Poland', in Mako, C., Warhurst, C. and Gennard, J. (eds). *Emerging Human Resource Practices: Developments and Debates in the New Europe*: 59–72: Budapest: Akademiai Klado.

Jankowicz, A. D. (1998). 'Issues in Human Resource Management in Central Europe. *Personnel Review*, 27, 3: 169.

Kabst, R. (2004). *Internationalisierung mittelständischer Unternehmen*. Munich: Hampp.

Kahancová, M. and van der Meer, M. (2006). 'Coordination, Employment Flexibility, and Industrial Relations in Western European Multinationals: Evidence from Poland'. *International Journal of Human Resource Management*, 17, 8: 1379–95.

Kamoche, K. (1996). 'The Integration–Differentiation Puzzle: A Resource-capability Perspective in International Human Resource Management'. *International Journal of Human Resource Management*, 7, 1: 230–44.

Karoliny, Z. (2003). 'The Nokia Way of Managing People: The Case of a Hungarian Subsidiary', in Makó, C., Warhurst, C. and Gennard, J. (eds) *Emerging Human Resource Practices: Developments and Debates in the New Europe*. Budapest: Akadémiai Kiadó, pp. 124–42.

Kim, Y. and Gray, S. (2005). 'Strategic Factors Influencing International Human Resource Management Practices: An Empirical Study of Australian Multinational Corporations'. *International Journal of Human Research Management*, 16, 5: 809–30.

Kiriazov, D., Sullivan, S. E. and Tu, H. S. (2000). 'Business Success in Eastern Europe: Understanding and Customizing HRM'. *Business Horizons*, 43, 1: 39–43.

Kopp, R. (1994). 'International Human Resource Policies and Practices in Japanese, European, and United States Multinationals'. *Human Resource Management*, 33, 4: 581–99.

Koubek, J. and Brewster, C. (1995). 'Human Resource Management in Turbulent Times: HRM in the Czech Republic'. *International Journal of Human Resource Management*, 6, 2: 223–47.

Koubek, J. and Vatchkova, E. (2004). 'Bulgaria and Czech Republic: Countries in Transition, in Brewster, C., Mayrhofer, W. and Morley, M. *Human Resource Management in Europe: Evidence of Convergence?* Oxford: Elsevier Butterworth-Heinemann, pp. 313–52.

Larsen, H. H. and Mayrhofer, W. (2006). *Managing Human Resources in Europe: A Thematic Approach*. London and New York: Routledge.

Laurent, A. (1986). 'The Cross-cultural Puzzle of International Human Resource Management'. *Human Resource Management*, 25, 1: 91–102.

Law, K. S., Tse, D. K. and Zhou, N. (2003). 'Does Human Resource Management Matter in a Transitional Economy? China as an Example'. *Journal of International Business Studies*, 34, 3: 255.

Letiche, H. (1998). 'Transition and Human Resources in Slovakia'. *Personnel Review*, 27, 3: 213.

Maisonrouge, J. G. (1983). 'The Education of a Modern International Manager'. *Journal of International Business Studies*, 14, 1: 141–46.

Mako, C., Warhurst, C. and Gennard, J. (eds) (2003). *Emerging Human Resource Practices: Developments and Debates in the New Europe*. Budapest: Akadémiai Kladó.

Martin, G. (20060. *Managing People and Organisations in Changing Contexts*. Oxford: Butterworth.

Martin, R. (2006). 'Segmented Employment Relations: Post-socialist Managerial Capitalism and Employment Relations in Central and Eastern Europe'. *International Journal of Human Resource Management*, 17, 8: 1353–65.

Martinez, Z. L. and Ricks, D. A. (1989). 'Multinational Parent Companies' Influence over Human Resource Decisions of Affiliates: U.S. Firms in Mexico'. *Journal of International Business Studies*, 20: 489–514.

May, R., Young, C. B. and Ledgerwood, D. (1998). 'Lessons from Russian Human Resource Management Experience'. *European Management Journal*, 16, 4: 447–60.

Mayrhofer, W. and Larsen, H. H. (2006). 'European HRM: A Distinct Field of Research and Practice, in Larsen, H. H. and Mayrhofer, W. (eds) *Managing Human Resources in Europe: A Thematic Approach*. London and New York: Routledge, pp. 1–17.

Mayrhofer, W., Brewster, C. and M. Morley (2000). 'The Concept of Strategic European Human Resource Management', in Brewster, C., Mayrhofer, W. and Morley, M. (eds), *New Challenges for European Human Resource Management*. London: Macmillan, pp. 3–37.

Meardi, G. (2006). 'Multinationals' Heaven? Worker Responses to Multinational Companies in Central Europe'. *International Journal of Human Resource Management*, 17, 8: 1366–78.

Mendenhall, M. E. and Stahl, G. (2000). 'Expatriate Training and Development: Where Do We Go From Here?' *Human Resource Management*, 39, 2/3: 251–65.

Mia, E. and Suutari, V. (2004). 'HRM in Foreign Affiliates: A Multiple Case Study among Estonian Affiliates of Finnish Companies'. *Journal for East European Management Studies*, 9, 4: 345–66.

Miah, M. K. and Bird, A. (2007). 'The Impact of Culture on HRM Styles and Firm Performance: Evidence from Japanese Parents, Japanese Subsidiaries/Joint Ventures and South Asian Local Companies. *International Journal of Human Resource Management*, 18, 5: 908–23.

Michailova, S. (2002). 'When Common Sense Becomes Uncommon: Participation and Empowerment in Russian Companies with Western Participation'. *Journal of World Business*, 37, 3: 180–7.

Milliman, J., Von Glinow, M. A. and Nathan, M. (1991). 'Organizational Life Cycles and Strategic International HRM in Multinational Companies: Implications for Congruence Theory'. *Academy of Management Review*, 16, 2: 318–39.

Mills, A. (1998). 'Contextual Influences on Human Resource Management in the Czech Republic'. *Personnel Review*, 27, 3: 177.

Minbaeva, D. and Michailova, S. (2004). 'Knowledge Transfer and Expatriation in Multinational Corporations: The Role of Disseminative Capacity'. *Employee Relations*, 26, 6: 663–79.

Minbaeva, D., Pedersen, T., Bjorkman, I., Fey, C. F. and Park, H. J. (2003). 'MNC Knowledge Transfer, Subsidiary Absorptive Capacity, and HRM'. *Journal of International Business Studies*, 34, 6: 586.

Morley, M. (guest ed.) (2004). 'Contemporary Debates in European Human Resource Management'. *Human Resource Management Review*, 14, 4: 353–498.

Morley, M. J. (2007). 'Of Infants and Adolescents: Progress and Pessimism in the Development Trajectory of International Human Resource Management'. Keynote Presentation to the *9th Conference on International Human Resource Management*, Tallinn, 12–15 June.

Morley, M. and D. Collings (guest eds) (2004). 'Contemporary Debates and New Directions in HRM in MNCs'. *International Journal of Manpower*, 25, 6: 487–559.

Morley, M., Gunnigle, P., O'Sullivan M. and Collings, D. (guest eds) (2006a). 'New Directions in the HRM Function'. *Personnel Review*, 35, 6: 609–17.

Morley, M., Heraty, N. and Collings, D. (eds) (2006b). *International Human Resource Management and International Assignments*. Basingstoke: Palgrave.

Morley, M., Heraty, N. and Collings. D. (eds) (2006c). *New Directions in Expatriate Research*. Basingstoke: Palgrave.

Mroczkowski, T. and Hanaoka, M. (1997). 'Effective Rightsizing Strategies in Japan and America: Is There a Convergence of Employment Practices?' *Academy of Management Executive*, 2, 2: 57–67.

Mroczkowski, T., Wermus, M. and Clarke, L. D. (2005). 'Employment Restructuring in Polish Companies during Economic Transition: Some Comparisons with Western Experience'. *Journal for East European Management Studies*, 10, 1: 37–54.

Ondrack, D. A. (1985). 'International Transfers of Managers in North American and European MNEs'. *Journal of International Business Studies*, 16, 3: 1–19.

Osland, A. and Osland, J. S. (2005). 'Contextualization and Strategic International Human Resource Management Approaches: The Case of Central America and Panama'. *International Journal of Human Resource Management*, 16, 12: 2218–36.

Paauwe, J. (1996). 'Key Issues in Strategic Human Resource Management: Lessons from the Netherlands'. *Human Resource Management Journal*, 6, 3: 76–93.

Paik, Y. and Teagarden, M. B. (1995). 'Strategic International Human Resource Approaches in the Maquiladora Industry: A Comparision of Japanese, Korean and U.S. firms'. *International Journal of Human Resource Management*, 6: 568–87.

Pearce, J. L. (1991). 'From Socialism to Capitalism: The Effects of Hungarian Human Resources Practices'. *Academy of Management Executive*, 5, 4: 75–88.

Pocztowski, A. (2008). 'From the Editor'. *Human Resource Management*, 60, 1: 7–9.

Poole, M. (1999). *Human Resource Management: Critical Perspectives on Business and Management*, vols I, II, III. London: Routledge.

Porter, G. and Tansky, J. W. (1999). 'Expatriate Success May Depend on a "Learning Orientation": Considerations for Selection and Training. *Human Resource Management*, 38, 1: 47–60.

Potter, M. (19990). *The Competitive Advantage of Nations*. New York: Free Press.

Puffer, S. M. (1993). 'Three Factors Affecting Reward Allocations in the Former USSR'. *Research in Personnel and Human Resource Management*, 3: 279–98.

Rosenzweig, P. and Nohria, N. (1994). 'Influences on Human Resource Managemetn Practices in Multinational Corporations'. *Journal of International Business Studies*, 25, 2: 229–51.

Rowley, C. and Warner, M. (2007). 'Introduction: Globalizing International Human Resource Management'. *International Journal of Human Resource Management*, 18, 5: 703–716.

Schuler, R. and Rogovsky, N. (1998). 'Understanding Compensation Practice Variations across Firms : The Impact of National Culture'. *Journal of International Business Studies*, 29, 1: 159–77.

Schuler, R. S. and Tarique, I. (2007) 'International Human Resource Management: A North American Perspective, a Thematic Update and Suggestions for Future Research'. *International Journal of Human Resource Management*, 18, 5: 717–44.

Schuler, R. S., Dowling, P. J. and De Cieri, H. (1993). 'An Integrative Framework of Strategic International Human Resource Management'. *International Journal of Human Resource Management*, 4, 4: 717–64.

Schuler, R. S., Budhwar, P. S. and Florkowski, G. W. (2002). 'International Human Resource Management: Review and Critique'. *International Journal of Management Reviews*, 4, 1: 41–70.

Schwartz, G. and McCann, L. (2007). 'Overlapping Effects: Path Dependence and Path Generation in Management and Organization in Russia'. *Human Relations*, 60, 10: 1525–49.

Shekshnia, S. (1998). 'Western Multinationals' Human Resource Practices in Russia'. *European Management Journal*, 16, 4: 460–5.

Shenkar, O. and Zeira, Y. (1987). 'Human Resources Management in International Joint Ventures: Directions for Research'. *The Academy of Management Review*, 12, 3: 546–57.

Simonyi, A. (2003). 'Patterns of Employment and Labour Initialization in Disadvantaged Villages in Hungary', in Mako, C., Warhurst, C. and Gennard, J. (eds) *Emerging Human Resource Practices: Developments and Debates in the new Europe*. Budapest: Akadémiai Kiadó.

Som, A. (2007). 'What Drives Adoption of Innovative SHRM Practices in Indian Organizations?' *International Journal of Human Resource Management*, 18, 5: 808–28.

Soulsby, A. and Clark, E. (2006). 'Changing Patterns of Employment in Post-socialist Organizations in Central and Eastern Europe: Management Action in a Transitional Context'. *International Journal of Human Resource Management*, 17, 8: 1396–410.

Sousa, J. and Richet, X. (2003). 'Economic Transformation, FDI and Local Supply Companies: The Case of Hungary', in Makó, C., Warhurst, C. and Gennard, J. (eds) *Emerging Human Resource Practices: Developments and Debates in the New Europe*. Budapest: Akadémiai Kiadó, pp. 157–72.

Sparrow, P. R. (2007). 'Globalization of HR at Function Level: Four UK-based Case Studies of the International Recruitment and Selection Process'. *International Journal of Human Resource Management*, 18, 5: 845–67.

Sparrow, P. R. and Hiltrop, J.-M. (1994). *European Human Resource Management in Transition*. Hemel Hempsted: Prentice Hall.

Sparrow, P. R. and Hiltrop, J.-M. (1997). 'Redefining the Field of European Human Resource Management: A Battle Between National Mindsets and Forces of Business Transition?' *Human Resource Management*, 36, 2: 201–19.

Stahl, G. K. and Caligiuri, P. (2005). 'The Effectiveness of Expatriate Coping Strategies: The Moderating Role of Cultural Distance, Position Level, and Time on the International Assignment'. *Journal of Applied Psychology*, 90, 4: 603.

Stephens, G. K. and Black, S. (1991). 'The Impact of Spouse's Career-orientation on Managers during International Transfers'. *Journal of Management Studies*, 28, 4: 417–28.

Suda, T. (2007). 'Converging or Still Diverging? A Comparison of Pay Systems in the UK and Japan'. *International Journal of Human Resource Management*, 18, 4: 586–601.

Szalkowski, A. and Jankowicz, D. (2004). 'The Development of Human Resource during the Process of Economic and Structural Transformation in Poland'. *Advances in Developing Human Resources*, 6, 3: 346–55.

Taylor, D. and Walley, E. L. (2002). 'Hijacking the Holy Grail? Emerging HR Practices in Croatia'. *European Business Review*, 14, 4: 294–303.

Taylor, S., Beechler, S. and Napier, N. (1996). 'Toward an Integrative Model of Strategic International Human Resource Management'. *Academy of Management Review*, 21, 4: 959–85.

Templer, A. J., Hofmeyr, K. B. and Rall, J. J. (1997). 'An International Comparison of Human Resource Management Objectives and Activities'. *International Journal of Human Resource Management*, 8, 4: 550–62.

Toh, S. M. and Denisi, A. S. (2003). 'Host Country National Reactions to Expatriate Pay Policies: A Model and Implications'. *Academy of Management Review*, 28, 4: 606–21.

Tregaskis, O. and Brewster, C. (2006). 'Converging or diverging? A Comparative Analysis of Trends in Contingent Employment Practice in Europe over a Decade'. *Journal of International Business Studies*, 37, 1: 111–26.

Tregaskis, O., Heraty, N. and Morley, M. (2001). 'HRD in Multinationals: The Global/Local Mix', *Human Resource Management Journal*, 11, 2: 34–56.

Tung, R. L. (1998). *The New Expatriates: Managing Human Resources Abroad*. Cambridge, MA: Harper and Row.

Tung, R. L. and Havlovic, S. J. (1996). 'Human Resource Management in Transitional Economies: The Case of Poland and the Czech Republic'. *International Journal of Human Resource Management*, 7, 1: 1–19.

Tung, R. L. and Lazarova, M. (2006). 'Brain Drain Versus Brain Gain: An Exploratory Study of Ex-host Country Nationals in Central and East Europe'. *International Journal of Human Resource Management*, 17, 11: 1853–72.

Tyson, S. (1995). *Human Resource Strategy: Towards a General Theory of Human Resource Management*. London: Pitman.

Vikhanski, O. S. and Puffer, S. M. (1993). 'Management Education and Employee Training at Moscow McDonalds'. *European Management Journal*, 11, 1: 102–8.

Warhurst, C., Darr, A. and Newsome, K. (2003). 'Towards a Better Understanding of the Cross-border Transfer and Diffusion of Soft Technology', in Makó, C., Warhurst, C. and Gennard, J. (eds) *Emerging Human Resource Practices: Developments and Debates in the New Europe*, Budapest: Akadémiai Kiadó, pp. 19–36.

Warner, M. (ed.) (2005). *Human Resource Management in China Revisited*. London: Routledge.

Weinstein, M. and Obloj, K. (2002). 'Strategic and Environmental Determinants of HRM Innovations in post-socialist Poland'. *International Journal of Human Resource Management*, 13, 4: 642–59.

Welch, D. (1994). 'Determinants of International Human Resource Management Approaches and Activities: A Suggested Framework'. *Journal of Management Studies*, 31, 2: 139–164.

Welsh, D. H. B., Luthans, F. and Sommer, S. M. (1993). 'Managing Russian Factory Workers: The Impact of U.S.-based Behavioral and Participative Techniques'. *Academy of Management Journal*, 36, 1: 58–79.

Wöcke, A., Bendixen, M. and Rijamampianina, R. (2007). 'Building Flexibility into Multi-national Human Resource Strategy: A Study of Four South African Multi-national Enterprises'. *International Journal of Human Resource Management*, 18 5 (May): 829–44.

Wu, C. C. and Chiang, Y. C. (2007). 'The Impact on the Cultural Diversity to Employees' Job Satisfaction between Mainland China and Taiwan: A Comparison of Taiwanese Invested Companies'. *International Journal of Human Resource Management*, 18, 4: 623–641.

Yan, Y. (2003). 'A Comparative Study of Human Resource Management Practices in *International* Joint Ventures: The Impact of National Origin'. *International Journal of Human Resource Management*, 14, 4: 487–510.

Yan, Y., Child, J. and Chong, C. Y. (2007). 'Vertical Integration of Corporate Management in International Firms: Implementation of HRM and the Asset Specifics of Firms in China'. *International Journal of Human Resource Management*, 18 (5): 788–807.

Zhu, Y., Warner, M. and Rowley, C. (2007). 'Human Resource Management with "Asian" Characteristics: A Hybrid People-management System in East Asia'. *International Journal of Human Resource Management*, 18, 5: 745–68.

Zupan, N. (1998). 'Human Resource Management in Slovenia'. *Journal of Human Resource Management*, 1, 1: 13–32.

Zupan, N. and Kase, R. (2005). 'Strategic Human Resource Management in European Transition Economies: Building a Conceptual Model on the Case of Slovenia'. *International Journal of Human Resource Management*, 16, 6: 882–906.

Zupan, N. and Ograjensek, I. (2004). 'The Link between Human Resource Management and Company Performance'. *Journal of East–West Business*, 10, 1: 105–19.

Managing human resources in Estonia

TÕNU KAARELSON AND RUTH ALAS

INTRODUCTION

Human resource management (HRM) in Estonia is a relatively young field. In the Soviet Union, during the period 1940–91, normal development processes in many fields, including human resource management, stopped. Soviet enterprises were large, overstaffed and inefficient. Effective use of human resources was not the aim. The aim was to provide everyone with jobs.

In 1991, everything changed. Estonia regained its independence, lost its Russian market and had to seek new ones. Most large enterprises were divided into parts and these parts were privatized. Massive downsizing began. The whole world changed. People started to realize how restricted their understanding was. Most people had to change their attitudes and behavioural patterns.

The functions that had to change the most in the management of organizations were marketing and sales, which were virtually non-existent in the Soviet era. Another function that required changes was personnel management – it had to change from its existing administrative function to that of HRM.

Fortunately, HRM did not have to start its development from scratch. There were people in both academic and practical circles who had had closer contact with the ideas and practices in this field in neighbouring countries, for example Finland. The development ideas acquired from management consultants in Finland were already being implemented here and there at the end of the 1970s.

The development of HRM was fostered by social changes that took place at the end of the 1980s, and these paved the way for entrepreneurship and foreign investment. During the 1980s, companies started to raise capital in the field of personnel management in order to be able to develop the function of HR management within the context of the liberal market economy characteristic of the 1990s.

After regaining independence at the beginning of the 1990s, three entrepreneurial psychologists established the HRM association PARE and started to provide basic one-year courses in HRM. The first course started in 1993 and was very popular. In the second half of the 1990s, the situation changed and several universities and business schools started to offer diploma and degree programmes in HRM. From 2001, the Estonian Business School in co-operation with PARE started the Executive MBA programme in HRM for HR managers in Estonian companies (Alas and Svetlik 2004).

This chapter provides an overview of the steps this function underwent during the development process. To help the reader understand these steps better, a historical overview is provided. The chapter also includes details on developments in management during the internationalization process. The largest Estonian bank, Hansabank, purchased the large Lithuanian bank LTB and started to integrate it into the Hansabank Group. Transformational change was required. The main focus of this case is the changes made to the organizational culture of LTB. We will focus on the activities of the personnel department in the process of improving the management of the Lithuanian bank.

THE TRANSITION PROCESS

Estonia is the smallest of the Baltic States with an area of 45,227 km² and a population of about 1.3 million. Approximately one-third of the nation live in Tallinn and about 67 per cent of the population reside in cities (Estonica).

Estonia had already experienced democracy and a market economy and enjoyed living standards comparable to other Scandinavian nations before its unlawful incorporation into the Soviet Union in 1940 (Zamascikov, 1987: 226). Although wages, income, housing and productivity in the Baltic republics were higher than in the other European republics of the Soviet Union (Gregory, 1987: 369), the Soviet occupation resulted in a significant decline in standards of living (Misiunas and Taagepera, 1983: 39).

Due to the fact that during the Soviet period the state was responsible for guaranteeing work for everyone, enterprises were internally overstaffed and passive and workplaces were over-secured (Liuhto, 1999: 16).

The Soviet regime was successful in eliminating private enterprise, introducing state-oriented socioeconomic institutions and having the population become accustomed to them. The very skills needed for private enterprise disappeared. What did not disappear was a dim sense of having lost something valuable. This sense was anchored in a Protestant work ethic that was much more deeply rooted than Lutheranism itself and was felt to be part of the besieged national culture (Taagepera, 1993: 108).

Education was strongly ideologised. In 1965, an eleven-year curriculum prevailed in Estonia (Taagepera, 1993: 95).

Estonia was at the forefront of reforms in the Soviet Union. Radical reforms in Estonia started in 1987–8 when a group of theoreticians and practitioners discussed the idea of economic autonomy for Estonia. The movement for autonomy gathered force in 1988 and developed into mass political movements in support of the restoration of independent statehood in all the Baltics (Taagepera, 1993: 311).

The transition to a market economy was supported by the re-establishment of independence in August 1991, and a currency reform based on currency board principles (fixed by law to the German Mark) in June 1992. The Estonian national currency is the Estonian kroon – EEK (€1 = 15.65 EEK).

During the transition, the resource-constrained and centrally planned economy had to become demand driven and market oriented. Outputs, which had formerly been mostly dependent on available resources, had to become demand driven and controlled by consumption in foreign and domestic markets (Rajasalu, 1995: 8). One of the main aims of the transition to a market economy was the formation of a competitive business sector based on private property in order to replace the strong state regulation with a combination of a strong market and only absolutely necessary state regulation (Taaler, 1995: 10–11). There was no room for slack resources in enterprises any more. The transformation away from central planning increased endogenous activity substantially, as the transition has both forced employees to be more active and at the same time created more favourable conditions for employee self-realization (Liuhto, 1999: 16).

The process of economic reform was radical and quick. According to Taaler (1995: 12), the government reduced its influence on economic and social life too quickly, and as a result the rate of economic liberalization was faster than the emergence of market competition. This was accompanied by the shock of losing markets to the East. The beginning of the 1990s saw a serious decline in the Estonian economy, which was accompanied by a decline in real income and growing income inequality (Rajasalu 1995: 17). This increased uncertainty about the future.

The next important steps involved lowering enterprise and individual income tax rates and abolishing progressive taxation for individual income (26 per cent); tax breaks for enterprises were eliminated and replaced by a more liberal depreciation policy. Since 2000, reinvested corporate profit has been tax free. Foreign trade was completely liberalized. Stress was laid on the state's non-intervention in business, essentially abolishing support and guarantees in any form (Taaler, 1995: 12).

Small-scale privatization began in Estonia in early 1991. In 1992, it was decided to implement the 'Treuhand' model for accelerating the process of large-scale privatization and a special body, the Estonian Privatization Enterprise, was established (Kein and Tali, 1995: 143). Privatization has been decisive. This is best illustrated by the fact that almost two-thirds of the nation's GDP comes from the private sector. The central element contributing to this progress has been a streamlined and centralized privatization process, which has welcomed foreign investment (Privatisation in Estonia).

As mentioned earlier, the process of economic reform was radical and quick. The beginning of the 1990s saw a serious decline in the Estonian economy – GDP declined by about 14 per cent in 1991, 18 per cent in 1992 and 2 per cent in 1993. In 1994, GDP finally started to grow (Rajasalu, 1995: 16).

Arguably one of the most successful transitions from a socialist economy to a market economy took place in Estonia (Leimann *et al.*, 2003). This liberal market approach in Estonia has emphasized the removal of trade barriers, the development of free-trade agreements, the introduction of favourable fiscal and monetary policies and the creation of macroeconomic stability.

According to the EU 2000 report, Estonia is a functioning market economy where market forces play their full role (Estonia). According to its overall index of economic freedom, the Heritage Foundation ranked Estonia among the freest countries in the world – fourth place in 2002 (Rajasalu, 2003: 18). According to the growth competitiveness index, Estonia's ranking rose from 27th in 2002 to 22nd in 2003 (IMD, 2004). By 2005, Estonia was ranked 20th.

The Estonian economy has advanced immensely since the beginning of 2000, when the member states of the EU decided to offer Estonia the opportunity to join in the EU in 2004. The main economic indicators before and after this period are provided in Table 2.1.

The period since accession to the EU has given rise to rapid growth in the economy. In 2005 and 2006, the Estonian economy was characterized by annual GDP growth of more than 10 per cent. The driving force behind this was the development of the real estate sector and increasing private consumption.

The free movement of people within the EU has caused an outflow of labour from the construction, services, transport and other sectors, so the existence of labour has become the most important factor in securing future growth. The decrease in the labour supply has caused a drop in the unemployment rate to the lowest level (5.9 per cent) since 1993. As a result, average wages rose by 17 per cent in 2006. This has caused higher consumer demand as well as increases in prices, which means the consumer price index rose by 4.4 per cent in 2006 compared to the previous year.

Table 2.1 Some economic indicators in Estonia, 1993–2006

Economic indicator	1993	1994	1997	2000	2004	2005	2006
Real growth of GDP (%)	–	−1.6	11.1	10.8	8.1	10.5	11.4
Unemployment rate	6.6	7.6	9.6	13.6	9.7	7.9	5.9
Average monthly gross wages and salaries (EEK)	1,066	1,734	3,573	4,907	7,287	8,073	9,407
Consumer price index (%)	89.8	47.7	11.2	4.0	3.0	4.1	4.4
Mean annual population (thousands)	1,494	1,463	1,400	1,370	1,349	1,346	1,345

Source: Statistical Office of Estonia.

In the long term, the current continuous economic growth and annual decrease in population will aggravate the shortage of labour.

STAKEHOLDERS IN HUMAN RESOURCE MANAGEMENT

Employers and their organizations

Changes in the legislative environment in the early 1990s encouraged the creation of new private enterprises by creating relatively simple conditions for establishing enterprises (Smallbone and Venesaar, 2003). The number of operating enterprises has increased year after year in Estonia. The most rapid changes took place at the beginning of the 1990s. In 1994–7, the number of enterprises grew slowly. In 2006, the number of operating enterprises reached 71,012 (*Statistical Yearbook of Estonia*, 2007).

If we analyse the commercial register in terms of the form of ownership, there were 70 state owned enterprises (0.1 per cent of all economically active enterprises) and 246 enterprises owned by local government (0.3 per cent) in 2006. By comparison, 65,482 enterprises were owned on the basis of Estonian private capital (92.2 per cent) and 5,217 enterprises on the basis of foreign capital (7.4 per cent). The share of government and local government owners has continuously decreased, while the share of foreign owners has increased (*Statistical Yearbook of Estonia*, 2007).

Table 2.2 indicates the number and percentage of enterprises according to size. If we look at the total number of economically active enterprises, 88 per cent have fewer than 10 employees and fewer than 0.3 per cent are large enterprises.

Table 2.2 The number of Estonian enterprises according to size

| Year | Number of employees | | | | |
	Total	Fewer than 10	10–49	50–249	Over 250
2000	46,853	39,235	6,313	1,134	171
2001	54,015	46,441	6,254	1,168	152
2002	57,183	49,484	6,386	1,157	156
2003	56,035	48,216	6,456	1,207	156
2004	60,882	53,153	6,304	1,258	167
2005	65,362	57,387	6,519	1,288	168
2006	71,012	62,609	6,901	1,323	179

Note: The data of economically active sole proprietors registered in the Commercial Register are included, but the data of economically active sole proprietors registered only in the Register of Taxable Persons are not included.

Source: Statistics Estonia, http://pub.stat.ee/px-web.2001/dialog/statfile1.asp

Estonia is a country where micro- and small enterprises make up 98 per cent of the total number of enterprises. The proportion of large-scale enterprises is only 0.25 per cent. Such a large percentage of micro and small enterprises has an effect on the overall human resource management situation. Generally, enterprises with such low numbers of employees do not have a full-time personnel specialist. The CEO is responsible for day-to-day activities in this field. Usually, companies that belong to the class of medium-sized enterprises based on the number of employees hire a personnel specialist. In general, enterprises with over 100 employees have employees specializing in the field of personnel management.

Entrepreneurial organizations have grown in Estonia since the end of the 1980s. The Estonian Association of Small and Medium-Sized Enterprises was established in 1988 for organizations employing less than 250 workers. It is a non-government, non-profit association for small and medium-sized enterprises (SMEs) and the self-employed, performing a representative, advocacy and lobbying function for SMEs as a social group (Estonian Association of SMEs).

The Estonian Chamber of Commerce and Industry (ECCI), which was originally founded in 1925, was re-established in 1989 in order to assist in creating a favourable business climate for the return to a market economy and to rekindle Estonia's traditional business relations with Europe and the rest of the world. The ECCI's membership of around 3,200 companies includes the majority of large enterprises, which account for over 85 per cent of Estonia's total exports (Estonian Chamber of Commerce and Industry).

In 1992, Estonia rejoined the International Labour Organization (ILO). Becoming a member of this organization meant that Estonia was obliged to acknowledge international labour laws, including the primary obligation of having to solve the core issues of social guarantees between the government, employers and employees via consultations and negotiations.

The Estonian Employers' Confederation is a non-profit, independent umbrella organization with the objective of protecting the common interests of employers. It represents 32 branch organizations that employ 35 per cent of private sector employees in Estonia. The Estonian Employers' Confederation is acknowledged by the government of Estonia and trade unions as a social partner and participates in tripartite and bilateral negotiations and commissions. It is the most representative employers' organization in Estonia (Estonian Employers' Confederation, www.ettk.ee/en).

Trade unions

The right to form and join a trade union or employee association exists on the basis of the Estonian constitution. Unions may freely join federations and affiliates internationally. There is a legal right to strike and retribution against strikers is prohibited. Unions are independent of the government and political parties.

Compared to the Soviet period, membership of trade unions has decreased dramatically. The union density rate is approximately 15 per cent (Eamets and Masso, 2004). According to a survey conducted by the International Network of Strategic Human Resource Management, CRANET, carried out in 27 countries, Estonia ranked last among European countries according to the number of people involved in trade unions: in two-thirds of the Estonian companies studied there were no trade union members at all (Alas, 2004).

Trade unions had to face challenges that dramatically affected their activities and membership: radical reform created a liberal market economy system, where the shift from state-controlled enterprise to privately driven entrepreneurship was caused by the foundation of new private enterprises rather than by the privatization of state owned enterprises. Only 7 per cent of all private enterprises were created directly as a result of privatization (Purju, 1998). In newly established enterprises, trade unions did not usually exist.

In the Soviet Union, despite defending the rights of its members, the trade union was an integral part of the management structure of the enterprise with the primary function of assisting in the fulfilment of production plans (Kiik, 2000). The issue of pay increases did not fall within the rights and responsibilities of Soviet trade unions. These matters were decided at the level of the Soviet government and Communist Party.

The Central Organization of Estonian Trade Unions (EAKL) was formed as a voluntary and entirely Estonian organization in 1990 to replace the Estonian branch of the official Soviet labour confederation, the All-Union Central Council of Trade Unions. EAKL is mainly a blue-collar worker organization.

The Confederation of Estonian Employee Unions (TALO) was established in 1992 and has 30,000 members according to 2005 data (Estonian Employees' Unions' Confederation). TALO is mainly a white-collar worker organization (Alas, 2003).

In spite of the modest role performed by labour unions in Estonian enterprises, it is still possible to speak about 15 years of experience in social dialogue between labour unions, employers and the government. In order to enhance the legal environment of this social dialogue, the Trade Unions Act has been adopted. It lays down the basic rights and legal status of trade unions, their relations with central and local government bodies and employers, as well as the provisions concerning their creation and function. Furthermore, Estonia has continued to promote and support social dialogue on both a tripartite and bipartite level, thus partially addressing the relevant short-term 1999 Accession Partnership. The first steps to establishing tripartite regional employment councils at county level have been taken in order to find solutions to regional socio-economic problems. These councils will define labour market measures including retraining and vocational training.

At the bipartite level, collective agreements have been concluded at branch level in the agro-food and road transport sectors. The direct collective bargaining coverage is around 29 per cent (Eamets and Masso, 2004).

CHANGES IN THE LABOUR MARKET

From 1993 to 2006, the population in Estonia decreased by 10 per cent. The most precipitous decline occurred directly following the restoration of independence between 1992 and 1993, when the population decreased by 2.3 per cent primarily as a result of the emigration of the ethnic Russian population. By 2006, the ethnic composition of the population was 68.6 per cent Estonian, 25.7 per cent Russian, 2.1 per cent Ukrainian and 0.8 per cent Finnish (Statistics Estonia, 2006)

The birth rate has been declining steadily over the past decade. The natural change in the population was last upwards in 1990. In recent years, the decrease in the population has slowed down, but still there were 2,439 more deaths than births in 2006 (Statistics Estonia, 2006).

The percentage of children in the population has decreased and the percentage of elderly people has increased quite steadily every year. In 2005, the figures were, respectively, 15.3 per cent under 15 years and 16.2 per cent over 65 years. Thus, the outlook for the next five to six years is that the number of people of working age will considerably decrease.

The percentage of women has remained constant – 53.9 per cent. The average life expectancy for women is 78 and for men 66 years (*Statistical Yearbook of Estonia*, 2006).

Changes in employment have broadly paralleled the output changes since the restoration of independence. Total employment fell by about 200,000 between 1989 and 1997, with the greatest part of the fall coming in the period up to 1993. Since 2001, employment has increased and unemployment decreased. By 2006, the number of employed had increased to 646,000. The primary sector (agriculture, hunting, forestry, fishing) constituted 5.3 per cent of total employment. The secondary sector (mining, manufacturing, electricity, gas and water supply, construction) constituted 34 per cent of total employment. The tertiary sector (wholesale and retail trade, services, etc.) accounted for 60.7 per cent of total employment. The number of employed by field of operation grew most in the fields of hotels and restaurants and real estate. The employment rate among the elderly (in the age group of 55 to 64) was one of the highest in the EU, at 56 per cent (Giaccone, 2007).

The education level in the labour force has increased in recent years. The percentage of the labour force with primary education has decreased and the percentage of labour force with tertiary education has increased (from 30 per cent in 2000 to 34 per cent in 2005). Unemployment was lowest among people with a higher education and a degree. The unemployment rate among this group was 3.9 per cent in 2005 (*Statistical Yearbook of Estonia*, 2006).

Economic growth has had a great impact on the labour market. The creation of new jobs has decreased unemployment to a critical level and the increase in wages has been too fast. These developments create a special context for HRM within enterprises. It is necessary to guarantee productivity growth in order to ensure sustainable development. On the other hand, the limited selection opportunities among the labour force create better conditions for employees compared to employers in the labour market, whose bargaining position has been most favourable in the last 15 years.

LABOUR LEGISLATION

The most important statutes and rules regulating activities in the labour market are the Constitution of Estonia and Conventions of the ILO. Several essential principles in labour legislation, such as a citizen's right to choose his or her field of activity, profession and workplace, are in accordance with the constitution. According to the constitution, working conditions are under state control and membership of employee and employer associations and unions is open to all. The Republic of Estonia has been a member of the ILO since 1921, and restored its membership status in 1992. Estonia has joined more than 30 ILO conventions, which means that their requirements are reflected in local labour legislation. One prerequisite for joining the conventions is their conformity with the constitution of the republic. The ILO conventions ratified in Estonia have had an influence, for example, on legislation and practice in the field of social dialogue, equality, labour safety, etc.

At the beginning of the 1990s, new labour legislation was adopted to govern relationships between employers and employees at the individual and collective levels under the new conditions of the market economy.

The majority of the essential laws regulating labour relations were worked out and adopted over a ten-year period (1991–2001). One of the most essential and voluminous acts of law in the labour law package is the Employment Contracts Act adopted in 1992. Over the years, the Act has been supplemented and amended several times, as with other acts. The largest amendments were introduced on 1 May 2004, and were related to the accession of Estonia to the EU. The Employment Contracts Act, which regulates the rights and obligations of the employer and the employee, has shaped HRM practices in Estonia to a very large extent: 'It has served us well throughout the establishing of free market principals. Perhaps now there is need for more flexible laws giving better opportunities for employers in the process of restructuring staff in companies' (Kirso, 2006). On the initiative of employers and with support from the government, the Employment Contracts Act has been amended to provide greater flexibility. The reasons for this include the changing nature of work and methods of working in society, as well as the large proportion of micro- and small enterprises and the extremely low number of large enterprises which is characteristic of Estonia. These moves have met with opposition from the representative employee organizations. Therefore the draft acts, which deal with the simplification of the processes of downsizing and making employees redundant and the abolition of the corresponding severance pay, have not yet been accepted.

According to the World Bank report *Doing Business 2007*, it is easiest for an employer to deal with labour in the United States of America. Denmark (15) and Great Britain (17) are also at the top of the list. Other Nordic Countries (Sweden, Finland and Norway) as well as Latvia and Lithuania are in the lower part of the table. Only Spain and Portugal are behind Estonia (151) out of the European countries. Problems with inflexible working time and the complexity of making employees redundant were the main causes for Estonia's lower ranking in the list (Zirnask, 2006).

Several aspects of the Employment Contracts Acts are dealt with more comprehensively in the Wages Act (1994), the Individual Labour Dispute Resolution Act (1995), the Occupational Health and Safety Act (1999), the Working and Rest Time Act (2001), the Vacation Act (2001) and others. The Labour Inspectorate is responsible for state supervision of compliance with the requirements of legislation regulating occupational health and safety in the work environment and labour relations and applies enforcement from the state on the basis and to the extent prescribed by law (the Labour Inspectorate). The labour unions also have occupational health and safety experts who assist workers to bring employers in line with legal standards. The Collective Agreements Act (1993), Employee Representatives Act (1993), Collective Labour Dispute Resolution Act (1993) and Trade Unions Act (2000) deal with the employees' right of association, collective contractual relations and representation in their relations with employers. The Health Insurance Act (1991), Social Protection of the Unemployed Act (2000), State Pension Insurance Act (2001), Unemployment Insurance Act (2001) and other related acts deal with social insurance issues. In 2002, the Estonian Unemployment Insurance Fund was established. Unemployment insurance is a type of compulsory insurance for the payment of benefits to employees upon unemployment, collective redundancy and the insolvency of employers. The benefits are financed via money received from unemployment insurance premiums. The unemployment insurance premium is 0.6 per cent of an employee's earnings and other fees for employees and 0.3 per cent of the gross payroll for employers.

In 2000, the government adopted the National Employment Action Plan following the European Employment Guidelines (Estonia). The priorities of the plan include the developing active labour market policies, supporting micro-enterprises, reducing administrative burdens for business, developing vocational education more suited to business needs, integrating disadvantaged groups into the labour market and improving the administrative capacity of the public employment services. In addition, the Employment Service Act was passed to provide the legal framework for functioning employment services.

IMPACT OF THE MOVE TO EU MEMBERSHIP ON HRM

EU enlargement in 2004 differed from previous enlargements because the income gap between the accession countries and EU countries was greater. For example, the hourly salary was eight times lower in Estonia than in the old EU countries and purchasing power was only 42 per cent of the purchasing power in the EU-15 (Svetlik and Alas, 2006). Therefore, there is a risk of a brain drain for the new EU countries. If too many young skilled and well-educated people leave the country, economic development and social security systems could be endangered. Mobility could increase in those segments where demand for labour massively outstrips supply in the old member states, such as in the information and communication technology field.

A study conducted in Estonia just before the EU enlargement in 2004 indicates that the willingness to emigrate or work abroad has decreased (Narusk, 2004). People have become more realistic about the opportunities in other countries and also more satisfied with life in Estonia. More than half of those previously willing to go abroad have changed their minds. This tendency can be seen in all age groups. Those who are eager to work abroad are young (72 per cent between 15 and 19 years), male (59 per cent), with a secondary education (60 per cent) or with an unfinished university education or are students. Estonians prefer Finland, Germany and Great Britain.

Unfortunately, the Estonian state does not have any official statistics on people working abroad. Anecdotal evidence suggests that the percentage is highest among construction workers. Workers leaving their jobs have seriously affected small and medium-sized enterprises, where the potential for increasing wages is much more limited than in large organizations. 'Finnish construction companies are actively looking for blue-collar workers from Estonia and now places far from Tallinn seem to be target areas where there is less economic activity and the unemployment rate is higher' (Kirso, 2006). Estonian companies, in turn, have looked to other countries with lower salary levels and higher unemployment rates, for example Poland, for labour to use in the construction area.

Not all construction companies have experienced a workforce flow abroad (Tüvi, 2006). The increase in wage levels in Estonia has kept some workers here, but has also noticeably decreased the cost-effectiveness of local enterprises: 'Workers that had left to work on construction sites, for example in Finland, have started to return as wages have begun to increase in Estonia in recent years, making working at home much more attractive' (Kirso, 2006).

Until now the most popular jobs among Estonians have been short-term jobs in Finland – 60 per cent of those going to Finland spend less than three months there. Only 10 per cent of those who had worked abroad spent more than one year there. The main attraction was higher wages (Svetlik and Alas, 2006).

The free movement of labour is a new factor within human resource management, a factor with which the Estonian government as well as those compiling personnel policy have had little experience. The movement of specialists abroad is, for example, a much more acute problem in the health care sector compared with the construction sector. Engaging specialists from abroad for vacancies in Estonia has been poorly prepared for in the legislation and insufficiently discussed in Estonia.

TRENDS AND DEVELOPMENTS IN HUMAN RESOURCE MANAGEMENT PRACTICE IN ESTONIA

In order to fully understand the peculiarities of human resource management today, one should take a close look at the developments in this field since the Second World War in Estonia. To characterize the stages in its development, the authors rely on the periods proposed by Vanhala (1995). She identified five stages in Finnish personnel management: the initiation phase, the pioneering phase, the self-criticism phase, the strategic HRM phase and the decentralization phase. In the present chapter the authors have adapted the suggested periods to Estonian conditions.

The personnel function in Estonia until 1991

In the period between 1945 and 1991 three stages have been identified in the development of the personnel function in Estonia. The main characteristics inherent in the personnel function in different periods are summarized in Table 2.3.

By the second half of the 1940s, institutions established before the Second World War during the time of Estonia's First Republic were brought down and the establishment of Soviet institutions was in full swing. Economic life took the form of

Table 2.3 Main characteristics of the personnel function in Estonia in different periods up to 1991

The stages	The main features
Administrative-ideological 1945–late 1950s	• Strictly administrative function aimed at achieving control over employees • Cooperation with repressive institutions • Recruitment and instruction of workers • Accountancy regarding staff issues
Initiation 1960–late 1970s	• Mainly administrative by nature • Taylor's approach to work • Handling of social problems of employees (housing, health care, etc.) • Complementary training for workers and specialists
Pioneering 1980–1991	• Complementary training for managers • Introducing new selection methods • Personnel appraisal • Organizational development

a centralized command economy. Instead of personnel management, the companies of that time were widely characterized by simple staffing which, on the one hand, had an administrative function and, on the other hand, served as a necessary means to achieve control over workers. By its nature, this was an *administrative-ideological* period, characteristic of the years between 1945 and 1960. The staff (cadre) departments existed in every organization. Besides administrative duties they were expected to perform certain ideological roles (Tepp, 2007). The staffing function dealt solely with issues of accounting and reporting, and the people responsible for this function had the lowest qualifications among other specialists and officials. Communist Party membership was in most cases a precondition for the position of department managers.

The political 'thaw' and a few economic reforms in the Soviet Union brought about changes also in the HR function. By its nature the function remained administrative, but from the new economic needs, progress and innovation were also required within this function. On a wider scale, the period could be characterized as an *initiation phase*, which lasted till the end of 1970s. The characteristic features included workers' training and the development of the system of complementary training. By the end of the initiation phase, complementary training for managers had also reached the agenda of personnel development. Taylorist methods – the improvement of work operations, setting working norms, implementing a piecework system, etc. – became widely used. In addition to the staffing function, companies embarked on a wide-scale social development of the enterprise – services for health care and leisure became common. From the middle of 1970s, through the work of qualified industrial psychologists in the staff departments of some big enterprises – recent graduates of Tartu University – the first signs of a professional approach to personnel management emerged.

The end of the 1970s and the beginning of the 1980s brought about the *pioneering phase*. The 1980s was greatly influenced by political developments globally and in the Soviet Union, which resulted in radical changes in both the economic and social life of the country. The end of 1980s was characterized by the beginning of entrepreneurship and the first rudiments of a market economy. While the economy was opening up, management and personnel management practices underwent changes. New methods of recruitment and selection were implemented and opportunities for complementary training and motivation of employees became more diverse.

The emergence of personnel management

With the restoration of independence and the appearance of a market economy, the previous phase of the HR function smoothly changed to become the phase of personnel management. Economic decentralization and privatization quickly led to economic restructuring and changes in the labour market.

Various and extensive direct foreign investment and the opening up of foreign markets provided a basis for rapid economic and technological development.

These factors also accelerated the development of the HR function. Compared with the staff administration during the Soviet period, the changes in the personnel management field were enormous. The disintegration and disappearance of existing organizations destroyed old staff departments, former personnel employees were mostly discharged and new labour laws were passed. The majority of typical role models in business were destroyed as well (Tepp, 2007).

Labour relations were characterized by weak trade unions, which had no influence over the arrangement of labour relations. A large number of employees were made redundant in privatized companies.

Following a period of rapid development of entrepreneurship and privatization of public enterprises, Estonian companies emerged as relatively small. Due to this fact some companies did not create the position of personnel manager/specialist and the tasks of personnel/HR management were shared between the managing director and heads of other functions. In companies with less than approximately 50–60 employees, the tasks of HR managers/specialists have been delegated to people in other positions (Alas, 1998).

The few large concern-like enterprises in the 1990s in Estonia were characterized by both vertical and horizontal division of labour in personnel/HR management. The person responsible for the central HR strategy and policy in the concern was the director of HR and the subsidiaries had their own HR managers or specialists. If necessary, the main areas of personnel management – training, selection and recruitment – had permanent staff responsible for these tasks (Alas, 1998).

In large companies there is a certain division of labour between line managers and HR experts. Line managers participate in decision-making processes in various areas of personnel management, such as, for example, HR planning, identifying training needs, performance appraisal, developing remuneration systems, etc. (Alas, 1998). The culture of personnel/HRM in this period was largely influenced by the subsidiaries of large Western enterprises in Estonia. The practices of these companies served as an example to a number of local enterprises while developing the HR function. Similarly, there was rapid development of HR managers and specialists. In Estonia, the first initiatives to interpret the new roles of HRM and create an understanding of HRM as a profession came from training and consultancy firms (Tepp, 2007). Besides continuous further training, professionalism was developed by obtaining practical experience – in this foreign companies played a great role. The services of companies providing further training in management came to the market faster and in a more flexible way than the faculties of economics at universities and business and management schools were able to offer. Since the middle of the 1990s, academic study programmes have provided subjects dealing with HRM and HR development, and a little later also the corresponding specialization options. Professional HR managers have had worthy challenges in companies with foreign ownership and these, in their turn, have facilitated a wider development of HR managers and the HR function as such in the whole country (Alas, 1998).

Slowly but steadily organizations started to view HR managers as advisors to managers and employees. HR managers proved to be of special value during periods of organizational change (Alas, 1998). The second half of the 1990s was rich in changes that took place in organizations. The changes were brought about both by the Western capital that started to pour into Estonia and by Estonian entrepreneurs who began to invest in neighbouring countries. The reason why the role of HR managers expanded was primarily the fact that implementing organizational changes required the preparation of employees. Some prerequisites for successful changes include communicating, informing, motivating and involving employees. Considering their preparation and responsibilities, HR managers in several large organizations were the most obvious people to handle the above-mentioned tasks and to advise other managers. However, this was far from the typical characteristic of HR in Estonia. Such a function primarily existed in larger organizations that employed competent HR managers, also recognized by top executives.

In the mid-1990s, there were but a few organizations in Estonia that viewed HR managers as strategic partners of senior managers. Similarly, there were not many companies with senior managers that would have accepted HR managers as business partners. It has to be noted that HRM was not one of the highest priorities among the many fields that required development (Alas, 2001).

One of the research studies of the last decade arrives at the conclusion that HR managers, as a rule, do not act as strategic partners to senior managers and that senior managers, in their turn, are not quite able to put their finger on those objectives where the expertise of HR managers could prove invaluable (Kalda, 2001). The situation of personnel management in Estonia in the 1990s has been presented in research data in the CRANET survey. Based on the data from the 1999/2000 survey, Ignjatovič and Svetlik (2003) have performed an analysis that divides the European countries that participated in the research into four clusters. The organizations that belong to the countries of the Western cluster enjoy a stable environment and represent a professional model in HRM. The characteristic feature of the Northern cluster is the model of employee-centred HRM. The Central and South European cluster is characterized by an approach that supports the management. The peripheral cluster includes countries where companies operate in a mostly dynamic environment and the management-centred model dominates. Based on the research carried out at the end of the last decade, personnel management in Estonia has found its place in the peripheral cluster.

From personnel management towards HRM

In Estonia a shift from personnel management to HRM most likely started at the turn of the century. The Estonian economy was on the increase; new institutions had been established and adapted to the requirements of the EU.

The results of the second CRANET survey carried out in Estonia in 2004 showed that the field of HRM witnessed a growth trend in its strategic nature (*Estonian CRANET Report*, 2004). The role of line managers was growing and companies invested greatly in training employees according to the needs of the business and in carefully selecting, recruiting and motivating managers and specialists.

Personnel/HR function

Relying on CRANET data, the number of people employed in HR departments on average was a little less than 1 per 100 employees. This number is extremely low compared to the European context, where the number of employees in HR functions per 100 workers is 2.52 (Svetlik, 2006).

Among different aspects of HRM, purchased (outsourcing) training and development services and the introduction of HR information systems are used by 95 per cent and 79 per cent of organizations, respectively. In the past four years, the number of organizations that have increased the practice of outsourcing is greatest in these particular aspects (see Table 2.4). In comparison with the results of the 2000 survey, outsourcing in aspects of HRM has become widespread.

The beginning of the current decade in HRM is characterized by the active development of HR strategies and policies to support overall business strategies. The development of HR policies is not the just creation of specialists in this field – other employees in the organization have also been included in this process (Alas, 2005).

Organizations and HR managers started to develop HR policies and strategies in order to support their strategic objectives. The number of organizations, where mission statements and strategies are defined and formulated in writing has increased (Table 2.5). A notable shift has occurred in the definition of HR strategies, which testifies to the aspiration of organizations to integrate HR strategies into corporate

Table 2.4 Outsourcing in HRM in Estonia, 2004 (% of organizations)

	Users of outsourcing	Increase in outsourcing in the past 3 years
Pay and wages	40	21
Pensions	20	8
Benefits	41	17
Training and development	95	53
'Soft' layoff	35	4
HR information systems	79	37

Table 2.5 Percentage of organizations with written strategies and mission statements

	2000 (%)	2004 (%)
Written corporate strategy	62	67
Written HR strategy	26	47
Written mission statement	62	72

strategies. On average, in the business sector every second organization had a written HR strategy in 2004 (Figure 2.1). This change is probably prompted by the business needs of organizations, which motivate the HRM function to design activities in the interests of the efficient implementation of corporate strategies.

Another characteristic is the movement of HR managers into the company management, thereby participating in and contributing to discussions. A slight shift has occurred in the involvement of HR managers on the management board of organizations (Figure 2.2). The involvement of a HR manager in the management of a company signals the recognition of him/her as a business partner and advisor to top managers.

Survey results in 2004 demonstrate that 34 per cent of HR managers in public sector organizations and 36 per cent of HR managers in companies considered themselves part of the management board or the equivalent in the organization. In 2000, the involvement of HR managers in the general management of organizations was somewhat lower.

Figure 2.3 demonstrates that no significant change has occurred in the beginning of the new decade in the involvement of HR managers in terms of organizational

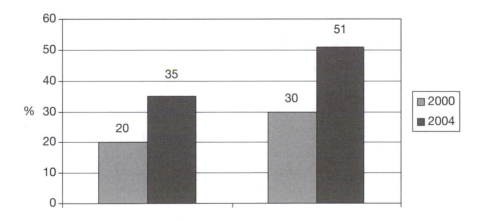

Figure 2.1 Existence of written HR strategies in business and public sector organizations in Estonia (per cent of organizations)

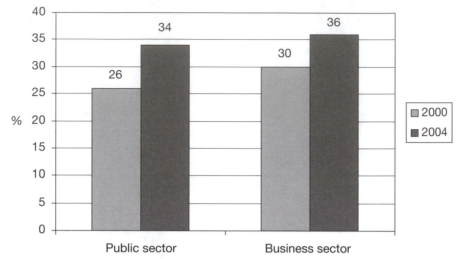

Figure 2.2 Involvement of HR managers on the management board of Estonian organizations (per cent of organizations)

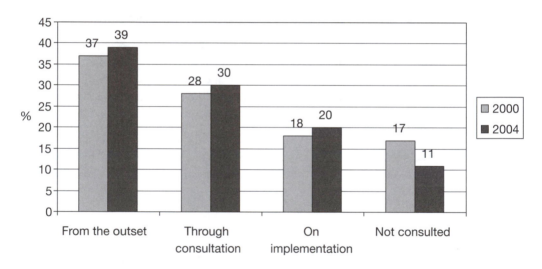

Figure 2.3 Involvement of HR managers in organizational strategy in Estonia (per cent of organizations)

strategy. Nearly 40 per cent of HR managers claim that they have been involved in organizational strategy issues from the outset. The role of line managers in the HR decision-making process indicates the growth in this tendency. The ones who implement HR strategies tend to be line managers rather than HR managers (Alas, 2005).

The CRANET survey also studied the distribution of responsibility in making HR policy decisions. The results demonstrate where responsibility for different HRM aspects lies with line managers or with HR managers, and where they share the responsibilities (Table 2.6). Data presented in Table 2.6 involve organizations with 200 or more employees for the reason that these organizations can be expected to have an HR department. Matters of pay and workforce expansion/reduction are issues where line managers have the first say and clearly carry the main responsibility. In principle, the distribution pattern of decision-making and responsibility between line managers and the HR function has changed little since 2000.

To sum up, one may say that in both the private and public sector the number of HR managers who have been included in the management of the organization has slightly increased, but there is no significant change in the number of HR managers being included in the process of strategy development. There is, however, a considerable step forward in formulating strategies, which is especially predominant in the growing number of organizations with a developed HR strategy. The position of HR managers in terms of business partnership has improved compared to the situation at the end of the 1990s. HR functions are more than ever being filled by way of outsourcing, which sets limits on the growth in the number of people working in the HR department.

The essence and level of HRM is more or less similar in the private and public sector – the organizations in the public sector have caught up with the practices pursued by the private sector. Essential differences in the levels of HRM are larger between small and large enterprises rather than between public and private organizations.

Recruitment and selection

The search for employees, selection and recruitment have become increasingly essential and complex tasks for organizations. As a rule, the demand for highly

Table 2.6 Main responsibility in making HR policy decisions in Estonian organizations with 200 or more employees (per cent of organizations, 2004)

Area of responsibility	Line managers	Line managers and HR department	HR department and line managers	HR department
Recruitment	7	47	42	4
Pay and benefits	27	47	22	4
Training and development	2	35	56	7
Labour relations	11	37	39	13
Workforce expansion or reduction	29	56	13	2

qualified specialists in a country with a developing economy is greater than the supply to satisfy the needs of the labour market. It is typical in Estonia, as well as in the rest of Europe, that organizations face difficulties in recruitment and retention of competent employees, especially professionals. There is a wide gap between the demand for and supply of specialists in Estonia. There is a disproportionate focus on higher education and vocational training, and social sciences compared with technology education (Vanhala *et al.*, 2006). The outflow of labour from certain sectors to countries offering better wages and salaries and the resulting rapid growth in the levels of wages and salaries in Estonia are additional factors making recruitment more complicated. Such a situation in the labour market provides the background for recruiting and selecting employees in organizations in Estonia. This is probably the reason why HR departments in different organizations spend most of their time searching for, selecting and recruiting employees.

Companies tend to use various methods while recruiting. The method most often used is public advertising, especially in circumstances where the company lacks employees with the necessary competency. Internal recruitment is also popular. Recruiting directly from universities or other institutions providing higher education has been marginal, but in the changing circumstances this way of recruiting has become increasingly popular.

The first recruitment agencies were established at the beginning of the 1990s. These agencies started to implement search and evaluation methods which were also accepted by Western companies. Therefore most of 'the agencies' clients comprised foreign companies setting up subsidiaries in Estonia.

In 1996, the first internet-based recruitment agency, CV-Online, was established by four students in Estonia in order to assist students in obtaining jobs. Today the company has expanded into eight Eastern and Central European countries and is the largest internet-based recruitment company in this region. Since the beginning of the current decade, internet-based searching has become widespread, and the use of print media as a channel for searching is common.

Interviews and background checks are the most preferred among selection methods. These are supplemented by methods displaying the applicants' skills and behaviour within a group. Tests of personality, abilities and behaviour type are also frequently used. When making a selection, the element most considered is the compliance of the applicant's personal qualities with the values of the organization (Alas, 2005). The three most frequently used selection methods are personal interview, letter of application with a CV and references.

Relying on the description of the situation in the labour market, one of the most important HRM issues today and in the future in Estonia is how to make oneself attractive as an employer in order to find people suited to one's business needs.

Reward and performance management

In the Estonian business sector there is a high level of decentralization and a large diversity of practices in establishing basic wages (Table 2.7). From 2000 to 2004, there have been no significant shifts in how pay is established. The national and regional levels are those least often used to establish wages. Managers' wages have become slightly more individualized. The majority of organizations follow the practice of fixing the salaries of managers and specialists according to individual wage agreements. In larger organizations, where the development of pay policies is more advanced, company level determination of basic wages is dominant. The pay for workers is mainly fixed on three levels – individual, organizational and according to structural unit. In the use of remunerative incentives, profit sharing demonstrates the most distinct change tendency (Table 2.8). The number of companies where profit sharing is applied grew by the year 2004. Nearly one-third

Table 2.7 Level at which basic managerial and employee wages in the business sector are established in Estonia (per cent of respondents)

	Managers		Manual employees	
	2000	2004	2000	2004
National/industry level	2	4	3	5
Regional level	2	3	2	–
Organization level	41	36	44	33
Structural unit level	14	15	30	27
Individual level	66	74	31	27

Table 2.8 Use of profit sharing and share options in business organizations in Estonia (per cent of respondents)

	Profit sharing		Share options	
	2000	2004	2000	2004
Management	19	31	7	10
Professional/technical	5	15	2	2
Office/administrative	3	10	1	2
Workers	3	5	–	2

of businesses include company management in the profit sharing scheme. The use of share options did not manifest any significant change, except for the managers.

Where they can, companies frequently use a system of pay-for-performance. To do so, a number of companies have implemented a system of performance assessments. The system depends on company results, personal results and a prerequisite of meeting the profit plan. In large enterprises pay systems are frequently based on job evaluation. The most widespread tool used is the Hay system. Since the beginning of 2000, companies have seriously started to consider competency models. Performance assessments and development discussions have become frequent. In addition to the assessment of the immediate manager, the importance of other assessors has increased. Changes that have taken place in employee performance assessment by the year 2004 demonstrate that the number of organizations where the principles of 360 degree assessment are applied has increased (Figure 2.4) On average, subordinates, co-workers and customers were involved in performance assessment in every fourth organization. The results of performance assessment were more frequently linked to determining employee training and development needs, career planning, pay calculation and rewards. Lately, different systems have been implemented to provide assessments via the e-environment.

Training and development

Employee training is the second most time-consuming area next to recruitment and selection within the scope of the HR function (Kalda, 2001). In Estonia, employee training may be considered the most advanced area of HRM. Due to the transition to a market economy at the beginning of the 1990s, an enormous demand for new

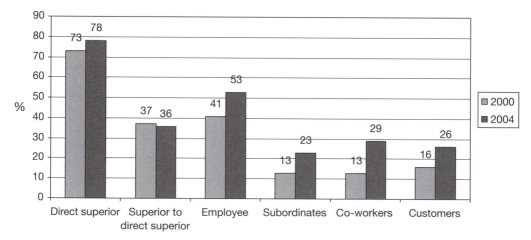

Figure 2.4 Use of different assessors in employee performance assessment in Estonian organizations (per cent of organizations)

knowledge and skills has emerged. The Adult Education Act was passed in 1993 and, in addition to regulating general and informal education, it also regulates the market and conditions for additional training.

The business needs of companies, both in strategic and short-term perspective have been a decisive factor when training employees. Estonian organizations tend to base their employee training on identifying training needs. While identifying and assessing training needs, companies have resorted to competency models and development discussions. Competency requirements have been developed to unite business strategies and employee training. Therefore it is safe to claim that the reasons for employee training rely on the development needs of companies and their employees. Training results are assessed via the results at work, and in this clients also provide a valuable source of information (Alas, 2005).

Employers accept significant expenditure to satisfy development needs. When developing the training budget, the measures are its ratio to salary expenses and the number of training days per year. The average ratio of training costs to salary expenses in Estonian organizations is around 3.5 per cent (*Estonian CRANET Report*, 2004).

As a rule, Estonian organizations offer their employees a relatively substantial number of training days each year. The average number of training days received by different employee categories has increased only slightly between the years 2000 and 2004 (Figure 2.5).

Training is considered important for all company employees. In order to train managers, specialists and teams, organizations use the help and services of training companies. Besides using training companies, in-house vocational training and additional training mainly involving workers are also practised.

The latest CRANET survey showed that the most important training areas in organizations in the near future have been defined as the need to improve customer service skills, leadership and teamwork skills and information technology literacy.

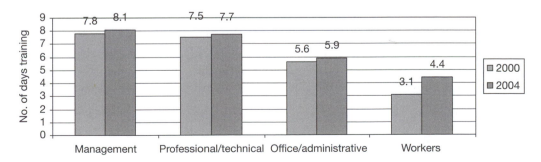

Figure 2.5 Average number of training days according to employee categories in Estonian organizations

THE FUTURE OF HRM IN ESTONIA

Conducting CRANET surveys in Estonia has provided the opportunity to look at the situation of Estonian HR management in the context of other European countries.

Based on the cluster analysis referred to in this chapter, Estonia belongs to the peripheral cluster along with a number of other Eastern-European countries (Ignjatovič and Svetlik, 2003). At the same time, the 'old' market economy countries form regional groups with common features, where the development of HR practices has been strongly influenced by regional and local factors. The relatively similar institutional conditions of Eastern-European countries have most likely defined the development of fairly similar HR patterns.

In principle, the peripheral cluster should fall apart and those countries should find their place in the clusters that are closest to them geographically and culturally. Based on the transition of HRM from the Eastern European cluster to that which is geographically closest, one may assume that in similar political and economic circumstances (democracy and market economy), the common features of HRM are mainly influenced by the cultural aspects of a region and by the institutional effects characteristic of the state.

Vanhala *et al.* (2006) point to an explicit convergence between HRM in Estonian and Finnish companies. Estonia is located in the same cultural area that has shaped HRM in the Nordic region. Therefore the developments and processes in Finland may also be expected in Estonia. We may probably assume that, although lagging behind a number of years, Estonian organizations will take the same route that organizations in Finland and other Nordic countries once did. One may find similar features in the rapid development of HRM strategies, accompanied by the trend of informing employees and involving them in decision-making processes.

Nevertheless, the convergence will not be consistent on all indicators. For instance, the totally different trade union landscape in Estonia compared to other Nordic countries will doubtless have a different effect and will create different practices in the field of labour relations. Estonian enterprises are characterized by direct relations between employers' representatives and workers. Therefore two powers – HR management professionals and managers at different levels – will remain central. The development of Estonian HRM has been greatly influenced by the implementation of information and communication technologies within the structure of organizations. Networks and virtual organizations, flexible working relations and working methods present the area of HRM with new challenges.

Hansabank Group privatizes Lietuvos Taupomasis Bankas

In 1990, when the replacement of the Soviet regime still seemed rather unrealistic in Estonia but the first blossoms of the market economy were already appearing, a group of young people had a plan to establish a new bank. Most of them had no idea about commercial banking. By 1994, Hansabank had become the biggest bank in Estonia, and by 1995, in the Baltic States. By the end of 2004, the net profit of Hansabank Group had reached €182.8 million (annual growth of 40 per cent). The rapid growth of the bank lured a major shareholder, and in 2005 Swedbank decided to acquire all Hansabank shares and withdraw the bank from the Stock Exchange.

Hansabank became the first bank to offer banking services in all three Baltic States: in 1996, Hansabank entered the Latvian market and by the end of 1999 it privatized Lietuvos Taupomasis Bankas in Lithuania.

Hansabank set the ambitious goal of integrating the LTB Bank into the Hansabank Group within one year. By this time the new group member was expected to have become profitable. Therefore a new team of managers, trainers, communicators and personnel staff was formed and sent to Lithuania to carry out the process of integration. The team was expected to be on site in Lithuania for three to four months.

The 'Estonian task force' consisting of specialists and managers was given training prior to their mission. The training sessions had to shape the attitudes of the integration team so that they would not feel like integrators, but part of a cooperative international team where the majority of the team members were Lithuanian. The session also focused on cultural differences – how to start communicating with the Lithuanians, which ice-breaking topics are the best and safest, etc. For instance, raising the topic of family and children, and showing a sincere interest in the private life of the communication partner can be very good techniques for bringing people together. It was important to approach counterparts from the human point of view rather than the rational.

Managers learned to differentiate between active and passive resistance, mitigate the straightforward approach of Estonian business culture, double-check that the tasks they had to implement had been understood and assess the importance of recognition and feedback. It was considered crucial to use face-to-face communication in such a complicated situation involving different cultures. In order to integrate LTB, Hansabank created executive committees in key areas such as information technology, human resources, public relations and communication, retail banking, risk management, leasing, factoring and e-banking.

HRM and internal communication areas worked as the source and transmitter of information. The HRM department as the source of information identified the problem and the internal communication department started to look for and offer solutions. For instance, the HRM department found that the Lithuanian employees felt

continued

uncomfortable and the internal communication department organized an article by a psychologist for the internal newspaper about the reaction of people to change. Similarly, the HRM department often discovered a need and the communication department offered ways to satisfy this need. For instance, the HRM department wanted to inform people about how job vacancies were filled. The internal communication department issued a special newsletter which gave an overview of all the vacancies and the terms and conditions for competition for these positions.

The task of the HRM and internal communication employees was to introduce the Lithuanians to the HRM and management culture of the Estonian organization and the practice of job evaluation interviews and competency patterns with the aim of implementing its management culture at LTB. This was not easy because the differences between the cultures of Hansabank and LTB were substantial.

The creation of a new structure

First a new structure was created and all personnel had to apply for the new positions. The top manager of the Lithuanian bank was appointed by Estonians. He then selected the members of the executive board. The remaining positions within the bank were available through open competition supervised by a 'fair selection committee'. At first, this committee was chaired by an Estonian, but later she was replaced by the head of the local HRM department. The committee had to fill in a selection explanation form about each of the selections made.

The new management was seconded by an integration team in all fields of activity. Every member of the board had a 'shadow' in the person of an integration team member. In reality it was often the case that at meetings the inner circle at the table consisted of Lithuanians, but behind them there was another circle of Estonian 'shadows' or consultants from the integration team. Prior to meetings, the Lithuanian manager discussed all the issues on the agenda with his/her 'shadow'. At the meeting Lithuanian people discussed the matters among themselves, but the consultants were constantly alert in order to assist with advice should it be necessary. The entire process of training the management and HRM department took place in the form of a consultancy.

For the position of HR manager, a person with experience in and knowledge of contemporary HRM was needed. There were no suitable people at LTB, and therefore it was necessary to send someone from Tallinn to handle the situation. The emergency HRM team consisted of four people and was sent to Lithuania for the whole summer. This task force consisted of the HR manager, personnel development manager, a personnel development specialist and a personnel information technology specialist.

The first thing to do was to fill the position of HRM manager. The new manager was a HR consultant from a consultancy company. At the beginning the other employees in the HR department stayed in their positions.

A similar system of 'shadows' to that practised with the management was also used with personnel. The new HR manager also had a 'shadow' from among the integration team. This practice could be to some extent compared to that of mentoring, although in this case the system was much more delicate. Besides instructing the Lithuanian people, it also aimed to make them feel that they were actually managing the whole system. This was one reason why the Estonian Hansabank integration team had to be present in Lithuania for only a few months, so as not to undermine the authority of the local management in the eyes of the Lithuanian employees.

On the first day, the four HR experts in the integration team had a meeting with the employees of the local HR department. The aim of the HR experts was to tell the locals that they had come to assist and have a look at how the integration could be carried out.

The second step was to go bowling with the local HR department employees in order to get acquainted. Unfortunately, the local employees had old Soviet attitudes and therefore entrusting them with key positions was out of the question. On the other hand, the integration team did not want to replace the whole department. The employees had to be motivated to adopt new ways of thinking and working. The Estonians wrote an article for the internal newspaper of the bank, edited by internal communication people. In this article they highlighted the work of the local personnel department, praising them and encouraging them to try even more.

The new HR manager, who had been recruited as part of the integration process, employed a new training manager and emphasized the training of his employees. All employees in the HR department were engaged in the process of recruiting new employees, which turned out to be a new experience for them and therefore called for special training. The training session was not carried out by Estonians, but subcontracted to a Lithuanian company. This was done by the new Lithuanian HR manager, who found the right partners in the market. He also introduced a new vision of HRM and managed to make old-fashioned people learn new things and see things in a new light.

All HRM processes at Hansabank were implemented at LTB. In addition, the Hansabank competency model was introduced.

There were a lot of meetings for employees aimed at introducing the values and goals of the new bank, and highlighting integrity and trust. For example, the oak doors on the Lithuanian managers' offices were replaced with glass doors.

To conclude, the goal was achieved and already in the first quarter of 2002 Hansa-LTB was in profit (€2.45 million). The number of employees was reduced from 3,500 to 2,231. The number of bank offices was reduced from 402 to 155, all operating on-line. The number of cash dispensers had increased from 70 to 268. The internet bank had 124,000 clients.

REFERENCES AND FURTHER READING

Alas, R. (1998). *Human Resource Management Handbook*, 1st edn. Tallinn: Külim (in Estonian).

Alas, R. (2001). Interview with Milvi Tepp. *Human Resource Management*. Tallinn: Külim (in Estonian).

Alas, R. (2003). *Employers' Organisations and the Challenges Facing Business Today*. Geneva: ILO. National report.

Alas, R. (2004). 'The Reasons for the Low Popularity of Trade Unions in Estonia'. *Journal of Human Resource Management*, 1–2: 14–28.

Alas, R. (2005). *Human Resource Management Handbook*. 4th edn. Tallinn: Külim (in Estonian).

Alas, R. and Svetlik, I. (2004). 'Estonia and Slovenia: Building Modern HRM Using a Dualist Approach', in Brewster, C., Mayrhofer, W. and Morley, M., (eds) *Human Resource Management in Europe: Evidence of Convergence?*, Oxford: Elsevier.

Eamets, R. and Masso, J. (2004). 'Labour Market Flexibility and Employment Protection Regulation in the Baltic States', available at: http://www.ettk.ee/upload/Uudiskiri/labour_market_flexibility.pdf.

Estonia, available at: http://www.gla.ac.uk/ecohse/estonia.pdf.

Estonia Page, The, available at: http://www.esis.ee/ist2000/einst/index.htm.

Estonian Association of SMEs, available at: www.evea.ee.

Estonian Chamber of Commerce and Industry, available at: www.koda.ee/.

Estonian CRANET Report (2004). Tallinn: Management Department of Estonian Business School.

Estonian Employees' Unions' Confederation, available at: www.talo.ee.

Estonian Employers' Confederation, available at: www.ettk.ee/en.

Estonica, Encyclopedia about Estonia, Estonian Institute, available at: http://www.estonica.org/eng/lugu.html?menyy_id=411&kateg=73&alam=75&tekst_id=412.

Giaccone, Mario (2007). 'European Foundation for the Improvement of Living and Working Conditions'. *Annual Review of Working Conditions in the EU: 2006–2007*, Dublin, available at: http://www.eurofound.europa.eu/ewco/studies/tn0702028s/tn0702028s.htm.

Gregory, P. (1987). 'Assessing Baltic Living Standards Using Objective and Subjective Measures: Evidence from the Soviet Interview Project'. *Journal of Baltic Studies*, 18, 4: 367–74.

Ignjatovič, M. and Svetlik, I. (2003). 'European HRM Clusters'. *Estonian Business School Review, People Friendly Management*. Tallinn: EBS.

IMD (2004). *World Competitiveness Yearbook*. Lausanne: IMD International.

Kalda, V. (2001). 'Situation of HR Management in Estonian Organisations Based on HR Managers' Evaluations'. Master's Thesis, Tallinn Pedagogical University (in Estonian).

Kein, A. and Tali, V. (1995). 'The Process of Ownership Reform and Privatization', in Lugus, O. and Hachey, G. A. (eds) *Transforming the Estonian Economy*. Tallinn: Majanduse Instituut, pp. 140–68.

Kiik, L. (2000). *Trade Unions under a Foreign Power 1940–1990*. Tallinn: Estonian Trade Unions' Confederation (in Estonian).

Kirso, K. (2006). Interview with Kärt Kirso, HR manager of YIT Estonia Ltd, on 3 July 2006.

Laar, M. (2002). *New Beginning of Estonia*. Wesseling: Konrad Adenauer Stiftung.

Labour Inspectorate, The, available at: http://www.ti.ee/index.php?page=10&.

Leimann, J., Santalainen, T. J. and Baliga, R. B. (2003). 'An Examination of the Dynamics of Transformation of Estonian State-owned Enterprises toward a Free-market Orientation', in Ennuste, Ü. and Wilder, L. (eds) *Essays in Estonia Transformation Economics*. Tallinn: Estonian Institute of Economics and Tallinn Technical University, pp. 49–69.

Liuhto, K. (1999). *The Organisational and Managerial Transformation in Turbulent Business Environments – Managers' Views on the Transition of Their Enterprise in Some of the European former Soviet Republics in the 1990's*, Publications of the Turku School of Economics and Business Administration. Series A–9. Turku: Turku School of Economics and Business Administration.

Misiunas, R. J. and Taagepera, R. (1983). *The Baltic States: Years of Dependence, 1940–1980.* London: Hurst; and Berkeley, CA: University of California Press.

Narusk, A. (2004). 'Foreign Country Attracts Estonians with Temporary Work', *Päevaleht*, 22 March (in Estonian).

Privatisation in Estonia, available at: http://www.esis.ee/ist2000/einst/economy/privatisation.htm.

Purju, A. (1998). 'Interrelationship between Privatization Methods, Ownership Structure and Economic Results – Evidences from Estonia. *Proceedings of First International Workshop on Transition and Enterprise Restructuring in Eastern Europe*, 22–22 August. Copenhagen: Copenhagen Business School.

Rajasalu, T. (1995). 'Macroeconomic Stabilization and Development', in Lugus, O. and Hachey, G. A. (eds) *Transforming the Estonian Economy*. Tallinn: Majanduse Instituut, pp. 16–51.

Rajasalu, T. (2003). 'Indicators of Economic Freedom and Economic Structure as Determinants of Growth and Convergence in Enlarging EU and Priorities for Estonia', in Ennuste, Ü. and Wilder, L. (eds) *Essays in Estonia Transformation Economics*. Tallinn: Estonian Institute of Economics and Tallinn Technical University, pp. 7–32.

Smallbone, D. and Venesaar, U. (2003). 'The State of Small and Medium-Sized Enterprises in Estonia on the Way to Accession', in Ennuste, Ü. and Wilder, L. (eds) *Essays in Estonia Transformation Economics*. Tallinn: Estonian Institute of Economics and Tallinn Technical University, pp. 71–91.

Statistical Yearbook of Estonia (2006). Statistical Office of Estonia, Tallinn.

Statistical Yearbook of Estonia (2007). Statistical Office of Estonia, Tallinn.

Statistics Estonia (2001). Available at: http://pub.stat.ee/px-web.2001/dialog/statfile1.asp.

Statistics Estonia (2006). Available at: http://pub.stat.ee/.

Svetlik, I. (2006). 'Introduction: Cracks in the Success Story', in Svetlik, I. and Ilič, B. (eds) *HRM's Contribution to Hard Work: A Comparative Analysis of Human Resource Management*. Bern: Peter Lang.

Svetlik, I. and Alas, R. (2006). 'The European Union and HRM: Impact on Present and Future Members', in Larsen, H. H. and Mayrhofer, W. (eds) *Managing Human Resources in Europe. A Thematic Approach*. London: Routledge.

Taagepera, R. (1993). *Estonia – Return to Independence.* Boulder, CO: Westview Press.

Taaler, J. (1995). 'Economic Reforms: The Main Stages, Programmes and Evaluations', in Lugus, O. and Hachey, G. A. (eds) *Transforming the Estonian Economy*. Tallinn: Majanduse Instituut, pp. 1–15.

Tepp, M. (2007). 'HR Profession in Estonia: Content and Contradictions', paper submitted to the 22nd Workshop on Strategic Human Resource Management, EIASM, Brussels, 19–20 April 2007.

Tüvi, E. (2006). Interview with Ene Tüvi, HR Manager of Merko Construction Ltd, on 4 July.

Vanhala, S. (1995). 'Human Resource Management in Finland'. *Employee Relations* (Bradford), 17, 7: 31–57.

Vanhala, S., Kaarelson, T. and Alas, R. (2006). 'Converging Human Resource Management. A Comparison between Estonian and Finnish HRM'. *Baltic Journal of Management*, 1, 1: 82–101.

World Bank (2007). *Doing Business 2007*, available at http://www.doingbusiness.org/ documents/DoingBusiness2007_Overview.pdf.

Zamascikov, S. (1987). 'Soviet Methods and Instrumentalities of Maintaining Control over the Balts'. *Journal of Baltic Studies*, 18, 3: 221–34.

Zirnask, V. (2006). 'Estonian Labour Legislation Is Hostile for Employers' (in Estonian), available at: http://www.ettk.ee/et/kommentaarid/2006/09/item23069.

3 Managing human resources in Lithuania

ASTA PUNDZIENE AND ILONA BUČIŪNIENĖ

INTRODUCTION

Lithuania is a country with a long and rich history going back to 2000 BC; however, the name of Lithuania was first mentioned only in AD 1009 in the Annales Quedlinburgenses. Since that time Lithuania has become a visible player among European countries. In 1236 Lithuania was united and became a kingdom under Grand Duke Mindaugas, who was later crowned king. In 1392–1430 Lithuania stretched from the Baltic to the Black Sea. In the sixteenth century, due to the growing strength of Russia, Lithuanian territories started shrinking. Finally Lithuania was annexed by Russia in 1795, and regained its independence only in 1918. However, in 1945 Lithuania suffered annexation for the second time, this time by Soviet Russia. In 1991 Lithuania gained its independence and since then it has operated as the independent Republic of Lithuania. In 2004 Lithuania joined the European Union.

Lithuania is located in Europe, with a total area of 65,300 km^2. Lithuania has borders with Belarus, Latvia, Poland and Kaliningrad region; the length of its Baltic Sea coastline is 90 km. The climate of the country is maritime: wet, moderate winters and summers. The terrain is lowland, with many scattered small lakes and fertile soil. There are 2,830 lakes larger than 0.5 ha in Lithuania. The country is not rich in natural resources, which mainly consist of peat, amber, oil, dolomite, limestone and timber.

The population is 3,607,899 (July 2004 est.). The age structure of the Lithuanian population is as follows: 0–14 years, 16.7 per cent; 15–64 years, 68.4 per cent; and 65 years and over, 14.9 per cent. The general demographical tendency echoes that of Europe – Lithuanian society is aging, which causes challenges for human resource management (HRM). Lithuania is still very much a homogeneous society, with only a few ethnic groups: Lithuanian (80.6 per cent), Russian (8.7 per cent), Polish (7 per cent), Belarusian (1.6 per cent) and other (2.1 per cent). The primary religion is Roman Catholicism; however, Lutheran, Russian Orthodox, Protestant, Evangelical Christian Baptist, Muslim and Jewish religions are practised as well. The official language is Lithuanian; it has Indo-European roots and belongs to the

Baltic language family. The most popular foreign languages are Russian, English, Polish, German and French.

The most developed industries in Lithuania are metal-cutting machine tools, electric motors, television sets, refrigerators and freezers, petroleum refining, shipbuilding (small ships), furniture, textiles, food processing, fertilizers, agricultural machinery, optical equipment, electronic components, computers and amber. The main processes that have taken place in the Lithuanian economy since 1991 are as follows: the collapse of mega factories, privatization, as well as growth of the entrepreneurial spirit that resulted in the development of the small and medium-sized enterprise (SME) sector. Another aspect to be mentioned is the reform of the research and development (R&D) system. The main goal of the reform has been to increase the efficiency of the R&D system and to strengthen links between research and industry, which will enable Lithuania to become a knowledge-based economy. So far the most successful results have been obtained in biotechnology and biochemistry, laser optics, chemistry and physics.

Along with economic reforms, changes have also taken place in people's minds as well. Lithuanian society has acquired new attitudes towards life values and work motivation. The above changes of social consciousness and organizational culture have been of the utmost significance in the country's transition to a market economy, as people's work attitudes towards fairness, sense of responsibility and work activity largely condition the quality of private and professional life and the pace of its economic growth.

The above period is unique not only for the development of Lithuania, but for the rest of Eastern and Western Europe as well. New challenges have arisen for all levels of management. At the international level, heads of governments and international organizations have sought means that would assist in the management of the labour force. At the national macro-economic level, governments have been trying to find the best solutions for national economic and industry-specific reforms that would lead to enhanced country and industry effectiveness and competitiveness.

THE TRANSITION PROCESS

After regaining its independence in 1991 and rejecting the centralized economy, Lithuania has undertaken the task of transforming its overall economy and individual industries, as well as returning to a market economy. This transitional period can be subdivided into the following three conditional stages:

1 1989–94 – destruction of the socialist economy;
2 1995–2001 – development of the market economy;
3 2001 to present – rapid growth of the economy and integration into the European Union.

Destruction of the socialist economy (1989–94)

In 1991 the Lithuanian government declared the start of economic reform, within which the year 1994 was scheduled as the primary date for ending the privatization process. At this stage, public property was denationalized and privatized, new market economy relations replaced those of the Soviet planned economy, the market was liberalized and many industries underwent restructuring. Under privatization, state-owned enterprises became joint stock or stock companies, wherein employees could purchase shares and become shareholders.

The period of 1991–3 witnessed labour transition from former large-scale state-owned enterprises to sole traders and joint stock companies who offered considerably higher pay. Moreover, a large proportion of the employable population were engaged in private business activities. At the time, numerous trading, service providing and manufacturing sole trader companies were set up, the produce of which was mainly exported to the former Soviet Union and Eastern European countries. Other characteristics of the above period comprise such phenomena as the emergence of the black market, tax avoidance and partially, or totally, unofficial labour remuneration. Consequently the liberalization of the economy, i.e. withdrawal from the price control mechanism, led to such outcomes as economic decline and inflation – prices began escalating in contrast to a relatively dilatory work pay increase, on the one hand, and growing unemployment, on the other hand (see Table 3.1). Moreover, due to the unstable and chaotic external environment, organizations were not engaged in long-term planning, employee development or motivation enhancement. As for the managerial attitude, it mainly focused on external factors, such as the search for new markets and suppliers, making large profits, while employee motivation was considered an issue of lesser significance (Bučiūnienė, 1996). Most Lithuanian industrial enterprises supported the Tayloristic approach to people as task executors, and strongly believed work pay to be the key driver of work motivation. Management competence was very low as well. Those who held managerial positions had either brought experience from the planned economy or had no management competence at all. For a while, it was believed that 'everything will be regularized by the market'. Employees' motivation was completely ignored, for they were expected to work hard in exchange for pay. In case of any dissatisfaction, employees were offered the option of leaving, as there were large numbers of people outside organizations willing to take their jobs.

The processes posed a great danger to the country, as the prestige status of knowledge and competence was declining, and the country faced the threat of becoming a cheap labour supplier. The above premise proved right at a later date when migration flows began to rise and some industries (e.g. textiles, furniture) became cheap labour providers.

Table 3.1 Lithuanian socio-economic indicators, 1991–2006

Indicators	1991	1992	1993	1994	1995	1996	1997	1998	1999	2000	2001	2002	2003	2004	2005	2006
Population (thousands)	3,736.5	3,746.9	3,736.5	3,724.0	3,717.7	3,601.6	3,575.1	3,549.3	3,524.2	3,499.5	3,481.3	3,469.1	3,454.2	3,435.6	3,414.3*	3,394.1
Labour force (thousands)	1,902.8	1,879.3	1,859.3	1,740.7	1,752.6	1,783.5	–	1,716.0	1,705.5	1,671.5	1,635.8	1,630.3	1,641.9	1,620.6	1,606.8	1,574.2
Inflation (%)	–	–	–	–	–	13.1	8.4	2.4	0.3	1.4	2.0	–1.0	–1.3	2.9	3.0	4.5
Average monthly net earnings (€)	–	–	37.0	72.7	104.6	135.2	167.0	198.0	209.2	200.5	202.6	211.0	227.76	242.0	268.0*	317.4
Average monthly gross earnings (€)	682.61	5,131.02	48.1	94.2	138.7	179.0	225.4	269.3	286.0	281.2	284.5	293.7	310.7	332.9	376.1	434.5
Average old-age pension (€)	–	–	16.13	31.4	42.6	55.7	70.3	83.4	89.8	90.5	92.0	93.6	98.6	107.6	121.7	138.1
Unemployment rate (%)	0.3	1.3	4.4	3.8	6.1	7.1	14.1	13.2	13.7	16.4	16.5	13.5	12.4	11.4	8.3	5.6
GDP at constant 2000 prices (€ million)	17,160.0	13,511.9	11,319.5	10,214.0	10,740.9	11,243.3	12,031.1	12,906.9	12,688.3	13,185.2	14,026.0	14,973.6	16,558.5	17,836.5	19,169.4*	23,746.2*
GDP change (%)	–5.7	–21.3	–16.2	–9.8	3.3	4.7	7	7.3	–1.7	3.9	6.4	6.8	10.6	7.0	7.6*	7.5*
GDP per capita at constant 2000 prices (€ thousands)	4,632.8	3,651.8	3,073.7	2,792.8	2,959.6	3,121.8	3,365.4	3,636.5	3,600.3	3,767.7	4,028.9	4,316.2	4,793.8	5,191.7	5,614.3	6,996.4*

Notes: €1 = 3.4528 litas.

*Provisional data from source: 1991–5 data provided from Department of Statistics to the Government of the Republic of Lithuania, 1997. *Statistical Yearbook of Lithuania.* Vilnius: Methodical Publishing Centre, Department of Statistics to the Government of the Republic of Lithuania; 1996–2006 data provided from Department of Statistics to the Government of the Republic of Lithuania, 2006. *Main Indicators of Economic and Social Development, 1996–2006,* available at: http://www.std.lt/en/pages/view/?id=1364 (accessed 10 August 2007).

Development of the market economy (1995–2000)

The year 1995 was a turning point for the Lithuanian economy: GDP started rising (Geralavičius, 1999) and the influx of foreign investment brought about new management methods, which, in turn, made a considerable impact on the labour market and managerial attitude towards employees. It was at this stage that labour relations based on a market economy developed, and companies started applying employee selection, recruitment and management methods. Foreign investment necessitated a qualitatively new workforce, as the managerial generation of the planned economy failed to meet the requirements that were created by the new environment. Subsequently opportunities opened for those who were fast to retrain, develop market-dictated competences and make good use of them. University graduates undertook activities that were completely unrelated to their education or qualifications. As in Soviet times the dominant foreign language in the country was Russian, foreign capital companies located in Lithuania were forced to offer managerial positions to graduates with a major in foreign languages.

Under the above conditions, a new managerial generation was born, which had either to develop or start business in a highly dynamic environment and to adapt foreign experience to specific national political and economic factors. In addition to gaining a good education, highly qualified and competitive specialists and managers underwent extra 'toughening training' in doing business at the time of the Russian recession in 1998–2000 (Geralavičius 1999).

Rapid growth of economy and integration into the European Union (2001 to present)

This stage can be best characterized by the rapid growth of the economy, a decrease in unemployment and a rise in the country's migration to Western Europe and the US. Though Lithuania has one of the highest unemployment rates in Europe, its rate has been falling at the fastest pace.

One of the consequences of the EU integration process is the growing rate of population mobility. Since Lithuania joined the EU on 1 May 2004, its citizens have been among the most active persons in the new member states to leave their country. No longer an isolated country, Lithuania is now facing more and more global tendencies, such as population decrease and a rise in the average lifespan. In 2004–6, Lithuania held a leading position in economic growth. However, in its turn, this rapid economic growth has resulted in a lack of highly competent as well as unskilled employees (Lithuanian Free Market Institute, 2006). Moreover, employees and employers have become equal partners, where both sides raise certain specific requirements and are in the position of having the power to choose.

The issue of finding employees with the right qualification is becoming more and more critical in Lithuania, as more and more highly qualified employees are taking the opportunity of foreign employment (Barcevičius, 2005). The level of unemployment has been constantly decreasing: in 2001 it stood at 16.5 per cent, while in 2006 it dropped to 5.6 per cent (see Table 3.1). Consequently employee retention and motivation have become key human resource management issues, as well as central conference and article topics. Organizations have started making heavier investment into human resources, striving to recruit, retain and motivate employees by spending more on employee development and on relationship building with current as well as prospective employees. The level of employee remuneration has risen as well (see Table 3.1). In addition, numerous companies have started conducting employee job satisfaction surveys and investing in staff and management training. Since 2005 the initiative has been taken to select the most desirable employer, which implies a concern about the public image among companies.

A favourable change can be noticed in the organizational attitude to employees. The majority of company managers have realized that human resources create a sustainable and inimitable competitive advantage.

THE CONTEXT FOR HUMAN RESOURCE MANAGEMENT

Stakeholders such as employers, trade unions and the industrial relations context

Industrial relations in Lithuania comprise both the social partnership and social dialogue. Both social partnership and social dialogue, in the Western European meaning, constitute a new phenomenon in Lithuania, as in other post-Soviet countries. The first legal document describing principles of social partnership and social dialogue was enacted in 1990. It was the Inhabitants Employment Law, legitimating principles of the social partnership and the functions of tripartite committees in the field of labour market policy. The system of the social partnership covering the Tripartite Council of the committees is regulated by the Labour Code of the Republic of Lithuania. Based on the agreement made by the social partners, the Tripartite Council is comprised of members with equal rights: representatives of trade unions, employers' organizations and the government of the Republic of Lithuania. In compliance with the procedures established in the law and collective agreements, other tripartite or bipartite councils (commissions and committees) may be established to examine and solve issues such as employment, health and safety at work, social policies issues, etc. In line with EU regulations, collective agreements in Lithuania may be concluded at the national, sector (production, services, occupational, etc.) or territorial (local government, country) levels, as well as at the enterprise or structural subdivision level. The Labour Code defines the collective agreement as a written agreement between an employee, employer and a collective regarding labour, its remuneration and other social and economic conditions (e.g. collective bargaining of pay, working time, job security, equal opportunities and diversity issues, and training and skills development). It also looks into legislative developments, the organization and the role of social partners, industrial action, employee participation and absence from work, harassment, new forms of work, etc. (European Foundation for the Improvement of Living and Working Conditions, 2004). There are three types of institution that consider collective disputes, conditions for their establishment and activities, and that legalize strikes. Collective disputes are resolved with the help of the following institutions:

- The Conciliation Commission (CC) is for hearing collective disputes. The CC should hear the collective dispute within seven days of its beginning. The CC is formed from an equal number of the authorized representatives of the parties in dispute. The decision of the CC should be adopted by the agreement between the parties and must be implemented within the time limit and procedures specified in the decisions.
- Labour arbitration (LA) is meant to carry on with the hearing when agreement between parties in dispute is not reached at the Conciliation Commission. It consists of a judge of a district court and six arbiters appointed by the parties to a collective labour dispute. After the hearing is over, a decision of the LA should be adopted by majority voting. The decision of the LA is not subject to appeal.
- The Court of Arbitration (CA) takes over the hearing of the collective dispute when an agreement between the parties in dispute is not reached at the Conciliation Commission. The parties should appoint one or several arbitrators to the Court of Arbitration. The decision of the CA is adopted by majority voting and laid down in writing and undersigned by all arbiters. The decision of the CA is binding on the parties in dispute.

If none of the mentioned institutions succeeds in resolving the dispute, a strike may be declared.

Trade unions have a long history in Lithuania, which goes back to Soviet times; however, with the regaining of national independence the system has become fragmented. With the Law on Trade Unions of the Republic of Lithuania, citizens of the Republic of Lithuania, as well as other persons who are permanently residing in the country, who are 14 or more years of age and who work under an employment contract, or other grounds, have the right to freely join trade unions and take part in their activities. Moreover, where an enterprise, or an institution, has no functioning trade union and if the staff meeting has not transferred the function of employee representation and protection to the trade union of the appropriate sector of economic activity, the employees are represented by the labour council elected by secret ballot at a general meeting of the staff. The legal side of trade union functioning is well established; however, no competence or best practices were inherited from Soviet times. In that sense present trade unions have to establish their practices anew and learn how to effectively operate in social partnerships.

Employers' organizations in Lithuania are comparatively young. Most of them were established at the beginning of the 1990s, with the regaining of national independence. Today we can name such organizations as the Lithuanian Chamber of Commerce, Industry and Crafts, which was established in 1992. The latter is a non-governmental organization uniting over 1,500 enterprises. In addition, another two employers' representatives can be identified: the Lithuanian Confederation of Employers and the Lithuanian Confederation of Industrialists. The former is a public body that unites over 500 enterprises and 100 associated structures. The latter is a union of associations. It unites about 40 branch associations, 9 regional associations and more than 60 non-associated structures. The main functions carried out by the above employer-representing bodies are the representation of employers' interests on various governmental committees, commissions, councils and ministries, as well as lobbying and expert delegation by different branches to industrial lead bodies working on vocational standards (Kaminskiene, 2005)

Key labour market developments

The main changes in the structure of the labour market occurred after the country regained independence. As has already been mentioned, the main features of the transition period were as follows: privatization and the development of new legal forms of organization. The industrial giants were replaced by small and medium-sized enterprises, including family businesses. At the beginning of the transition process, the labour market was going through the difficult period of fine-tuning of unbalanced supply and demand processes in the labour force. Due to the restructuring of the economy and inertia of economic growth, unemployment was growing rapidly. Re-qualification and adaptation to the new labour market requirements took some time, until 1999, when the growth of the economy became noticeable. In line with global tendencies of the development of the knowledge economy and society, the nature of work was changing as well. The world of work demanded creative, intelligent individuals, able to solve problems and acquire new meaningful perspectives (Adomaitienė and Tereseviciene, 2002). Supply did not match demand either in competence needed nor in its quantity. Since Lithuania joined the European Union, recruitment and retention have become a major problem for employers (Pundziene et al., 2006). The migration of the labour force to EU countries has become a threat. It is interesting to note that the peak of emigration from Lithuania was the year 1992; in 1999 it decreased noticeably and then started to grow again in the past three years (Stankūnienė, 2004).

The annual reports of the Lithuanian Labour Exchange (LLE) indicate that the number of vacancies for permanent jobs registered on the LLE in 2005 was 101,900, and 22,200 for temporary jobs. In 2005, compared to the same period of the previous year, the number of vacancies for permanent jobs increased by 700, and 6500 for temporary jobs. In 2005 the LLE was able to offer vacancies to as many as 75.7 per cent of the unemployed addressing the LLE; in 2004 the figure stood at 64 per cent, while in 2003 it was 54 per cent. (See Figures 3.1 and 3.2.) The structure of workplaces is changing as well.

The economy has been improving at a fast pace in recent years. The growth of the country's economy has encouraged the growth of employment. It is forecasted

Per cent

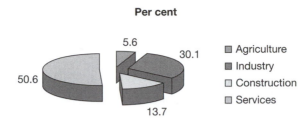

Figure 3.1 Vacancies registered in Lithuania according to economic activities, 2005
Source: Lithuanian Labour Exchange, 2005.

Per cent

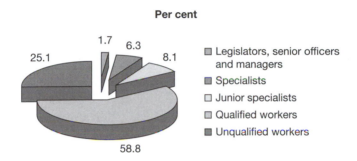

Figure 3.2 Vacancies registered in Lithuania according to professional groups, 2005
Source: Lithuanian Labour Exchange, 2005.

that Lithuanian GDP increase will remain one of the highest in Europe. The growth of the labour demand for labour, productivity increases and the convergence of prices upon accession to the EU will keep making a positive influence upon the growth of wages. The national average monthly wage will grow at an increasing pace.

The balance of the established workplaces, which is 44,000, is currently the highest it has been in the 10 years since the first forecast was carried out. A positive balance of new workplaces is planned in both small and large companies (see Table 3.2).

Key legislative provisions

Labour relations in the country are regulated by the Constitution of the Republic of Lithuania, adopted by the citizens of the Republic of Lithuania in the referendum of 25 October 1992, and the Labour Code, which was amended in line with the EC requirements in 2003 (Labour Code of the Republic of Lithuania, 2003). Ratification of the Labour Code marks an epoch of renouncing legal acts inherited from the Soviet system and accepting European law. The provisions of the Lithuanian Labour Code conform to EU Acts and Directives. The Labour Code provides that all people

Table 3.2 Forecast of workplaces to be established in Lithuania

In services	*In manufacturing*
Wholesale and retail trade	Wood products
Transport, warehousing and communications	Food production
Computers, IT	Clothes makin
Business services	Metal articles
Hotels and restaurants	Electronic equipment

For specialists	*For service employees and qualified workers*
Warehousing servants	Shop assistants
Sales, marketing, tourism and commerce managers	Carpenters, builders and joiners
Physicians	Bricklayers
Accountants	Painters
Engineers	Drivers
Insurance agents	Tailors
Computer equipment operators	Welders
Technicians in construction engineering	Wood processing machine and equipment operators

Source: Lithuanian Labour Exchange web page (http://www.ldb.lt/LDB_Site/index.htm (accessed May 2006).

are to be treated equally irrespective of their gender, sexual orientation, race, national origin, language, citizenship and social status, religion, marital status, age, opinions or views, political party or public organization membership, and factors unrelated to the employee's professional qualities. Article 48 of the Constitution provides that 'Each human being may freely choose a job or business, and shall have the right to have proper, safe and healthy conditions at work, to receive fair pay for work and social security in the event of unemployment'.

Work time

The Lithuanian Labour Code provides that the working time of a person shall not exceed 40 hours a week, where a daily period of work shall not be more than eight hours. The maximum working time per week including overtime may not exceed 48 hours (Labour Code of the Republic of Lithuania, 2003).

The pay for overtime and night work has to be at least one and a half times the hourly pay/monthly wages established for the employee. The pay for work on a rest day or a holiday which has not been provided for in the work schedule has to be at least at double rate, or compensated by granting the employee another rest day in the same month or by adding that day to his annual paid leave.

Annual leave

Article 49 of the Constitution guarantees that each working person has the right to rest and have leisure as well as to take annual paid leave. The minimum annual leave is 28 calendar days. Employees under 18 years of age, single parents raising a child under the age of 14 and/or a disabled child under the age of 16, and disabled persons are granted 35 calendar days of annual paid leave. An extended annual leave of up to 58 calendar days can be granted to certain categories of employees whose work involves greater nervous, emotional and intellectual strain and professional risk, as well as those working under specific working conditions.

Maternity pay

Women shall be entitled to the following maternity leave: 70 calendar days before the birth and 56 calendar days after the birth (in the event of complicated confinement or birth of two or more children, 70 calendar days).

Work pay

The Lithuanian government determines the minimum hourly pay and the minimum monthly wage. Since 2005, the minimum pay in Lithuania has been €145.

Severance pay

Severance pay is one of the legal means that ensure employment safety. The Lithuanian Labour Code (Article 140) provides that a dismissed employee shall be paid severance pay in the amount of his or her average monthly wage (from one to six months) taking into account the continuous length of service of the employee concerned at that workplace.

Labour relations

The rights and interests of employees may be represented and protected by trade unions. Trade unions shall be freely established and shall function independently. They shall defend the professional, economic and social rights and interests of employees (Article 50 of the Constitution, 1992). Where an enterprise, establishment or organization has no functioning trade union and the staff meeting has not transferred the function of employee representation and protection to the trade union of the appropriate sector of economic activity, the employees shall be represented by the labour council elected by a secret ballot at the general meeting of the staff (Article 19 of the Labour Code). While defending their economic and social interests, employees shall have the right to strike (Article 51 of the Constitution, 1992). The procedure for organizing strikes is described in detail in the Lithuanian Labour Code.

The impact of the move to the EU membership on HRM

Integration into the European Union has provided Lithuanian citizens with an opportunity to move freely and find employment in other EU countries. One of the key reasons for emigration is the quite considerable work pay differences. Based on Eurostat data, the minimum work pay is 3.5–10.1 and the average pay 2.4–9.1 times lower in Lithuania than in other Western European countries. In 2004 Lithuanian emigrants comprised 15,165 persons. While findings of the 2001 survey aimed at evaluating the consequences of the EU citizen free movement demonstrated that 63.1 per cent of the population would like to leave the country for 'good' or 'temporarily' (Ministry of Social Security and Labour, 2001), the results of the 2005 survey revealed a downward tendency in migration (Ministry of Social Security and Labour, 2005) where 1.3 per cent of the population would like to leave the country for good and 14.9 per cent temporarily. An assumption can be made that the majority of those who intended to leave the country have already done so. In addition, increasing demand for labour and work pay have a negative impact on intention to leave the country.

Lithuania has already faced the negative consequences of emigration: a large part of the emigrants comprise young able people, which has led to a fall in the number of potential taxpayers (Civil Society Institute *et al.*, 2005). Along with lower birth rates, emigration contributes to the population decrease in Lithuania. The greater part of Lithuanian enterprises have been affected by workforce emigration (Lithuanian Free Market Institute, 2006). It reduces the unemployment rate and increases managerial anxiety over qualified workforce scarcity, which is reflected in recent newspaper headlines, such as 'Escaping Minds are Irreplaceable', 'Lithuania Holds the Leading Position in Labour Drain to the EU', etc.

Emigration also contributes to increases in work pay not only because of declining employee numbers, but also because of rising labour mobility in the domestic market – higher job supply encourages people to change jobs more often. In 2005–6 employee retention became the number one HR issue (Hay Group, 2005; TNS Gallup, 2006).

By way of concluding, a presumption can be made that Lithuania's joining the EU induced employers and the country to pay considerable attention to increasing their attractiveness. At the national macro-economic level, the government is trying to find solutions for national economic and industry-specific reforms, leading to an increase in the country's and industries' effectiveness and competitiveness.

TRENDS AND DEVELOPMENTS IN HUMAN RESOURCE MANAGEMENT PRACTICE IN LITHUANIA

The nature of the HR function

The HRM function in Lithuania has followed the history of the country and its transformations. The state of HRM practices is related to the Soviet heritage and negative attitudes to HRM. In the Soviet period, the department that was responsible for personnel issues in companies in all ex-Soviet Union republics was called a 'cadre department'. Along with administrative functions, such as employee recruitment, dismissal and employee data collection and recording, cadre departments used to develop employee training and reserve plans, were responsible for developing employee qualification and produced staff CVs. Cadre departments carried out political and ideological roles: they developed employees in the spirit of socialist values. As a rule, the above departments were managed by members of the Communist Party, who had previously held such positions as a company communist party or young communist secretary, or trade union chairman. In companies with a military status, cadre departments were associated with the KGB and performed the function of employee history and reliability check-ups. During this period, HRM was considered a scientifically and practically irrelevant domain and was not taught as a discipline at educational establishments.

Since Lithuania's independence, HRM has been taught at Kaunas University of Technology and Vilnius University, but HRM specialization is not popular among students. In 1999 a human resource management study programme was developed at ISM University of Management and Economics. This master of management programme is gaining more and more popularity among HRM practitioners and managers in other fields. Nevertheless, Lithuanian enterprises still suffer a lack of HRM professionals, which was revealed by a TNS Gallup survey carried out in 2006 during which managers with an HRM responsibility in 304 Lithuanian companies with over 50 employees were interviewed (TNS Gallup, 2006). The scarcity of HRM professionals is particularly perceived in large trade and services industry companies.

Following the results of the HRM practitioner survey, in the majority of companies (71 per cent), the HR department was given the same level of importance as other departments (TNS Gallup, 2006). It seems that the significance of the HRM department is no longer doubted in Lithuania. However, according to research data, 41 per cent of the respondents pointed out insufficient attention to HRM. Lack of time, resources, knowledge and skills was indicated as the main reason related to this issue. Twenty-one per cent of the respondents pointed out that currently HRM is not relevant to their companies and 13 per cent noted that top managers do not favour this area. The above-mentioned facts prove that HRM still does not have the same importance as other functions in Lithuanian organizations.

In their daily duties HRM practitioners allocated most of their attention to administrative functions such as the registration of employees' records, composition of work contracts, work safety and time administration, employees' recruitment and selection (TNS Gallup, 2006). Employee orientation, career planning and change management are those areas which get the least attention from HRM practitioners.

HRM practitioners ranked their knowledge and skills in HRM administration, i.e. registration of employees' records, composition of work contracts, work safety and time administration, employees' recruitment and selection, as best mastered. The weakest point in the HRM practitioners' competence was change management. The present finding shows that HRM practitioners give attention and allocate time to the HRM areas that they feel most competent in. The above fact should be taken into consideration when developing HRM education and training programmes.

Most enterprises considered employee retention, performance and reward management as the most critical human resource areas, while equal opportunities and relationships with unions were least problematic for HR practitioners (Hay Group, 2005; TNS Gallup, 2006).

To determine the key roles of HRM in the largest Lithuanian organizations, a survey of employees with an HRM responsibility or company managers in case of their absence, was carried out in May 2006 (Bučiūnienė and Bigelienė, 2006). A sample of 89 enterprises was selected from an overall population of the 500 largest Lithuanian companies listed in the company directory of leaders of Lithuanian business. HRM roles were measured following Conner and Ulrich's (1996) model, which is based on the following two dimensions: strategic, i.e. competing demands of future focus; and operational, i.e. operational focus, defining four HR roles – strategic partner, change agent, administrative expert and employee champion. The levels of all HR roles in Lithuanian companies were rather low (6.2–6.4 on a 10-point scale). Survey results did not reveal differences between the role means. The roles of administrator, business partner and change agent were given higher scores in organizations that had a human resource manager (see Figure 3.3). This leads to an assumption that the development of HRM roles is dependent on the managerial attitude to personnel. The level of significance attributed to the HRM function by the top-level managers is reflected in the duties of the employee responsible for the performance of HRM functions, i.e. his or her status in the company. Where companies do have HR managers, it means that the significance of HR is considerably higher, which in turn affects the HRM role and performance.

HRM roles are associated with the form of company ownership. Taken together, the HR role scores were lower overall in Lithuanian capital companies than they were in mixed and foreign capital companies (see Figure 3.4). The roles of change agent and strategic partner were ranked highest in the mixed and foreign capital companies. The results of this study show that differences in HRM between Lithuanian and foreign capital companies still persist. Lithuanian capital companies lack experience in the HRM field, and their HRM roles are less developed.

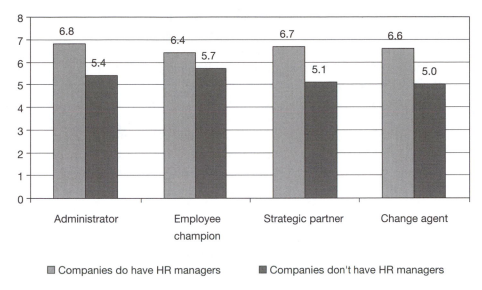

Figure 3.3 Rank means of HR department role distribution in Lithuania based on the existence of a HR manager

Note: A 10-point Likert-type scale was used, where 1 stood for 'completely disagree' and 10 for 'completely agree'.

Source: Bučiūnienė and Bigelienė, 2006.

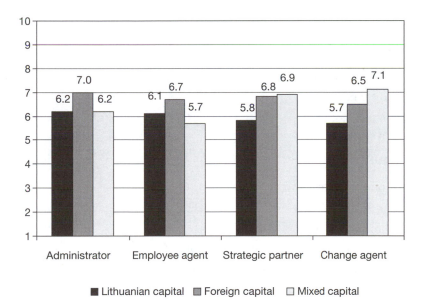

Figure 3.4 Rank means of HR department role distribution in Lithuania based on company ownership

Note: A 10-point Likert-type scale was used, where 1 stood for 'completely disagree' and 10 for 'completely agree'.

Source: Bučiūnienė and Bigelienė, 2006.

The survey was also aimed at measuring HRM outcomes to assess how HRM roles are related to performance outcomes. HRM outcomes were measured following Guest's (1997) model, which includes three groups of HRM performance outcomes: HRM outcomes (commitment, quality and flexibility), behaviour outcomes (effort/motivation, cooperation, involvement and organizational citizenship) and performance outcomes (high productivity, quality, innovation and low absence, labour turnover, conflict, customer complaints). A correlation coefficient was calculated to determine the relationship between HR roles and HRM performance. As provided in Table 3.3, HRM roles bear the strongest relationships with HRM and behaviour outcomes, employee motivation in particular. The strategic partner role was found to have the strongest association with HRM outcomes. It bears a moderate correlation

Table 3.3 Relationship (Spearmen's correlation coefficient) between HRM roles and HRM outcomes in Lithuania (Bučiūnienė and Bigelienė, 2006)

HRM performance outcomes	Mean (standard deviation)	Adminis-trator	Employee agent	Business partner	Change agent
HRM outcomes					
Commitment	6.8	0.177	0.261(*)	0.305(**)	0.197
Work quality	7.4	0.304(**)	0.279(**)	0.381(**)	0.280(**)
Employee flexibility	7	0.242(*)	0.371(**)	0.427(**)	0.335(**)
Behaviour outcomes					
Employee motivation	6.6	0.352(**)	0.500(**)	0.483(**)	0.394(**)
Communication among employees	7	0.248(*)	0.334(**)	0.407(**)	0.349(**)
Employee involvement	6.8	0.284(**)	0.311(**)	0.465(**)	0.333(**)
Performance outcomes					
Employee productivity	7	0.185	0.239(*)	0.401(**)	0.274(**)
Level of innovation	7.2	0.167	0.117	0.292(**)	0.268(*)
Employee turnover	4.9	0.198	0.204	0.004	−0.015
Conflict frequency	3.9	−0.061	0.222(*)	−0.259(*)	−0.234(*)
Customer satisfaction	7.7	0.246(*)	0.307(**)	0.233(*)	0.144
Employee competence	7.8	0.218(*)	0.299(**)	0.271(*)	0.175
Difficulty in recruiting new employees	4.3	0.225(*)	0.013	0.1	0.055

Note: $*p < 0.05$, $**p < 0.01$.

with employee flexibility, motivation, cooperation, involvement and productivity. As for the employee champion role, it was found to correlate with employee motivation.

It can thus be stated that the role of the HRM strategic partnership is highly significant for organizations. The more power it is granted in an organization, the easier it will be to increase not only employee motivation, cooperation, involvement, and flexibility, but productivity as well. Therefore organizations have to put all their effort in the consolidation of the above role.

Recruitment and selection

Due to the current labour market situation as well as growing requirements for employee competence, recruitment and selection (R&S) are becoming more and more difficult and sophisticated processes, especially for employment agencies. The main challenges for recruiting and selecting employees are high demand and low supply of the necessary competencies in the labour market. The R&S process itself has become more and more professional since 1991.

A survey (Kupelyte *et al.*, 2006) was carried out to test what kind of recruitment and selection methods are employed by Lithuanian managers. Fifteen enterprises from different sector and of different sizes (2 small, 9 medium and 4 large) were surveyed. The questionnaires were distributed to managers responsible for the HRM function, or those specializing in recruitment and selection.

Surveyed managers reported that the most popular source of recruitment is advertisements in local newspapers (29 per cent of the sample; see Figure 3.5). The second most popular source comprises employment agencies as well as personal contacts. In comparison with other research data (Dessler, 2005), quite a high number of Lithuanian managers rely on educational institutions and internal recruitment sources (respectively, 13 and 11 per cent, in comparison with 8 and 12 per cent reported in the literature). The main reasons provide by managers for using the above recruitment sources are as follows:

- advertisements in newspapers are regarded as a highly convenient, rapid and not too expensive channel to reach the majority of the target group;
- employment agencies have broad databases and a highly personalized selection of best candidates, which saves managers' time, but is more costly;
- the labour exchange is easy accessible, but its clients are mainly low-qualified workers;
- personal contacts are very reliable, convenient, time saving and costless, but access to the competence pool is limited;
- educational institutions are a convenient way to access young, potential employees with the necessary competence, and there is a broad variety;
- internal recruitment sources are more reliable, for the candidate is well known, which indicates less possibility of being mistaken.

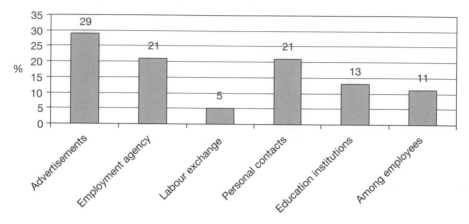

Figure 3.5 Recruitment sources reported by Lithuanian managers
Source: Kupelyte *et al.*, 2006.

Enterprises are still keen to recruit and select employees by themselves. Most of the
time employment agencies are utilized by medium-sized and large enterprises,
especially those with foreign capital. Enterprises that use the services of employment
agencies report that it saves time, and that agencies guarantee a more competent
process of selection, as they have specific knowledge and experience in the field.
Those that do not refer to employment agencies report that the main reason for this is
sufficient in-house competence to carry out the selection process by themselves. Also
they believe that carrying out recruitment and selection by themselves saves the
enterprise money and time. The survey showed that enterprises lack information on
the services that employment enterprises provide, which suggests a low level of trust
in agency work. Small enterprises admitted that they do not feel the need for help
from employment agencies (Kupelyte *et al.*, 2006). In enterprises that do not use the
services of employment agencies, recruitment and selection is carried out by the
manager (see Figure 3.6)

The most popular and most used selection methods in Lithuania are personal
candidate interview (87 per cent of all respondents) and probation period (60 per cent
of all respondents) (see Figure 3.7). The least popular selection methods are self-
administered questionnaires and tests (respectively, 27 and 13 per cent). The results
very much interrelate with enterprise intentions to select employees by themselves.
Most of the time enterprises do not possess sophisticated knowledge on modern
selection tests or competence to administrate them. Besides in-house expertise on
selection methods varies from everyday managerial knowledge on the issue to
professional knowledge of human resource management and organizational
psychology held by human resource managers, if such exist in the enterprise.
Employment agency staff typically hold management and/or organizational
psychology qualifications. Methods employed by employment agencies during the
selection process are as follows:

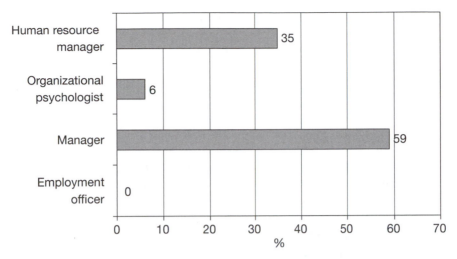

Figure 3.6 Staff responsible for recruitment and selection in Lithuanian enterprises
Source: Kupelyte *et al.*, 2006.

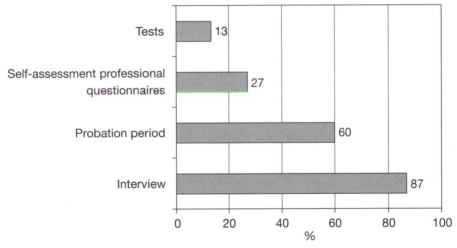

Figure 3.7 Most popular selection methods within Lithuanian enterprises
Source: Kupelyte *et al.*, 2006.

- interviews (un-structured, semi-structured, structured, etc.);
- examination of professional competencies (self-administered professional questionnaires etc.);
- psychometric testing (the most common are the MMPI, California test; however, recently more suitable tests have come to the Lithuanian market, e.g. DiSC), etc.

In that sense employment agencies have expertise on recruitment and selection and the demand for their services should grow in the near future.

Reward and performance management

Several basic factors influence the design and the level of reward: cost of living (inflation); legal factors and government actions; labour market conditions and job differences; strength of the trade union; organizational change; regional, industry-specific and company ownership factors.

Cost of living (inflation)

National inflation affects the cost of living. In 2002–6 inflation was low in Lithuania (see Table 3.1). According to the data provided by the Hay Group obtained from a survey of 212 companies from different industries employing in total over 68,000 employees, i.e. 5 per cent of the total Lithuanian employee population, which was carried out in 2005, the great majority of Lithuanian companies are constantly reviewing their base employee pay. Improvements in company/individual performance constitutes the largest part of the work pay raise, i.e. 76 per cent, whereas the cost of living/inflation increase constitutes only 19 per cent.

Legal factors and government action

The Lithuanian government sets the minimum monthly work pay and controls the amount of state officers' work pay. Under the government's decree, in July 2006 monthly work pay rose to €173, and by the end of 2007 it should reach €231 a month. The above government actions have a considerable impact on the work pay market as well as the national average work pay.

Labour market conditions and job differences

The labour market is one of the determinants of financial compensation. The recent work pay increase has been influenced by the dramatic rise of emigration, which has led to a decrease in the unemployment rate as well as labour market supply: in the past three years there has been a scarcity for such jobs as qualified technical specialists with professional experience, knowledge of English, and/or managerial skills; qualified and experienced middle- and top-level managers, as well as sales and marketing specialists in the Lithuanian labour market (Hay Group, 2005). Job abundance was reported among administrative jobs, lower-level accountant jobs without knowledge of English, lawyers, economists without language skills, recent graduates of universities without previous working experience, and sales representatives without any specific qualification. Looking into jobs with above-average salaries, these comprise finance, marketing and administrative jobs. Lower salaries are paid to employees in R&D, engineering, production and quality.

Organizational factors

The average monthly net and gross wage is higher in enterprises with larger numbers of employees (Department of Statistics to the Government of the Republic of

Lithuania, 2006). This tendency can also be observed in both the public and private sectors. Still, it is possible to trace a consistent pattern illustrating that the work pay in SMEs operating in the public sector is higher than that in the private sector, whereas in large enterprises it is quite the contrary.

Regions and industries

There exist considerable regional differences in the work payment rates. The highest work pay is in Vilnius, the capital of Lithuania, and Klaipeda, the seaport, while in other cities work pay comprises 80 per cent of the above amount (Hay Group, 2005), which in turn has led to production relocation in lower-level work pay regions, as it provides companies with the possibility of economizing. However, enterprises have to meet other challenges in those areas, i.e. scarcity of qualified workforce.

Company ownership factors

In addition to classical work pay divergences, the Lithuanian pay market varies along lines of ownership. Clear differences stand out between multinational and indigenous Lithuanian companies. In 2004 and 2005, the work pay of companies in the capital of Lithuania comprised about 80 per cent of the national average, while among multinationals it stood at 125 per cent (Hay Group, 2005).

Unofficial payment of wages

According to the European Industrial Relations Observatory (2006), the scale of the 'shadow economy' in Lithuania may be close to 20 per cent of the gross domestic product (GDP). Some companies pay part of employees' wages in an unofficial manner, thereby evading personal income tax and social insurance contributions. Shortages in the labour force – which are becoming more pronounced due to rapid economic growth in recent years and emigration of the labour force – reduce the problem of illegal payment of wages.

We will analyse the use of some elements of the employee reward system in Lithuanian companies.

Bonuses

Most Lithuanian companies pay bonuses once a year only, which in the case of top-level management is true of 71 per cent of companies, while annual bonuses for manual workers are paid in 31 per cent of companies. Monthly bonuses are paid to top-level mangers only in 11 per cent of companies, while 50 per cent of companies offer it to their manual-labour workers (Hay Group, 2006).

In Lithuanian companies profit-sharing plans are implemented in the case of top-level management, management, specialists and clerical staff. For manual workers profit-sharing plans are applied in only 8 per cent of companies.

Employee stock ownership plans are applied in a relatively small number of Lithuanian enterprises. The most popular practices include stock option plans and stock purchase plans, which are offered to top-level management in 12 and 8 per cent of companies, respectively (Hay Group, 2006).

Benefits and services

Enterprises tend to offer benefits to facilitate the process of attracting, maintaining and motivating employees and managers. As for insurance-related benefits, travel insurance for business trips seems to be the most favoured form. Supplementary life insurance is offered in about 40 per cent of service enterprises, supplementary disability insurance is given to employees in about 30 per cent of enterprises, and supplementary medical insurance is provided to 33 per cent of top managers and 16 per cent of manual workers (Hay Group, 2006). Employees in approximately 45 per cent of companies are offered sports and cultural activities at company expense. Among other benefits, the most popular ones are company cars, fuel allowance, discounts on company products (applied in 55 per cent of enterprises).

Family benefits are still rather unpopular in Lithuania. Childcare is applied exclusively to the top-level management in 2 per cent of companies, extended/flexible maternity leave in 7 per cent and special children's programmes in 3 per cent.

Lithuanian companies spend only 1.5 per cent of the overall employee-related costs on their non-financial motivation (Eamets and Philips, 2005). However, in comparison with such countries as Belgium and Great Britain, Lithuania is still lagging behind (7 to 14 per cent).

Performance management

Lithuanian enterprises apply quite an array of performance appraisal forms: annual performance evaluation interviews, competence development and evaluation, management by objectives, etc. Some organizations have started using balanced scorecards. The most advanced performance appraisal methods are applied in telecommunication, IT and pharmaceutical companies, which fall under the industries where retention of competent employees plays a significant role. Being aware of the impact of managerial competencies on employee job satisfaction and relations with the company, these companies pay considerable attention to employee appraisals of their supervisor performance. To develop and exploit managerial potential, more and more enterprises are employing a 360-degree method. In accordance with appraisal results, management development programmes are being introduced.

Branches of multinational corporations tend to adapt performance appraisal systems applied in their headquarters. An example is the case of Philip Morris Lithuania. Despite the fact that Philip Morris was established in Lithuania in 1993, the performance appraisal system was implemented only in 2001. The company started with the top management performance appraisals and moved to all employee-level assessments. Performance management and appraisal systems are not separate.

The corporate system is adapted for Lithuania. Appraisal consists of three major parts: objective setting, performance appraisal, competence assessment (seven competences of all employees and three additional managerial ones are evaluated) and carrier aspiration. Consistent with the appraisal results, pay increases and carrier possibilities are planned for the coming year. The appraisal system allows differentiation between good and bad employees. A system of poor performance management is designed for poor performers, where individual performance development programmes are developed.

Small and medium-sized Lithuanian enterprises usually confine themselves to appraisal interviews and based on the results, employee merit pay is defined. In small Lithuanian enterprises performance management is less developed as their management lacks the necessary competence for it.

Training and development

Reorganisation of the Lithuanian economy to the market economy had an impact on training and development issues. In general six economic development phases with implications for the training and development system can be identified (Sakalas, 1998) (see Table 3.4). The main attention should be paid to the competence supply and demand relationship and dynamics. The deficit in the competencies needed in the new economic situation, chaotic supply of competencies, a rising need for standardization to obtain training and development quality, normalizing the labour market as well as education and the training system, developing awareness of competence need within organizations and the world of business are the main stages that Lithuanian training and development has been going through since 1991. Successful completion of the cycle should mean a balanced demand and supply of competence as well as a closer and more fruitful cooperation between the worlds of business and education.

In 2003, a survey was conducted in two different sectors (Pundziene, 2005), the transport and the food industry, in order to assess more than 60 managers' attitudes towards workplace learning. The respondents were top- and middle-level managers of selected enterprises. The main instruments employed for the assessment included a questionnaire constructed on the basis of lifelong learning indicators (European Commission, 2001), which describe managers' attitudes to non-formal and informal learning. In 2005, an additional survey was conducted using the same research model and tool to supplement the results of the original study (Pundziene *et al.*, 2005). Eighteen top and middle managers representing telecommunications and information technology (IT) as well as public education sectors were surveyed. Both surveys were organized around five main scales:

- content of learning;
- place of learning;
- preferred teaching/learning method;

Table 3.4 Training and development dynamics

Development in the economy	Changes in training and development practices
Political changes. Liberalization of the system; support from foreign countries (European Union, USA, etc. in Lithuania's case)	Collapse of existing education and training system
First steps towards market economy – 'Law of the jungle'	Deficit of competencies (foreign languages, IT, social skills, etc.) in the new economic situation; chaotic supply of competencies; private education establishments are founded
Control of inflation	Rising need for standardization to obtain training and development quality; need for customer security services
Stabilization of the market	Normalizing labour market as well as education and training system
Stabilization of economic policies	Development of national qualification system, accreditation and quality assurance system; close links with the world of business
Growth	Developed awareness of competence need within organizations and the world of business

Source: Adapted from Sakalas, 1998.

● perceived effectiveness of learning;
● main obstacles to learning.

As noted in Figure 3.8, the dominant content of the education and training within both sectors in 2003 was technical knowledge and skills. In the selected food-industry enterprises core skills are seen more important in comparison to the selected transport sector enterprises; however, selected transport sector enterprises pay more attention to management and leadership skills. In 2005, in the above sectors, the main focus was laid on core as well as management and leadership competencies, and in the same year respondents pointed to financial, sales and customer services competences as especially important. This finding is partially due to the specifics of telecommunication and IT as well as public education sectors, as companies in these sectors are going through major changes and extensive growth. Moreover, the telecommunication and IT sector as well as the public education sector are heavily dependent on new knowledge due to the intellectual nature of business.

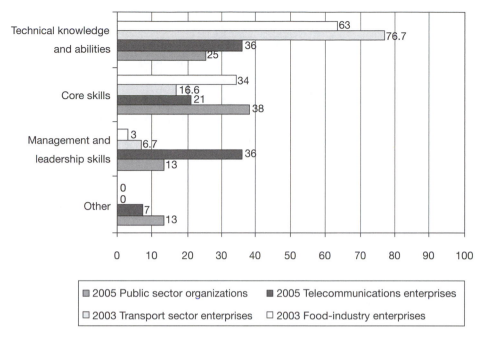

Figure 3.8 Content of the training in Lithuanian enterprises
Source: Pundziene *et al.*, 2005.

Traditional forms and methods of education and training are preferred. Approximately 80 per cent of training is carried out through lectures, courses and seminars delivered mainly at educational institutions (see Figure 3.9). It is interesting to note that workplace learning is not as popular as is advocated in organizational learning theory. Distance learning is not practised at all in the selected enterprises that participated in the first survey; however, it takes place in organizations included in the second survey (see Figure 3.9). The perceived level of the effectiveness of education and training in the selected enterprises is low (see Figure 3.10). Only 7 per cent of the transport sector enterprises reported that it was effective. Food-industry enterprises reported a higher level of effectiveness, 30 per cent; however, the results are still not satisfactory.

The second survey reveals the effectiveness of two different providers of training services: consultancy agencies and educational institutions. According to responses, training services provided by educational institutions are perceived to be more effective. None of the respondents was of the opinion that training services are totally ineffective. The following main learning obstacles were reported by respondents:

● already recruited highly qualified experts;
● high workload of employees;
● lack of financial resourses (priority is for development of production);
● lack of training institutions capable of carrying out effective training;

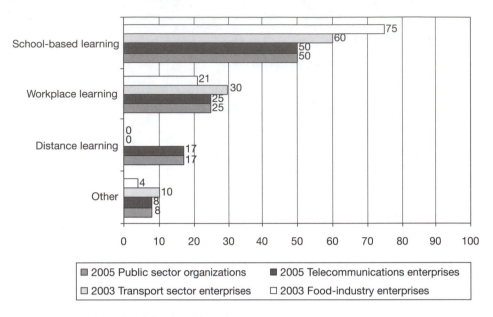

Figure 3.9 Location of training in Lithuania

Source: Pundziene *et al.*, 2005.

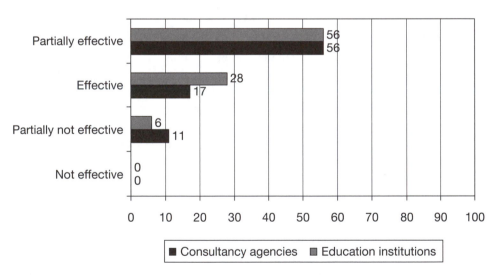

Figure 3.10 Effectiveness of training in public sector organizations and telecommunication enterprises in Lithuania

Source: Pundziene *et al.*, 2005.

- inability to apply new knowledge in practice;
- lack of employee interest;
- language barriers.

The main obstacles to learning identified by managers from the telecommunications sector are as follows:

- high workload of employees;
- Inability to match learning time with work time;
- Lack of employee interest.

The obstacles reported by public sector respondents include a lack of financial resources, high workload of employees and a lack of training institutions capable of carrying out effective training.

'Inability to apply new knowledge in practice' as well as 'Lack of employee interest' could be a consequence of inappropriate content and teaching/learning methods in education and training experienced by employees. 'Lack of Training institutions capable of carrying out effective training' is probably a question of cooperation between the enterprises and external training providers. The results of the survey are a good indicator, which should be taken into account by enterprises themselves as well as training providers. Workplace learning, as well as work-based learning, should be more often used by enterprises and training providers. In addition, special attention should be paid to the content and teaching/learning methods when addressing training.

Integrating work and learning is a natural outcome of social-economic changes going on in the world. The main reasons for these kinds of changes are the rapid progress of knowledge and technology development influencing human abilities and needs, which means that training needs are changing rapidly. Education and training should help to meet strategic goals and major changes in the enterprise, and workplace learning is one way to increase the effectiveness of organizational learning. Lithuanian food-industry and transport enterprises showed that education and training are taking place in enterprises; however, the content and teaching/learning methods are very traditional and, finally, the results of the training are perceived as insufficiently effective by the enterprises themselves. Learning should become 'tailor made' and attractive: increasing the diversity of training and learning approaches, employing internal company trainers, increasing the use of informal training, responding to individual needs, evaluating learning, etc. A repeat research study in 2005 indicated changing tendencies – a relative share of formal and non-formal learning through 'school'-provided lectures and seminars was decreasing; instead, more informal learning activities such as reading, fairs, work, etc. were reported. However, we have to take into account variances between sectors; the education and telecommunication and IT sectors are much more dependent on the intake of up-to-date knowledge, which influences their learning habits.

THE FUTURE OF HRM IN LITHUANIA

Intensive migration is forecast to continue until the year 2010 in Lithuania (Svidlerienė, 2004). Due to labour migration and competitiveness, labour demand will grow too. Therefore Lithuanian enterprises will be forced to increase their attractiveness and work pay. A survey of HR practitioners enabled key HRM future tendencies to be identified (Bučiūnienė and Bigelienė, 2006).

The growth of the role of human resource as a key organizational success factor

A widening gap between demand and supply in the labour market will make organizations view their employees as a key success factor and make them pay greater attention to them. Taking into consideration the likely growth of competition in the labour market among enterprises, they will have to enhance their attractiveness in the eyes of their employees.

Changes in employee–organization relationships

A new generation of employees is currently developing in Lithuania, who hold new attitudes to work and employers. Employees are becoming more committed to work and career rather than the employer, and their key goal is to increase their personal competence and competitiveness in the labour market. The above change in employee work attitudes has been influenced by the decline of long-term job security and social guarantees that companies provide to their employees. Thus, on the one hand, among their priorities organizations include the significance of employee recruitment and retention and seek employees' commitment to the organization, while, on the other hand, individuals tend to value independence and the possibility gaining exclusive competences that would be saleable and in demand in the market. Accordingly the employer's attitude to the employee is bound to undergo substantial changes as well, i.e. organizations have to look upon their employees as individuals with their own interests and life strategy, and view employees as equal partners.

Development and consolidation of organizational culture

Recently numerous Lithuanian organizations have started focusing on the development of organizational culture and the dissemination of values. Nurturing a healthy and strong culture provides potential to organizations, and assists them in developing the spirit of devotion, innovation, and inspiration. The above tendency should develop further in the future.

Increase of the significance of employees' and managers' development

Employee training is becoming one of the key job motivators. In the future greater attention will be given to the development of leadership skills among all levels of management. Leadership is now perceived not merely as leadership in business, but leadership among people. Managers should therefore become co-workers and team coaches. Managers also face greater responsibility in developing, motivating and retaining employees. They are accountable not only for financial results, but human relations too. In developing their employees and management, organizations should make better use of the available EU structural funds, a rather large part of which is allocated for this activity.

New management generation

A new generation of managers is now taking managerial positions at all levels. These managers entered the labour market during the years of Lithuania's independence, which means they studied business management at universities following Western traditions or gained experience from their former managers who ran many organizational units after the influx of foreign investment. This generation is thought to have more management skills and leadership competences. The outputs of the above competences should incorporate improved management quality, which in turn should have a positive impact on employees' satisfaction with their managers and organizations. Such a situation should also assist in building company attractiveness among employees. Better competence should also increase flexibility and work effectiveness, which should enable organizations to employ a wider range of motivational means, raise work pay and reduce the threat of labour emigration to higher paying countries.

Enhancement of employer attractiveness

As it is becoming more and more complicated to find, recruit and retain employees, efforts and competences of the HR department are not sufficient to manage these processes. Top-level management, marketing and finance department specialists will eventually have to get involved in the enhancement of employer attractiveness and search for new effective HRM methods. Organizations will also focus their effort on students and young people in an attempt to attract potential employees, which will necessitate paying greater attention to the establishment and cultivation of relationships with educational institutions, for instance offering grants to students, developing student internship programmes, etc.

Increasing role of trade unions

The impact of trade unions is likely to grow. The establishment of trade unions should be especially speedy in the service sector, in retail and among industry workers, i.e. sectors in which the workforce is paid a minimum wage, working conditions are poor and working hours are quite long. Another essential issue is the dialogue between employees, their representatives and employers. Employee representatives, i.e. trade unions, will eventually gain real valid power representing employee interests. Their opinion will have to be taken into account; moreover, companies will have to search for trade-offs. The legal side of HR management will gain more attention, which will make it a rather relevant aspect of HR department activity. The significance of social responsibility in business will grow too.

Further increase in the significance of the HR department role and new challenges for the HR department

The human resource department will be ascribed an increasing number of functions. Even companies who for a long time considered human resource management as administration will have to enlarge their HR departments by granting them broader functions. Human resource departments will have to form a partnership with management in meeting various business challenges. However, organizations may face the problem of insufficient HR department experience and competence in the area of business management.

To become a strategic partner with management, as well as a change agent, HR managers will have to possess better leadership skills, i.e. make decisions and search for ways to make them attractive, inspiring and influential. Thus a person with decision-making power in managing the development of the unique and inimitable competitive advantage, i.e. human resources, will need certain qualities – leadership features – that will assist him or her in attracting followers, instead of merely confining him- or herself to managing employees by means of administrative legal means.

Human resource management transformation: from start-up to successful business

The case illustrates human resource management specifics in today's highly dynamic Lithuanian business environment (developed by Pundziene, Morkunas, Ragulskytė-Pavliuk, Kaseliauskas and Simkonis in 2006)

START UP: a short history of the entrepreneurs

ABC is a successfully growing consultancy firm established seven years ago by two partners. The number of clients is constantly increasing. As a result the portfolio of products as well as the variety of specific knowledge and skills needed is also growing. Currently the firm employs 12 highly qualified consultants who are able to lead consultancy projects as well as to consult. People who joined the company seven years ago have stayed with it until today. However, meanwhile a number of young and energetic colleagues have joined the team.

Gradually with the increasing number of clients as well as workload, the entrepreneurs started hiring administrative help. Having gained experience and training, some of them have become consultants themselves. In the beginning there was no sophisticated organizational structure – relationships and roles depended on the actual needs of the firm.

The above structure was suitable when the firm had four or five employees, as it was very flexible and allowed the company to meet clients' needs, which could not be met by big competitors. When the number of personnel was small, due to everyday contacts and intensive communication, they were able to stand in for each other in all running projects. In the long run that kind of relationships became impossible – the enlarged team had to split into different projects. A need for specific knowledge arose. When suddenly the firm grew to 12 employees, a new way of operating was needed.

With the help of an analysis of the experience of their competitors as well as foreign consultancy firms, managers are usually not only competent administrators but also consultants able to manage large-scale projects, innovate, develop and implement new products, and provide high-quality services. The development and retention of high-quality competence within ABC as well as maintaining the pace of growth constitute the firm's current challenges to be solved.

Human resource management transformation

An interview was held with the CEO and the owner of ABC, who was asked how he reacted to such successful and rapid growth of the company. What were the main steps made to sustain success? The CEO was relatively young, but a very strong character with a clear opinion of his own on the surrounding events. The CEO of ABC was a determined person, committed to the growth of the firm as well as to his own professional development. His slogan was 'everything is possible for a good lawyer'.

continued

The CEO looked at the consultant and started to answer in a very clear manner as if he had a pre-arranged answer:

> The enterprise was established seven years ago by two guys, that's why most of the changes were implemented very slowly, sometimes spontaneously without any formal plan – most of the time the decisions were taken in order to immediately respond to the clients' needs. Of all the developments of the firm I would like to mention the three most important. The first changes that gave impetus to the development of the firm were the decision of the owners to expand the enterprise – to hire external people apart from the founders and to train them to serve clients. In this context some of the competitors' experts were attracted to work for ABC. The second change was to set the firm's offices in different regions of Lithuania. This step enabled us to review development plans and reallocate resources. The third change was related to technological innovations. Open attitudes of ABC towards informational technology (IT) enabled to reorganize the firm's activities so as to be able to make use of them.

The next pending change is integration, i.e. foreign experience shows that consultant firms consolidate their integration efforts by optimizing their activities to meet internationally operating client needs. It is obvious that the integration process will both be beneficial and require some losses as well. The integration should be planned very carefully to be a success.

One of the examples of the technological innovations being implemented in the firm is the Labour Time Accounting System (LTAS). On the one hand, along with organizational growth, the Performance Time Accounting System based on manual reports became ineffective due to the time not declared by consultants, while, on the other hand this was due to the enormous amounts of time needed to analyse and interpret the reports, not to mention the specific skills needed.

To eliminate the deficiencies, a decision was taken to implement an electronic LTAS that would store data on the services provided to clients as well as enable data to be analysed across different aspects. For the implementation of the system, a project was developed comprising a description of the main processes concerned as well as resources needed. The authors of the project had envisaged that the implementation of the LTAS would directly effect the employees of the firm. What would be the employees' reaction to the forthcoming change?

In the opinion of the employees, certain issues were of particular interest. With the extensive growth, employees reported a loss of the sense of unity and team spirit within the firm. New upcoming young, energetic and persistent employees were looking for changes. Authoritarians with long experience within the firm perceive 'dynamism' as disturbing and forthcoming changes as drawing back progress. Moreover relationships with the firm management became frustrating. Some of employees commented that in the beginning decisions were made without delay and in consultation with them; but the process had became bureaucratic. The managers made decisions related to the firm's future development without asking for the employees' opinions: 'In our firm decisions are taken by Managers who consider themselves to know best what the firm needs.' They were often not consulted on decisions. Their task was to focus on production. The result of this managerial–employee divide was that employees felt that the attitude towards them as people had changed and they were now viewed as a simple means to production – lemons to be squeezed.

A lack of communication among the management and employees is also an issue to be considered: 'I think that there is a need to talk more with people; there should be a possibility for employees to reveal their opinion of the decisions taken.'

A lack of understanding of the processes taking place among the firm's employees has a twofold interpretation – some of them, especially based on previous experience within the firm, regard changes as a managerial intention to control and worsen the present situation. Younger employees, who are ambitious for promotion, view the changes as part of the process of appraising people's performance and motivating them to produce.

Successful business

One of the ABC employees said: 'In my opinion, changes are very useful to the enterprise, because the main aim of the new Labour Time Accounting System (LTAS) is an effective use of working time.' Another employee supported the first statement, remarking: 'I am waiting for change, because the outcome should make our work easier. With the new LTAS there will be a possibility of serving more clients, which means I could earn more.' A survey showed that half of the employees had positive attitudes towards the LTAS and were ready to actively support changes needed for further successful growth of the enterprise. In addition to clear support some of the employees addressed several important issues for further successful growth of the company: 'I think that support [for the change processes] develops only when employees of the enterprise may influence the decision of the managers'; 'I have worked for the company for many years and also have plenty of ideas how to make the enterprise more effective even without introducing the LTAS'; 'Employees had no opportunity to discuss the planned change – we were informed by e-mail.' The survey conducted on the initiative of the enterprise ABC management resulted in several conclusions regarding future HRM policies for fast growing enterprises: it is very important to see and to use the potential of your employees, especially those with long experience in the enterprise, involving them in the process and gaining their support and expertise; to give employees a possibility of discussing all critical issues that come up in the enterprise and to reason their positive or negative attitudes to the upcoming events – constructive communication increases process awareness as well as potential personal benefits, and thus decreases their willingness to withdraw. The higher the degree of change, the more personal communication should be, taking into consideration employee previous experience on change – memories of harmful, unsuccessful change management makes employees suspicious and reluctant to commit.

REFERENCES AND FURTHER READING

Adomaitienė, J. and Tereseviciene, M. (2002). 'Labour Market requirements for Changes in Teaching and Learning Methods for Vocational Training'. *Vocational Training: Research and Realities*, 4: 38–52.

Barcevičius, E. (2005). *The Means of Encouragement of Economical Emigrants to Return to the Mother Country.* Research report. Available at: http://www.migracija.lt/ MD/Informac/Integruotas%20migrantu%20tyrimas%20-%202%20versija.pdf (accessed 10 April 2006) (in Lithuanian).

Bučiūnienė, I. (1996). *Changes in Employees' Motivation of the Lithuanian Industrial Companies during the Transition to the Market Economy.* PhD dissertation. Kaunas University of Technology (in Lithuanian).

Bučiūnienė, I. and Bigelienė, K. (2006). *Human Resource Management State in Lithuania. Research Report.* Kaunas: ISM University of Management and Economics.

Civil Society Institute, Information Analysis Department to the Seimas of the Republic of Lithuania (2005). *Lithuanian Emigration: Challenges and Opportunities.* Vilnius: Civil Society Institute, Information Analysis Department to the Seimas of the Republic of Lithuania 48 (in Lithuanian).

Conner, J. and Ulrich, D. (1996). 'Human Resource Roles: Creating Value, Not Rhetoric'. *Human Resource Planning,* 19, 3: 38–49.

Constitution (1992). Constitution of the Republic of Lithuania adopted by citizens of the Republic of Lithuania in the referendum of 25 October 1992. Available at: http://www.regione.taa.it/biblioteca/minoranze/lituania1.pdf (accessed 10 August 2007).

Department of Statistics to the Government of the Republic of Lithuania (1997). *Statistical Yearbook of Lithuania.* Vilnius: Methodical Publishing Centre, Department of Statistics to the Government of the Republic of Lithuania.

Department of Statistics to the Government of the Republic of Lithuania (2006). *Main indicators of economic and social development, 1996–2006.* Available at: http://www.std.lt/en/pages/view/?id=1364 (accessed 10 August 2007).

Dessler, G. (2005). *Human Resource Management.* Upper Saddle River, NJ: Pearson Education International.

Eamets, R. and Philips, K. (2005), *Company Investment in Human Capital.* Institute of Economics, University of Tartu. Available at: http://www.eiro.eurofound.eu.int/ 2005/05/feature/ee0505102f.html (accessed 10 August 2007).

European Commission (2001). *Task Force on Measuring Lifelong Learning: Report of the Eurostat.* European Commission Statistical Office of the European Communities. Available at: http://circa.europa.eu/Public/irc/dsis/edtcs/library?l=/public/measuring_lifelong (accessed 10 April 2006) (in Lithuanian).

European Commission (2007). *General and Regional Statistics.* Available at: http://epp.eurostat.ec.europa.eu/portal/page?_pageid=0,1136162,0_45572076&_dad=portal &_schema=PORTAL (accessed 10 August 2007).

European Foundation for the Improvement of Living and Working Conditions (2004). *Annual Review for Lithuania.* Dublin: European Foundation for the Improvement of Living and Working Conditions.

European Industrial Relations Observatory On-line (2006). 'Employee Dismissed for Alleging Company Tax Evasion'. Available at: http://www.eiro.eurofound.ie/2006/04/ articles/lt0604019i.html (accessed 10 August 2007).

Gabartas, R. (2006). Lithuanian and European Salaries Are Separated by the Decennaries'. *Kauno diena*, 12th October (in Lithuanian).

Garavan, T. N. and Morley, M., Gunnigle, P. and McGuire, D. (2002). 'Human Resource Development and Workplace Learning: Emerging Theoretical Perspectives and Organisational Practices. *Journal of European Industrial Training*, 26, 2/3/4: 60–71.

Geralavičius V. (1999). *Lithuanian Economy: The Present and the Future Prospective.* Available at: http://finansai.tripod.com/ekonomika.htm (accessed 10 April 2006) (in Lithuanian).

Guest, D. E. (1997). 'Human Resource Management and Performance: A Review and Research Agenda'. *International Journal of Human Resource Management*, 8, 3: 263–76.

Hay Group (2005). *Hay Group Compensation Reports. Lithuania.* Vilnius-Praha: Hay Group.

Hay Group (2006). *Hay Group Compensation Reports. Lithuania.* Vilnius-Praha: Hay Group.

Kupelyte, I., Klipc, O., Urbanaviciute, J. and Pundziene, A. (2006). *Recruitment and Selection.* Research report. Kaunas: Vytautas Magnus University.

Labour Code of the Republic of Lithuania (2003). Kaunas: Poligrafija ir informatika (in Lithuanian).

Lithuanian Free Market Institute (2006). *A Survey of the Lithuanian Economy 2005/2006 (2).* Vilnius: Lithuanian Free Market Institute.

Lithuanian Labour Exchange (2005). *Lithuanian Labour Exchange Reports 2004/2005.* Available at: http://www.ldb.lt/LDB_Site/index.htm (accessed 25 May 2006).

Matiušaityetė, R. (2003). 'The Migration of the Labour Force in Lithuania and the European Union'. *Ekonomika*, 63. Available at: http://www.leidykla.vu.lt/inetleid/ekonom/63/straipsniai/str4.pdf (accessed 10 August 2007) (in Lithuanian).

Ministry of Social Security and Labour (2001). *Evaluation of Potential Move of Labour Force to EU Countries.* Vilnius. Available at: http://www.socmin.lt/socmin/Migracija-prezentacija1_files/frame.htm (accessed 10 August 2007) (in Lithuanian).

Ministry of Social Security and Labour (2005). *Intentions to Emigrate. Representative Survey of Population.* Vilnius: Ministry of Social Security and Labour (in Lithuanian).

Pundziene, A. (2005). 'Workplace Learning: Concepts and Attitudes'. *The Humanities and Social Science. Scientific Proceedings of Riga Technical University*, 8, 8. Riga.

Pundziene, A. and Dienys, V. (2003). 'Work and Learning: The Changing Nature of the World of Work and Education Interaction'. *Vocational Training: Research and Realities,* 6: 38–52.

Pundziene, A., Barvydiene V. and Alonderiene R. (2005). 'Organisational Learning: How Competence Comes to the Workplace'. *International Journal of Learning*, 12, 2005/2006.

Pundziene, A., Kundrotas V. and Lydeka Z. (2006). 'Management Challenges in Rapidly Growing Lithuanian Enterprises'. *Baltic Journal of Management*, 1, 1: 34–48.

Putelyte, G. (2006). 'Promise the perspectives for the employees in 2007'. *Veidas*, 50.

Sakalas, A., (1998). *Personnel Management.* Vilnius: Margi Rastai.

Stankūnienė, V. (2004). *The Outline of Strategy of Lithuanian Population Policy.* Vilnius: Institute of Labour and Social Research. Available at: http://www.sti.lt/leid_pristat/Tekstai/Strategija/mak_1D_a.pdf (accessed 10 April 2006) (in Lithuanian).

Svidlerienė, D. (2004). *The Forecast of the Population of Lithuania for 2005–2030 year.* Vilnius: Department of Statistics to the Government of the Republic of Lithuania (in Lithuanian).

TNS Gallup (2006) *Human Resource Management Survey. Research Report.* Vilnius: TNS Gallup (in Lithuanian).

Managing human resources in Poland

TADEUSZ LISTWAN, ALEKSY POCZTOWSKI
AND MARZENA STOR

INTRODUCTION

The primary goal of this chapter is to describe the nature of human resource management (HRM) practice in Poland. After World War II Poland, together with many other Central and Eastern European countries, fell under Soviet influence as a consequence of the Yalta agreement. But after 45 years Poland appeared to be the first country to liberate itself from those fetters in 1989 and started substantial economic reforms toward a market economy. The vast scale of defaults that had been made before this breaking year as well as transformations that Poland has come through since then – all these make significant conditions for changes in the scope of contemporary HRM practices. This is why we recognized outlining these conditions as reasonable and decided to engage a good deal of attention on them. We believe this will bring readers to a better understanding of the present state of affairs. Nonetheless, the main emphasis is on contemporary HRM practices and their context. The context, appearing at the beginning and throughout the whole chapter, is discussed with reference to various environmental factors, namely macroeconomic, legal, social, cultural, educational and technological, all set against the backdrop of internationalization and globalization.

First, we discuss the key phases of the Polish transition process to outline the general context for HRM. Then, we focus on some selected aspects of this context, namely legislative provisions, the concept of social partners involving labour unions and employers' organizations, the social security system, labour market developments and the impact that Polish accession to the EU has had on HRM. We then turn to core HR activity area, namely recruitment and selection, reward and performance management, and training and development. These activities are examined in different types of business organizations. The chapter ends with a brief discussion about the future of HRM in Polish organizations and it is based on findings presented in the previous sections.

Unfortunately, because of space restrictions, we couldn't go deeper into some other areas of the personnel function, such as placement, personnel audit and, in particular, employee deployment, which are salient characteristics and significant problems in restructuring organizations. However, we hope the structure and content of the chapter will provide a rich description of the traditions and transitions characterizing Polish HRM.

The main sources of reference in this chapter derive from widely accessible statistical data published by various statistical offices and departments (Eurostat, OECD Databases, Polish Central Statistical Office, Department of Economic Analyses and Forecasts at the Polish Ministry of Economy and Ministry of Labour and Social Policy) and from longstanding research conducted by the authors and the academic departments they work for.

THE TRANSITION PROCESS

Early political and economic changes

Poland – together with other post-communist countries – represents a case of dual transition to a market economy and democracy. However, this is the first country in the communist block to undertake comprehensive reforms designed to dismantle the remnants of the command economy and introduce market and democratic developments instead. The dual transition process started with the collapse of state socialism in 1989 and the Round Table Talks between the government and the opposition which led to partially free elections in June of that year and the formation of the first non-communist government in the Soviet bloc. The country and its society have experienced a dramatic change in its political and economic activities since then.

After a radical set of reforms that were launched in late 1989 and early 1990 – known as the 'big bang' – the last decade and a half has brought Poland to a very different position in the world of Nation States. In theory the transformation process consists of three phases: stabilization, adjustment-related recession and expansion. But in Poland it is thought to cover four major phases of development which took place in consecutive periods: 1990–3, 1994–7, 1998–2001 and 2002–3 (Bukowski, 2007; Baka, 2004).

In October 1989 the government presented a programme of fast and deep reforms, the so-called Balcerowicz Plan – its author being the Minister of Finance at that time and in early 1990s. The reforms were based on macroeconomic stabilization and liberalization of the national economy, accompanied by measures for building market economy institutions. Over the course of the next few years, the fiscal system was reformed, with the introduction of personal income tax, corporate income tax, and value-added tax (VAT). Meanwhile, in January 1990 state-controlled prices were lifted and from then on the price of goods and services was largely shaped by market forces. The market reform plan assumed that prices would rise on average by 50 per cent. In fact, they rose at that time by 78 per cent and some goods and services by even as much as 600 per cent. At the end of 1990 GDP growth was –11.6 per cent (see Table 4.1). But it was a first step towards prices as they operated in developed capitalist economies. Furthermore, demand and supply were again activated. There was also a revolution in the liberalization of international trade. The zloty became convertible to other currencies and internal convertibility was also established, providing the platform for a more dynamic economic growth.

The beginning of the 1990s saw a wave of small businesses being established by individual entrepreneurs. This phenomenon became one of the most important causes of eventual economic advancement in Poland.

In those days self-employment amounted to 26 per cent of the total employed workforce in Poland, whereas in the EU the equivalent figure for self-employment was 11 per cent (Stor, 2004: 95). It appeared that a significant number of the Polish people were full of initiative and willing to take responsibility for their own financial affairs. Starved of business, political and individual freedom for a protracted period of time, they had an opportunity to become masters of their own lives once again. That was what Professor L. Balcerowicz believed in – when a business' financial success depends on its owner's single-handed economic efforts and responsibility, when the government lets people manage their own affairs and doesn't claim to know what is the best for them – these make good foundations for a country's economic growth (Balcerowicz, 1988: 120).

While the number of privately owned businesses was increasing, both employment and the number of people active in the labour market were declining and unemployment was rising significantly. This was largely due to restructuring in state enterprises which revealed hidden unemployment that could not be absorbed in the short term by emerging private sector companies (Bukowski, 2007: 23).

A striking aspect of macroeconomic policies in the early years of the Polish transition was a sharp increase in the level of government cash transfers to individuals. This initiative was designed to mitigate the increase in overall income inequality that would have resulted from the increase in labour earnings inequality. Much of the transfer was due to an increase in pension expenditures. Older people had the most to lose from the privatization and closure of state-owned companies and would have been most adversely affected by enterprise restructuring. But the increase in the generosity of state pensions (relative to prevailing average wages) in 1991–2 induced a large number of older workers to take early retirement. Thus, despite the negative implications of a large budget deficit, the economic expansion and other government initiatives may, on balance, have actually facilitated transition, first, by removing potential opposition to reforms by a powerful interest group and, second, by helping to reduce employment in enterprises to more efficient levels and promoting other aspects of enterprise restructuring (Michael *et al.*, 2001)

Ups and downs of the 'Tiger of Europe'

The achievements of the initial period of transition were quite remarkable. So much so that by the mid-1990s Poland had become known as the 'flying Eagle of Europe'

Table 4.1 Selected key Polish economic statistics, 1990–2008

Indicator	Data as of the end of the year																		
	1990	1991	1992	1993	1994	1995	1996	1997	1998	1999	2000	2001	2002	2003	2004	2005	2006	2007	2008
GDP growth	–11.6	–7.0	2.6	3.8	5.2	7.0	6.2	6.8	4.8	4.1	4.0	1.1	1.4	3.8	5.3	3.6	6.1	6.5*	5.5*
Unemployment	6.5	12.2	14.3	16.4	16.0	14.9	13.2	10.3	10.4	13.1	15.1	17.4	18.3	20.1	19.1	17.6	14.9	12.7*	9.0*
FDI in US$ billion	x	x	x	2,830	1,491	2,510	5,197	5,678	9,574	7,891	10,601	7,118	6,064	6,420	7,858	9,602	13,922	x	x

Note: *Estimation by the Ministry of Economy; x = data unavailable.

Source: Kochanowicz et al., 2005: 11; *Main Macroeconomic Indicators . . .*, 2007: 1; *Koniunktura . . .*, 2007; *List of Major Foreign Investors in Poland, 2007.*

and the 'Tiger of Europe'. The 'fat years' of the second stage of transition appeared to be a success.

And yet at the end of the decade Poland's success proved to be fragile one. After the very favourable years of 1995–7, when annual GDP growth ranged from 6 per cent to almost 7 per cent, the country saw a dramatic slowdown at the end of the 1990s (see Table 4.1), bringing GDP growth down to 1.1 per cent in 2001. At the same time, there was a sharp increase in the budget deficit, which in 2001 amounted to 5.5 per cent of GDP, as well as growing balance of payment problem. The unemployment rate climbed in 2000–1 and became the highest in Europe (17.4 per cent as of the end of 2001).

Finally, while the economic transformation undoubtedly brought benefits to sizable segments of society – especially to a small but growing middle class – it also produced very significant social costs. These included a very high rate of unemployment, mentioned above. This was the single most important factor contributing to poverty, which was quite extensive, and reached 15 per cent in 2001 (*Structural Reforms . . .*, 2004: 13).

The third stage of Polish transition brought changes in social insurance and political services, including four major reforms in the areas of pension provision, health care provision, education and public administration.

The Polish economy entered the last phase of transition at the end of 2002 and the beginning of 2003. Statistical analysis indicates that the negative trend in the labour market had already stopped in the last quarter of 2002, when both labour activity and the employment rate stabilized. Although as of the end of 2003 unemployment stood at 20.1 per cent (declining in 2004 to 19.1 per cent), GDP at the same time rose from 3.8 to 5.3 per cent.

The positive effects of the transition process became visible in the educational level of society as well. The percentage of the population with completed higher education increased from about 2 per cent in 1990 to about 12 per cent in 2004 as more and more people wanted to gain a better position in the labour market[1] (Berger *et al.*, 2004: 37–8).

All the above has been accompanied by an increasing growth in access to technology developments. Although in 2005 only 40 per cent of individual households had a personal computer, 62 per cent mobile (cell) phones and 30 per cent the technical possibility of internet access, the number of devices has been growing dramatically since then. With respect to businesses – 93 per cent of enterprises employing 10 persons or more in 2004 were using computers, and 99 per cent had internet access (*Statistical Yearbook . . .*, 2006).

But what was especially common in the last two phases of Polish transition was a deep rewriting of existing legislation as part of the process of accession to the EU. This continued to be very intensive with the adoption of many new laws in 2004 due to EU membership, especially in the case of laws on state aid, freedom of economic activity, tax on goods and services, excise tax and many others.

From the perspective of the many years of transition in Poland, it can be said that the privatization process is complete in many fields. The changes in the ownership structure of enterprises has resulted in a new structure of employment as depicted in Table 4.2. Ongoing state ownership and involvement in relation to sectors and enterprises of strategic importance to the economy and to state security is envisaged. Some public utility enterprises will remain in the possession of the State Treasury as well.

The present state of affairs

Poland – the largest economy among the wave of new member states to join the EU in 2004 (GDP of almost PPP[2] $500 billion in 2006), the largest land area (312,685 km²) and the most populated country (38.2 million inhabitants) – is a remarkable story of transition. The reforms gave rise to extensive structural change in the economy. This included, most importantly, the fast rise of private businesses, accompanied by a dramatic shift of employment from the public to private enterprise sector (see Table 4.2), the inflow of foreign investment in various forms (in 2006 about $13 billion of FDI came into Poland – see Table 4.1), the restructuring of foreign trade, the bulk of which is now from Western Europe (in contrast to the predominant importance of Eastern Europe and the Soviet Union under socialism), the emergence of a modern banking system (now predominantly in foreign hands), and the restructuring and privatization of state-owned enterprises (although this process is still far from complete today).

Another aspect of restructuring is the relative decline in the share of manufacturing in GDP and the concomitant increase in the importance of the service sector (see Figure 4.1) contributing to a trend which mirrors global developments.

Nowadays, being a member of the EU, the main goal of Poland's long-range economic strategy in the EU is to achieve a high and stable rate of economic growth, which is necessary in order to eliminate the gap dividing Poland from the EU

Table 4.2 Structure of employment in enterprise sector by ownership in Poland, 1990 and 2006

Sector by ownership	Data as of the end of the year	
	1990	*2006*
Public sector	52.06	18.6
Private sector	47.94	81.4

Source: Calculated from *Statistical Yearbook . . .*, 1999; *Statistical Yearbook . . .*, 2006.

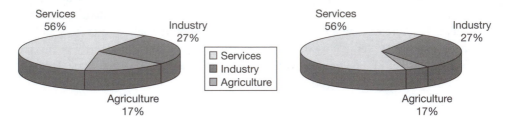

Employment by sectors of the economy

Value added by sectors of the economy

Figure 4.1 Sectoral structure of employment and value added in Poland, 2006

Source: *Poland in the European Union . . .*, 2007.

countries. Therefore the strategic aim of the National Development Plan is to develop a competitive economy based on knowledge and entrepreneurship, and to create long-term harmonious development, ensuring growth of employment and improving social, economic and spatial cohesion with the EU at the regional and national level.

THE CONTEXT FOR HUMAN RESOURCES MANAGEMENT

Some key legislative provisions

The Constitution of the Republic of Poland is the supreme Polish legal document and the basis of the political system of the Polish state (JoL[3] of 1997, no. 78, item 483). The Constitution protects and guarantees respect for all the civil rights – the personal, political, economic, social and cultural rights and freedoms – regarded as standard for a democratic country. Therefore any deed concerning HRM, both directly and indirectly, is subordinate to the Constitution.

The basic regulations of labour relations are provided for in the Act of 26th June 1974 establishing a fundamental Labour Code (LC).[4] Article 18 §2 of the LC provides that conditions of a contract of employment, or any other document forming the basis for the establishment of employment relations (e.g. covered in collective bargaining agreements, internal company rules, regulations, statutes), that are less favourable to the workers than those provided by the labour law, are null and void; the corresponding provisions from the LC are applied instead.

Polish legislation provides also for mandatory and voluntary insurance. Nearly all occupational groups are covered by this mandatory insurance. The details of this insurance are provided in Table 4.3.

Table 4.3 Insurance contribution rates in Poland, 2008

Specification	Contribution rate (per cent of wage)	Rate by payer (per cent of wage)	
		Employer	Employee
Social insurance			
Pension insurance	19.52	9.76	9.76
Disability insurance	6.00	3.00	3.00
Sickness insurance	2.45	–	2.45
Accident insurance	0.97–3.86	0.97–3.86	–
Health insurance	8.50	–	9.00
Guaranteed employee benefits fund	0.15	0.15	–
Labour fund	2.45	2.45	–

Source: Act of 13 October 1998 on Social Insurance System (JoL no. 137, item 887 with further amendments), Act of 27 August 2004 on Health Care Benefits Financed by Public Funds (JoL no. 210, item 2135).

Nevertheless, the LC is the main source of regulation governing employment contract types, duration, and termination. But it's worth mentioning that employment contracts can be also concluded within the scope of the Civil Code (CC)[5] and the Act on the Employment of Temporary Workers (ETW).[6] The most common types of employment contracts are given in Table 4.4.

Working time in Poland is limited to 40 hours per week and eight hours a day. The exceptions of this rule are strictly limited. Hence, an employer is obliged to organize working time schedules accordingly. Similarly, timetables for holiday leave need to be drawn up according to adequate legal schemas and, even more, consultation with employees in advance. Special attention should be paid to young people (under 18) and persons bringing up children who enjoy particular protection under the law.

The law in Poland prohibits discrimination against any individual based upon race, skin colour, religious affiliation, sexual preference, age, marital status, political orientation, labour union membership, ethnicity and national origin in all aspects of employment. If it comes to the court, the burden of proof is placed on the employer to show that selection practices have been fair and that individuals have been selected on merit.

Table 4.4 Types of employment contracts in Poland

Type of contract	Period of contract	Termination of contract
Contract for a probationary period of time (Art. 25 §2 LC)	No longer than 3 months (Art. 25 §1 LB)	< 2 weeks – 3 days notice period (Art. 34 LC) > 2 weeks – 1 week notice period (Art. 34 LC) 3 months – 2 weeks notice period (Art. 34 LC)
Contract for a limited period of time (Art. 25 §1 LC)	● to a date specified in a contract ● in the case of a pregnant worker the termination date is extended until the date of her confinement (Art. 177 §3 LC) Employment contract for employee substitution	● with the time specified in the contract (Art. 30 §1 p. 4 LC) ● if the contract is concluded for > 6 months – two weeks prior notice may be appropriate (Art. 33 LC) 3 days notice period (Art. 33 LC)
Contract for specified time of work performance (Art. 25 § LC)	● determined in a contract by work performance ● in the case of a pregnant worker the termination date is extended until the date of her confinement (Art. 177 §3 LC)	● until the date the work is completed and for which the contract was concluded (Art. 30 §1LC)

Contract for an unlimited period of time (Polish – Art. 25 §1 LC)	● only the starting date is determined	● termination with prior notice (Art. 36 §1 LC), depends on the period of employment:
		  < 6 months – 2 weeks
		  6 months to < 3 years – 1 month
		  > 3 years – 3 months

Contract for temporary work (contract with a contingency worker) (Polish – ETW)	Maximum for 12 months in consecutive 36 months (Art. 20 ETW)	3 days termination notice

| Contract for specified service (Art. 734 CC), including agency contract and contract for management | The period of performing the legal act (rendering services) | An order-giver may dissolve the contract at any time but an order-taker should be paid for the expenditures that he/she has incurred in order to perform the service or should be paid compensation for the activities undertaken so far (Art. 746 CC) |
| Contract for specific work performance (Art. 627 CC) | The period of performing the work | Until the work is performed, an order-giver may withdraw from a contract (Art. 644 CC) but paying previously fixed remuneration; no such financial consequences in the case it's probable the work won't be completed when due, the work has been performed defectively or its starting date is being delayed (Art. 635 CC & Art. 636 §1 CC) |

Source: Stor, 2004: 316.

The employer is also obliged to establish clear rules and regulations regarding compensation, work order and norms, job execution and responsibility, training and promotion, performance appraisal and many other things. Some basic obligations of employees as well employers are shown in Table 4.5.

Social partners and internal stakeholders

A special role in Polish legislative provision is assigned to social partners. Partners of social dialogue are: self-governing bodies, self-governing professional bodies, labour unions, employers' organizations and other social organizations. The basic deeds concerning the social partners are: the Act of 23 May 1992 on Labour Unions,[7] the Act of 23 May 1991 on Employers' Organization,[8] the Act of 6 June 1991 on Solving Collective Labour Disputes,[9] the Act of 6 July 2001 on the Tripartite Commission for Socio-Economic Affairs and Voivodship Commissions of Social Dialogue,[10] the Act of 7 April 2006 on Informing Employees and Holding Consultations with them, the Act of 5 April 2002 on European Works Councils.[11] These deeds, in principle, comply with European standards. An organizational core of social dialogue in Poland is the Tripartite Commission for Socio-Economic Affairs. Its major role is to reconcile the interests of the employees, employers and the commonwealth. The Commission's competences include:

- conducting social dialogue concerning wage and social benefits;
- quarterly evaluations of the growth of average wages in entrepreneurs' businesses;
- reconciling levels of average annual wage growth ratios for the state budget area for the following year;
- reconciling minimum wage levels for the following year; and
- reconciling the pension indexation ratio for the following year.

The scale of unionization and coverage of the labour force with collective agreements have diminished dramatically since 1990 (see Table 4.6). This phenomenon is related to a change in the institutional environment of labour unions and the scope of their influence as well as to a shift in employment from industry to services (see Figure 4.1), increased unemployment (see Table 4.1), privatization (see Table 4.2), individualization of employment relationships and the emergence of flexible forms of employment (see Table 4.4). Labour unions are rather absent in small firms and hardly visible in the foreign-owned companies. Their strongholds are the state-owned enterprises and public services, where they represent the corporatist interests of various professions. Currently, the largest existing labour unions are NSZZ 'Solidarność' (Solidarity), OPZZ and Forum Związków Zawodowych.

On the other side there are employers' organizations that are very active in Poland. Among them, it is worth mentioning the Confederation of Polish Entrepreneurs, the Polish Confederation of Private Entrepreneurs and the Business Centre Club.

Table 4.5 Basic obligations of employers and employees in Poland

The employer's obligations	*The employee's obligations*
1 New workers should be instructed concerning their obligations, work rules and basic rights	1 Perform their work conscientiously and carefully
2 Organize work in a such way as to use the working time and workers' skills and abilities effectively	2 Comply with instructions given by superiors in connection with employees' work if the instructions are not against the law or employment contract
3 Provide safe and healthy conditions and train workers regularly in rules and regulations of such conditions	3 Conform to the hours of work observed in the establishment
4 The compensation must be paid when due and according to the rate determined in the employment contract	4 Comply with the company's order as well as its rules and regulations
5 Facilitate upgrading of professional skills for employees	5 Comply with provisions governing occupational health and safety as well as fire regulations
6 Create favourable conditions for graduates to let them familiarize themselves easily with work demands	6 Have regard for the welfare of the establishment
7 Satisfy workers' social needs according to the company's means and available resources	7 Take proper care of the company's property
8 Use objective and equitable criteria for employees and performance appraisal	8 While employed not to divulge business secrets whose revelation would be detrimental to the employer
9 Maintain records of labour relations and personnel files for employees	9 Keep secrets covered by other provisions of the law
10 Influence on forming rules and good social relations in a company	10 In the framework of a separate contract an employee cannot conduct activities that are competitive with the employer, independently on legal bases for such activities (work or activity under a civil law contract or in connection with self-employment) (an agreement not to compete/non-compete clause)
11 Provide a worker with a certificate of employment on termination of the employment relationship	11 Comply with the rules of social interrelation in the enterprise
12 Render the legal acts of equal treatment of men and women in employment relations accessible to employees	12 After termination of the employment relationship an employee is obliged to keep secret information the revelation of which would be detrimental to the employer; the period of such a prohibition is determined by a separate agreement

Source: Stor, 2004: 324–325.

The representatives of both labour unions and employing organization (coming mostly from big establishments; see Table 4.7) take part in many Seym Commissions, referring to taxes, labour market regulations, public finance, etc.

As is shown in Table 4.7, although the biggest enterprises in Poland make up only 2.51 per cent of all active establishments in the market, and employ about 32 per cent of the total labour force, while the SME sector, comprising as much as 97.49 per cent of the total number of establishments, employs about 68 per cent of the workforce. Analysing some research data on HR function in these companies, it may be concluded that the most advanced developments in the context of the transition process and major internal stakeholders (employees, employers, labour unions, business owners) in most cases refer to large companies, especially to those which are privately owned and with foreign capital (see also Listwan, 2005). In general, employee participation in management is recognized, employees are considered a most valuable asset and major HR activity is shared between HR professionals and line managers.

Table 4.6 The percentage of workers belonging to labour unions in Poland, 1990–2005

Year	1990	2000	2006
Degree of unionization	33%	14.8%	11%

Source: Bukowski, 2007; *Poland in the European Union . . .*, 2007.

Table 4.7 Establishments in Poland by size and rate of employment in 2006

Specification	Total	Number of employed			
		49 and fewer (small enterprises – SE)	50–249 (mid-sized enterprises – ME)	SME (SE + ME)	250 plus (large enterprises – LE)
Per cent of establishments	100	83.16	14.33	97.49	2.51
Per cent of employed	100	45.90	22.15	68.05	31.95

Source: Calculated from *Statistical Yearbook . . .*, 2006.

The impact of the EU membership on HRM

The basic deficiencies of the personnel function in the communist era included the predominance of political and ideological criteria of selection, promotion, performance appraisal, training and development instead of criteria based on individual merit (Koziński and Listwan, 1993: 205). Nowadays Poland represents, in cultural terms, a transition between East and West, between socialism and capitalism. It is also a European country with the most differentiated population within the range of values, preferences, patterns of behaviour, self-esteem, professional aspirations shared by people. The analysis of research findings provided by some well-known Western authors (see Hofstede and Hofstede, 2005; Trompenaars and Hampden-Turner, 1997; Inglehart and Wenzel, 2005) have concluded that the Polish are characterized by a high level of uncertainty avoidance, a middle level of power distance, individualism, masculinity, inner control, are traditionalists rather than secular-rationalists, and mostly survival-oriented, emphasizing economic and physical security rather than focusing on self-expression and quality of life. But there is also a wide layer of society that doesn't fit that 'average profile'.

Some other empirical data reveal that university students are an example of those who present low uncertainty avoidance and power distance, a high level of individualism and masculinity, and are more oriented toward self-expression and quality of life than survival-oriented.[12] Yet, another study shows that together with Polish managers working for private and foreign companies in Poland they also make up a group of people who are secular-rationalists, give high priority to tolerance of diversity, raise demands for participation in decision-making, are career development-oriented, open to change and innovation, value individual dignity and equal rights, while putting significant emphasis on family ties.[13] Expatriate managers working in Poland perceive students as very inventive and responsible employees with a high level of entrepreneurship (Stor, 2006).

Interestingly, as a result of a positive experience with Polish workers after Poland's accession to the EU in 2004, many private international employment agencies were set up in some Western European countries to serve companies wishing to hire the Polish. This is not only because the Polish workforce may be cheaper than the local one, but due to the fact that Polish employees are assessed as professional, responsible, creative and hard-working.[14] But it is a threat to Polish companies. Some of them complain that too many good and highly educated people have left Poland, resulting in a so called 'Brain Drain'.

Hence, changes in the area of a company's personnel function also stem from the process of Poland's integration with the European Union has had a significant impact on how the HR function operates in Polish organizations and on the environment in which they operate. Implementation of the principle of the free movement of people has had a direct impact on labour market activities and on employment in the company, but this should not be examined in isolation from the benefits that membership of the union has brought. Professionals responsible for human resource management in Polish organizatons have focused a considerable amount of their effort on assessing the risk of an exodus of the best workers from the company. Although opinions regarding the potential for a 'brain drain' following accession are mixed, aside from those voicing fears of a deepening of this phenomenon there are those who think that the risk is negligible because even before the accession Polish specialists had no real difficulties in receiving work permits and many had emigrated.

Holding on to the best managers and specialists in the most important areas of the organization may necessitate the development of high standards in the realm of HRM. Standards with respect to attracting talent, sophisticated remuneration strategies and related policy areas must meet the expectations and aspirations of people who are better educated, are aware of their value and who know how to move through a competitive labour market. There can be no doubt that the international market is already moulding standards with respect to people with high potential and it should be expected that in the future they will encompass an increasingly large share of employees. Moreover, modern methods of solving personnel issues – not mandatory in European Union legislation, but a prerequisite for achieving high standards of HRM – must be implemented in the personnel function.

Labour market cultural diversity has increased in line with Poland's entry into the EU. The emergence of conditions for Polish specialists to undertake work in different cultural contexts and the influx into Poland of workers with differing cultural qualities have created new tasks related to preparing all workers to function under conditions of growing cultural diversity in employment for those charged with HRM responsibilities. This is a very important issue as many studies show that there is a large share of managers and specialists who are unsuccessful when delegated by their parent company to work in the markets of host and third countries. One of the reasons for this lack of success in multicultural or culturally different environments is a lack of knowledge and skills in surviving the 'cultural shock', as well as lack of awareness that an appreciation of diversity can not only limit the potential for conflict, but may even be a source of competitive advantage.

One of the greatest challenges in the area of personnel is the raising of company competitiveness through improved work productivity and a rationalization of work costs. The weight of this problem comes from the significantly lower work productivity per employee in Poland compared with the average in the European Union. The challenge of improved productivity also applies to the way in which it is to be achieved. If such growth is to be achieved mainly by way of reductions in employment, then highly visible side-effects include increased unemployment and a falling employment rate, which in Poland is currently lower than the average for the European Union. Moreover, the importance of lower labour costs as a competitive factor should not be overestimated as this is cancelled out by lower work productivity.

Poland's accession to the EU opened access for Polish entrepreneurs to a much larger market, but also exposed the lack of qualifications of both management and lower-level employees. The European Social Fund (ESF) provides a means of reducing the shortcomings of Polish business personnel. Thanks to the ESF, training courses are now undertaken by a much larger number of employees than before. At present, the management at many companies have decided to introduce entire training packages intended for all employees, starting from the lowest level on up. Everything from individual employee development plans through training seminars is prepared by external training experts, in cooperation with the HR department. Their eventual recommendations are based on in-depth analyses that include research, interviews and sessions. The overall objective is to raise the competitiveness of a given firm in its given market. The ESF covers up to 80 per cent of the costs of such training for small and medium-sized businesses, and up to 60 per cent for large enterprises. From 2004 to 2006 some €250 million from the European Social Fund was allocated to Poland to co-finance training and postgraduate studies, but only a small proportion of firms have taken advantage of these funds. In 2005, only 7 per cent of firms accessed this support, mainly due to a lack of awareness of the funds available. Medium-sized and large companies took best advantage of this opportunity, 21 per cent and 28 per cent, respectively. It is envisaged that into the future, companies will use EU funds to a considerably greater extent than was the case heretofore (Masłoń, 2006).

TRENDS AND DEVELOPMENTS IN HRM PRACTICE

The nature of the HRM function

The systems changes taking place in Poland since 1989 have also made their mark on the organizational level HR function. The current state of HRM theory and practice in Poland is the result of several factors. The first of these is past experience, which in the realm of HRM, was characterized by such qualities as the dearth of a systems approach, the influence of political factors and a high level of centralization. The effect was that the HR function was a low level function in the organization, over-employment was commonplace and high fluctuation and low efficiency characterized the production function. Looking over the years of the transformation, it may be stated that the impact of this factor, though continuously visible, is decreasing. The second important factor embodies changes in the environment of the companies in Poland, which are creating new challenges, especially in the field of HRM. An aspect of these changes is the emergence of a service market in the area of HR consulting offered by both foreign and domestic agencies. The solutions they propose are gradually becoming a standard with respect to the HR function. The third major factor is the state of knowledge about managing people, which is applied by persons lecturing in this field at colleges and various courses, thus moulding the way the personnel function is thought of in organizations.

In endeavouring to outline the most important qualities of HRM in Poland, it is necessary to say they are examined in the context of strategic, organizational and cultural conditions in the functioning companies. Most economic and other organizations found themselves facing the challenge of introducing major changes into their action strategy or even building it from scratch during the 1990s. What is noticeable is the impact of such strategies on the HRM field, primarily on a reorientation of the view of the role and importance of people in the organization towards perceiving them as significant company resources of strategic importance. Put simply, the organizational HRM conditions in Poland come down to one huge challenge in the form of restructuring – a prerequisite for achieving the already-mentioned strategy. Restructuring in the scope of the HR function usually means change (often restrictions, not growth) in the state and structure of employment. Among the cultural conditions underpinning HRM, the first that should be mentioned are the changes taking place in the consciousness of society during the transformation process. Changes occurring in the value system have an impact on the organizational culture of companies that are active there, and collide, often dramatically, with elements shaped during past periods.

The importance ascribed to the HR function by companies may be also studied by analysing the professional position of the person dealing with HRM. The evidence from empirical research confirms the general view that HRM and declarations regarding its great significance still do not occupy a sufficiently strong position in the institutional sense in Polish companies (Pocztowski et al., 2001). These studies show that in most cases HR issues are placed at the middle-management level (in 41.6 per cent of the companies under study); in 20.8 per cent of the companies the person responsible for HR matters occupies a non-managerial post. Further, in 27.9 per cent this kind of issue is dealt with by a director at the highest management level, while in only 11.9 per cent by a member of the executive board. In analysing the structure of work time devoted by the HR department staff to their various tasks, it was discovered that administrative work occupies the bulk of their budgeted time. A total of 64 per cent of respondents state that its share is over 50 per cent. Almost half of the respondents devote between 20 per cent and 30 per cent of their time to planning day-to-day activities. Most of the companies examined (almost 80 per cent) do not devote more than 25 per cent of their time to matters of strategic importance. In the case of 33.3 per cent of the companies, only 5 per cent to 10 per cent of that time is given to this purpose. A total of 67.4 per cent of the companies examined report the participation of line managers in moulding principles of HRM. In assessing the frequency of contacts of the HR department with line managers, almost half point to continuous contacts. A total of 35.4 per cent consider such contacts to be irregular, 14.6 per cent as rare, and 4.2 per cent as very rare. External HR consultants have become important partners of the HR staff over recent years. In the case of the companies studied, however, only 5.9 per cent benefit regularly from such services, while 38.6 per cent use the services, but sporadically, and 55.4 per cent state that they do not utilize them. In assessing the manner of implementation of the HR function in the above-sketched context of organizational strategy, structure and culture, it should be stressed that most HR tasks, such as employing workers, their appraisal and compensation, and their training, are basically conducted in the company at an operational level. Worth noting is the growing awareness of the importance of an appropriate approach to HRM in both the privatized state enterprises and newly established private companies. The above study shows that 83 per cent of the companies examined declared the importance of HR strategy but at the same time 45 per cent of them did not have any form of HR strategy.

As has already been mentioned, a significant factor impacting the emergence of HRM refers to the degree of restructuring being undertaken in the organization. This creates an opportunity for the penetration of new practice in this field of management. The size of an enterprise is also an important factor differentiating the approach to solving specific HR issues. Empirical studies show that large enterprises utilize a broader arsenal of specialized techniques and have developed procedures for basic processes (Listwan, 199: 45). Similarly, it has been demonstrated that international companies have more systemic and innovative HRM systems (Obłój and Weinstein, 2001: 48).

Recruitment and selection

In the centrally planned economy the key positions in enterprises were mostly reserved for those who exhibited political and ideological loyalty toward the governing Communist Party. Additionally, nepotism became an official standard for a good number of those whose position was strong enough to decide about the hiring and promotion of others. In practice, even lower managerial posts were rarely available to non-members of the governing party. Furthermore, either hiring or promoting somebody on his or her merits was less important. Hence, a quip about managerial staff buzzed among workers – BMW, pronounced in the same way as a well-known car make. The abbreviation stood for Polish words – bierny (passive), mierny (mediocre) but wierny (loyal). Therefore, the process of filling vacancies was not based on objective selection criteria, but on the so-called 'agreed-upon method'. This method relied on the enterprise management (usually managing director) and a political organization agreeing on a certain candidate. That kind of approach to recruitment and selection resulted, on the one hand, in very limited access to a valuable reservoir of talented people that enterprises would have benefitted from recruiting. On the other hand, those capable individuals were deprived of development, advancement and promotion opportunities.

Not surprisingly, one of the main causes of the society-wide protest in 1980 (that Solidarity was born out of) was the demand that merit qualification criteria be used to fill managerial posts. This created a momentum to work out a selection method, the so-called 'selection by competition', to be used in the case of managerial vacancies (Listwan et al., 1986). Although this method was approximate to an assessment centre process (AC), it used some different procedures and involved some different participants. Yet its validity was rather high and similar to AC's. This conclusion was drawn after the period 1980–1, in which many managerial posts, especially at the top management level, were filled. Further events in the country, chiefly the imposition of martial law, made continuation of the above practices impossible.

It was not before 1989 that the rationalization of the staffing process started. It is necessary to bear in mind that it was a time of radical changes in Poland. The socio-economic transformation of Poland, meaning the transition from a centrally planned economy to a market economy, resulted in significant unemployment as a result of excessive and unreasonable employment in companies functioning in the former system as well as low productivity of the employed labour force and enterprises themselves. That was another reason, among those mentioned in the previous sections, for the sizeable unemployment that has characterized the Polish labour market since the beginning of the 1990s.

Together with the employment practices deriving from the socialist past, all these created very specific conditions for the early staffing activities in the early transition period. What is more, the labour market lacked a managerial cadre with the required market economy experience. Needless to say, the educational institutions were unable to provide managers immediately with appropriate knowledge and skills. That is why solving this problem necessitated engaging Western educational institutions that offered training, both at home and abroad. A significant role should be also ascribed to international companies that located in Poland, and that facilitated the transfer of know-how into Poland.

At present, recruitment and selection face some new problems. The Polish labour market is characterized by low occupational and spatial mobility of employees, in particular those with few qualifications. Moreover, the phenomenon of a high unemployment rate is accompanied by an increasing demand for highly qualified workers in the New Economy sectors that considerably exceeds the available supply. This is partly due to the educational system in Poland.

The structure of degree programmes is dominated by the social sciences, business and law. In the academic year 2006/7, the above-mentioned disciplines were studied by about 40 per cent of all students. Additionally, as many as 21 per cent of all the students followed degree programmes in the humanities, arts or education studies. As a result, the characteristic distinctively differentiating Poland from EU member states is its low percentage of students following technical, engineering, natural sciences, computer science or mathematical degree programmes. Only about 14 per cent of all the students follow a programme in technology, industry and construction, and only about 6.8 per cent in sciences, while on average in the EU 27 the share of students in engineering and science constitutes 26 per cent of the total (see Figure 4.2). Nevertheless, 14.2 per cent of Polish citizens aged 13 and over are university graduates (see Figure 4.3), while the equivalent share in EU countries amounts to about 20 per cent on average. At the same time the total population aged 25 to 64 having completed at least upper secondary education in Poland amounts to 85.8 per cent and in the EU is up to 70 per cent. The group most prone to unemployment and economic inactivity in Poland, as in other countries, consists of poorly educated people (basic vocational or lower education level). Such people constitute as much as 59 per cent of all the unemployed, 67 per cent of those economically inactive and only 43 per cent of the employed, while their share in the entire population constitutes 56 per cent (in 2006). This means that people with low professional skills are strongly under-represented in employment and over-represented among those who are economically inactive. People with low skills in all age groups are the only group under-represented in employment and over-represented in inactivity. The situation is reversed for people with tertiary education (Bukowski, 2007: 59).

Research based on newspaper advertisment analysis also shows that in 2004 employers preferred graduates of information science, engineering or technical studies, public service, economics and administration (Sztandera *et al.*, 2005).

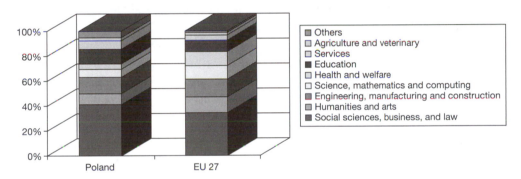

Figure 4.2 Structure of education by field of higher studies in Poland and the EU 27 in the academic year 2006/07

Source: Calculated from Eurostat Education Indicators Database.

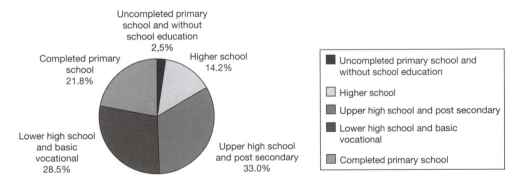

Figure 4.3 Population in Poland at age 13 and over by level of education, 2006

Source: Calculated from *Statistical Yearbook* ..., 2006: 118.

The highest percentage of job advertisements were addressed to IT and telecommunication specialists and graduates of technical studies (32 per cent of the offers), and to economic, financial, marketing and sales specialists (23 per cent). What differentiates the advertisements to people with a technical background from the others is the emphasis on specific skills, both inherent in this occupation and those that go beyond the category of universally applicable skills. The candidates for economists' positions are more often expected to have organizational skills, to be able to work in a team and to be creative. In almost all adverts, the employers emphasize that they require work experience, which partly shows that they perceive hiring a person without experience as risky and, moreover, that they see the majority of graduates as not having suitable work skills. Work experience seems to be a signal for the employer that the person in question is able to carry out the entrusted task by him/herself.

The other factor influencing recruitment and selection in Polish companies is connected with the presence of public and non-public institutions of the labour market. The latter include recruitment agencies for work either in Poland or abroad, career-counselling agencies, job-counselling agencies and temporary work agencies. All of them have been present in Poland since the early 1990s, when the monopoly in public employment services was broken (*The Structure of the Labour Market . . .*, 2005). Both the increase in the number of private recruitment agencies and the growing number of people taking up temporary work indicate that there has been a remarkable development of this sector of the market in recent years.

In the light of the research on staffing practices in Poland, the contemporary features of recruitment and selection may be characterized, in principle, as follows (Pocztowski *et al.*, 2001):

- in most organizations, planning HR needs is the recognized antecedent to recruitment and selection, and plans usually cover a short time horizon (up to one year);
- fewer than half of the companies (45 per cent) make use of job analysis and job description as instruments of staffing, whereas nearly 30 per cent use job requirement profiles for the same purpose;
- firms indicate internal sources of recruitment as the most preferred, while no specific preferences toward recruitment come second and preferences toward applicants from outside the organization are rarely reported;
- among methods of recruitment – advertising position openings in newspapers and magazines prevails (in about 75 per cent of companies), using the help of people already employed was reported by 53 per cent of the companies, whereas 39 per cent reported using employment agencies, 27 per cent job agencies and 20 per cent direct contact with schools;
- application forms are the most popular way of selecting applicants, accompanied by qualification certificates, application letters and references;

- the other reported techniques of selection are: interviews (about 75 per cent), personality tests (26 per cent), knowledge tests (18 per cent) and intelligence tests (14 per cent).

Staffing practices tend to vary, depending on the ownership of the firm, the size of the establishment as well as the kind of employees being sought.

State-owned companies and those which have some State Treasury share in their ownership structure usually use a very limited set of advanced HRM solutions. This is different in private companies, and especially in those with foreign capital. They expend a great deal of effort in the field of recruitment and selection. In these companies HR needs are analysed more often and HR planning is conducted for longer time horizons. Their recruitment and selection procedures are more advanced and the selection instruments and techniques they use are of high predictive value. It is worth mentioning that this state of affairs is more common in large enterprises (employing over 250 workers) when compared to small businesses. In the latter, even though the recruitment and selection process seems to be rational, it is often less systematic for the most part (Listwan, 2005).

It is also noticeable that the resourcing of the managerial cadre is more sophisticated than the resourcing of non-managerial employees. As in the previous cases, this is a particularly distinctive feature of both large and international companies in Poland, rather than enterprises in the SME sector. The preparation and realization of managerial staff resourcing are conducted to standards applied in Western European business organizations.

On the whole, it has to be emphasized that the recruitment and selection process is more rational nowadays than it used to be in the former political and economic system. Nonetheless, there are some weaknesses in this aspect of HR activity that result in, among other things, from a wide gap between supply and demand in the labour market, imperfections in the educational system, mediocre activities undertaken in the preparation phase of recruitment and selection, and a poor range of devices used in this process itself. No less important is the relatively low level of qualifications of staff working in HR departments and the frequently instrumental approach to employees.

Reward and performance management

Reward management is one of the key issues appearing in HRM practice in organizations operating in the Polish market. According to the Constitution, the minimum wage in Poland or how it is set is regulated by the law: the Act on the minimum wage of 10 October 2002,[15] according to which wages are set each year by the Tripartite Commission for Socio-Economic Affairs, or the government if the Commission is unable to set them within the required time.

The minimum wage increases year on year and the increase is not lower than the rate of inflation. As of 2007, the minimum wage is 936 PLN before tax (€244). The level, structure and rules of payment are determined by collective bargaining agreements and internal company rules and regulations.

Reward systems in particular enterprises may vary significantly as they depend on such factors as the form of ownership, company size, sector of the economy, company location, and HR department and its position within an organizational structure. In most cases higher payments are more common in:

- large companies, especially those with foreign capital;
- businesses operating in or near cities, like Warsaw, Krakow, Wrocław, Poznań and Gdańsk;
- companies from such sections of the economy as pharmaceuticals, fast-moving consumer goods (fmcg), computing and IT;
- departments dealing with marketing, finance, IT and telecommunication technologies.

As is shown in Table 4.8, the average wage may also differ depending on the occupational group of the labour market it refers to.

In short, the highly paid groups in both public and private sectors of the economy are senior officials, managers and specialists – all of them above the national average, whereas service workers, salespeople and labourers are paid much less than the average. However, comparing wages from the two sectors with an average wage in the economy, it must be concluded that occupational groups requiring high qualifications are paid better in the private sector, while those demanding lower qualifications are paid better in the public sector. But, on the whole, workers employed in the public sector units earn on average more than workers from the private sector (*The Structure of the Labour Market . . .*, 2005).

With reference to education, university graduates get higher wages on condition that they work in professions requiring high and medium skills levels. If the skills they have are inadequate and if they work below the level of acquired qualifications, highly educated workers are paid accordingly lower wages. If they work as office workers or technical staff at the medium grade (where the majority of employees have post-secondary education), their remuneration is still somewhat higher than that of the low-educated workers carrying out similar tasks, but this difference is not significant. It means that a highly educated worker can expect a higher wage for the work performed, much higher than in the case of other workers, provided that he or she works in a profession requiring a high level of knowledge, occupational qualifications and specialist skills. Individuals in managerial positions, university teachers and specialists in law, administration and management are generally highly remunerated. Specialists in science and engineers earn somewhat lower wages,

Table 4.8 Average wages by the main occupational groups of labour market and ownership sectors of economy in Poland, 2005

No.	Specification of occupational group	Wages as a per cent of an average wage in the economy		
		Total	Public sector	Private sector
	Total	100	107	98
1	Senior officials and managers	232	205	249
2	Professionals	134	126	154
3	Technicians and associate professionals	99	94	106
4	Office workers (clerks)	85	90	82
5	Service workers and shop and market sales workers	57	71	54
6	Skilled agricultural, gardening and fishery workers	68	75	64
7	Craft and related trades workers	78	101	72
8	Plant and machine operators and assemblers	85	97	80
9	Elementary occupations	57	59	56

Source: Calculated from *The Structure of Labour Market . . .*, 2005.

although physicists and chemists earn exceptionally high net wages in their first job (compared with net managerial earnings) (Bukowski, 2007: 121–2).

It is also worth noting that the private sector, although it generally pays less on average, creates much better remuneration conditions for workers with the highest levels of education than the public sector (see Figure 4.4).

The rate of inflation is another critical factor influencing the rate of pay increases. Within the last few years inflation has stabilized at a low level (of 2–3 per cent a year). This has translated into relatively low pay increases in Polish enterprises. It makes a difference, since inflation hovered at the level of 20 per cent 15 years ago.

The basic elements of the reward package are: base pay, merit pay, rewards and benefits. The proportions between them depend on all factors enumerated previously, but the share of base pay is rather high, reaching about 80 per cent on average. The variable part of remuneration is mainly correlated with the position that the post has in the organizational hierarchy and usually ranges from 15 per cent (for

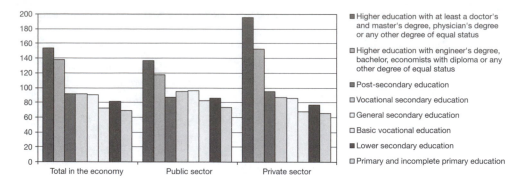

Figure 4.4 Average wages by education and ownership sectors of the economy as a percentage of the average wage in the Polish economy, 2005

Source: Calculated from *The Structure of the Labour Market ...*, 2005.

non-managerial posts) to 30 per cent (for managerial posts); however, in particular companies these proportions may vary.

Reward strategies are predominantly oriented toward providing support to organizational strategy achievement through attracting talented employees, motivation to increase productivity and effectiveness, and employee development (Urbaniak and Bohdziewicz, 2005: 84). This concerns companies distinguished by a high level of HRM and using best practice in this field of management.

Typically, job evaluation is the basis for establishing base pay. Here, companies are likely to draw up job and grade description manuals and pay schedules. But currently the movement toward consolidating salary grades and ranges into just a few wide levels, each of which contains a relatively wide range of jobs and salary levels (broadbanding), is one of the most visible remuneration trends in Polish companies.

With regard to variable elements of remuneration and pay increases, decisions are made according to performance and determined by the performance-based incentive plans which have been agreed. Here, performance results achieved by individuals, internal organizational units (e.g. teams) and the entire organization may all be examined. However, individual results usually come first, and in the case of managerial staff the results gained by the whole company play an important role as well. Furthermore, there are more and more examples of companies that use competency-based incentives schemes to manage payment increases. Among the most popular perks and other benefits granted to employees regarding the posts they occupy are mobile phones, professional training, language courses, laptops and company-owned or leased cars for business use. Relatively less popular are such forms of incentives as employee stock ownership plans, stock option plans, supplemental life and health insurance, employee pension plans, although one may observe growing interest in them.

Noticeably, the number of companies making use of market research on pay rates is increasing. This is due to the fact that some businesses are forced to make the choice about how much to pay employees with respect to their competition. Some of them want to pay the highest wages in the market to ensure that they attract and retain the most qualified employees, while others want to compete on low labour cost. This phenomenon is accompanied by the dynamic growth of the HR consulting market, mentioned in the last section. Consulting agencies conduct research and publish data covering salary and wage differentiation by occupational group, education level, geographical location and many others.

Building an effective reward system, particularly its variable elements, demands that this system be integrated with performance management. This issue is often discussed in the context of employee appraisal systems. Many companies have implemented some elements of performance management, for example goal setting, effectiveness-oriented appraisal criteria, appraisal interviews and appraisal feedbacks that provide information to the ratee on his or her performance.

The research conducted in Polish companies revealed that in 2000 as many as 32 per cent of companies reported result-oriented appraisal systems, whereas 34 per cent did not. The remaining percentage of companies reported that they were either in the process of working out such a system or planned to implement one (Pocztowski *et al.*, 2001: 48).

Numerous other studies also show the growing interest of companies in appraisal systems, which is reflected in the implementation of periodic appraisal systems. To quote some comparable data, 95 per cent of companies applying the most advanced methods of HRM and taking part in the Polish Competition for the title of HRM Leader in 2005 had formalized employee performance appraisal systems, and the remaining 5 per cent were in the process of implementing them (Urbaniak and Bohdziewicz, 2005: 68). These systems, as a rule, covered both result- and competency-oriented criteria, and often referred to management by objectives. The distinguishing feature of these appraisal systems is their all-employees character, where the overwhelming practice relies on employees being appraised by their immediate supervisors and relatively little involvement of other participants. An appraisal interview, also called a development interview, is an integral part of formalized performance appraisal systems. The major role of this activity is to provide feedback information on employee achievements as well as to support professional development. The results of employee periodic appraisals are further used in such areas as training, career planning and pay.

The reward and performance management practices described above are not universal. Still, there is a group of enterprises whose HR practices are far behind the

contemporaneous standards of professional HRM. This varied picture issues from
some specific cultural conditions and organizational practices – deriving from the
pre-transformation period – and partly from deficiencies in the knowledge and
competences of those who are responsible for managing employees, especially in the
SME sector. The reward and performance management practices in these companies
are very simplified and in most cases based on discretionary criteria. This is so
because they are right at the initial phase of building effective reward systems
connected with performance management. This situation necessitates support from
universities, consulting agencies and professional associations because, referring back
to the beginning of this chapter, the SME sector is the one that generates the highest
rate of employment.

To summarize reward and performance management practices in Poland it may be
stated that there is no homogeneity in this area. The companies that take advantage of
formalized performance management systems make use of these systems' results to
form appropriate reward policies and plan employees' development. An increasing
necessity to apply such systems is also perceptible in enterprises that have used
traditional and intuitive methods of HRM so far.

Training and development

The goals of the training and development programmes of nearly all Polish business
organizations are to maintain or improve the performance of individuals and, in so
doing, improve that of the organizations. According to the latest research,[16] employee
training has become standard in the overwhelming majority of Polish companies.
The research findings show that more than 90 per cent of companies with nine or
more employees report organizing staff training. The only exception is a group of the
smallest firms, in which participation in training programmes was reported by 59 per
cent. The research also reveals that half of micro businesses don't organize training
because they see no need to develop qualifications. They exhibit lack of awareness of
the role that improving knowledge and skills can have on business development and
success.

Apart from the size measured by employment rate, the stage of growth and level of
revenues differentiate the companies as well. Employee qualifications are improved in
92 per cent of dynamically growing companies, in 84 per cent of established
enterprises experiencing linear growth, in 61 per cent of those that are classified as
start-ups and those in the early stage of growth, and in 74 per cent of enterprises in
stagnation or the crisis phase. Next, 90 per cent of companies with revenue ranging
from 2–10 million PLN and 100 per cent of companies reporting revenue over 10
million PLN take advantage of training. Thus, high-revenue firms train their
employees more often, whereas the cost of training remains a barrier for micro-firms,
with every fifth firm indicating excessive cost as the reason for not participating in
training programmes. This is also why the most prestigious customers of training
firms are definitely the largest companies (with more than 250 employees). In 2005

nearly 50 per cent of them spent at least 50,000 PLN on training, and nearly one-third 100,000 PLN or more, whereas 67 per cent of all companies spent below 5,000 PLN on average. The plans for the forthcoming year look similar,

Interestingly, it is rather rare that an employee will ask to attend a training workshop by submitting a direct request to a supervisor. In about 20 per cent of the companies under study it is the immediate supervisor who makes the decision about what kind of training and who should attend. It is also worth emphasizing that in the overwhelming majority of companies, the final decisions concerning organization and participation in training seminars are made by the company president. This pattern of practice does not apply to the largest companies where decisions are made by the HR department.

When planning their training needs, companies exhibit a preference for externally run courses. They are altogether used by 81 per cent of medium-sized firms and 93 per cent of large firms. The most popular form of this type of training is open training courses, which account for 70 per cent of all forms of external training.

As for in-house training, it is organized by 57 per cent of companies. The proportion is considerably higher in medium-sized companies (at 84 per cent) and large companies (90 per cent).

Although MBA programmes are considered to be very effective, they are significantly less popular with companies. Only 2 per cent of respondents send their managers on these programmes. This is partly due to the fact that most such programmes are directed at managers who already have a lot of experience in high-level positions and come from the corporate world. Moreover, the most prestigious programmes cost up to €20,000. Similarly, distance education via the internet is of the lowest interest. E-learning is utilized in only 1 per cent of companies and the probable reason is that it is considered to be the least effective of all forms of qualification development.

However, the conclusion that the low percentage using the internet for distance learning can be extended to other training activities is false. A survey carried out in 2004[17] revealed that about 40 per cent of companies use the internet for training. The rate is highest for large enterprises, where about 60 per cent use it for that purpose, while for medium-sized and small enterprises the proportions are 46 per cent and 32 per cent, respectively.

With reference to the structure of training needs that are realized, the most popular training activities concern administration-related questions and obligations in workplace health and safety. Vocational and professional training courses directly related to work performed by a given company are also in high demand. Notably, more than 40 per cent of companies perceive the need for 'soft' courses, as well as in HRM, marketing, promotion, advertising, PR and sales techniques (see Figure 4.5).

Coming back to the research mentioned at the beginning of this section, the most popular employee training method is on-the-job training. This form is most often directed by senior employees or managers. In companies this method is recommended for low-skilled jobs. Nearly 70 per cent of firms consider this method

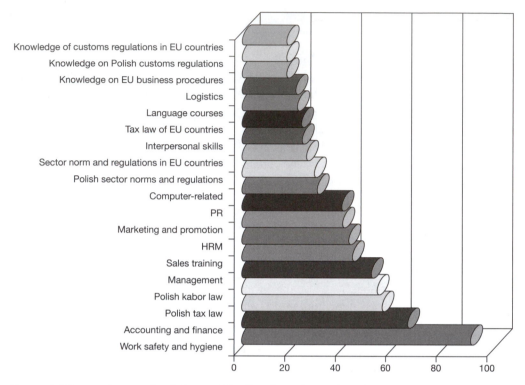

Figure 4.5 Types of external training used by firms' employees in Poland, 2005

Note: Only values above 10 per cent are shown on the chart; multiple responses were allowed.

Source: Calculated from Tokaj-Krzewska and Pyciński, 2006; *Szkolenia w Polsce . . .*, 2006.

as effective. Meanwhile case studies, workshops, games and simulations, which permit employees to practice new skills, are thought to be less effective than traditional training methods. This means that training has been first and foremost treated as a means of providing a new employee with the required practical skills. Exceptions are the businesses experiencing dynamic growth. They appreciate workshops that include games and simulations.

Research conducted in 2005[18] concluded that in the SME sector, lower-level employees are trained more often then others, namely 81 per cent of companies provide training just for them, while 52 per cent provide it for professionals and 46 per cent for managerial staff (Tokaj-Krzewska and Pyciński, 2006).

Most companies claim they analyse future training needs. Their identified priority areas include: work health and safety, accounting and finance, management, marketing and promotion, quality systems, sales and customer service, law, computer skills, interpersonal skills and HRM. This may indicate that companies regard upgrading their employees' skills and knowledge as a category of development rather than training itself in order to meet the organization's general long-term needs. Probably, this is also how organizations understand career development. These findings support some earlier research data on careers in which about 60 per cent of companies declared that a career is understood as qualification development and hierarchical progression (Pocztowski *et al.*, 2001: 69–70).

As for responsibility, this research revealed that in most cases it is both the organization and the individual who are responsible for career development (see Table 4.9). However, the employee must always accept full responsibility for his or her own career development. This was indicated by about 30 per cent of companies. The requirements to be promoted to some higher position are, in order of importance, as follows: distinguishing results achieved on the present post, upgrading qualifications and employees' own efforts and initiative. Further, to plan career development most organizations use such plans as education and training plans and employee succession plans (Pocztowski *et al.*, 2001: 94).

The general conclusion that may be made concerning training and development in Poland is that among different types of organizations it is mostly large organizations, and especially those with foreign capital, that exhibit the highest level of training and development activities. In these kinds of organizations training and development is often preceded by analysing and planning training needs as well as by performance appraisal. The plans usually issue from the company mission and business strategy. The training process is often focused on systems issues and makes use of both on-the-job and off-the-job methods. The companies also use the support of renowned external training centres, often agreeing contracts covering many years. With today's emphasis on measuring HRM's financial impact, it is crucial that some organizations make provisions to evaluate training effectiveness.

The above types of organization pay special attention to management development. The ultimate aim is, of course, to enhance the future performance of the company itself. The general management development process consists of assessing the company's strategic needs (e.g. to fill future executive openings, or to boost competitiveness), appraising the managers' current performance and then developing the managers (and future managers). Some development programmes are company-

Table 4.9 Responsibility for career development in organizations in Poland in 2000

Who is responsible for career development	*Per cent of indications*
Mostly the employee	31.7
Mostly the organization	2.0
Both the organization and the employee	61.4
No answers	4.5

Source: Pocztowski *et al.*, 2001: 70.

wide, and involve all or most new (or potential) managers. Other development programmes aim to fill specific positions, such as senior-level openings, and involve succession planning. Management development can begin using managerial on-the-job training and include job rotation, the coaching approach and action learning. For many, the off-the-job method is the most popular, including apprenticeship training programmes abroad.

It is clear that preparation and training for cross-cultural interactions and gaining an ability to operate in new conditions are critical; however, foreign companies display certain weaknesses in this part of their training activities. Because of the fact they apply an ethnocentric approach to staffing their local units in Poland, this sometimes causes misunderstandings and lengthens the process of adaptation to the new environment.

To summarize, the training and development process in Polish companies operates on a relatively good level and contributes to the increase of organizations' personnel potential. However, in the light of challenges deriving from past and current conditions particular activities are still insufficient.

THE FUTURE OF HRM IN POLAND

The future of HRM in Poland is determined by the challenges that Polish companies need to face, the challenges that create the context for emerging personnel issues.

The changes in the Polish economy have translated to labour markets, have been visible in enterprises' activities, have covered methods of work performance, and have been exhibited by employees' value systems. The significant field of changes, from an HRM perspective refers to transformation of the condition and structure of employment. This is reflected in changing proportions between lifelong employment, part-time employment and limited-time employment, with a growing preference for the latter.

Currently, hiring people is increasingly based on an organization's real need to complete some tasks, hold certain ventures, realize concrete goals and services – in contrast to the practice of permanent contracting the enterprises have used so far. This results in a decreasing number of workstations and reductions in a fixed part of employment. Employment is becoming more flexible as a result of applying new technologies which make work independent of time and place. Flexible contracts and flexitime in employment are accompanied by flexible reward systems, and, even more, by an increasing difference between the remuneration of low-skilled workers and highly skilled professionals. Thus, stimulating and maintaining organizational commitment in the context of employment getting more and more varied becomes a daily problem.

In the near future the effectiveness of the knowledge worker will be the key success factor for businesses. This means that HRM will have to work out a system capable of identifying, developing and mobilizing talents in an organization – thus covering activities which are called talent management. Managing talents requires the creation of conditions that enhance the development of entrepreneurial attitudes in an organization. The contemporary worker is not only a subordinate that performs devolved work. He or she becomes a resourceful partner and entrepreneur who actively participates in the company's activities.

One of the biggest HRM tasks is the transition from traditional training to lifelong learning. It necessitates not only revising the incremental cycle of learning, widely used in practice, and providing it with so-called double loop learning, but also making learning a part of business. Hence, the typical and currently dominating training practices should evolve toward practices associated with lifelong learning, which will become an integral part of professional life.

Although a traditional and reactive approach to training is still predominant, it is important to recognize that there have been some changes introduced in HRM practices within the last few years. One of them is the growing recognition of personal commitment as a key element of the learning process. Notably, changes within the range of training objectives are visible among which are the need to improve employees' competences and stimulate creativity, initiative and even ways of thinking.

Creating entrepreneurial attitudes among workers, managing talents and knowledge effectiveness all demand a new kind of leadership. But this refers not only to particular skills, but also requires new ways of thinking. Developing such leadership is a great challenge to HRM. In many organizations the supply of talented people seems to be sufficient, and it is rather the lack of people who are able to find, motivate and develop talent that is the real problem. Securing efficient managerial staff is a priority task for HRM.

Managing companies in the globalized economy, and especially managing human resources, raises the issues of how to attract and retain competent managerial and professional staff that are capable of realizing the company's goals in different cultural environments. This problem is getting bigger in the context of two major phenomena, namely Poland's accession to the EU and increasing internationalization of the Polish market, both of which require cultural awareness skills.

In the future HR professionals will also have to pay much greater attention to so-called socio-professional stressors, that is, factors causing stress and tension release. They should be able to answer the question of how to cope with stress, and consequently provide workers with appropriate knowledge and tools. It is enough to enumerate only the most important factors of stress to understand the problem:

- employees are continually required to adjust to rapid and incremental changes, both inside and outside the organization;
- they have to cope with lack of employment security;
- they observe or personally experience employee redundancies;

- they must undertake jobs which are often widely dispersed;
- they have to deal with new patterns of professional career.

HRM will also have to solve problems connected with balancing the professional and personal lives of employees. Therefore, all the main internal stakeholders should be involved in developing a system that allows a balance to be maintained, including line managers and HR managers.

The issue of strategic importance to HRM is the measurement of the effectiveness of the HR function itself. The problems that appear here are one of the barriers to strategic thinking and action in the area of the company's functioning. Since the main criterion of the function's evaluation is its contribution to value creation for stakeholders, measurement and evaluation of this contribution become a critical question.

The future of HRM relies on creating and providing value to the recipient, who turns out to be more and more varied and demanding. To meet the needs of such recipients it will be necessary to provide them with values that are unique, crucial, individualized, and to upgrade the quality of life and work. If we assume that the essential source of values is non-material resources, then a justified conclusion may be that there is a clear necessity to introduce change in HRM and make it more effective. This activity should be reflected in creating conditions that facilitate and stimulate fast and open inflow of ideas from outside the organization while maintaining their free flow inside the organization. There are two ways to achieve this. The first one, which is hard, requires applying modern IT instruments to HR processes. The second – which is soft – relies on creating an organizational culture that stimulates learning and knowledge-sharing in the entire organization.

In the course of events, change will be required in traditional duties, tasks and functions that are typical of current HRM, and roles played by particular actors; moreover, the entire system will evolve toward a value creating network. Among the elements comprising this network, and at the same time being the places of value creation, will be introducing new forms of work service, outsourcing the activities which are cost-consuming and of secondary importance to value creating, ensuring an effective system of intraorganizational communication, implementing programmes of organizational commitment covering, among others, reward systems, career development plans and orientation programmes preparing for work in a multicultural environment.

ComputerLand: a child of the Polish changes

Introduction

The case of ComputerLand is an example of a Polish company that was able to start and develop its business thanks to the economic and social transformation processes begun in the 1990s. It is also an outstanding example of a company that has experienced in its growth all phases of the Polish transition process and managed to win a leading position in the market. Without any doubt, one of the most important factors bringing this organization to success are the advanced HRM policies and practices that ComputerLand has been employing in its business practice since the very beginning.

Regarding the business profile, ComputerLand provides advanced IT services to corporate and institutional clients. It operates in six sectors of the economy: banking and finance, health care, industry, public administration and services, telecommunications and utilities, chemicals, insurance.

Company mission

ComputerLand has experience and creative potential, and understands the goals of its customers, therefore is able to create long-lasting relationships with customers and shares responsibility for their future, allowing them to develop and operate on the European level.

History in short

ComputerLand has been in the Polish market since 1991 and since 1995 has been listed on the Warsaw Stock Exchange. A year later it was rewarded with the greatest stock price increase. In 1995 ComputerLand began to build the ComputerLand Group, which has become the second biggest IT company group in Poland. In 2000 it was rewarded with the highest return rate among WIG 20 companies (an index of the 20 largest companies on the Warsaw Stock Exchange). In 2005 ComputerLand was granted five stars, which is the highest possible result and won the Trustworthy Company title. It sales have grown dramatically since the company was established (see Figure 4.6).

Industry leader

ComputerLand is the leader in the Polish IT market. It has earned this position by performing the most complex IT projects with large significance for the Polish economy and quality of life in the country, having an excellent base of large institutional customers. The company earned the title of one of the 100 top employers in the global IT industry (according to the American edition of the weekly *Computerworld*). The ComputerLand Group's position in the Polish IT market is reflected in top places in industry rankings. In *Computerworld*'s 2004 Top 200 ComputerLand was placed in the highest positions for gaining revenue from servicing the following sectors: industry

continued

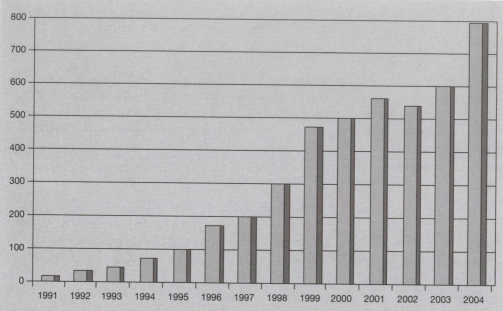

Figure 4.6 ComputerLand's sales, 1999–2004 (millions of Polish zloty)

(1st place), utilities (1st place), business and finance (2nd place), public administration (2nd place), heath and care (2nd place). It also gained 3rd place among Tailored Software developers.

Corporate social responsibility

ComputerLand's efficient operation is based on corporate governance and responsible human resources management. Internal values observed by the management board and all employees are the foundation of social responsibility for the entire company. Therefore ComputerLand has participated in various charity endeavours almost since the company's establishment. The company's employees have been giving a part of their salary to the United Way foundation each month for over 10 years. This activity resulted in the company receiving the title of Gold Donor in 2004.

Employment structure and potential

When the company started it employed 12 persons. The current potential of ComputerLand and of the companies making up the Group is over 2,000 employees, 15 regional offices in every corner of Poland, three offices abroad and perfect industry competences. ComputerLand Group's employees form a young team with diverse, broad education, both in IT and in economics, capable of reacting effectively and flexibly to their customer's needs. ComputerLand alone employs over 800 experts working in project implementation, including implementation experts, computer scientists working as IT solution developers and designers, analysts and project managers (see the Figure 4.7).

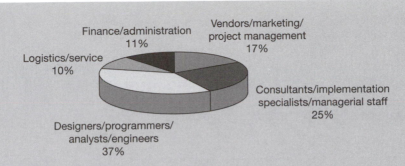

Finance/administration
11%

Vendors/marketing/
project management
17%

Logistics/service
10%

Consultants/implementation
specialists/managerial staff
25%

Designers/programmers/
analysts/engineers
37%

Figure 4.7 Employment in ComputerLand by occupational group

The aforementioned resources enable the company to provide comprehensive services to its customers – starting with needs analysis, through IT strategy creation, solution development and deployment, to system maintenance and improvement. The average age of an employee is 33. The proportion of managerial staff by sex is 30 per cent women and 70 per cent men. About 70 per cent of all employees have completed higher education.

The HRM department

There are 12 people in the HRM department specializing in various areas of HRM. The department's mission is as follows:

> The main goal of the HRM department is to support the management board in building a company with a culture of open communication and competent managerial staff that understand and identify with the company's objectives and strategies.

The main areas of HR department activities are creating value with the employees, facilitating the system of intraorganizational communication and managing human potential effectively. To realize the above goals the HR department engages the managerial staff of different organizational levels. The involvement of line managers is of significant interest.

The company believes that building value with the employees is conditioned by specific organizational culture and characteristics of the employed workers. It is assumed that in the environment of very ambitious and open-minded people the most important ways to create value with the cadre are staffing, training and development, and motivating systems.

The employees are perceived as strategic assets and it is believed that special care should be devoted to them. To realize the goals and tasks of the personnel function the following procedures have been elaborated and implemented: planning personnel needs; preparing staffing and training plans; working out the adaptation process of the newly hired; career planning; performance appraisal; forming a reward system;

continued

administering personnel documents; grievance and conflict-solving steps; monitoring of the personnel function.

The company has also introduced a Human Resources Management Information System (HRMIS) that allows it to collect and store different kinds of information that may be used by employees and management. Every employee can complete information about him- or herself with current data.

Staffing

The staffing process issues from planning personnel needs. The employment plans are strictly connected with business activities for consecutive years. The employment plans are included in a document prepared by a team of HR professionals and in consultation with managers of the key organizational departments. This document consists of: strategic goals of staffing; methods, techniques, and procedures that are to be used; methods of measuring staffing practices effectiveness; forms and blanks needed for staffing process.

The staffing process covers three phases: recruitment, selection, and placement. The company uses both external and internal recruitment but the latter is preferred. Only when it is impossible to find a worker to fill the vacancy internally does the company look for an employee from outside the organization.

The general criteria used in the selection process are: continual learning needs, readiness to share knowledge, team-working skills, ability to stand by obligations and willingness to face challenging goals.

The staffing process starts with analysis of the applicant's documents. Next, an HR specialist conducts a psychological interview supported by a psychological test. This is to verify various skills and abilities, i.e. problem solving, organizing work, team-working, communication skills, creativity, inventiveness, motiation to achieve results, building relations with a client, quality orientation; as well as technical and foreign language knowledge and skills. It enables HR to draw up a psychological profile of an applicant. Then the applicant is interviewed by the manager of a particular department, the HRM director and an HR professional specializing in recruitment and selection. Finally, a complex assessment is generated that leads to the final employment decision.

After the work is contracted the placement process starts. It covers three phases:

- induction;
- acclimatization to work tasks;
- verifying accomplishment and expectations after a probationary period.

The application documents of those who are not hired are stored in the company's database to be used in the next recruiting process.

ComputerLand also organizes student apprenticeships. They are directed to students of such disciplines as computer science, economics, human resources management, sociology, psychology, and management and marketing.

Training and development

The training and development process covers identifying training needs, planning, realizing, and evaluating training programmes. Planning career paths is a significant element of this process as well.

For planning and implementing training programmes the company uses a document entitled 'Training policy'. This document outlines the goals of the training policy, the procedures for conducting internal and external training, the roles of training participants and the elements of the training system.

The main goals of training and development are: supporting the adaptation process of the newly hired, widening and enriching knowledge in the scope of products and services offered to clients, upgrading qualifications associated with an occupied post and tasks being executed, and promoting the company's core values, namely continual training and development, knowledge-sharing, innovation and creativity.

The training budget is elaborated for each independent organizational unit, excluding special training prepared by the HRM department (i.e. workshops for new employees). The person responsible for budget realization is a manager of each unit. Monitoring of training policy realization is conducted every half year. Everybody in the company may initiate his or her own training and development.

Employees can attend externally run and internally run training programmes. The programmes can be open as well as in-company. ComputerLand cooperates with many professional consulting agencies and training companies.

It was ComputerLand in which in 1999 an application of 'learning space' was implemented for the first time in Poland. It is an e-learning system whose main goal is to ensure every employee access to information needed to complete work on particular posts. It makes learning possible at any time, any place and for any worker.

Currently the e-learning system provides training in internal clearance procedures, legal services, merchant loans, periodic employee appraisals, software programming procedures, and the basics of the quality system and many others. Every e-learning session ends with exams.

Motivating systems

The motivating system comprises material and non-material instruments for motivating staff. The main goals of this system are: delivering opportunities for continual development, promoting the company's core values, attracting and retaining the best employees, and creating good working conditions and a friendly atmosphere.

continued

In non-material motivation managers use various instruments, i.e. delegation of managerial authority, oral praise, diplomas with gratitude, letters of special reference, material awards and company cars. Once a year, at a special company-wide gathering, the most outstanding employees are granted awards, statuettes, extraordinary diplomas, etc.

Thanks to high standards and the very high service quality of employees, ComputerLand has received many prizes and mentions. These motivate the company to make further improvement and development efforts.

In 2002 ComputerLand received a mention in the ranking of the best IT companies prepared by the American edition of *Computerworld*. ComputerLand was included in the prestigious group of 100 world's best IT employers, as well as named among 100 companies that offer their employees the most competitive employment conditions. When selecting the best employers, such criteria as employee satisfaction, personnel fluctuation, the percentage of employees working in the company for over five years, career planning, recruitment methods, new employee introduction methods, employee performance evaluations, the percentage of female employees, training policy type and non-salary employee benefits were considered.

In 2002 ComputerLand received an amber statue for 'outstanding achievements in modern human resources management' in the 'Human Resources Management Leader' competition. It is the most prestigious competition related to human resources management. It is organized by the Institute of Labor and Social Studies. The competition is administered by the President of the National Bank of Poland, Leszek Balcerowicz. The goal of the competition is to further foster knowledge and best human resources management practices, as well as to improve the effectiveness of HR management.

In 2004 ComputerLand was named the best 'Company for an Engineer' in a vote organized by the Polish branch of the Board of European Students of Technology. The prestigious title of a 'Company for an Engineer' has been awarded for the fourth time. It is the best result ComputerLand has achieved during the last few years.

Material motivation is connected with employee performance appraisal, managing by objectives, and remuneration. Employee appraisal covers periodic employee appraisal based on two-way communication between superiors and subordinates. The HR department has employed the 'Code of Periodic Appraisal System' which includes the goals of appraisal, instruments and measures, methods to be used, obligations concerning the participating individuals and a manual for users. The company uses a competency-based model of employee appraisal. Managerial and professional staff are appraised using the 360-degree method. Apart from fixed pay, the company pays merit pay amounting to 30 per cent of the total payment. The merit pay depends on the commitment and contribution that was made by an employee to a particular project and on profits generated by this employee. Apart from that, the company provides full medical care to its workers.

For people with an economics education ComputerLand offers the acquisition or upgrading of skills associated with IT and computer technologies that bring benefits both to the company and employees. It is also possible to participate in 'soft skills' training workshops, such as customer service, negotiations, assertiveness, sales techniques, project management and quality management. The company also finances higher education for outstanding or promising workers and encourages its employees to upgrade their knowledge and skills.

NOTES

1 To compare, gross enrolment increased from 12.9 per cent (in 1990) to 46.4 per cent (in 2004), and net enrolment from 9.8 per cent to 35.3 per cent, respectively.
2 Purchasing power parity (see more: http://poland.gov.pl).
3 *Journal of Laws*.
4 JoL of 1998, no. 24, item 141, as amended.
5 JoL of 1964, no. 16, item 93, as amended.
6 JoL of 2003, no. 166, item 1608.
7 Consolidated text: JoL of 2001, no. 79, item 854 with subsequent amendments.
8 JoL of 1991, no. 55, item 235 with later amendments.
9 JoL of 1993, no. 55, item 236.
10 JoL of 2001, no. 100, item 1080 with amendments.
11 JoL of 2002, no. 62, item 556.
12 The research covered about 800 students on HRM and Sociology courses conducted by Dr Marzena Stor at Wrocław University of Economics during the years 2003–6 within the research interests of the HRM Department at this University.
13 The research covered 35 large foreign companies operating in Poland. The project was completed by the HRM Department at Wrocław University of Economics within the framework of a research grant financed by the Polish State Committee for Scientific Research in the period 2004–6, and supervised by Prof. Tadeusz Listwan.
14 The research is based on interviews in some selected British companies by the staff of the HRM Department at Wrocław University of Economics, headed by Prof. Tadeusz Listwan within the research grant entitled *European Career Gatway*, financed by the EU within the program *Leonardo da Vinci*.
15 JoL no. 209, item 1679, with later amendment.
16 Research conducted in February 2006 on a representative sample of 546 businesses, commissioned by the Fundacja Obserwatorium Zarządzania (see *Szkolenia w Polsce*, 2006).
17 The survey was carried out in strict accordance with the requirements of the European Statistical Office (Eurostat) and covered about 6,000 enterprises with at least 10 employees (and was obligatory for them).
18 The research conducted on a sample of 600 companies in 2005 within the work ordered by the Polish Agency for Enterprise Development.

REFERENCES AND FURTHER READING

Baka, W. (2004). *The Economic Agenda for the Polish Round Table 15 Years Later: Lessons for the Future*. Warsaw: Tiger, Transformation, Integration and Globalization Research Center.

Balcerowicz, L. (1998). *Wolność i rozwój. Ekonomia wolnego rynku.* [Liberty and Development. Economy of the Free Market.]. Kraków: Wydawnictwo Znak.

Berger, K. *et al.* (2004). *Raport o stanie sektora małych i średnich przedsiębiorstw w Polsce w latach 2002–2004* [The State of Small and Mid-Sized Enterprises in Poland in 2002–2004 – Report]. Warsaw: Polska Agencja Rozwoju Przedsiębiorczości.

Bukowski, M. (ed.) (2007). *Employment in Poland in 2006 – Productivity for Jobs*. Warsaw: Ministry of Labor and Social Policy, Department of Economic Analysis and Forecasts.

Hofstede, G. and Hofstede, G. J. (2005). *Cultures and Organizations. Software of the Mind*. New York: McGraw-Hill.

ICT Usage in Enterprises in 2004. Investing in People (2004). Polish Central Statistical Office, http://www.stat.gov.pl.

Inglehart, R. and Welzel, C. (2005). 'Exploring the Unknown: Predicting the Responses of Publics Not Yet Surveyed'. *International Review of Sociology* (March), 15, 1.

Kochanowicz, J., Kozarzewski, P. and Woodward, R. (2005). *Understanding Reform: The Case of Poland*. Warsaw: Center of Social and Economic Research. No. 59/2005.

Koniunktura gospodarcza w państwach Unii Europejskiej w 2006 roku. [Economic Trends in EU Countries in 2006] (2007). Warsaw: Ministerstwo Gospodarki. Departament Analiz i Prognoz.

Koziński, J. and Listwan, L. (1993). 'Poland'. In Peterson, R. B. (ed.) *Managers and National Culture. A Global Perspective.* Westport, CT: Quorum Books.

List of Major Foreign Investors in Poland. (2007). Warsaw: Polish Information and Foreign Investment Agency.

Listwan T. (1993). 'Funkcja personalna przedsiębiorstwa w okresie zmian systemowych'. [Personnel Function in Companies in the Transition Economy]. (In *Przegląd Organizacji*, [Organization Review], 3.

Listwan T.(1999). 'Zarządzanie kadrami w okresie transformacji gospodarczej w Polsce' [Human Resources Management in Polish Economic Transition]. In *Zarządzanie Zasobami Pracy – Humanizacja Pracy* [Human Resources Management – Work Humanization], 1–2.

Listwan, T. (2005). 'Praktyka zarządzania kadrami przedsiębiorstw w czasie transformacji ustrojowej w Polsc' [The Practice of HRM in the Transition Economy in Poland. In Listwan, T. (ed.), Dylematy transformacji systemowej w Polsce. [Dilemmas of Systems Transformation in Poland]. Poznań – Wrocław: Wydawnictwo Forum Naukowe.

Listwan, T., Koziński, J. and Witkowski, S. (1986). *Konkursy na stanowiska kierownicze* [Managerial Selection by Competition]. Warsaw: PWE.

Main Macroeconomic Indicators – Republic of Poland (2007). Ministry of Economy, Analyses and Forecasting Department (June).

Masłoń, A. (2006). 'Benefiting from the EU funds'. *Warsaw Voice. Training and HR.* http://www.warsawvoice.pl/view/11485.

Michael, P., Keane, P. and Prasad, E. (2001). 'Poland: Inequality, Transfers, and Growth in Transition'. *Finance and Development* (a quarterly magazine of the IMF) (March) 38, 1.

Obłój K. and Weinstein, M. (2001). 'Strategy and Human Resource Management in Polish Enterprises'. In *Zarządzanie Zasobami Ludzkimi*, no. 1A.

Pocztowski, A., Miś, A., Sapeta, T. and Purgał, J. (2001). *Praktyka zarządzania zasobami ludzkimi i jej wpływ na rynek pracy* [The Practice of Human Resources Management and Its Influence on the Labour Market]. Warsaw: Instytut Pracy i Spraw Socjalnych.

Statistical Yearbook of the Republic of Poland (1999). Warsaw: Polish Central Statistical Office.

Statistical Yearbook of the Republic of Poland (2006). Warsaw: Polish Central Statistical Office.

Stor, M. (2004). 'Prawne i etyczne aspekty zarządzania kadrami'. [Legal and Ethical Aspects of Human Resources Management]. In Listwan, T. (ed.) *Zarządzanie kadrami* [Human Resources Management] Warsaw: Wydawnictwo C. H. Beck.

Stor, M. (2004). 'Amerykańska i europejska koncepcja przedsiębiorczości'. [American and European Conception of Entrepreneurship]. In M. Juchnowicz (ed.) *Kapitał ludzki a kształtowanie przedsiębiorczości*. Warsaw: Wydawnictwo POLTEX.

Stor, M. (2006). 'Międzykulturowe problemy kadry menedżerskiej w Polsce'. [Cross-Cultural Problems of Managerial Staff in Poland]. In Listwan, T. (ed.) *Sukces w zarządzaniu kadrami. Kapitał ludzki w organizacjach międzynarodowych* [Success in HRM. Human Capital in International Organizations]. Prace naukowe no. 1130. Wrocław: Wydawnictwo Akademii Ekonomicznej we Wrocławiu.

The Structure of the Labour Market in Poland in 2004 (2005). Warsaw: Polish Ministry of Economy and Labour.

Structural Reforms on the Products and Services Market and on the Capital Market (2004). Warsaw: Ministry of Finance.

Szkolenia w Polsce – kompendium 2005/2006. Raport 2006 [Training in Poland. The Report of 2005/2006] (2006). IPSOS. Fundacja Obserwatorium Zarządzania.

Sztandera, U., Minkiewicz, B. and Bąba, M. (2005). *Oferta szkolnictwa wyższego a wymagania rynku pracy* [Higher Education Offer Against Labour Market Demands]. Instytut Społeczeństwa Wiedzy na zlecenie Krajowej Izby Gospodarczej.

Tokaj-Krzewska, A. and Pyciński, S. (eds) (2006). *Raport o stanie sektora małych i średnich przedsiębiorstw Polsce w latach 2004–2005.* Warsaw: Polska Agencja Rozwoju Przedsiębiorczości.

Trompenaars, F. and Hampden-Turner, C. (1997). *Riding the Ways of Culture. Understanding Diversity in Business*. London: Nicholas Brealey Publishing.

Urbaniak, B. and Bohdziewicz, P. (2005). *Zarządzanie zasobami ludzkimi. Kreowanie nowoczesności. Raport 2005* [Human Resources Management. Creating Modernity. 2005 Report]. Warsaw: IPiSS.

Managing human resources in the Czech Republic

5

JOSEF KOUBEK

INTRODUCTION

The Czech Republic provides an example of a country which became underdeveloped as a result of an externally imposed system. Before the Second World War the Czech part of former Czechoslovakia belonged to the most developed areas of Europe not only from the point of view of gross national product (GNP) per capita, technology, standard of living, etc., but also from the point of view of personnel management. There were firms whose personnel management systems were very advanced, and it is possible to say that those systems had many features of the present human resource management. The leading firm in the introduction of the most effective personnel management system was the Bata Company (at present known as Bata International, whose headquarters were transferred to Canada after the communist takeover in 1948), but also Škoda Company, CKD, Tatra, etc. had very advanced personnel management systems. The characteristic feature of the systems was an emphasis on performance through systematic performance appraisal, performance based compensation, systematic training, careful selection and placement and very extensive care of employees (benefits, working environment and working conditions). It was also possible to see a purposeful effort to harmonize the company goals and the individual goals of employees, to improve the quality of working life and employees' satisfaction.

After the communist takeover organizations lost their independence in decision making. The imposed Soviet model of management centralized any decision making and made it uniform. The central authorities even decided details concerned with individual organizations, and if the management of an organization wished to change anything it was necessary to ask the central authorities for approval. Concerning personnel management, the centralization of decision making was particularly strict and it meant that personnel management in companies degenerated into personnel administration. During the period of communist rule the personnel agenda in individual organizations was dispersed step-by-step or distributed into different, relatively independent organizational units. So-called personnel departments ensured some administrative services only (personnel records and documents of individual employees, statistics, etc.). The spheres of compensation and work organization were administered by departments of labour and wages (or departments of labour economics). Special departments organized the training and development of employees. Manpower planning was ensured as a rule by departments of planning, but their roles were formal only because of the system of central planning and central distribution of jobs and human resources. Departments of employee care administered benefits and social activities. Many organizations had specialized departments of health and safety. A very important and powerful department in any organization was the department of personnel policy (so-called cadre department), which systematically analysed and evaluated first of all the political reliability of every employee. This department was probably the only decision making unit among the above-mentioned departments concerned with the personnel agenda in the organization. It used to decide selection, placement, promotion, training and development, termination, etc., taking into account first of all political criteria before the professional characteristics, expertise or performance. Some personnel activities were underdeveloped, some of them existed formally only and some of them had a different form and different tasks than in West Europe. Employee relations were disregarded and trade unions' main role was in employee care or the social policy of the organization. Any normal collective bargaining did not exist and so-called collective agreements were formal only. A characteristic feature was the absence of any formal performance appraisal system. There were four reasons for this: socialist egalitarianism, resulting in wage and salary levelling; the full employment policy (nobody was afraid of any negative appraisal, because there was no danger of unemployment); scarcity of labour in a badly planned and managed economy; and the centralized system of compensation, which was unable to compensate adequately better or worse performance. All these factors made any formal performance appraisal system unnecessary. In connection with the central planning system, as a rule very good and very comprehensive unified personnel information systems were developed (from the 1950s until the beginning of the 1980s the so-called Unified Labour Force Records [JEP – Jednotná evidence pracujících], replaced since 1980 by a computerized system, the Unified Database of Organizations with Sub-system Labour, Compensation and Social Affairs [JÚZO – Jednotná údajová základna organizací, subsystém práce, mezd a sociálních věcí]).

During the period of communist rule some specific personnel practices were developed. First of all, the weak pressure on performance and lack of attention to motivating employees resulted in a poor and ineffective compensation system, ambiguous responsibilities and taking a person on, or promoting them, was based not on performance and competence, but on political loyalty and connections.

Unfortunately, both the dispersed personnel agenda and underdeveloped personnel functions or poor personnel practices have a tendency to survive, not only in the present public sector, but many employees and managers are willing to continue with them until now, even in the private sector.

THE TRANSITION PROCESS

The revolution in 1989 had several motives. First of all, there was a need for both individual and national freedom. But a very important motive was the need to change the ineffective economic system. Already during the political changes period in November and December 1989 the principal goals of the economic transformation aiming at increase in productivity, efficiency and competitiveness of the Czech economy were presented. Those were, above all:

- to give full opportunity for individual (private) entrepreneurial activities and to support them;
- to create a radical economic transformation from a centrally planned economy to a market one;
- to ensure the privatization of property;
- to enable the internationalization of the Czech economy and to integrate it with Western economies.

On the macroeconomic level top priority was placed on a strict anti-inflationary policy, restrictive monetary policy, budget surplus and a convertible currency. On the microeconomic level the need to induce efficient allocation of resources and minimize the social costs and consequences of transformation was stressed. The main measures identified in this context were, among others:

- better utilization of national resources, including human resources;
- reduction of over-employment and retraining of the redundant labour force;
- establishing a normal labour market and its institutions;
- legalization of collective bargaining;
- restructuring of the social security and health care systems and their gradual separation from the state budget.

As can be seen, human resource, labour market and social policy issues were considered as the most important aspects of the economic transformation. Consequently, HRM had a very important role in the economic transformation in the Czech Republic and its role increased in the subsequent period, i.e the period of stabilization and development of the market economy.

What were the results of the transformation process in the sphere of labour? A normal labour market and all its institutions were rapidly established. Since 1991 two very important acts have been brought in: the Employment Act and the Collective Bargaining Act. They are nearly identical with the equivalent acts abroad. The Labour Code has been adapted step-by-step to the new situation and recently (2006) a totally new and 'European' Labour Code was approved by Parliament. Unfortunately, the social security and health care systems have been changing very slowly and the process has not yet been finished. Since the second half of the 1990s the rules and directives of the EU have been gradually adopted and already before entering the EU in 2004 the 'European' legislation existed in the Czech Republic.

Concerning the other objectives of transformation it is possible say that all the above-mentioned objectives were realized very rapidly, especially the process of introducing the market economy and the process of privatization. Since the end of the 1990s the characteristics of the Czech economy have been very similar to those of the 'old' EU countries. The Czech Republic is a very popular area for international investors and, on the other hand, Czech investors are developing their activities abroad. As part of this internationalization process, Czech exporting activities have grown significantly. While in the 1980s about 80 per cent of Czech exports were oriented towards CMEA (Council for Mutual Economic Assistance) countries and Third World countries, now approximately the same percentage is oriented towards the 'old' EU countries and the other developed economies. The Czech Republic was among the most developed economies of the former communist countries, having had the highest real GDP per capita. The growth rates of real GDP per capita have been recently highest also, with the exception of the Baltic countries of the former Soviet Union (see Table 5.1).

The majority of the economy has been privatized, but some companies where the state owns shares still exist.

THE CONTEXT FOR HUMAN RESOURCE MANAGEMENT

The changes in the Czech Republic have had their source predominantly in the step-by-step learned importance of human resources and its proper management for the success of companies. The process has been accelerated by imitating foreign firms existing in the Czech Republic and by extensive training of Czech managers (abroad and at home). But, in any case, the process of change in HRM has not been too rapid.

Concerning the position of HRM in the system of organization management, it is possible to see that HRM is still not fully considered as a priority by managers, in

Table 5.1 Growth rate of real GDP per capita in the Czech Republic, 2000–2005 (per cent)

	Year					
	2000	2001	2002	2003	2004	2005
Czech Republic	2.3	4.5	0.0	4.3	4.2	6.0
EU 15	3.0	1.5	1.0	0.5	1.4	0.9
EU 25	3.5	1.7	0.6	1.1	1.6	1.1

Source: Eurostat.

spite of its increasing importance influenced by the market environment and other factors. Many organizations and managements prefer such fields as marketing and sales, new technologies, finance or business administration, because they are seen as a more rapid way to become successful.

In addition, the transformation situation threatened managerial positions, the mobility of managers was very intensive, and consequently the managers, who felt an early loss of their positions, were not willing to take any steps with long-term returns and to save work for their successors. Another negative factor infuencing HRM is connected with managers attempting to gain success as soon as possible to prove their competence. A concentration on sales, in the first instances, over a concentration on human resources, was to be expected in order to impact foreign investments and new technology, financial operations, etc.

But there are still other reasons such as the belittling and deprecation by managers, particularly top ones, of HRM. Top managers are often technical specialists and prefer the technical aspects of organizational functioning. They often don't respect personnel departments as partners in management, but only as a service which administers personnel records and staffing. It is very difficult to convince them of the importance of HRM. They simply don't know (and often don't want to know) anything about modern HRM. As well, a consequence of the former role of the communist personnel policy departments is that the approach to HRM is often belittling and it needs an enormous effort to establish a normal personnel department and its functions.

Nevertheless, some influences have shown the increasing importance of HRM and consequently the need to take it more into account. What have been the influences?

- One of the typical features of Czechs is an entrepreneurial spirit and a high tendency towards individualism. Many Czechs recall the existence of their private business or the private business of their parents before the communist takeover. And many of them have been struggling to restore and to run such businesses. Others see an opportunity to do something more independently and more efficiently (and more profitably, too) than is possible in the position of employee. Consequently, the most dynamic, most experienced, skilled and generally the best employees have been leaving their former employers for their own private businesses. And the small businesses have attracted other good people from large employers. It is no wonder that the traditional employers have been suffering from a lack of skilled craftspeople, specialists and other professionals. The situation has drawn the attention of large employers and managers to personnel management activities. One of the most urgent problems of large organizations has been how to stabilize (retain) skilled employees, how to recruit them and how to motivate and compensate them.
- Foreign organizations and foreign capital entering extensively into the Czech economy have had a similar effect. Some of the foreign organizations have offered better compensation and also more creative, more interesting and more independent work than the Czech organizations and therefore they have been rather

attractive employers. This has resulted in an outflow of the best employees from the other organizations, too. And the other organizations have had to look for measures to be able to avert or at least moderate the outflow.

● The rapidly increasing market environment in the 1990s forced management to change its approach to human resources. Managers were increasingly aware of the importance of human resources for the market success of their organizations and consequently for their individual careers. Neglecting the appropriate personnel management could jeopardize not only the results and the future existence of the organization, but, first of all, the positions of managers.

● The changing approach to HRM was caused, a little paradoxically, by mistakes made in this sphere some time ago. The typical phenomenon under socialism was over-employment. Many organizations felt this over-employment all the time, but even the first stages of economic transformation forced them to search for a solution to the situation. Consequently, it was necessary to save labour and reduce the number of employees. But there was a problem: what criteria should be used for selecting which employees to make redundant? The managers had no experience with such problems; many of them were managers with little expertise surviving in positions from the communist period, and consequently they often used 'socialist' and very strange criteria. Concerning individual employees, they used, for example, the social situation of individual employees, personal likes and dislikes; they often preferred to make women redundant, plus employees of retirement age, employees 50 years and older or young (single) employees. Because there was a firm conviction that there was a surplus of clerical and other non-productive workers (even managers and specialists) in organizations, this category of employees were reduced first of all. The individual units (workshops, teams, departments, etc.) were evaluated from the point of view of a presumed prospective usefulness and then some of them were closed and very often all the employees were discharged without any selection. This approach led to the loss of many skilled and experienced employees directly and also indirectly, because many employees felt insecure in such organizations and left as soon as possible. All this had an impact on the performance of such organizations and later forced the managers to pay attention to personnel management and look for modern and effective methods. The organizations with this experience are now more aware of the importance of HRM and they often belong to the most progressive organizations in applying modern approaches to managing people. They also serve as a warning to other organizations.

● New tasks of independent organizations influenced needs in the training and development of employees, particularly managers. Training and development have a very long-term tradition among the personnel functions in Czech organizations and it seems that this area of personnel management was particularly favoured by management. Unfortunately, training and development have been focused mostly on managerial or professional and technical groups of employees, trained first of all in marketing and sales or computers and new technology, but languages have also been a very important area of training and development. Languages in particular enable a transfer of new knowledge and experience, including new approaches to human resource management. It is already possible to see some favourable consequences of the intensive training and development in general or non-personnel managerial skills, because both Czech and foreign instructors stress the human resource aspects of the matter concerned.

- Managers have been exposed to systematic inducement, systematic propaganda concerned with modern HRM and its importance for organizational efficiency. Since the beginning of the 1990s many educational activities, both international and national, have been developed aimed at introducing business management know-how. Different kinds of HRM courses have been very frequent among these educational activities. HRM issues have been included particularly in the courses for top and middle managers. It is also possible to see a systematic stress on HRM in different articles published in both professional and general journals and newspapers (at present there are eight specialist HRM journals and several journals and newspapers have a regular HRM section). Universities play a very important role in this field. They are not only educating, but also organizing educational activities, providing up-to-date information and consulting managers or other educational institutions. Foreign companies working in the Czech Republic play a very important role, too. Their approach to HRM is often imitated and their experience is utilized in Czech companies. But this effort also has a very strange consequence: HR and HRM become a matter of fashion. Every organization declares it has an HR department, HR management and HR managers. But it is only a label. The changed name doesn't mean changed practice.

Unfortunately, some problems in HRM in Czech organizations have been caused by the existing staff of personnel/HR departments. On the one hand, there are some personnel managers, as a rule new ones, who are mostly very interested and engaged in HRM progress and bringing modern HRM systems into organizations. Their need for information and experience and their effort to change the situation in organizations is striking. They are mostly active members of professional associations, for instance the Club of Personnel Managers, the HRM section at the Czech Managers' Association, the Czech Society for Human Resources Development, etc. The professional associations organize different kinds of education and discussions and develop an intensive effort to improve the HRM situation in organizations. On the other hand, there is another group of personnel managers, or, more exactly, personnel officials, who continue the traditional paperwork practices, who don't want to change anything and who don't want to learn anything.

A similar situation can be seen in organizations where the personnel managers are not qualified for their job. After the revolution many organizations discharged the former staff (or rather former heads) of the personnel policy departments appointed by the Communist Party secretariates. Because of lack of specialists in personnel management, very often individuals with an inadequate education (for instance a technical one) were appointed to personnel positions, above all the top ones.

Inexperienced individuals gained most of their information and instructions from colleagues or subordinates, who survived in the personnel job from the communist period. Consequently, such new personnel managers and heads of personnel departments maintain traditional personnel management practices and cannot assert any new personnel functions and improve the position of human resource management in organizations. Many of them are aware of their incompetence and are afraid of more competent individuals in their domain and therefore they don't want to recruit young graduates specializing in HRM (see the case study on pp. 000–000).

Fortunately, it seems that the first, more progressive group of personnel managers is increasing as a result of both educational activities and the current situation in organizations.

EMPLOYERS, TRADE UNIONS AND INDUSTRIAL RELATIONS

During communist rule, only the unified so-called Revolutionary Trade Unions Movement existed, but no unions of employers (because the state was the principal employer) and no normal industrial relations. All employees were members of the trade unions, because membership was compulsory.

During the first half of the 1990s it was possible to observe some substantial changes in trade unions. The former unified trade unions were diversified and different interests of individual groups of employees caused relatively independent individual unions to be established mostly under the umbrella of the Czech–Moravian Confederation of Trade Unions (which represents a substantial majority of 33 trade unions). Besides the Confederation there exists a small group (the Trade Union Association of Bohemia, Moravia and Silesia) of non-associated individual trade unions. However, the Confederation is considered the principal partner in negotiations among trade unions, employers and the government.

Institutions such as employers' unions emerged as a consequence of the privatization process. But they are mostly multipurpose institutions, because they represent not only the interests of employers, but also the interests of individual industries or branches in partnership with the government and other institutions. Several such unions exist, but only one of them has the word 'employer' in its name (the Union of Employers in the Mining and Oil Industry). The others don't declare formally in their names that they represent the interests of employers. One of the most important unions of this kind is the Union of Industry and Transport of the Czech Republic. The union develops different activities; for instance, it runs a special institute, which serves as a centre of training and education for managers and organizes – among other things – courses in HRM. The representatives of all these unions are partners in collective bargaining, especially in three-party bargaining. A 2003 survey containing only a small group of respondents signalled that about two-thirds of organizations might be members of an employers' union (see Table 5.2).

Table 5.2 Percentage of staff in Czech firms organized in trade unions

Percentage of organized employees	Year		
	1993	*1996*	*1998*
0	0	7	14
1–25	1	6	10
26–50	4	19	25
51–75	30	40	34
76–100	65	26	14
Don't know	1	2	3

Source: Cranfield Project on European HRM. Unfortunately the data from the last survey in 1993 are not representative because of the very small number of respondents.

As has already been mentioned, membership of trade unions was compulsory during communist rule. Since the beginning of the 1990s a long-term decline in membership has occurred.

While in 1993 95 per cent of organizations had 51 per cent or more employees with membership in trade unions, in 1996 this had fallen to 66 per cent of organizations and in 1998 to 48 per cent of organizations. The 2003 survey results were not representative, but they showed that the decrease in membership had continued and the proportion of organizations with 51 per cent or more employees with union membership might be about 30 per cent in the first half of 2000s.

The decline in union membership was caused by several different factors:

- It could be a reaction to the previously compulsory membership in trade unions. Many people left the institutions connected with the former communist system, not only trade unions, but also youth organizations, sporting and social organizations, women's unions, etc.
- There emerged quite new companies built on 'green grass', which had no tradition of industrial relations.
- Changes in ownership; new owners innovated their business programmes, which resulted in less need for manual workers, who were the typical members of trade unions.
- Many skilled craftsmen – former employees organized in trade unions – left their employers to run their own small businesses.
- Introduction of flexible forms of employment and work organization; fewer of the people working in the flexible regimes are organized in trade unions.
- Decomposition of large manufacturers into small and middle-sized businesses; employees in the small and middle-sized businesses are more under the control of

their employers and are in smaller groups which makes it harder to have the courage to establish trade unions or to continue in membership.

- Many trade union members felt that the trade unions are not fully able to defend their interests; on the other hand employers began to offer some benefits and advantages to eliminate the influence of trade unions.
- International recruitment, selection and hiring of employees who would not probably be interested in trade union membership (young people, highly educated people, women, people from traditionally agricultural regions, foreigners etc.).
- Some employers, particularly international ones, often openly declared that they didn't want any trade unions in their companies and even forbade membership.
- There has been a massive campaign by right-wing political parties against trade unions; they give them different labels, such as 'bolshevic', 'communist', 'red', and blame them for damaging economic development etc.

On the other hand, a relatively high percentage of organizations recognized trade unions for the purpose of collective bargaining (99 per cent in 1993; 91 per cent in 1996) and it seems that the percentage has not changed since that time. It seems as well that the influence of trade unions in organizations was declining during the 1990s, but since the Social Democratic Party has been in government (since 1988) the influence and activity of trade unions have improved and employers have to respect them a little more. After all, the support of trade unions and the Social Democratic Party is mutual. In fact trade unions were forced into mutual support by the above-mentioned campaign of right-wing parties.

At present, it is possible to see that trade unions have a very similar legal and political position as in most developed countries.

KEY LABOUR MARKET DEVELOPMENTS

The unemployment rate was surprisingly low (at about 3–4 per cent) during the 1990–7 period, but it has increased since 1998 (to a maximum of 8.8 per cent in 2000). In January–March 2006 it was about 8 per cent. The low unemployment rate in 1990–7 is interpreted as a success of the then conservative government's policy (by the conservative Citizen Democratic Party, which was in power at the time) and the rapid growth after 1998 is interpreted as a failure of the Social Democracy government policy (by the same conservative Citizen Democratic Party, which was then in opposition). But in fact the low unemployment rate in the first period was a consequence of some different positive factors (individual activity, entrepreneurial spirit and flexibility of people, followed by the tradition of small family businesses, a rapid increase in the number of young people attending universities and other institutions of education, etc.) and also negative factors (a low rate of personal savings among citizens and a high level of participation in state-sponsored social employment schemes which masked real unemployment figures). Unfortunately there were very serious latent factors and symptoms of rapid unemployment growth in the next period. Even in the first half of the 1990s some estimates of a higher future unemployment rate were published (official estimates by the Czech Statistical Office and presented by the government predicted about 6–8 per cent, but some estimates presented by independent labour market specialists predicted more than 10 per cent, or even 17 per cent unemployment rate at the beginning of the 2000s).

What are the causes of the unemployment rate increase since 1998? There are several:

- Demographic causes. The very numerous generations born during the 1970s began to enter the labour market, while the much less numerous generations born in the 1930s had been leaving the labour market since the mid-1990s. The ratios between the two amounts reached their peak in 1997 and 1998 (see Table 5.3). At that time the yearly increase represented about 90,000 new labour resources on the labour market. Even in 2005 – in spite of some decline – the increase in the labour force was about 20,000. The increase during 1995–9 was about 430,000 and during 2000–4 about 260,000 new labour forces. It was too large an increase considering the total labour force (about 5,200,000) in the Czech Republic and of course too large for an economy in transformation.
- Delaying some transformation steps during the first half of the 1990s practised by the then right-wing government. The right-wing parties wished to win in the 1996 elections and therefore they avoided transformation steps which would have a negative impact on the social welfare of the population, particularly on employment. In fact they conserved the former over-employment and left the dangerous problem to their left-wing successors.
- Means of privatization. The privatization realized by the right-wing government in the first half of the 1990s, particularly the voucher privatization, destroyed large numbers of jobs, firms and even some industries. The small owners of shares from voucher privatization were in fact eliminated by groups of so-called investment funds, but the objectives of the investment funds were not to run the controlled firms, but to trade with them. This led to many bankruptcies.
- Excessive liberalization of import by the right-wing government. This resulted in nearly uncontrolled import of cheap comsumption goods from East Asia, which nearly destroyed some traditional Czech industries (particularly textiles, clothing and shoemaking). Liberalization of trade with the EU (unfortunately one-sided) led, for example, to difficulties in agriculture and the food industry. This all resulted in a substantial decrease in the number of jobs in the pertinent branches and industries.
- Step-by-step shortening and finally abolition of compulsory military service and the establishment of a small professional army led to an increase in the free labour force in the market, because the professional army has fewer than half the number of previous army staff.
- Last, but not least, there were causes connected with introducing the full-value market economy during the second half of the 1990s. The market and competitive environment forced owners and managements of organizations to apply modern

Table 5.3 Unemployment rate and working age population in the Czech Republic 1991–2006 (per cent)

Year	1990	1991	1992	1993	1994	1995	1996	1997	1998	1999	2000	2001	2002	2003	2004	2005	2006
*Unemployment rate Czech Republic**																	
	–	2.6	3.0	4.3	4.3	4.0	3.9	4.8	6.5	8.7	8.8	8.1	7.3	7.8	8.3	7.9	8.0
*Unemployment rate EU 15***																	
	–	–	–	10.5	10.1	10.2	9.9	9.3	8.6	7.7	7.3	7.6	8.0	8.1	7.9	–
*Unemployment rate EU 25***																	
	–	–	–	–	–	–	–	8.4	9.1	8.6	8.4	8.8	9.0	9.1	8.7	–
*Working age population replacement ratio ****																	
1.28	1.32	1.38	1.50	1.63	1.78	1.91	2.00	2.01	1.95	1.82	1.66	1.51	1.35	1.22	1.16	1.07

Notes: *Czech Statistical Office (www.czso.cz), resp. Eurostat For 2006 January–March average; **Eurostat; ***Working-age population replacement ratio is the ratio between the number of individuals reaching working age and number of individuals over working age as a consequence of population development. 2005 and 2006 preliminary data.

approaches to managing and utilizing human resources and to save labour costs, in order to be competitive not only in national but in international markets. This began a period of mass redundancies, with its influences on unemployment.

Considering all the causes of the development of unemployment in the Czech Republic, one could say that an unemployment rate not exceeding 9 per cent is something of a miracle. It could be said that it is a merit of the Social Democratic governments after 1998 and of the good condition of the Czech economy. Recent unemployment rates are lower than the rates in several 'old' EU countries (Belgium, Germany, Greece, Spain, France, Italy and Finland) and are among the lowest of the new EU members.

Population changes will positively influence the future development of the unemployment rate. During the second half of the 2000s the less numerous generations born in the 1980s and 1990s will enter the labour market, while the very numerous generations born in the 1940s and 1950s will be leaving. This will even result in a negative replacement ratio. It will potentially lead to a decrease in the unemployment rate.

IMPACT OF THE MOVE TO EU MEMBERSHIP ON HRM

The majority of the legislative provisions – including provisions concerned with the sphere of labour and employment – made during the 1990s and the early 2000s were focused on the harmonization of the Czech legislation with EU legislation. After all, those were necessary terms of membership of the EU. Consequently, there were nearly no impacts of entering the EU in 2004 on labour and employment.

Some 'old' EU member countries feared a massive inflow of labour from the 'new' members, but the fears proved totally groundless, particularly in connection with the Czech Republic. Czech people have liked working abroad for some time, but this is in order to gain experience, to learn something new or to learn languages. Czechs don't like to live outside their country for a long time or even permanently (emigrants from the communist period mostly returned home after 1990). They are home country oriented and they prefer to live and work among their 'own people'.

The preference for not moving abroad has been supported by very positive economic development since the early 2000s. In spite of some negative phenomena (e.g. an unemployment rate considered too high, but much lower than in the majority of other post-communist EU countries and an ongoing State Budget deficit) it is possible to see very visible economic and social progress. The standard of living is relatively high (even higher than in some old EU countries) and continues to increase, there are very positive indices of economic growth, the currency is sound and the exchange rate is improving, but it has only a little influence on the permanently increasing export of Czech products. The Czech Republic is a favoured country among foreign investors, because of skilled labour and some incentives; it is also a favoured country among foreign tourists – the income from tourism is permanently increasing and it is one of the key industries. Recent positive economic development has resulted in changes in the World Bank's classification of the country. The bank placed the Czech Republic among rich countries (so called nett contributors) in 2005.

The consequence is that Czechs need not search for jobs, better economic conditions or a higher standard of living abroad. On the contrary, the Czech Republic is a favourite destination for labour from Slovakia, Poland, Ukraine, as well as from the 'old' EU countries or even from North America. The actual estimates concerning foreigners living and working in the Czech Republic are about 250,000–300,000, which corresponds to about 2.5–3 per cent of the total number of Czech citizens.

After all, two years of EU membership is a very short period for observing and evaluating any changes.

TRENDS AND DEVELOPMENTS IN HUMAN RESOURCE MANAGEMENT PRACTICE

The following discussion is based on the results of three surveys organized in the Czech Republic in 1993, 1996 and 1998 in connection with the Cranfield Project on European Human Resource Management. Unfortunately, the last survey in 2003 suffered from lack of funds and therefore the Czech organizers decided to use an electronic questionnaire. The response rate was only 3–4 per cent and it resulted in data which were not representative and comparable with the data of the previous surveys. The low response rate was caused not only by using electronic questionnaires, but also by the increasing general tendency of Czech organizations to be unwilling to give any information because of their experience with different research agencies and researching consultating firms (mostly international), which abused the information given to favour their clients – mostly foreign investors or competitors. Consequently, the results from the 2003 survey will be mentioned with some reservation only and the results could be influenced by the fact that respondents were probably organizations with more developed HR functions.

The nature of the HR function

The proportion of organizations with a human resource/personnel department or at least with a HR/personnel manager was 96–8 per cent during the 1990s and since that time it has been relatively constant. The number of people employed in HR departments increased during the 1990s, but the reverse tendency is observable, because of the outsourcing of some HR functions and transferring some HR responsibilities on non-personnel management, especially to line managers.

Concerning the position of the HR function in organizations a schizophrenic approach can be seen: there is a substantial difference between rhetoric and practice. Everybody stresses the importance of HRM and the HR function (because it is fashionable), but in reality many organizations continue to belittle HR matters and the HR function and top management doesn't care about the quality of people employed in HR, particularly about the quality of heads of HR departments. The heads of the departments are often managers who have been sidelined due to lack of success in the other fields of the organization. It seems as well that the HR function is considered a 'woman's' job.

All the surveys organized in the 1990s showed that the head of the HR function had a place on the main board of directors in more than 60 per cent of organizations. It seems that it is fashionable for the head of the HR function to be on the board. The phenomenon is more frequent in Czech organizations than the average for EU countries.

The cardinal problem of the HR function in Czech organizations (including international ones in the Czech Republic) is first of all the competence of heads, but also the competence of all HR staff. Their knowledge of modern HRM and their HR skills are often questionable. The people who came into HR during the first half of the 1990s, before new young specialists had graduated, have been surviving there and defending their territories against potential new competent incomers.

The competence of HR department heads is documented in Table 5.4, which shows that the majority of the HR/personnel department heads were incompetent people in 1990s. The insufficiently representative group of respondents from 2003 confirmed the tendency towards improvement, but in any case about 50 per cent of the heads of HR departments were still incompetent (see also the case study on pp. 154–156).

Table 5.4 Origin and experience of the most senior HR manager in Czech organizations

From where was the most senior HR/personnel manager recruited?	Year		
	1993	1996	1998
From within the HR/personnel department	27	27	30
From HR/personnel specialists from outside of the organization	8	18	18
She/he had some experience in HR/personnel management	35	45	48
From non-HR/personnel specialists in the organization	54	33	31
From non-HR/personnel specialists from outside of the organization	7	15	14
She/he had no experience in HR/personnel management	61	48	45
Not declared	4	7	7
Total	**100**	**100**	**100**

Source: Cranfield Project on European HRM. Unfortunately the data from the last survey in 2003 are not representative because of the very small number of respondents.

An increasing proportion of organizations had a business strategy: while in the mid-1990s about two-thirds of organizations had one, at the end of the 1990s three-quarters did. The less reliable 2003 survey showed that nearly all respondents had a business strategy, of which about 90 per cent had one in written form.

It seems that the HR functions are important contributors to business strategy formulation and implementation and their importance is moderately increasing. While in the 1990s HR functions were involved from the outset in the development of business strategies in about 55 per cent organizations, recently this has risen to around 60 per cent of organizations. If we consider as well the role of consultants, the HR function influences business strategy in more than 80 per cent of organizations.

There has been a considerable increase in the proportion of organizations with an HR strategy, particularly with a written strategy. While in 1993 only 61 per cent organizations had an HR strategy, in 1996 70 per cent did and in 1998 76 per cent. The 2003 survey (with reservations due to the small group of repspondents) signals that the figure could be more than 90 per cent. The pronounced increase is due to the existence of written forms of HR strategy (26 per cent of organizations in 1993; 39 per cent in 1996; 45 per cent in 1998; and 73 per cent in 2003).

The existence of a mission statement has increased from 52 per cent of organizations in 1993 to 75 per cent in 1998 and perhaps 90 per cent in 2003 (concerning the written form, there was an increase from 31 per cent of organizations in 1993 to 55 per cent in 1998 and about 74 per cent in 2003).

If we could rely on the 2003 data, then corporate values statements were more frequent in Czech organizations than in organizations of any other country which participated in the Cranfield Project (about 95 per cent of organizations had a written form of the statement in the Czech Republic).

There is an increasing responsibility of line managers for human resource management. This is connected with the transformation of HR departments from large departments responsible for everything in HRM to rather smaller ones focused on concepts and professional, organizational, monitoring and consultation issues. The increase in the HR responsibility of line managers can be seen particularly in recruitment and selection and performance appraisal (performance management), but also in training and development and HR planning. In any case it seems that the line managers' HR roles are closely supported by the HR departments and most of the decision making is shared.

Recruitment and selection

Concerning recruitment there has been some increase in the shared responsibility of HR departments and line managers, but concerning decision making in selection the responsibility has been transferred to line management – in spite of continuing resistance from HR departments. If the collaboration of HR departments and line managers goes well and all participants in the process are well trained and informed there are no problems. But – unfortunately – well-trained and informed participants in recruitment and selection processes are a little rare in Czech organizations. Consequently, the processes suffer from incompetent approaches, amateurism and dilettantism of participants.

But there is also a strange phenomenon in recruitment and selection. There is a group of HR managers who don't like to take responsibility for such an important process. Maybe they are aware of their incompetence or it is simply buck-passing. They leave the whole process of recruitment and selection to external agencies or consultants. Unfortunately the majority of external agencies and conultants are not real experts in recruitment and selection methods (HR consulting is not a licensed or certified business in the Czech Republic and nobody has to prove his or her qualification or competence to do it, but it is an attractive business and therefore there are many individuals and groups involved in it). They are not able to prepare effective recruitment advertisements and they offer rather 'mysterious' methods of selection. They very often assert that the methods have more than 90 per cent reliability and validity (for commercial reasons). They use not only different questionable psychological or psychometric tests and questionnaires (often translated from foreign languages and constructed for another mentality and environment), but also some 'universal' assessment centres or even graphology and typology (frenology). They present them as 'scientific' methods or 'foreign know-how'. This is very convenient for HR managers or other managers in organizations, because it offers answers, even unequivocal ones. If anything goes wrong with the selected individuals in the future, the agency or consultant is blamed, not the HR manager or any other manager in the organization.

The majority of selection interviews are one-to-one unstructured and badly prepared interviews (used in more than 80 per cent of organizations); well-prepared structured or semi-structured interviews are rare. The interviewers usually don't appreciate the necessity of preparing for interviews. Consequently, the selection process is full of subjectivity.

In spite of the fact that there is relatively strict anti-discrimination legislation in the Czech Republic, many organizations try to avoid the legislation and practise very special methods of recruitment and selection. Unfortunately, many such organizations are international ones. The typical example in the case of age discrimination (it is forbidden to mention any age limit in advertisements) is the formulation that the 'organization offers interesting work in a young dynamic collective'. This means that if you are older than 'young' you will not fit in. There is a well-known international company, which normally accepts all candidates, but among the candidates actually selected more than 80 per cent are men, in spite of the fact that a considerable majority of all the candidates were women. Another international company asks candidates about membership of potential membership in trade unions (declaring an interest in building strong and effective trade union organization in the company), another one asks women candidates about their family plans (declaring that this is connected with planning for its 'maternity career' programme of services), etc.

It is necessary to consider all the facts when looking at the survey data. The data alone cannot display fully the reality of recruitment and selection in Czech organizations.

What are the most frequent recruiting methods? It seems that the most popular methods for recruiting manual and clerical employees are advertisement in newspapers, word of mouth and collaboration with state job centres. Managers, particularly middle and junior ones, are recruited internally, but it seems that external recruitment is increasing a little. The use of advertisements in newspapers or professional magazines is still increasing and an increasing proportion of managers, particularly senior ones, are recruited in collaboration with recruitment agencies or consultants. Recently there has been an increase in the use of electronic recruitment.

Among selection methods, the most popular are application forms and interviews (with the popularity of interview panels increasing). References are relatively popular, too. It seems that there is some increase in the popularity of psychological and psychometric testing. On the other hand, assessment centres and graphology are used for only a few appointments (see Table 5.5).

Recently there has been an effort to improve the image of employer's organizations. So called 'HR/personnel marketing' is increasing in popularity among large organizations. It is an attempt to apply some marketing approaches in HRM,

Table 5.5 Selection method used in Czech organizations

Selection method	For every and most appointments		For few appointments and not used	
	1996	*1998*	*1996*	*1998*
Interview panel	17	25	32	28
One-to-one interview	81	81	3	–
Application forms	83	78	3	6
Psychometric tests	7	10	45	46
Assessment centre	1	–	55	62
Graphology	1	–	59	63
References	32	33	8	12

Source: Cranfield Project on European HRM. Unfortunately the data from 1993 are not comparable and data from the 2003 survey are not comparable and representative because of the very small number of respondents.

particularly in recruitment, retention and motivating people, and it is oriented towards two areas: marketing the organization's image and labour market research.

Reward and performance management

Employee rewards were determined centrally during communist rule. The process of privatization and the transition to a market economy destroyed the old system and introduced a totally decentalized system of reward determination, with the exception that the public sector was funded from the State Budget (public administration, public education, public health services, army, policy, etc.). The minimum wage is also determined centrally by the government. But the public sector also uses collective bargaining and the trade unions apply some pressure in this area. In the private sector, the rewards are fully determined by individual companies or even by their organizational departments. National or industry-wide collective bargaining has some influence, but regional bargaining is not important. Consequently, there are many different reward systems in Czech organizations and there are some regional differences among the levels of pay. Partly it depends on the regional level of unemployment and partly there are regional differences in the intensity of competition on the demand side of the labour market, but mainly it is connected with regional differences in the education and skills of the labour force. It seems that the reward systems increasingly offer some opportunities for managers to influence the rewards of individual employees. Maybe this is a consequence of the increased use of variable pay and performance-related pay. There is also an increasing tendency towards individually negotiated pay (particularly among managers and specialists). There has been a strange trend in the use of non-money benefits. In the beginning of the transformation non-money benefits were recognized as a tool of so-called 'socialist paternalism', and the stress was laid on normal pay. Liberal economists and right-wing politicians proclaimed that an orientation towards normal pay would enable people to decide better about satisfaction of their needs. Their mistake was that they regarded non-money benefits as social measures and didn't see them as an important tool for motivating and attracting people and as a tool to increase the competitiveness of organizations in the labour market. Consequently, there was a decline in the use of non-money benefits during the 1990s. Nevertheless, there are some signs of increasing use of such benefits since the end of the 1990s. First of all, there were different benefits for managers and highly educated specialists, but gradually there has been some renaissance of benefits for clerical and manual employees (see Table 5.6).

There are long-term popular incentive schemes in Czech organizations. The most popular among them is merit pay, which is used by approximately two-thirds of organizations. It is the typical incentive scheme for manual employees (about three-quarters of organizations, compared to half of organizations for managers). About one-third of organizations use profit sharing. This scheme is rather typical for managers. On the other hand, employee share options are relatively rare (about 6–7 per cent of organizations).

Table 5.6 Percentage of organizations where there has been a change in the share of variable pay or non-money benefits in the total reward package in the last three years

Character of change	*Year*		
	1993	*1996*	*1998*
Variable pay			
Increased	59	60	50
Decreased	34	23	13
Same	4	16	32
Non-money benefits			
Increased	9	25	27
Decreased	10	53	6
Same	52	9	39

Source: Cranfield Project on European HRM. Not surveyed in 2003.

Concerning benefits, it seems that the above-mentioned renaissance since the end of the 1990s has brought some changes. The traditional benefits oriented towards family, child care, recreation and culture were replaced by very popular additional company old age insurance (recently about one-third of organizations) and benefits connected with training and development, including special learning leave. Additional holidays (usually one week) is popular, too. Recently, there has been an increasing occurrence of special programmes for women on maternity leave, including some additional maternity leave.

Performance management as a concept is not applied in Czech organizations or in international organizations in the Czech Republic. Organizations practise (if at all) traditional performance appraisal, but it seems that the proportion of organizations with formal performance appraisal systems has been increasing since the 1990s. While in the second half of the 1990s about 50–60 per cent of organizations had such a system, the actual estimates suggest more than 80 per cent do so (the non-representative 2003 survey showed as much as 90 per cent). It seems as well that performance appraisal schemes are more focused on managerial and professional staff, while manual staff are less often included.

The appraisers are immediate superiors (100 per cent of organizations having the formal performance appraisal) or next-level superiors (50–60 per cent of organizations), but there is an increasing tendency towards self-appraisal (50–60 per cent of organizations) or even to apply 360-degree feedback.

Performance appraisal results are used increasingly first of all for compensation (recently more than 90 per cent of organizations), identification of training and development needs (in the mid-1990s about 60 per cent, actually about 80–90 per cent of organizations), career progression or promotion.

It seems that processes of performance appraisal are full of formality and subjectivity. The opinion of the majority of managers and staff is that it is a necessary, but useless paperwork exercise. The appraisers are, as a rule, not well trained.

Training and development

'Training and development are considered the most important HR functions for the twenty-first century.' The phrase is repeated daily in Czech organizations, in government, in the media – everywhere. But, as a rule, it is rhetoric only. In fact, training and development are a little neglected in Czech organizations. Many liberal economists, representatives of right-wing political parties and particularly company owners and managements have another belief: 'If you want be employable, you have to be concerned for your own training and development.' The training and development provided by organizations are insufficient, focused on mostly managers (manual staff are as a rule neglected) and undertaken only if there are funds. Consequently it is an unsystematic, random and ad hoc process full of formality. While in the 1993 survey the Czech Republic was among the better half of countries participating in the Cranfield Project for training and development, in 1996 it was last among them (see Table 5.7).

There was a substantial decrease in the average proportion of the annual salaries and wages bill spent on training and development in the 1990s. Because the situation has

Table 5.7 Percentage of organizations spending a proportion of the annual salaries and wages bill on training and development (valid per cent)

Proportion of the annual salaries and wages bill	*Year*		
	1993	*1996*	*1998*
0.01–0.50	26	28	37
0.51–1.00	24	27	22
1.01–2.00	19	22	21
2.01–4.00	14	13	11
4.01 and over	17	11	9
Total	**100**	**101**	**100**
Average	1.97	1.65	1.44

Source: Cranfield Project on European HRM.

not changed since that time, it is a little surprising that the proportion was 2.5 per cent in the 2003 survey. This could be due to the influence of a small group of respondents with more positive characteristics of HRM than is usual among Czech organizations.

Although from the perspective of expenditure on training and development the Czech Republic was behind the other countries which participated in the Cranfield Project, from the perspective of time spent on training and development (particularly among managers and professional/technical staff) it was among the leading countries. The not fully reliable 2003 results confirmed the situation reflected by the 1998 results. The contradiction in the international comparison from the perspective of expenditure and the perspective of time spent could be explained either by the fact that training and development are cheaper in the Czech Republic or by the fact that the cheaper processes are used. Another explanation could be that the absolute amount of funds spent on training and development has not been increasing in proportion with the increase in wages and salaries. But there could be another reason: the money spent on training and development doesn't include the costs of increasing training on-the-job, but only really paid costs spent on different courses and off-the-job activities.

Table 5.8 confirms the above-mentioned feature of training and development in Czech organizations: the activity is focused on managers and professional/technical staff; clerical and particularly manual staff are ignored.

Table 5.8 Percentage of organizations giving a number of days per year to training and development (valid per cent)

Proportion of the annual salaries and wages bill	Year											
	1993				1996				1998			
	MG	P/T	C	MN	MG	P/T	C	MN	MG	P/T	C	MN
0.01–1.00	–	3	14	25	3	6	21	40				
1.01–3.00	10	16	22	39	13	20	30	38	47	57	87	92
3.01–5.00	18	21	29	19	21	22	27	13				
5.01–10.00	29	30	27	13	29	28	16	7	31	29	10	5
More than 10 days	44	30	8	4	34	24	6	2	22	14	3	3
Total	**101**	**100**	**100**	**100**	**100**	**100**	**100**	**100**	**100**	**100**	**100**	**100**
Average	10	8	5	3	9	9	4	2	9	7	4	3

Notes: MG = managerial; P/T = professional/technical; C = clerical and MN = manual.

Source: Cranfield Project on European HRM. The 2003 survey indicated that there had been almost no changes in comparison with the 1998 survey (average number days for managers was 8, for professional/technical 8, for clerical 4 and for manual 3).

The basic method of training needs identification is demand by line managers or employees. Also, the evaluation of training and development is rather informal and depends on participants' and their immediate superiors' opinions.

A very typical feature of training and development in Czech organizations is a shift from off-the-job methods to on-the-job methods. Another typical feature is rapidly increasing computer use in the process of learning.

THE FUTURE OF HRM IN THE CZECH REPUBLIC

There have been some positive changes in human resource management in the Czech Republic and there is some convergence with the practice existing in most developed economies, but some negative features remain. It seems that the transformation of HR functions will be a long-term process because there is too much inertia and too many obstacles. First of all, it will be necessary to change the top managers' approach to the HR function and HR management. Second, it will be necessary to continue to educate HR management and to replace the old ineffective heads and staff in the function. It will be necessary to ensure that personnel agencies and consultants become real professionals, not incompetent 'gold-panners'. Last, but not least, it will be necessary to ensure that international organizations respect not only Czech legislation, but also the mores of most developed countries. A very positive contribution to improvements in the sphere of HRM is represented by the very intensive publication of books and articles written both by Czech and foreign authors and the existence of several professional magazines. There is also a relatively good offer of different training and development activities. Simply put, there are quite good opportunities, but there are obstacles among organizations and their managements.

Personnel management in a glass company

Case study

The case described is typical of many Czech companies and other organizations. Particularly senior positions – but also other ones – in personnel departments are occupied by incompetent individuals and good graduates specializing in HRM cannot find adequate jobs. This practice can be observed even in international companies.

The company GLASSTON originated from the merger of two relatively large glass producers, GLAvanova sklárna (GLAvan Glass Work) and Sklárny TONdl a syn (Glass Work TONdl and Son), in 1927. Both owners had the very good idea of creating a new name for the company partly from their family names so as to inform the public about their production. In addition, the Czech word 'ton' means 'der Ton' in German and 'tone' in English. The slogan of the company was 'GLASSTON – skvělý ton' in Czech,

'GLASSTON – prächtig Ton' in German and 'GLASSTON – splendid tone' in English. The company exported about 80 per cent of its production of traditional Czech cut glass, pot-metal glass, sheet glass, household glass and different kinds of utility glass. The company became a share company in 1937. In 1948 (the communist take-over) it was nationalized and some time afterwards it changed its name. From 1948 to 1992 it was United Glassworks, a state company.

The company was privatized in 1992–3 by a group of top managers (mostly appointed during the communist period).

There were almost no changes before 1993 in the staff of the Personnel Department, compared with the former communist Personnel and Cadre Department – with the exception of its head, who was dismissed in February 1990, but replaced by one of his subordinates. The new owners decided to appoint a new head of the Personnel Department shortly after privatization. The new Personnel Director was originally the long-term head of the Department of Planning and he had no qualifications or experience in personnel management. Consequently he relied on his subordinates (all of them had secondary education) and let them continue with established practices, i.e. paperwork. In fact, he didn't manage anything and he was not willing to learn anything or change anything. On the other hand, he inherited a very important place on the board of directors (the former communist head of the Personnel and Cadre Department was a very powerful individual and very important decision maker in Czech companies and also the principal member of the top management), where he contributed by repeating clichés about the importance of human resources. The 'brilliant' Personnel Director held the position until the end of 1998, when he retired on an old-age pension.

The new Personnel Director (now Human Resource Director) was appointed in 1999. Before his appointment he was a Vice-Director in the Department of Sales and Marketing and he graduated from the Czech University of Technology. He had no experience in personnel management either, but he was considered an individual able to manage and to motivate people. In addition he had just begun MBA study and it was possible to expect that he would learn something about HR.

The first action the new HR Director undertook was a meeting with his subordinates. He told them that it would be necessary to change the work totally, and consequently everybody would have to participate in some HRM courses. The courses were organized about two weeks after the meeting. The staff of the department were divided into two groups and every group spent one day in lectures. The lecturer was asked to tell them all about modern HRM during a period of eight hours. The HR Director didn't participate in the courses. In the meantime it turned out that the MBA course was too time-consuming and he stopped it. Nevertheless, he decided to study modern HRM approaches individually and he bought a textbook and subscribed to one of the specialist journals.

continued

In spite of some effort to learn at least a basic knowledge, he realized he was not able to answer most of the questions asked by his subordinates or other managers and to help them. He began to become aware of his incompetence. One day he was visited by a student of the University of Economics who needed some information for his diploma thesis. The HR Director realized that the student had a much better knowledge of HRM than him. He came up with a wonderful idea: to utilize students preparing diploma thesis as unpaid consultants, instructors or even problem solvers. The HR Director approached the university and offered to organize an opportunity for a good student preparing his or her diploma thesis. He informed the university that the management of the company would prefer students who were willing to prepare their thesis focusing on specific problems of HRM in the company. He promised as well that he would function personally as a mentor of the student.

Of course, the university accepted the offer, because it is often difficult to convince organizations to allow students to practise in them.

So, for several years the HRM Director has taken advantage of students' knowledge and work. The students have solved some specific problems for the HR Department and functioned as consultants to the HRM Director, because they were mostly better professionals than he was. It might be expected that the HRM Director would develop some effort to recruit to the HRM Department some of the good students after they graduated. But it is not his policy. The opposite is the case.

The HR Director prefers to recruit individuals with secondary education (particularly women) and doesn't recruit and hire anybody who could be a potential threat to him. He tries to be the irreplaceable feudal lord surrounded by loyal and dependent people, because he is one of the incompetent people who defend their territory regardless of the consequences for the company. In fact, he is paid for his cliché-making, as his predecessor was.

Why haven't owners realized that the HR Department works inefficiently and only formally? Because they don't know anything about modern approaches to HRM, they have a dismissive approach to it and they are not able to recognize the consequences of the situation in the HRM Department. After all, the company is still a successful producer and exporter and it has relatively good economic results. The employees may be dissatisfied, but they are afraid of unemployment and therefore they don't protest. It would be risky because of their specialized profession and the monopolist position of their employer in the region.

REFERENCES AND FURTHER READING

Brewster, C. and Koubek, J. (1995). 'Human Resource Management in Turbulent Times: HRM in the Czech Republic'. *International Journal of Human Resource Management*, 6, 2 (May): 223–47.

Hegewisch, A., Brewster, C. and Koubek, J. (1995). 'Industrial Relations in Turbulent Times: Changes in Postcommunist Europe'. *Documents of the 10th Congress of the International Industrial Relations Association 'Learning from Each Other'*, Washington (USA), 31 May–3 June.

Hegewisch, A., Brewster, C. and Koubek, J. (1996). 'Different Roads: Changes in Industrial and Employee Relations in the Czech Republic and East Germany Since 1989'. *Industrial Relations Journal*, 27, 1 (March): 50–64.

Koubek, J. (1990). 'A Brief Outline of the Main Contemporary Problems Relative to the Labour Sphere in Czechoslovakia'. *Documents of the OECD Conference 'Labour Market Flexibility and Work Organisation'*. Paris, 17–19 September.

Koubek, J. (1991). 'Demographic Trends and the Problem of Labour Force Reproduction and Utilization in Czechoslovakia 1990–2010'. *Documents of the Conference 'Human Resources in Europe at the Dawn of the 21st Century'*. Luxembourg, 27–29 November.

Koubek, J. (1995). 'Elevating the HR Function'. *People Management*, 27 July: 39.

Koubek, J. (1997). 'Human Resource Management in the Czech Republic'. In Hanel, U., Hegewisch, A. and Mayrhofer, W. (eds) *Personalarbeit im Wandel. Entwicklungen in den neuen Bundesländern und Europa.* Munich and Mering: Rainer Hampp Verlag. Personalwirtschaftliche Schriften (herausgegeben von Dudo von Eckardstein un Oswald Neuberger), Band 11, pp. 95–113.

Koubek, J. (2000). 'Human Resource Management in Transforming Economy – Convergency or Divergency? (Example of the Czech Republic)'. In *International Conference: Human Resource Management – an Important Factor for European Integration*. Varna (Bulgaria): International Business School 'Transbusiness-E', pp. 43–6.

Koubek, J. and Vatchkova, E. (2004). 'Bulgaria and Czech Republic: Countries in Transition'. In Brewster, C., Mayrhofer, W. and Morley, M. (eds) *Human Resource Management in Europe. Evidence of Convergence?* London and New York: Elsevier/Butterworth/Heinemann, pp. 313–51.

Managing human resources in Slovakia

6

ANNA KACHAŇÁKOVÁ, OLGA NACHTMANNOVA,
ZUZANA JONIAKOVA, ZUZANA ROBY,
DARINA ZUBRIKOVA AND JANA BLŠTÁKOVÁ

INTRODUCTION

Slovakia has come through significant changes in its business environment in the last two decades. First came the transformation of the National Economy System from centrally planned to market economy in 1989. Later came the creation of an independent state, the Slovak Republic, in 1993. Then came membership of the European Union in 2004, and preparation for the entrance to monetary union, planned for 2009.

These changes, especially the transformation process, had an essential impact on the everyday lives of Slovak citizens. A centrally planned economy brought many certainties and social safety for many future years. The labor market did not report any unemployment, education was free and medical care was available for everyone. The state owned all the strategic enterprises and other businesses where state citizens were employed. There were no housing issues, since the state guaranteed and subsidized proper living quarters for everyone. There were only a few sole proprietors who ran their own businesses, but they carried the burden of great tax on their incomes, and other state measures which neither forbade nor supported small and medium-sized enterprises. Cooperation with other companies abroad (besides the Eastern Bloc countries) was quite impossible for enterprises, as was travel to Western Europe for ordinary citizens. With long-term planning and long-term safety came no flexibility and limited choices. In moving from a self-imposed centrally planned economy to a market economy, Slovakia had to accommodate to an essentially different system, not only in its economy and politics, but in everyday life and the thinking of its citizens.

When it comes to human resource management (HRM) we must understand the enormous change caused by this transformation. In the centrally planned economy, personnel departments were created in enterprises covering only administration. We can hardly talk about management here. The employees' performance, payroll and attendance records in the workplace should have been included in their competencies.

After the transformation, this understanding of the HR department's stature within a company had to be changed.

We must also mention the labor market situation. Since unemployment was forbidden, everyone had to work, which meant guaranteed openings in a particular enterprise for graduates after finishing school. This was called administrative workforce allocation. Therefore, the choice among candidates for working positions was quite limited. Open positions were very often filled not with the best candidates but with those available. After the change in the economic system people had to start looking for jobs themselves. Enterprises had to learn how to create their own personnel plans, how to fill their openings with the right people, how to manage their performance, train and educate them, how to measure their performance, and how to motivate them in order to gain and maintain competitiveness in not only the domestic but also the international marketplace, which Slovakia has just entered.

Three years later Slovakia became an independent state when Czechoslovakia split into two republics. The former Czechoslovakia had been strategically planned to maintain self-sufficiency in any economic area. Therefore all the industrial state-owned enterprises had been built in the Czech part of the country, and the Slovak part was oriented to agricultural production and supplying the whole country's grocery products. Since the country split, there have been many other challenges for the Slovak Republic as an independent state with a population of five million. The business environment had to be developed from its very foundations.

Slovakia managed to enter the EU in 2004, which opened great possibilities and placed great demands on Slovak entrepreneurs. All these events have caused essential changes in the business environment. Slovak companies need to accept and adapt to these changes in order to keep their competitiveness. Competitive HRM is currently necessary for the success of a company in the marketplace.

Our goals within this chapter are to provide the reader with a view of the HRM system in Slovak companies, to reveal its development since the National Economy transformation, and to point out the challenges which Slovak companies face in this area. The chapter describes the progress reached in the business environment in Slovakia and explains the political and economic reasons for the changes. HRM had to be reviewed, re-evaluated and redesigned to be understood properly in our companies.

We also provide the reader with a case study describing HRM in a successful Slovak company. The enterprise is also an example of quality HRM as a precondition for success in the conditions of the market economy in Slovakia. Like many enterprises in Slovakia today it is not owned by a Slovak creator, but it is a 100 percent subsidiary of an international concern. Its management is adjusted to the Slovak business environment. We consider this particular enterprise a good example of the way companies in Slovakia can succeed in the currently challenging business environment. Nevertheless adopting the principles of experienced and progressive HRM systems from companies from Western countries is one of the ways we believe Slovak companies could reach the desired HRM quality.

All the findings and conclusions published in this chapter are based on our continuous research focused on HRM functions in Slovak companies. We have been monitoring functions of HRM in Slovak companies since 1998 in a survey every year. Therefore we are now able to provide the reader with tendencies observed during this period of time. Since our team (Team for Personnel Management, Department of Management, Business Management Faculty, University of Economics in Bratislava) has joined the Cranfield Project and has become a CRANET member, we are able to compare findings from our domestic research with tendencies in other European countries. We are now capable of evaluating the situation in Slovak companies in the context of European tendencies.

EXTERNAL ENVIRONMENT OF HRM IN SLOVAKIA

Current HRM in Slovakia has been formed in a process where it is possible to identify three significant phases:

1 The conditions for starting this process were created after 17 November 1989 as a consequence of the 'Velvet Revolution,' which led to the transformation of the national economy from a centrally planned economy to a market economy.
2 The second phase began with splitting the Czechoslovak Federative Republic into two separate republics in December 1992.
3 The third phase started with the entrance of the Slovak Republic into the European Union in May 2004.

Human resource management in Slovak companies after the National Economy transformation process in 1989

The transformation of the Slovak economy into a market economy started after the year 1989, when we were still a part of Czechoslovakia. Its impact appeared in this early period particularly by opening both countries, the Czech Republic and Slovakia, politically and economically to the world. Later on, the administrative allocation of the workforce was replaced by the law of supply and demand. The process of ending state paternalism began, while the privatization of state property started. In January 1991, economic reform in the context of a market economy was introduced.

Another part of the economic reform was labor market policy formation, which meant employment management liberalization, creation of systems for checking employment history, making jobs socially beneficial, retraining employees, the creation of social security systems for the unemployed, and macro regulation of the labor market by intervention in labor price and demand.

During the existence of the Federation of Czech and Slovak Republics, the focus of labor market creation was to maintain full but effective employment and sustaining the right socially useful and effective work contributing to aggregate economic efficiency. This meant there was a need for a state employment policy, which caused changes in the structure of manufacturing and the technical base, created conditions for job intermediation, retrained employees for employment in different areas, and instituted a system of social security for those who were made redundant, influenced supply in the labor market through innovative working regimes, and finally created conditions for changes in the quality of the education system and for an anti-inflation policy.

Against the backdrop of ongoing social and economic reform, labor market reform progressed, but in doing so had an initial negative effect on employment. Naturally, this rise in unemployment raised the risk of an emerging social tension.

HRM in Slovak companies after the creation of the Slovak Republic on 1 January 1993

The next phase, connected with the Slovak Republic's independence, meant a continuation in transforming the economy and proprietary structures following the original plans from the time of Federation. These plans were modified according to Slovak conditions.

The policy of intensive labor market reform, coupled with a supportive legislative framework, had been pursued in Slovakia since 1990. After Slovakia became independent, the basic strategic goals of labor market policy continued to improve in the context of new conditions.

The system of employment had been essentially changed in a short time of labor market creation, and it had created basic preconditions for its future development within a market economy. However, the labor market efficiencies finally achieved fell somewhat short of intentions.

The transformation process continued by influencing the labor market using measures of employment policy via the system of macroeconomic policy influencing labor demand and legislative statutes influencing the extent and structure of labor supply as well. Later on, interventions were made within the area of job intermediation, consulting, retraining, programs for supporting new jobs, organizing public service jobs and other labor market tools.

Social aspects of employment were emphasized by job loss for many people, which meant loss of the key source of income. The state gained the position of guarantor of citizens' rights to adequate income security in case of unemployment, which was an absolutely new role for the state, since there had not been any unemployment in the former regime.

HRM in Slovak companies after the Slovak Republic joined the European Union in 2004

A certain improvement in quality appeared during the transformation of the economy and labor market in Slovakia in the third phase, which is related to joining the European Union in 2004. It is not possible to expect huge changes in the performance and competitiveness of the Slovak economy and noticeable changes in the labor market in such a short time after entry into the EU. Individual EU countries have opened their labor market for Slovak citizens only very slowly. According to the latest estimate, at the end of 2008 (in comparison to 2001) approximately 170,000–180,000 new jobs should be available. The unemployment rate should continue decreasing (in 2005 it was 16.2 percent).

The content of most of the main measures on employment policy and labor market policy taken within the transformation process in the last 15 years has mostly focused on the following:

● reaching a tolerable level of unemployment;
● inserting the core of employment issues into economic policies;
● supporting new jobs via the revitalization of investment policy;
● support for public services;
● support for long-term job stabilization via structural changes in the national economy;
● solving polarization of regional unemployment;
● supporting enterprising activities as a source of job opportunities; by effective stimulation via the tax system and policies regarding prices, loans, and salaries;
● changing the education system to ensure better adaptability of graduates in market economy conditions;
● increasing the efficiency of active labor market policy measures;
● increasing the efficiency of retraining programmes;
● developing services of intermediation and consulting in the area of choosing profession and employment;
● increasing the efficiency of solving long-term unemployment;
● creating an adequate institutional and legislative labor market framework.

The process of transformation has not always run without problems, and not all principles or their modifications have been positive. All in all, people have shown quite notable ability to adjust to new business conditions and apply their entrepreneurial and managerial skills. A significant factor was also the aim to maintain social cohesion, which enabled less popular measures to be realized, such as raising energy prices, involving patients to financing their medical treatment to a greater extent, pension reform, etc. The positive impact of these measures should appear in the very near future. The essence of most of these measures is the redistribution of social responsibility between the state and its citizens. Measures taken should stimulate people to reconsider their consumption, especially with an orientation to the future. It also makes them participate in some services, which are currently entirely covered by the state via the tax or obligatory insurance system. A positive impact should appear in raising the quality of medical care, education, and the social security system.

MANAGING HUMAN RESOURCES IN THE CONTEXT OF THE TRANSFORMATION TO A MARKET ECONOMY

The history of HRM in Slovakia is related to the process of transforming the Slovak economy. During the period of socialism, few preconditions had been created which would allow for the smooth transition of administrative personnel management to a more strategic function. This means that while socialism aimed to plan every activity in a company several years in advance, the market economy demands a flexible reaction to actual demands and tendencies in the market. While central planning created an artificial business environment, the market economy basically works naturally according to the law of supply and demand. Managing human resources in a turbulent market economy creates different preconditions for and places different requirements on the skills of both the subject and object of management, as opposed to those which existented under the conditions of centrally planned management.

According to surveys conducted to establish the extent to which HRM was developing in Slovak organizations in the past 15 years, there is evidence of a number of systems and management practices that suggest the emergence of elements of HRM. Results of the research in this area show very positive tendencies.

The situation in the area of HRM was quite difficult in Slovak organizations in 1989, and management was moving from minimum interest in HRM to systematic work in this area. This situation was influenced by owners of organizations, top managers, and line managers, who were not always selected for their positions according to the requirements of a market economy. Since almost all the enterprises were owned by the state and managed by directors installed by the only political party (the Communist Party), transferring these competencies to the private sector required that the managerial skills of new managers and owners be developed. The education system was not prepared for providing its students with economic knowledge. There was an enormous lack of specialists in the area of market economy and management. The only apparent option was to search for information abroad in Western Europe and America. Slovak management pioneers faced another challenge: They had to deal with the language barrier. English as the international business language was not very popular in the Eastern Communist Bloc. Even nowadays companies find it necessary to invest great finances and time into the development of their employees' ability to communicate in English fluently.

After 1990, although paperwork and rigidity feature in the work of a human resources manager, this was not typically the case for HRM specialists. The responsibility of human resources departments has changed, and they have started to use knowledge from the practice of organizations in developed countries. The status of these departments has also risen in the hierarchy of organizations.

On the basis of research after 1998, it is possible to draw the conclusion that top managers in Slovak organizations have started to realize that well-managed human resources mean substantial help in solving all the problems which they have to deal with within their positions. The tendency to delegate authority to HRM appears to be growing. These departments obtain the right to take charge of all the management activities, such as to directly intervene by organizational strategy determination in the area they manage. The growing professionalism of HR managers also raises their ability to convince an organization's top management of the need to invest in human resources to the degree necessary for continuous change.

BASIC RELATIONSHIP BETWEEN EMPLOYERS AND TRADE UNIONS

Top managers, as the representatives of shareholders, can significantly influence the extent of centralization and decentralization, corporate culture, management style and also the system of HRM of an organization. These attributes depend on the industry in which an organization operates, but also on the HQ of the organization. One of the ways of communicating with employees (used by shareholders to communicate key changes, economic results and strategic goals of an organization) is through meetings with representatives of trade unions. These meetings help trade unions to understand present problems, which later creates a space for local managers to bargain for better working conditions for the employer. In 1989, membership of employees in trade unions was very common, but their function was rather formal. Trade unions did not have realistic possibilities of influencing the creation of social and economic working conditions, because legislation was centrally directed. It was not possible to agree on individual conditions and requirements. Everything was determined by very strict and exact labor norms and standards. Actually there was no space for collective bargaining at all. Trade unions covered activities which now belong on the agenda of HR departments, i.e. organizing trips for employees, presentations, and camps for children, and other such activities.

The amendment of the Labor Law in 1990 got rid of the monopolistic position of trade unions. The plurality of trade unions was continuously established. Yet as Slovakia was a part of Czechoslovakia an act was passed regarding collective bargaining. This act was the second passed after the radical change of the political regime in Slovakia (the first one was the Wage Act, which legally defines the term 'wage'). This proves the awareness of its importance for Slovakia, the aim of the legislative approach to other countries of Europe, and the fulfillment of obligations to the International Labor Organization. The act was passed in 1991 under the first democratically elected government led by Prime Minister Vaclav Klas. First, there was a need to establish a legislative framework for salaries and wages. Many norms and regulations were cancelled and many institutions dealing with regulation of the price of labor (wages and salaries) were closed down. The state lost its monopoly position in the determination of wages and salaries; it has kept only a few regulatory mechanisms (such as the institutionalization of the minimum wage and determining the working week). All these mechanisms are stated in the Labor Law. There has been a need for such regulation, since in Slovakia only a few companies have an employer–employee relationship covered by collective bargaining. Issues regarding rewards for employees have become a part of trade union and employer responsibility, with minimal state intervention in modern Slovakia. The state has created the basic legislative framework by passing an act regarding collective bargaining. Besides a policy in the area of wages and salaries, the social partners started to influence decisions in the area of social and economic working conditions. Later, the principle of introducing a broad-ranging labor agreement establishing a minimum floor of rights for employees was accepted.

According to the Collective Negotiation Act, in Slovakia there are two kinds of labor agreements. Labor agreement on a higher level concerns working and economic conditions for trade unions and an organized group of employers in a particular industry (there are no labor agreements on the regional level in the Slovak Republic). Another kind of labor agreement is concluded on the level of a particular organization, and it deals with its working and economic conditions. There is no principle of superordination in the application of these agreements. However, there is a rule that if something is agreed upon in the labor agreement at a higher level and the labor agreement at the level of an organization guarantees lower claims for employees, in this matter it is the labor agreement at the higher level which is obligatory for the organization. Social partners for each labor agreement themselves determine the areas of interest which they are going to deal with in the agreement.

The issue of working relations between employee and employer is closely dealt with in the Labor Law. The last part of the Labor Law focuses on the role of trade unions. The participation of employees in labor–law relations is realized in two forms: via trade unions or employees' councils. In an organization both forms can be created, but an organization is not obliged to create either of them. Trade unions have the right to collective bargaining, ensuring the implementation of working agreements, and informing employees. The employees' council has the right to participate in decision-making, negotiation, information, and monitoring.

In the last few years, employee interest in trade union membership has decreased. The results of our survey showed that 26–50 percent of employees are organized in trade unions in 14 percent of the organizations in the sample; in another 14 percent of organizations, the figure was 51–75 percent of employees; 76–100 percent of employees were members of trade unions in only 8 percent of organizations; over 49 percent of organizations do not negotiate with trade unions at all.

The low level of employee membership in trade unions causes a decrease of their influence in an organization. Trade unions are very often presented as a barrier to free business and the prosperity of enterprises. According to our survey, during the last three years the influence of trade unions has increased in only 4 percent of organizations, the situation has not changed in 38 percent of organizations, and it has decreased in 15 percent of organizations from the sample. Trade unions have had no influence at all in 43 percent of organizations. Here, it is possible to understand the role of trade unions as a formality. Employees in this case keep their membership in trade unions only because this has been a tradition. This occurs especially in organizations with foreign ownership, where keeping particular standards of working conditions is considered a part of competitiveness in the labor market. Here the primary role of trade unions is as a partner to provide employees with consulting services, information about changes made at the national and international level, and to give them notice about better working conditions.

Only 53 percent of all organizations in the sample which stated that their employer–employee relationship is covered by collective bargaining in the sample answered that they accept trade unions as a partner. It is obvious that if trade unions are not considered as an equal partner for collective bargaining in an organization this leads to decreasing trade union influence.

In Slovakia there are two associations of entrepreneurs. Not all organizations from our research sample are members of such associations. Only 35 percent of organizations from the sample are members of an employers' association. One of the causes of such a low interest in membership of these associations is the absence of provision of adequate consulting services. Among our sample, 15 percent of organizations stated that services currently provided by these associations are not convenient for them at all; 56 percent stated that their influence was low. This means 71 percent of organizations are not satisfied with these services; 28 percent of organizations are quite satisfied, and 1 percent are absolutely satisfied.

LEGISLATIVE FRAMEWORK FOR HRM IN SLOVAKIA

The transformation to a market economy in 1989 influenced all areas of economic life. Many enterprises were privatized, and enterprises owned by the state became public limited companies. The first and second phases of redistributing common national property were realized by "coupon privatization," where all adult citizens of Czechoslovakia had the opportunity to buy a coupon book and invest these coupons in purchasing company shares. It was not an exception that employees invested in companies which they worked for, in order to support these companies. Employees trusted management, production plans, and opportunities for the realization of production in the market. In this period many companies have been or are being either downsized or closed down, and their employees released. Despite the fact that the majority of companies have closed down, there are still companies which remained on the market by an investment of domestic private capital or international capital.

The first act which reflected democratic development was not passed until 2001. It was renewed in 2003. Both acts were passed under the government led by Mikulas

Dzurinda. In 2007 the act was renewed again under the government led by Robert Fico. This novelization has set an equitable position for employees and employers in their professional relationship with each other.

Another phase of privatization was selling companies to an owner determined by the government. The government has also stopped the second phase of privatization as it formerly was planned, and it has replaced shares of minor shareholders by securities owned by the state. Payable after five years and covering their purchase, it used the profit from privatized companies. The new government in 1998 continued selling state property via public tenders, with criteria defined in advance.

With the change of ownership of enterprises, there were obviously great changes in many areas of management, not excluding HRM. There was a need to create a regulatory legislative framework adjusted to the new conditions of private ownership. The regulation of the labor law relationship between employer and employees is covered in the Labor Law. Some key issues regulated in the Labor Law are: working agreements and their conclusion, working conditions and changes to them, working time, and the minimum wage.

In Slovakia, we have a work shift length determined by the Labor Law. Working time may not exceed 40 hours per week. The Labor Law also covers other issues regarding working time, such as work breaks during shifts, overtime, and vacation. The Labor Law currently also regulates the following areas of work: work stoppages, work security/job protection, social policy, work-related injuries, and the role of trade unions.

Before 1989, there were over 800 norms and acts regarding the employee reward system in Czechoslovakia. The reward system was strictly regulated for every kind of employment. In 1991, the Wage Act was passed, the only regulation for the employee reward system. The majority of issues regarding employees' rewards were negotiated by collective bargaining. As a consequence of the simplification of legislation, the Wage Act was canceled in 2001, and the employee reward regulation became a part of the Labor Law.

The content of the Labor Law is quite large, because of a lack of labor agreements in many organizations in Slovakia. The Labor Law regulates basic issues of employing people in the commercial sphere. There are employees who do not work directly in the business environment. There is a separate legislative framework regulating employment of people working in state services and public services. The Labor Law plays a subsidiary role in these cases.

The entrance of Slovakia into the European Union is reflected only very slowly in adjustments in the legislative framework. A significant effect of this has been access to the EU labor market. Employing foreigners has become simpler, which not only enables the transfer of foreign professional knowledge, but also positively influences foreign investors in decision-making regarding investment in our country. The migration of the domestic workforce to other EU member countries is still quite influenced by many regulatory protective measures in individual countries. Despite this fact, the movement of the workforce is increasing, and it has many positive impacts. However, there are also many negative consequences of opening the labor market, especially that many university graduates or specialists are leaving our country to find better paid working opportunities elsewhere.

Slovak legislation after entrance to the EU had to adjust to the norms and standards of the EU. Changes had to be made to the Labor Law in the following areas: prohibition of discrimination, working agreement for a limited period, working time, redundancy agreements, and relations between employer and trade unions.

The entrance of Slovakia into the EU had a positive influence on the inflow of foreign investments caused by tax reforms and a cheaper but highly qualified workforce. Since the education system in Slovakia has been very demanding, high quality, and free of charge (therefore available to anyone), Slovakia currently disperses a qualified workforce in many industrial and agricultural areas. Slovakia also has a very attractive potential for foreign investment when it comes to location, because it is situated in the heart of Europe. Our south-western region for example, surrounding the capital city Bratislava, has come through a quite remarkable period of development and economic growth. Foreign investment is still attractive to the Slovak economy, mostly because it means new jobs for Slovak citizens, but also because there is also an inflow of knowledge in enterprise, technologies, and management. When it comes to managing HR, the transfer of modern systems of HRM from headquarters is quite common. Quality HRM creates preconditions in a company for Slovak employees to fulfill their career plans, enables their professional growth, and provides them with modern workplace conditions.

To stimulate foreign investment, the Slovak government has prepared several measures, such as supporting early completion of freeway connection of major Slovak districts, which will also help other regions in their development and prosperity. The Slovak government is also trying to allocate EU-funded grants to less-developed regions to stimulate their attractiveness and further prosperity. For foreign investors, tax-related and subvention-related stimulation is also used. However, Slovakia is aware that the advantage of a cheaper workforce is not long-lasting, and therefore in the near future it will be necessary to stress other advantages.

TRENDS AND DEVELOPMENTS IN HUMAN RESOURCE MANAGEMENT PRACTICE

Adequate human capital is necessary for the survival and prosperity of organizations. Adequate human capital means not only a certain number and structure of employees, but also their talent, knowledge, skills, motivation, and a will to develop. Creating such potential, which would guarantee effectively fulfilling tasks according to an organization's goals, is not possible without an effective system of management. Creating a human resources system requires knowing its present status, predicting, searching, and solving potential problems which might disturb the system's smooth and productive running.

The complex systems of HRM, its particular functions, and their linkage have been the objects of our research based on the questionnaire survey for seven years. We believe that knowledge of the actual status of HRM and its confrontations with the latest tendencies in this area is the essential precondition for its improvement and continued approach to the level of organizations in developed countries in the world. We have focused on the main areas of the HRM system. These are initial characteristics and activities, by which it is possible to fundamentally influence the concept and the level of the whole system of HRM (the position of the human resources manager on the management board of an organization, the existence of a corporate culture and personnel strategy, and methods of job analysis). Other areas of interest are human capital formation and staffing practices, and formal employee appraisal as a necessary precondition for their development and performance management, including training and motivating employees. A third area of interest is flexible working practices, which are related to the currently actual requirement for employee flexibility not only in Slovakia but also in the European context. The following findings regarding particular areas of HRM are based on tendencies which were discovered in questionnaire surveys repeated every year within a three-year period.

The concept of HRM is, to a great extent, determined by the relevance which is assigned to it by top management in managing the whole organization. One of the indicators in this area is whether or not a human resources manager is involved in the top management of the organization, where there is space for participation in making strategic decisions at all management levels. The human resources manager has a responsibility for the whole system of personnel functions, their efficiency, strategic integration, and methodology. The human resources manager guarantees the achievement of goals and fulfillment of the strategy set by top management in his or her area. Besides other tasks, his or her main task is the coordination and professional guidance of all subjects involved in managing people. Therefore, if the meaning of managing people depends on its orientation on management support of an organization based on integrated system of cultural and personnel techniques, then it is logical to require a creation of adequate conditions to reach a synergy effect based on these techniques, which means attaining the goals of an organization and individual employees as well.

The results of our research convince us that the top management of Slovak organizations does not always appreciate the importance of human resources, and therefore it does not always create the proper conditions for solving strategic tasks in this area. This situation has not practically changed since 2000. (According to the results of the survey in 2003, only 54 percent organizations from the sample involved the HR manager in top management.)

In the area of forming working potential of an organization, many activities of HRM are still marked by an incomplete and unsystematic approach, often not following the latest tendencies in this field. This approach appears also in the function of job analysis, which should create a basis for the whole system of HRM.

The major precondition for modern HRM is well-designed job improvements. Job improvements and functions are essential units of any organizational structure. Only if they are well planned and covered are their objectives successfully reached. This requires that HR managers are well informed about the content of a particular job, which will lower the risk of mistakes. Information about particular jobs and preconditions for performing the job are gathered on the basis of complex job analysis. Job analysis creates a basis not only for job identification, but also for personnel decision-making in many other areas, such as project improvement and job methods, organizational structure creation, recruitment, selection and adaptation of employees, their evaluation, training, reward, and creating secure working conditions. Because of previous experience, we are convinced that even if the job analysis is conducted in personnel praxes, its results are usually not appropriately interpreted or utilized. Various methods are used by job analysis for gathering relevant information about a job (job descriptions written by the job-holder and by the manager, interviewing, creating questionnaires, observing job performance, and performing the job). Among the major criteria for choosing adequate methods are: the purpose of their use, effectiveness in gaining the information, their actuality, objectivity, accuracy, and comprehensibility. It is usually possible to use several combinations of methods to obtain a complete concept of tasks, physical, psychological, mental, and social requirements of the job.

The quality of job analysis depends on the whole system of HRM, and therefore this process of searching should come from gathering and evaluating various information about a job, its parts, and its requisites. Job analysis in Slovak organizations is mostly based on the subjective assessment of managers. Information obtained in this way is sufficient neither for particular work improvements nor for the development of integrated human resources systems. There are great reservations, for instance, in the use of questionnaires and also in the method of observation and measurement. The present situation in this area appears to be a certain underestimation of this function within the whole human resources system.

In modern organizations, the managers focus on effective motivation of employees in activities according to organizational strategy and goal setting. An employee evaluation system is considered a very important foundation. The goal of an evaluation system is reaching long-term growth in employee performance based on continuous improvement of employees' skills and competencies and their working behavior. On the basis of real disposable working potential balance and required working potential according to set goals, it is possible to develop skills, attitudes, values, creativity, motivation, cooperation, and other characteristics of every employee. Besides workforce development evaluation, employees could have a positive influence on the whole system of HRM. First of all they could have a positive influence by providing feedback and improving performance, and then by providing information for job analysis and personnel planning. This helps to clarify goals, to solve apparent problems of working positions, to improve the process of selection, and to solve tasks regarding rewarding employees and such. For the purpose of appraising employee performance an effective, reliable, and generally accepted evaluation system should be established in every organization as the foundation of continuous improvement of performance, based on the continuous development of employees' skills and competencies. Formal performance evaluation should be understood as a process where an organization appraises performance and also the required competency and working behavior of an employee. The criteria used for appraising should express facts which realistically and relevantly contribute to performance. Appraising must be simultaneously practical and comprehensible for both evaluators and appraised employees. In many organizations in Slovakia evaluation systems for all employees don't exist yet (in 2003 they existed in only 60–65 percent of organizations).

The efficiency of evaluating employee performance is to a great extent dependent upon the subject who performs the evaluation. In general the choice of evaluators is determined by the capacity of a certain evaluator to monitor employee performance, his or her ability to evaluate and to use the information in practice. The direct superior is considered the most competent position for the evaluator. He or she knows best the situation of the evaluated employee's workplace; he or she is able to provide the employee with feedback regarding his or her performance. He or she can suggest various remedies and other activities in order to manage the employee's performance. At the same time, the direct superior gains awareness of the performance results of subordinates, which is a necessary precondition for making correct decisions, especially in areas such as job organization, reward systems, employee training, development, and career planning.

It is also possible to involve other competencies in the employee's evaluation. Utilization of multidimensional employee evaluation is connected with new approaches within performance management. It is based on systematic gathering of information about the performance and behavior of an employee or a group of employees from various sources (i.e. direct superior, personnel manager, colleagues, and subordinates) to gain a complex view of the performance of evaluated employees. The aim is to obtain feedback from several evaluators, which is called a 360-degree evaluation (feedback). It is possible to extend this space for evaluators by involving external evaluators, for instance customers and clients. As a part of the evaluation process it is also possible to use an employee's self-evaluation, where similar criteria are used as with other evaluators. Using these methods, it is possible to obtain valuable information which enables a full picture of the characteristics of an employee or a group of employees to be completed. However, their practical application should be effective and should provide a real view of evaluated employees.

In Slovak organizations the main evaluator in the process of employee evaluation is the direct superior (in 2003 this was the norm in 65 percent of the organizations surveyed), although other respondents such as semior managers and employee self-evaluation were also recorded (as was the case in 2003 in 32 percent of the organizations). Despite these tendencies, it is possible to state that in Slovakia a complex employee evaluation system has not noticeably appeared. We believe the reason for this still remains the fact that the corporate culture in many organizations does not support the employee's perception of the evaluation system as a part of their education and development. Since companies in the former political and economical regime were not particularly oriented towards high-quality employee performance, evaluation was a formal and administrative task, rather than a strategically elaborated and continuously realized process.

The use of information obtained in the employee evaluation in Slovak organizations is quite wide ranging in many areas of HRM. This information is mostly used in rewarding employees according to individual performance (62 percent of organizations), also in identifying training needs (51 percent of organizations) and improving job organization (43 percent of organizations), and less often in career management (35 percent of organizations).

The issue of a flexible workforce occurs frequently in the world, and it also appears in Slovak organizations, mostly in the context of opening the European labor market. Employee flexibility means not only systematic training, development, and adjustment to actual changes, but also to a great extent using a flexible work regimen. Because of the influence of a turbulent business environment, organizations will be forced not only to change the number and structure of their employees. They will also be forced to offer them the possibility of time flexibility, which means creating the possibility for working a legislatively determined shift adjusted to the needs of the organization and the employee as well. Stepwise, this should be reflected for instance in the greater use of personnel leasing, external employees, and in greater involvement of subcontracting and outsourcing. Under the conditions of the Slovak economy, the most preferred flexible working agreements are part-time jobs (65 percent of organizations), flexitime (59 percent of organizations), temporary work (59 percent of organizations) and subcontracting (44 percent of organizations).

In the following text, we compare particular HRM functions in conditions in the Slovak Republic compared to the situation in organizations in more developed EU countries. We will describe these functions: recruitment and selection, the compensation and benefits system, and workforce training and development.

Recruitment and selection

Organizations in Slovakia prefer to fill vacancies for managerial positions by recruiting internally from among their existing workforce. Their trend shows that the existing workforce is used most often in this category of employees. According to the analyzed sample, 54 percent of the organizations look for a potential manager inside the organization itself. We believe that this is a good approach, since there are many advantages, e.g. higher motivation of employees and their identification with the organization, open opportunities to reach personal career plans, and relatively lower costs of the process. It would be an oversight not to mention disadvantages of the use of internal personnel sources for recruiting managers. There is a limited inflow of new ideas and new approaches to reaching set goals. Using internal sources might cause a lack of new experience and contacts, a necessity highly questioned more than any other employee category. An additional disadvantage can be seen in creating conditions for rising pressure and competitiveness among employees, which are not always desirable and could be even counterproductive.

It is obvious that organizations in developed countries (which have preconditions for well-established, long used, and accepted strategic approaches to HRM) are more likely to choose several methods rather then one certain method for their recruiting activities. There is no preferred method, but internal sources for managerial positions dominate. If external sources are used, then the services of headhunters and executive search agencies are used to a large extent for this employee category. In Slovak organizations, it is recruiting and selection where outsourcing services are used most often to cover HRM functions. However, we have to admit that the extent of the use of outsourcing is less than its utilization in organizations in more developed European countries. As a consequence of the changing business environment, the trend towards specialization and professionalism forces our organizations to change their attitude, and the tendency to use outsourcing utilization is rising.

Based on the analyzed sample, the second most used method in recruiting managerial employees is specialized personnel agency services. Almost 27 percent of the sample uses this method. If we focus on the research results, it is possible again to state that services of personnel agencies are used by Slovak organizations to a much lesser extent than on average within other European organizations. We have searched for an explanation for this phenomenon. It is understandable that there should be distrust as well as suspicion about the quality of this kind of service, since they have only been active in the market for a few years. Another probably very frequent reason is enterprises' aim to cut their operating costs to a minimum. Therefore they would prefer a promotion within the career plans of their employees to investing in the recruitment process, the selection process, and following the process of adaptation and orientation of a newly hired employee. This attitude is a consequence of lasting short-termism among organizations in Slovakia, which is unfortunately distinctive in the area of HRM.

Another employee recruiting category we have analyzed is the recruiting of professionals. According to our survey performed in 2005, in Slovak organizations professionals are recruited mostly by advertising methods (40.6 percent). It is a traditional and very commonly used method in Slovak organizations not only for this category of employees. Well-designed advertising should lead to a relatively tight pool of properly qualified applicants. At the same time it should bring expected results inexpensively and quickly. An advertisement which creates a 'flood' of application letters is not wanted, because the organization will have to spend much time, energy, and money to conclude the process of recruitment with satisfactory results. If we wanted to compare the situation in organizations in Slovakia and the situations of organizations in other developed European countries we would not find much difference. It is also because advertising is a universal method appropriate to almost any kind of enterprise and any working position. It has become the primary method for the majority of organizations from the sample. It is not necessary to analyze recruitment methods for the clerical employee category, since they are comparable with the category of professionals. Fifty percent of the polled organizations chose advertising as a primary method for recruiting clerical employees.

The ideal methodology for recruiting employees in the conditions of the Slovak business environment has appeared to be a combination of several suitable methods. This is the finding which was confirmed by our research results. Nowadays organizations prefer internal sources, references, and personnel agency services for acquiring applicants.

The process of selection is critical in the formation of an organization's human capital pool. The goal of this process is to select those applicants who not only match the requirements of the working position, but also who can contribute to improving the workplace environment and social climate in an organization as well. The effort spent on a precise selection process has appeared to be well invested and might bring outstanding returns as well.

The core of any selection process in Slovak organizations for any position is an interview, whether in a wider or reduced form. Over 54 percent of the organizations analyzed use an interview panel as a key method for selecting applicants for managerial positions. This method is a precondition for comprehensive, more objective and fair and impartial selection. Very few organizations use other selection methods more. Therefore we may say that applicants for managerial positions are selected also by one-to-one interviews and references, along with interview panels.

For the category of specialists the most often-used selection method is also an interview, but very rarely in the form of a panel. Usually it happens as a one-to-one discussion with the aim of gaining as much information as personal contact can provide. Since this method is based on one person's evaluation, no matter how professional he or she is, it always brings quite a bit of subjectivity into the selection process. There is a danger of an incorrect, hasty or too subjective decision. Based on the survey results, the situation in Slovak organizations does not differ from the situation in organizations in more developed European countries. A questionnaire is not as commonly used in Slovak organizations as it is in other developed European countries from the sample. In Slovak organizations the interview is still the second most used method of selection for the professional employee category, but especially in the form of a panel. Questionnaires appear to be very often used in almost all countries participating in the survey.

We would recommend that Slovak organizations consider using questionnaires in order to provide as much information as possible in a set form. This is irreplaceable by any other method of selection. A questionnaire is mostly structured into certain parts which request the particular phases of professional life and personality of an applicant. The form is adaptable to the needs of any organization, and it is able to provide as much detailed information as is required. References are also very often a part of questionnaires. They are also favored and therefore very often used as an additional method of selection for the professional/technical employee category in Slovak organizations. Many authors would not recommend using references as the only method of selection for any working position. Information gained by this method should not be used as the only source and criterion for a final decision. The method is too subjective, and if used as the only method it could provide distorted information.

The analysis has led us to conclude that the methods for selecting candidates for clerical employees do not differ much from the methods used for professional/technical category candidates. The most common method is the one-to-one interview. We believe that this is due to the aim of gaining verbal and nonverbal information straight from the applicant.

It might be interesting to note that the least favorite and least used method for selecting candidates is graphology, which is a very difficult, lengthy and specific method. Only 1.2 percent (only three) of all organizations surveyed said that they used this method. Compared to the situation in other countries, this percentage is extremely low.

Rewarding employees

Rewarding employees has essentially changed during the last several years. Because of economic and social changes in the 1990s managing employees rewards has became a competence of organizations. This system was no longer centrally regulated. This enables organizations to create a compensation policy which is suitable for individual conditions and the requirements of their particular organization. Organizations in practice don't always use mentioned opportunities, which is reflected not only in the efficiency of their compensation policy, but also in aggregate economic results.

"Reward" is generally understood as wage, salary, or other benefits and incentives in financial form received by an employee as a reward for his or her performance. The present theory of HRM and also the practice in Slovak organizations extend this definition, understanding a compensation system as a more complex system containing also various forms of intangible rewards and benefits. These forms have been recently analyzed by many organizations, because managers have realized their advantages for rewarding employees.

The majority of successful organizations use a "package system" of employee compensation, where each employee receives a "package" of many forms of compensation as a reward for his or her performance. Compensation systems in Slovak organizations have become connected with organizational strategy, declared by three-quarters of the organizations in the sample. The linkage between compensation system and corporate culture is weaker, appearing only in one-third of the organizations from the sample. By creating a compensation system, organizations take into consideration mostly macroeconomic indicators and their business environment. Research (2005) indicates that about 50 percent of organizations have developed such a compensation system and a further 40 percent monitor employees' satisfaction levels with the compensation system in use.

The quality of human resources is one factor which at present significantly influences the competitiveness of organizations. Therefore, it is the aim of every organization to recruit the best candidates in the labor market. This leads the organization to focus on external competitiveness in the decision-making process regarding how high their employees' wages are. In the Slovak labor market there are fundamental differences in rewarding employees from an industrial and regional perspective. Organizations use various supplements such as regional coefficients to regulate wages. The highest level of wages is in the region of our capital, Bratislava. The greatest differences in the level of wages are in the category of professionals. As has already been mentioned, 50 percent of the organizations from the analyzed sample set the level of their wages by taking into consideration surveys of wages performed by specialist personnel agencies, reviewed annually. Under the pressure of external conditions, the level of wages is regulated nearly once a year.

If an organization wishes its wage rates to have an incentive effect, it will have to create a compensation system that combines the optimal proportion of base compensation and pay incentives. Base compensation is mostly in the form of wage rates. It reflects the value of a particular job for an organization, which is set by methods of job evaluation. These methods are not sufficiently used in Slovak organizations. A survey (2005) showed that a formal system of wage rates was used by the majority of organizations for the employee category of workers (66 percent), clerical employees (64 percent), and professionals (46 percent). Wage rates are used less often for rewarding managerial employees (30 percent).

A variable component of the salary must be set as a percentage of the wage rate, and it must be based on specific conditions of an organization and reflect priorities of wage policy. According to our survey, the pay incentives are between 20 and 25 percent of total salary, and there are quite significant differences among individual employee categories. Pay incentives are mostly used in the category of managerial employees and also for employees in trade departments. Pay incentive programmes are designed to reward employees for good performance; 40 percent of organizations apply pay incentives to reward individual performance, and 30 percent of organizations reward team performance. One of the latest tendencies in employee compensation is to reward employees for organization performance, which is apparent also in Slovak organizations: 60 percent of organizations from the sample say that they use this form for managerial employees, with a decreasing tendency down through the hierarchy of an organization (24 percent of organizations use this form for workers). The application of pay incentives demands a purposive evaluation system and its connection to a compensation system. This precondition also creates suitable conditions for supporting the use of pay incentives in the structure of total employee compensation. However, 41 percent of organizations say that it has recently increased.

The practice in employee compensation distinguishes quite a number of forms of wages and their modifications which vary according to their incentive influence and mechanism of stimulation. A task of each organization is to include a suitable combination of wage forms in its compensation system according to its character and needs, but also according to the needs and characters of its employees. The choice of a convenient combination of wage forms can essentially influence the efficiency of the whole compensation system, and it is a source of efficiency differences among particular systems.

Wage forms in Slovak organizations are also reflecting the latest tendencies in involving pay incentives to a greater degree. Formerly, frequently used forms such as 13th and 14th wage (a form of bonus payment) are no longer claimed, but they depend more on the performance of the whole organization. Approximately one half of organizations include 13th wage in their compensation system; 14th wage is used by a very low percentage. An hourly wage rate still prevails in Slovak organizations, even if supplemented with various forms reflecting performance, according to specific conditions of a particular organization. Pieceratewages are used quite rarely. Only 23 percent of organizations use this form of wage, which is probably related to qualitative changes in the character of the transformation process in the business environment.

Results of the survey by personnel agencies in the Slovak market show the tendency towards wage equalization. Therefore, organizations nowadays prefer to use many non-financial forms of compensation, and include benefit systems and employee services in their systems. These rewards are not directly related to the employee's performance, but an employee receives them from the title of his employment in the organization. This form is very popular, and therefore it has become quite an item in labor costs, requiring adequate attention from management.

Some very popular benefits in Slovak organizations are, in particular: lunch tickets, additional retirement insurance, sport activities, cultural events, and health insurance. If an organization wants to use fully the whole potential of employee's benefits, it must adopt the principle of a "cafeteria system" of benefits and indirect compensation. This principle enables an organization to finance its system of benefits more effectively, while widening its range, making it more attractive for employees. Only 16 percent of organizations in the research sample use the cafeteria system in their system of indirect compensation. This fact shows that Slovak organizations do not use opportunities of managing a system of benefits as much as they could. However, this fact is also influenced by the recent change in tax legislation, which has limited the number of items excluded from the imposed income tax. This has consequently influenced the structure of offered benefits and complicated the implementation of a flexible compensation system.

Development and training of the workforce in conditions of an integrated Europe

If the Slovak Republic has the ambition to participate in the evolving European Union and develop the competitiveness not only of Slovak organizations, but also of the whole EU, it must fundamentally reappraise its policy in the area of education.

Workforce training and development are part of an organization's strategy and policy. Skills and knowledge development is beneficial for the whole organization and for individual employees as well. It is important to realize that training and development mean first of all investing in employee benefits which are provided by an employer. Here appears a question which all managers should be able to answer: "How should we manage training which will be useful, effective and bring competitive advantage for the organization?" These are the basic steps for managing effective workforce training and development:

1 Identification of training and development needs and defining goals.
2 Training activity design planning.
3 Realization of training activities.
4 Evaluation of realized training activities.

Based on the survey, we may assert that Slovak organizations are still very conservative in delegating training activity design to the HR department, which would help to make the line managers' responsibilities more effective. This phase of the training and development cycle is covered by line managers consulting on the issue with the HR department in the majority of organizations. We believe that here the responsibility is too centralized, and the extent of delegating competences should be greater. Concrete forms of training and development activities are stated in training and development programmes. The content of the training programme and training attendants are determined according to training and development policy. Slovak organizations are getting closer to the training and development system in organizations in developed countries of the EU in the phase of realization of training activities.

Throughout the whole training and development cycle, the question of costs is quite important, since effectiveness needs to be demonstrated. Education and research in general have a great influence on economic growth and employment. As EU leaders have remarked in Lisbon: "Investing in people and development of active and dynamic state welfare are decisive for the economy based on knowledge." This means that EU members should focus on increasing investment in human resources and emphasize the priority of lifelong education, because better knowledge and skills increase the chance of getting employment. Slovakia belongs unfortunately among those countries which do not invest sufficient sums in education. We believe that this is the critical area where organizations are making the greatest mistake. Slovak managers are still not aware of the importance and seriousness of employee training and development. The average amount spent on employee training and development in Slovak organizations is only 2.1 percent of annual salaries. It is on average 1.7 percent below the average for developed organizations in EU countries.

Within the survey there was also a question regarding training days per year per employee. After the entrance of our Republic into European structures, there is enormous pressure to adjust to European legislative norms and standards. Especially for managers, knowledge of foreign languages is essential. Training in language skills is lifelong training. Those European countries which were founders and charter members of the EU already have language education managed very well in schools. Their international orientation is a part of their culture, institutions providing foreign languages education have a long tradition, and the business environment is set on the need for international communication. All of this is reflected in the good language skills of a manager.

Slovak organizations are nowadays in a very turbulent and difficult business environment, where the pressure of modernization and continuous scientific progress demands more than only 4.9 days of training per professional/technician per year, which is the typical situation in Slovak organizations. Compared to other countries within the survey, Slovakia is below the average, which is 6.2 days of training per professional/technician per year. The number of training days received by clerical employees does not differ so much in Slovak organizations compared to organizations in more developed EU countries. It is on average 4 days per person per year. However, changes in legislation and the entrance of Slovakia into EU structures requires an increase in the number of training days for the category of clerical employees. We believe that for categories of clerical employees and workers this is unfortunately the number of training days which is necessary to obtain the basic knowledge stated in labor legislation.

The final employee category whose training and development we have analyzed within the survey is that of workers. We expected the lowest number of training days to be received by employees in this category. But we did not expect that it could be lower than 2 days. The typical Slovak worker receives only 1.7 days per year on average. This amount is very low compared to the average of organizations in more developed EU countries, where the average per employee per year is 4.1 days.

In our research we were also interested in the methods which organizations use to train their employees. There are great hidden reserves in the area of training and development in Slovak organizations. The proportion of employees trained using internal methods was 31 percent, which is over 12 percent lower than the European average. Internal training methods are the most used methods in Slovak organizations. The proportion of employees trained externally is 16.5 percent. There could be an explanation why organizations just do not have enough finances to cover more expensive external trainings.

Based on particular findings from the analysis, we may state that if Slovak organizations want to survive in difficult competitive conditions they will have to reappraise their strategy of workforce training and development.

THE FUTURE OF HRM IN SLOVAKIA

We believe that future development depends on respecting and implementating the following tendencies:

- globalization;
- professionalizing managers;
- advanced methods and procedures.

Globalization is related to international management application in Slovak organizations, but they also apply procedures which are used by similar organizations in developed countries. The principal integrated components of globalization policy are values preferred by corporate culture, compensation and benefits, rewarding performance, and career planning. Some activities of an international HQ management can sometimes be considered as directive. Therefore the transfer of these activities to local offices is not always simple. Strategy integration into global strategy must therefore be very sensitive and cautious. Practice shows that a convenient way to integrate it can be to apply the experience of the best components of an organization. The transfer of positive results of HRM creates the most natural way to integrate global organization strategy via reciprocal support and cooperation.

Even if the globalization is mostly connected with economic aspects, it also has political, social and cultural dimensions. The corporate culture is even more significant when the organization operates in the international market. Managers have begun to realize that corporate culture can be a source of competitive advantage, in particular when it is considered valuable, rare, and hardly imitable. This kind of corporate culture represents a connection between the strategic perspective of an organization and HRM, which create conditions for the adequate behavior of quality managers and other employees. Corporate culture influences all activities of strategic HRM, which may be reflected, via the competency and motivation of workforce, in the economic results of an organization.

Employee motivation, in this context, gains special meaning, which is tightly related to the corporate culture of an organization. Corporate culture itself has a motivational influence, and it can support certain motivational factors. Preconditions for good working motivation are properly set goals and their elaboration into particular tasks and objectives of a team and its members. A strong focus on employee involvement, including delegated responsibility for planning and structuring work, is seen as a critical requirement.

The professionalization of managers and the development of work with human resources should continue. The training of managers should be oriented on the following key areas of knowledge management, habits, and behavior in the market economy: How can a person become an effective manager? What steps should be chosen in the career advancement of a manager? How does one make decisions? How does one manage time rationally? How can a person present his or her own ideas?

How does a worker learn to cooperate with superiors and subordinates? How does a worker find satisfaction in his or her work? How can we develop the will to raise efficiency and the quality of work among people? How do we provide employees with opportunities for their professional growth? How do we find people to develop enterprises and apply new ideas, people to increase productivity, delegate responsibility, and develop communication? It will be necessary for an organization's development plans to focus on the professional development of employees and also on their professional career, which does not automatically need to mean promotion within the hierarchy of responsibilities, but it may also mean promotion in the hierarchy of professionalism and delegation to more demanding tasks. This tendency is currently obvious for good employers. An important task in the process of professionalizing managers is also the extent of the utilization of knowledge and skills in practice and their influence on work performance improvement. Particular attention will be paid to managerial motivation to use soft skills, and also to creating adequate conditions in order to enable the use of obtained skills in practice.

The area of HRM needs to acquire a European type of management and its use for every organizational level in practice. Business practice needs, in particular, the following methods and procedures for the effective creation and development of human resources:

- Transformation of personnel activities means the continuous transfer of delegation of operative tasks regarding HRM to line managers. We believe that conceptual, analytical and methodological-consulting activities of the HR department will strengthen. However, this process of the change of HR manager from an administrator to a consultant does not always run without problems. Line managers are not always willing, or even able, to perform personnel functions, and HR managers may feel that their position is losing its relevance.
- Strategic planning, measuring, and benchmarking will need to be applied within the framework of HRM. To gain a view of human capital in an organization and on the efficiency of particular activities in managing human resources, it is important to monitor the costs, productivity indicators, and indicators of effective management in particular areas of HRM.
- Outsourcing of personnel activities is joined by monitoring the effectiveness of particular activities of HRM. Some personnel activities will be excluded from the responsibility of HR departments and will be provided by commercially based external agencies.
- Personnel marketing is becoming a tool for shaping and maintaining the required workforce, due to the employees' good reputation and labor market research. It is a method for recruiting quality employees, retaining them and strengthening their loyalty to the organization. Via personnel marketing only those candidates who meet specific requirements of the open position are sought. Therefore, not only is analysis and evaluation of working positions required, but also analysis of the needs, interests, expectations and attitudes of potential candidates. Shaping working potential based on personnel marketing leads to the creation of a specific

corporate culture. It is related not only to the process of staffing, but also to releasing employees, where it is necessary, to help those employees to reintegrate into the work process elsewhere. It is relevant, in particular, in the conditions of the transformation of the Slovak economy and systematization tendencies in HRM in Slovakia.

- An assessment centre is used, more often, as a method to shape the workforce of an organization. This method may be used in the process of selection, and as a method for managerial employee evaluation. An assessment centre, as the basis of a combination of interviews, tests, and various team games, role playing and solving logical tasks, enables the evaluation of all candidates, or training of all managers, at the same time and the same conditions. These methods are among the most objective methods, because several evaluators are always involved in the process of assessment. Its cost is the reason why this method isn't used to an even greater extent in Slovak organizations.

- Managing performance is a new strategic process enabling employees to understand what they should be oriented toward and what objectives should be reached. In this approach there is also a continuous process of communication between an employee and his or her superior. The goal of this integrated process is reached by the continuous improvement of performance. A part of this process is a performance plan and its monitoring during the whole year, complete performance evaluation, workforce training and development, and a reward system. This approach to managing performance leads to increased employee performance by providing employees with information about set goals and training, which helps them to reach these goals, as well as providing each employee with the opportunity to be coached by managers and receive feedback.

- Permanent, lifelong education becomes necessary. Knowledge and information are becoming a preferred economic category in Slovakia also. They are very important factors in economic prosperity. Therefore, it is necessary to recognize and elevate education as a key important process in an organization. Only by this means is it possible to deal with a turbulent business environment. Nowadays, it is not sufficient to set the strategy of workforce training and development for an organization. It is necessary that every employee determines his or her own strategy of development, to start the intervention of an organization in employee education.

- Strengthening of collective bargaining began after the entrance of Slovakia into the EU. Even if the position of trade unions in many organizations has recently weakened as a consequence of many influences, we do believe in the continuous growth of trade union significance.

Case study

As an example of a systematic approach to HRM functions by a young Slovak enterprise we would like to describe the system of HRM in Hella Slovakia Front-Lighting. We have chosen this enterprise as an example for this case study because of its success in the Slovak market and for its continuous growth, which are supported by following and practicing the latest tendencies in HRM with regard to national and regional particularities. The enterprise is also an example of quality HRM as a precondition for success in the conditions of the market economy in Slovakia. Even though Hella Slovakia is not owned by a Slovak owner and it is a 100 percent subsidiary of an international concern, its management is adjusted to the Slovak business environment. Precisely because of this fact, Hella Slovakia is a perfect representative of the group of enterprises which were established by the entry of foreign investors after the transformation from a centrally planned to a market economy.

Hella Slovakia Front-Lighting was established on the Slovak market as a subsidiary within absolute ownership of the concern Hella Group. Hella Group is an internationally reputable partner of the automobile industry and after sales. The core activity of the concern is the production of floodlights and electronics for the automobile industry. The concern asserts the strategy of international growth. In the form of subsidiaries and joint ventures, it owns 65 production plants. The strategy is oriented to high-quality production and new service concepts. In order to achieve these goals, it uses and supports the innovative potential of its employees. Fast decisions, flat organization structures, and involved employees are a guarantee of success and a leading position on the market, which the concern consistently builds. Hella Group employs 23,000 people worldwide and 2,000 specialists working there as engineers and technicians.

Hella Slovakia Front-Lighting is a Greenfield Project. It was established in 2003 as a subsidiary within full ownership of the concern Hella Group. When it was established, Hella employed 70 local people; in 2005 it employed to 376 people.

Hella Slovakia is based near the village of Kocovce in the district of Nove Mesto nad Vahom in the county of Trencin. The western part of the district shares a border with the Czech Republic. This county has an advantageous geographical position within the Slovak infrastructure. It spreads out in the middle of economically developed regions which are along the corridor of the big cities from Bratislava to Trnava to Trencin to Zilina. In this area is located the transportation connection joining the north and south, west and east of Slovakia. Hella placed its factory near the D1 freeway, which provides the key transportation connection.

This area provides Hella Slovakia with sufficient and quality sources of working potential. Several manufactories were placed in the district in the production of

continued

air-conditioning, mechanical engineering, and research and development in the area of automation and mechanization. These plants were closed after the transformation of the centrally planned economy to a market economy, and many employees lost their jobs.

Slovakia has recently become very interesting to foreign investors, particularly in the automobile industry. In the neighboring counties of Trnavsky and Zilinsky, two automobile producers have established their production plants. Therefore the market in which Hella operates is still growing and provides wide opportunities of demand in Slovakia.

The employees of Hella Slovakia are educated mostly in technical training institutions or at high schools with technical specialization. Hella employs people aged mostly from 25 to 45. The largest number is represented by workers in production, then professionals and technicians. Only 4 percent of the total number work in administration.

Because Hella Slovakia operates in the Slovak market as a part of a larger group, in order to understand its HRM system it is relevant to know how lines of authority for HRM functions are drawn. The international headquarters sets the policy regarding compensation and career management only. Any other function of HR management is managed by the subsidiary.

The enterprise has created a human resources department which is actively participating in decision-making for setting goals and determining enterprise strategy. It participates in the form of membership on the board of directors. A human resources manager has been recruited as a personnel specialist outside of the enterprise, where she has been leading the HR department as well.

The strong orientation of the enterprise toward motivation, contentment, and support of innovative employee potential is a consequence of its approach to managing the workforce as a key creator of enterprise value. This approach is projected into every HRM function. The cost aspect is not always key. Someone responsible for managing human resources is always involved in strategic decision-making. He or she is not only involved in the role of consultant or in the phase of strategy realization, but is also present from the very beginning of strategy making. This approach proves a strong orientation of the enterprise toward employee matters. The enterprise communicates its mission, strategy, personnel strategy, and the concept of corporate culture in written form to its employees. This creates preconditions for greater identification of employees with the enterprise and also space for their loyalty. The representative of the human resources department and line manager are always involved in making essential decisions in particular functions of HR management. Tight cooperation of these two HRM positions is necessary for choosing and applying the correct HR policy.

At present, the main HRM challenges for Hella Slovakia are human capital development and its greater identification with the enterprise. These goals will be achieved by raising the number of employees according to the plan for enterprise growth in the next three years. This will be realized by using personnel marketing, education and training activities, and changes in motivation programs and the evaluation system. Fulfilling the strategic aims for the next three years, which is growth, is therefore not limited only to hiring new people, but means especially developing human capital quality and integration.

The realization of a majority of HRM functions is being supported by an integrated information system organized in partial modules. Providing actual, relevant, and exact information, as well as utilizing data archives and data distribution, helps the decision-making process and its communication to target subjects. At present, utilization of a quality information system is an absolutely necessary precondition for being competitive in the Slovak market.

Since Hella is an enterprise with a strong growth orientation, creating potential by increasing the number of employees is a key issue. The enterprise also uses outsourcing for recruitment and selection. Indeed, the use of this method is steadily growing. Headhunting and executive search services are used for recruiting employees in managerial categories and also partly for the category of professionals and technicians. Professionals and technicians are recruited mostly by cooperation with institutions providing education and by using references. There are several high schools specializing in the technical fields, providing graduation in professional education. A combination of recruiting methods is used for other categories of employees, including the services of the "office of unemployment." Because this is a region with a suitably qualified workforce, as well as unemployment caused by the closure of manufactories by the former regime, the employment registry is a good source of applicants for Hella Slovakia. The process of selection is realized by using a combination of standard methods for every employee category: one-to-one interviews, panel interviews, and references. In selecting employees for managerial positions, the most often used method is an assessment center, which enables an organization to test several aspects of professional abilities as well as personal skills.

The enterprise focuses on the system of employee evaluation very precisely. It is performed regularly for every employee category. A 'motivation interview' is used as the main source of information for employee evaluation. This method assures higher objectivity of evaluation and provides space for feedback. Therefore, it is very useful in employee evaluation. Reports are another source of information on all evaluated subjects, who are, besides line managers, also subordinates, colleagues, and customers. The output gained by employee evaluation is also used as a source of information for the reward system, education and training, carrier management, personnel planning, and job analyses. Part of the motivation interview is an agreement between an employee and his or her subordinate regarding identification of training needs, which, of course, is based on job description, enterprise strategy goals for the next period and the employee's career plan.

continued

Thus the line manager is not solely involved in defining training needs, since the aims of an employee are also taken into consideration. The human resources department is responsible for the realization of education and training activities.

Coaching as an in-the-job method of employee training is mainly used for all employee categories. Other methods used are job rotation, self-managed education, and e-learning. E-learning is not yet used for the category of workers. The enterprise precisely evaluates the effect of employee education and training activities directly afterwards, but also a few months later. The effectiveness of these activities is analyzed also by the following ratios: costs of education per employee, the percentage of realized trainings to planned trainings, the rate of costs of education and training activities to operation costs of the enterprise. Because of high-tech technologies used in the enterprise, training employees professional abilities is the most important area of education. Next most important are language skills, which are related to the customer's portfolio, and also soft skills training assigned to managerial employees and project management training for project team leaders.

A proof that Hella Slovakia sees its employees as a key source of the enterprise's success is that it uses the compensation system as its main motivation tool. Internal equity and external competitiveness are covered by analyses of all relevant information, such as enterprise strategy, personnel strategy, external surveys of wage level, internal surveys of employee contentment, macroeconomic ratios and line managers' professional advice.

Salaries are set at the level of each individual for all employee categories, except for workers. In this way the enterprise practices an individual approach to employee motivation. Depending on the character of a particular position, pay per hour and contractual wages are used. The enterprise tries to involve its employees in economic activities. A variable part of the salary for each employee category is related to the enterprise's economic results. Individual performance is reflected in a variable part of the salary according to the attainment of set goals by an employee for a period of time. For employees working in teams, a variable part of the salary depends on the performance of the team. The system of benefits is realized by a form of cafeteria system, which helps to raise the effect of benefits. This form of employee motivation has lately increased. The enterprise also considers non-material forms of compensation important.

Hella Slovakia is an important employer in the region of Nove Mesto nad Vahom. By its successful business activities and strategic approach to HRM, Hella has created a very positive image for local citizens, which is not only another stimulation tool, but also a source of success in the market.

REFERENCES AND FURTHER READING

Armstrong, M. (2002). *Managing Human Resources*. Praha: Grada Publishing.

Figel, J. and Adamiš, M. (2004). *Slovakia on the Way to European Union. Chapters and Associations*. Zastúpenie Európskej komisie v SR.

Joniaková, Z., Blštáková, J. and Werflová, A. (2005). *Employee Compensation System – Textbook*. Bratislava: EKONÓM.

Kachaňáková, A. (2001). *Human Resources Management: Human Capital and the Success of a Company*. Bratislava: SPRINT.

Kachaňáková, A. (2003). Human resources management: Human capital and the success of a company. Bratislava: SPRINT.

Kachaňáková, A. and Blštáková, J. (2004). "Theory and Praxis in the Area of Human Resources Management". *Proceedings from International Conference: Managing Workforce*, Zvolen.

Kachaňáková, A. and Blštáková, J. (2005). "Development of Human Resources Management in the Context of European Tendencies". *Proceedings from International Conference: Managing Workforce in Organizations*, ŽU in Žilina.

Kachaňáková, A. and Blštáková, J. (2005). "Development of Practical Application of Theoretical Knowledge in the Area of Managing Human Resources". *Economics and Management*, 1. FPM EU in Bratislava.

Kachaňáková, A. and Blštáková, J. (2005). "Human Resources Management in Slovakia. Present and New Trends". *Proceedings from Inernational Conference: Human Resources Management in Conditions of Forming New European Labor Market*, Trenčín.

Kachaňáková, A., Nachtmannová, O. and Joniaková, J. (2002). *Human Resources Management: Managing Workforce and the Success of a Company*. Bratislava: SPRINT.

Kachaňáková, A., Nachtmannová, O. and Mulíková, M. (2002). "Latest Tendencies in Human Resources Management Evolution in Slovak Organizations". *Economic Journal*, 2.

Kachaňáková, A., Nachtmannová, O. and Mulíková, M. (2003). "Theorie und Praxis in Organisationen der Slowake". *Personal* (Forcheim, Germany). 4.

Majtán *et al.* (2005). *Management*, 2nd edition. Bratislava: SPRINT. Chapter 9. Human Resources Management.

Nachtmannová, O. and Zúbriková, D. (2005). *Job Organization – Textbook*. Bratislava: EKONÓM.

Sedlák *et al.* (2006). *Company Economy*. Bratislava: MERKURY Ltd.

Textbook for e-learning elaborated within the framework of KEGA 3/103403, chapter Human Resources management. Bratislava, CĎV 2006.

Zúbriková, D. and Blštáková, J. (2006). Anwerben und entwickeln PERSONAL Zeitschrift fur Human Resource Management Verlagsgruppe Handelsblatt Hefft 4/06, April 2006.

7 Managing human resources in Hungary

JÓZSEF POÓR

INTRODUCTION

There are visible differences between the levels of development in the human resource management (HRM) practices of different East European (EE) countries. These may be attributed to a variety of differences – in tradition, in levels of economic development and in the degree of centralisation in the previous economic and political systems of the various individual states. In these countries only traces of the characteristics of modern HRM could be detected within the framework of the systems then in force. Typically, approaches similar to the School of Scientific Management were also dominant in Hungary. In general terms HRM activity in this country prior to the changes which occurred at the end of the 1980s was very tightly controlled by the state. 'The years following the political changes', according to Antal (2004: 96), 'were characterised by disintegration in every post-socialist country – and also in Hungary. Today, the shrinking of the national GDP has slowed to a halt and inflation has moderated. This situation has enhanced the value of these markets, which face a probably slow convergence in that they will not be able to catch up with Western countries in the near future, but, rather, in the space of two or three decades.' During recent years it has become widely acknowledged that, in addition to traditional production-related factors, HRM is becoming more and more important for success to be achieved and for domestic and international competitiveness to be retained or strengthened. In this chapter we shall pay special attention to highlighting both the convergent and divergent trends of the development of HRM in Hungary. We propose to present an overview of HRM policies and practices in Hungary in the light of three different research projects. Our first HR benchmark survey offers insights into HR practices between 1997 and 2001, the second provides information on the HRM functions of multinational corporations operating through their Hungarian subsidiaries from 1988 to 2004, whilst the third comprises statistics, analytical detail and a stochastic analysis of Hungarian data *vis-à-vis* HRM practice in East European countries and in the whole CRANET (Cranfield Network on Comparative Human Resource Management) database also.[1]

ABOUT THE COUNTRY

Before we move to our major discussion topic a brief overview of Hungary might be useful. The country's population is approximately 10.1 million. In the early 1990s the economic performance of Hungary was weaker than before the political changes of 1989. Inflation and unemployment showed a sudden increase when compared to previous years, whilst at the turn of the millennium the most important feature of the economic and labour processes in Hungary was subordination to the requirements of EU accession. In this context, as an acceding country (according to Berki, 2004), Hungary had to pay special attention to maintaining economic processes on a predefined track, implementing the harmonisation of the legal environment and complying with the norms and requirements determined by various organisations and representatives of the EU.

Aided by accelerating privatisation and structural changes, Hungary experienced significant growth in GDP. Nowadays and in the near future Hungary's growth rate as a newly acceded country will, according to various forecasts (Palánkai, 2004), exceed the EU average. However, one further feature of the Hungarian transformation is that this significant growth in GDP was achieved in this country at the cost of decreasing employment.

The wave of dramatic change in the political, legal, social and economic systems of Hungary created many opportunities for business, but it also posed many challenges. In order to meet these, Hungarian companies were required to adopt new methods, systems, policies and expertise. Nowhere were these demands greater than in the management of an organisation's human resources.

Most international financial institutions have agreed that the country has successfully completed its transition from a centrally directed economy to a fully functioning and prosperous market economy. By the end of 2005 the economy had grown by approximately 4 per cent, unemployment had fallen to 6.5 per cent, and inflation had dropped to 4 per cent.

The private sector accounts for more than 85 per cent of GDP. However, despite the economy's performance, an estimated 25 per cent of the population lives in poverty, with the elderly, larger families and the Roma minority most seriously affected. GDP per capita was approximately $6,500 (1.3 million HUF) in 2005.

The situation in the Hungarian economy has drastically changed during the last two years. Economic growth has slowed to 1.4 per cent (BBJ, 2007), its lowest for 11 years. The government has begun to address several critical problems in relation to agriculture, healthcare, tax reform and the budget deficit, and today budget consolidation dominates the political agenda. Current tax increases and spending cuts are temporarily dampening growth, although, if all goes according to plan, the programme will bring dividends to the economy in the longer term (OECD, 2007: 1)

THE TRANSITION PROCESS

A series of reforms began in Hungary in 1968, creating an economic system which has been termed 'market socialism'. The pace of experimentation and change – political, social and economic – accelerated in the 1980s during what is commonly known as the period of 'reform communism' and by 1990 the Hungarian economy had a substantial private sector of small entrepreneurial companies. Hungary, far more than its former communist neighbours, experienced economic and political changes which were more evolutionary than revolutionary.

In Hungary in the old system, the work ethic was built on two significant foundations: (1) workers had little respect for supervisors, employers and the party and (2) even jobs without meaning or responsibility were maintained in order to achieve 'full employment'. A large number of workers operated in the black economy, either as workers or as customers (Hethy and Mako, 1972). In the 'shortage economies' of former socialist states there was a disparity between the amount demanded for a product or service and the amount available in a market. This same disequilibrium existed also in the labour market. In Hungary and in other Central and East European (CEE) countries the real hero of the company or business was the manual worker.

Historically, economic transactions in Hungary worked through bureaucracy and the various state ministries rather than through markets. There was limited competition and dysfunctional organisational politics were pervasive. Key positions in companies were tightly monitored by the Party and by state bureaucracy, and management was not regarded as a profession. Promotion decisions traditionally were not based on performance appraisal, and in many cases the professionals' selection and staffing decisions were strongly influenced by the Party, by government policies and objectives. The Hungarian Socialist Workers' Party maintained its authority over managerial cadres in order to control not only the vast bureaucracy but also business life. Managers were instructed by the Party to combine one-person leadership with collective leadership. Managers and employees were rewarded for conforming rather than for performing. Managers' efforts and skills were focused more on pleasing superiors than on profitability or customer service (Pearce, 1991).

The traditional HRM philosophy followed an industrial, production economy bias (Kovari, 1995). Social goals focused on the production of industrial and consumer durable goods, applying bureaucratic processes of increasing labour specialisation. The traditional view of job analysis is closely related to the scientific management concept of mass production in business and to the model of effective bureaucracy in socialist public administration. The duties and responsibilities of a job were identified and then assigned to several job-holders simultaneously. Worker initiative was replaced by 'the single best way of task performance', which was included in the job description. Consequently, broader job descriptions and higher personnel commitment were new to employees working in Western-owned joint ventures.

The traditional Hungarian personnel department consisted of two separate systems, one for white-collar employees and one for blue-collar workers. The white-collar group reported to the so-called 'Personnel' Office, whilst the blue-collar employees reported to the director of economic affairs (Bangert and Poór, 1995). Under the former system personnel departments were directly supervised by the CEO and were usually responsible for traditional personnel functions including selection, career management, etc. These high-profile employees belonged to the category of politically important managers and professionals. Special emphasis was placed on creating professional development opportunities which required them to attend annual off-site training programmes. Figure 7.1 depicts the formal structure of a typical organisation. While it may seem odd to anyone from another economic system, the chief executives in each of the state-owned enterprises had no control over the wages that were paid to most of their employees and little influence over non-wage benefits.

High levels of performance were rare, and so, in the absence of exceptional quality and ability, mediocrity was the normal expectation. Payment-by-performance simply did not exist, and egalitarian pay structures were a high priority. Employees who merely showed up for work kept their jobs, and if supervisors wanted them to do any serious work the supervisors had to 'pay' for it in the form of a bonus. Such bonuses were sometimes as much as 200 per cent of the employee's basic pay. Since these bonuses were individually negotiated, an atmosphere of suspicion and mistrust developed – based on the fear that others were enjoying better deals.

Individual responsibility and accountability were avoided whenever possible (Pearce, 1991), and few managers took risks, even when it would have been appropriate to do so. Employees, supervisors and managers seldom had sufficient information to make informed decisions, and communication tended to flow only in one direction, that is, downwards.

Key representatives of trade unions were nominated and selected by the Hungarian Socialist Workers' Party, and it should be explained that union membership was, in practice, obligatory, even though not officially so. (The main exception to this general principle, of course, lay outside Hungary, that is, in the Polish 'Solidarity' Trade Union). Trade union representatives, in fact, were part of state bureaucracy (Laszlo, 1995).

In Hungary the one-party political and power system collapsed at the end of the 1980s, and the first free parliamentary election, held in May 1990, was a form of

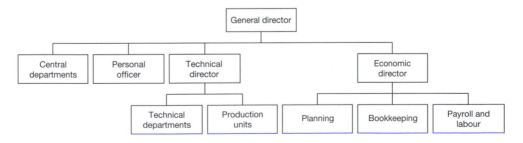

Figure 7.1 Typical HR infrastructure within state-run enterprises in Hungary, pre-1990

plebiscite on the communist past. Hungary is now well on the way from dictatorship to democracy, being a parliamentary democracy with a freely elected legislative assembly. The bewildering speed of the renaissance of capitalism over the past 15 years has bound Hungary more closely to the West than for decades, and such a rapid transition from centralised state control and national economic planning to free market, globally competitive capitalism is unprecedented in the history of mankind. This difficult political and economic process has a number of basic elements, of which four major ones should be highlighted in respect of human resources at the macroeconomic level.

First comes the creation of a new labour law environment. The New Labour Law was implemented in Hungary in 1992 and covers all aspects of employment in the private (although not in the public) sector.

In respect of the latter, a separate law was enacted regarding the status of civil and public servants, including the establishment of educational and promotional requirements. Both laws (Hungary, 1992a, 1992b) were adopted in the same year. Different governments (all coalitions) issued their own government decisions on reform of the public sector, including No. 1100/1996, No. 1052/1999, No. 1057/2001 and No. 1113/2003, although these government decisions have had no serious effect on the framework of HRM within the civil and public service.

However, the current socialist-liberal coalition government introduced a drastic reform programme for the public sector in June 2006. This programme contains several items which will influence the framework and management of the government HRM function at both the central and local level in Hungary and in the short or medium term.

Second is the ending of the egalitarian pay structures which had been a priority during the early years of socialism. Pay differentials are now more common and have, in fact, increased from 1:5 up to 1:15/20 between highly paid managers and skilled workers.

Third came the end of the era of the right to work – job entitlement. In parallel with the right to change jobs there came for many workers considerable difficulty in finding jobs as unemployment became common in Hungary, although currently there is single digit unemployment in Hungary.

Fourth came the restructuring of the social welfare system – something which is now placing a tax burden on both employers and employees. The relatively cheap labour force is made more expensive by increasing payroll taxes for services once provided entirely by the state. Employers' social security contributions for health and pensions in Hungary total some 33.5 per cent. Political and economic changes have created unprecedented issues and demonstrated the need for a total reconstruction of the whole social and welfare system. East European countries in general have enacted some form of pension reform since the change of their political and economic systems, and the broad picture resulting from recent social and welfare practices in

Hungary is of a system partly in a state of flux. Our experience confirms that the former state-dominated pension system has been transformed into a three-tier scheme. Normal pension schemes in Eastern Europe, including Hungary, usually include the following key elements:

- Pillar 1: a reformed state pension system (pay-as-you-go);
- Pillar 2: a mandatory, individually focused non-state system (mandatory individual);
- Pillar 3: a voluntary employer-focused framework with fiscal incentives (voluntary) (see Table 7.1).

Table 7.1 Pension systems in Western and Eastern Europe

3 Pillars (pay-as-you-go + mandatory individual + voluntary) 12 countries		*Pillar 1 and Pillar 3 (pay-as-you-go + voluntary) 7 countries*	
Austria	Ireland	Cyprus	Malta
Belgium	Netherland	Finland	Norway
Denmark	Spain	Italy	Portugal
France	Sweden	Luxembourg	
Germany	Switzerland		
Greece	UK		

3 Pillars (pay-as-you-go + mandatory individual + voluntary) 12 countries		*Pillar 1 and Pillar 3 (pay-as-you-go + voluntary) 4 countries*	
Bulgaria	Lithuania	Czech Republic	
Croatia	Poland	Serbia	
Estonia	Romania	Turkey	
Hungary	Russia	Ukraine	
Kosovo	Slovakia		
Latvia	Slovenia		

Pillar 1 (pay-as-you-go) 3 countries		*Pillar 1 and Pillar 2 (pay-as-you-go + mandatory individual) 1 country*	
Albania		Macedonia	
Bosnia and Herzegovina			
Montenegro			

Source: Szegedi, E., 2007.

On the one hand, the state guarantees certain minimum levels of pension and medical services, whilst, on the other hand, employers and employees are expected to take responsibility for any additional pension and healthcare benefits required beyond those modest levels provided by law.

THE CONTEXT FOR HUMAN RESOURCE MANAGEMENT

Stakeholders

Trade unions

In 2004 there were 550,000 trade union members in Hungary. (Prior to the political transition in 1990 data from the National Office indicate that 3.9 million – 83 per cent of the 4.8 million employed – paid union dues). Our latest CRANET figures show an even lower percentage in respect of the former. (See details later on p. 209.)

The national tripartite forum, currently known as the National Interest Reconciliation Council (OET), is a central element of the Hungarian industrial relations system. Labour laws permit collective bargaining at company and industry levels. The OET is a forum for representatives of employers, employees and the government and sets both minimum and recommended wage levels in the public sector.

Foreign capital as a key driver

The total stock of highest foreign direct investment (FDI) in Hungary increased from €100 million in 1989 to 47.5 billion in 2005, which is the second FDI per capita figure in the region (following only the Czech Republic) (UNCTAD, 2005), and foreign capital established significant positions in the fundamental sectors of the Hungarian economy (see Figure 7.2). In addition to investments in manufacturing and technology, the foreign entities concerned have carried out significant restructuring in the incentive scheme management practices of the companies under their control.

A new component of corporate strategy has emerged recently: outsourcing (Peng, 2006). Developed countries started to outsource or near-source to Eastern Europe.

Key labour market development

'This region has seen enormous improvements in economic outcomes since 1990,' says Arup Banerji, the supervisor and sector manager of the report in the Human Development Economics Department of the World Bank's Europe and Central Asia region (ECA). 'But unless there are more and better jobs created in the region, the poverty reduction we have seen in recent years could grind to a halt – and this in turn

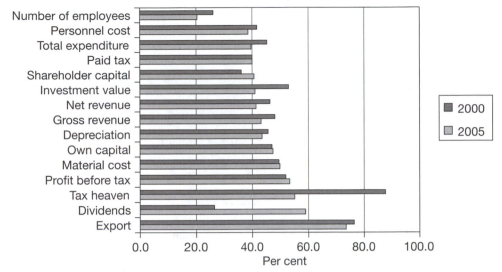

Figure 7.2 Role and influence of foreign capital in the Hungarian economy
Source: Pitti, 2007

would really undermine the political support for reforms,' he warns. Overall, the report says that the greatest change since transition has been the shift from secure, though not highly rewarding, employment, to less stable jobs with greater earning potential (World Bank, 2005).

Key legislative provision

The Hungarian Labour Code was introduced in 1992. This Code, as amended in 1997 and 2004, recognises the right of unions to organise and bargain collectively and permits trade union pluralism. Workers have the right to associate freely, choose representatives, publish journals, and openly promote members' interests and views. With the exception of military personnel and the police, they also have the right to strike. Due to the Labour Code, 'normal working hours' is the period during which the employee is expected and authorised to work. In extraordinary cases, the employee can be employed beyond normal working hours.

There are three types of contract: employment contracts, independent contractor contracts and assignment contracts. The normal working time is 40 hours per week and eight hours per day. In areas of particularly arduous or unhealthy working conditions, the employee may be given a shorter working week, although the shortening of the working week does not imply a reduction in wages. Working hours may vary from day to day in accordance with the needs of the employees and of the enterprise, but, in the case of full-time employees, the daily working time must be at least four hours. Shift work is allowed, although shift schedules must be communicated seven days ahead. A maximum of an eight-week schedule can be determined in advance (Mercer, 2005).

The Labour Code prohibits any negative discrimination against employees due to their sex, age, family status, disability, minority, nationality, race, origin, religion, political conviction, trade union membership/activity (or any opinion, wealth or language) or any other circumstance unrelated to their employment. Opportunities for promotion to a higher position must be offered solely on the grounds of professional ability, experience and performance.

In addition to the Labour Code, which covers almost 79 per cent of employed people in Hungary, there are ten laws which exclusively regulate the employment of people (21 per cent) in different areas of the public sector. It is likely that all of these regulations will be amended or replaced by new laws.

As detailed previously, the Hungarian pension system consists of three pillars. Pillars 1 and 2 are mandatory whilst Pillar 3 is voluntary. The first step towards this system was taken in 1993 when Parliament accepted the Law on Voluntary Mutual Pension Funds (VMPFs), which enabled voluntary supplementary pension funds to be established (Pillar 3). The reform of the pension system was completed in 1997 when Mandatory Pension Funds (MPFs) were established as a further pillar of pension provision (Pillar 2). The active members of the pension system belong to two separate groups depending on age: they can participate either in the Pillar 1 only or in Pillars 1 and 2, according to Hungarian legislation. Due to the low replacement ratios of the first two pillars, additional company retirement plans are, in general, widespread, with 43 per cent of companies surveyed by Mercer (2005) having already established a supplementary retirement plan. The first and second pillars are mandatory, whilst membership in the third pillar is voluntary.

TRENDS AND DEVELOPMENTS IN HUMAN RESOURCE MANAGEMENT

Empirical research aimed at determining and analysing the operation and management of organisations in Hungary has been conducted since the 1960s. Within HR some quite large-scale empirical surveys took place from the standpoints of factory and work sociology, company culture, communication and HR (Bakacsi et al., 2002; Karoliny et al., 2003).

Our research into Hungarian HR practice has been conducted for the past 17 years by means of surveying organisations, and these data and findings serve as the basis for the present chapter. The first research into the subject was conducted at the beginning of the 1990s, and the results were published, with Hungarian and foreign co-authors, in Hungarian and foreign forums (Bangert and Poór, 1993; Kaucsek et al., 1992). One of the basic aims of these surveys was to describe Hungarian HR practice with the help of statistical indices (benchmarks) (Poór and Roberson, 2003). In the following we shall use three different sources of empirical evidence to explore the trends in Hungary.

Research project 1: the changing role of HRM in Hungary (1997–2001)

Since 1997 the same questionnaire has been employed, thus permitting direct comparisons over a number of years. Prior to 1997 a different set of questions was employed. During each survey the usual respondent was the most senior HR manager of the company, or the HR expert designated by him or her. On one occasion we also asked for the opinion of the other side, that is, of line management.

In our analysis – wherever possible – we tried to draw a comparison between the development of HR in Hungary and international practice. When we conducted our very first surveys, there was no real need for this type of information from the companies' side, but by now the situation has changed completely. Large Hungarian companies also show an interest in practices undertaken in their partner companies when they plan to restructure their own system, and, as a consequence of the ever-increasing need for cost-efficiency, many companies are no longer reluctant to use outsourcing. To provide a basis for this, benchmarking data showing Hungarian and international HR practices are indispensable (see Table 7.2).

Between 1997 and 2004 we conducted surveys among large Hungarian companies several times, using a questionnaire. The methodology of these surveys had the following basis:

● The questionnaire used between 1997 and 2004 was first tested in 1995. In subsequent years, influential factors and explanatory variables of the questionnaire – company turnover, headcount, form of ownership, industrial sector – remained unchanged. However, the method of collecting opinions on HR practice was modified in that on one occasion not only HR managers but also the managers of various departments in the participating organizations responded to the distributed questionnaire. Further, the 2002 survey was conducted with the assistance of interviewers, whereas, previously, the participants themselves filled in the questionnaires.
● Companies participating in the surveys were selected randomly from among those companies in the 'Top 10' List published by the Hungarian *Business Week* (Figyelö) in the given year and from companies where the authors of this article had undertaken any other type of research, survey or consulting work.

The characteristics of the companies responding are as follows:

● a total of 409 companies participated in the seven surveys, amongst whom 13 participated each year;
● the number of participants varied between 27 and 112;
● the majority of those questioned or responding came from the medium-sized or large company sectors;
● the majority of participating companies were in foreign ownership;

Table 7.2 Characteristics of companies participating in our research surveys, 1997–2004

Year	Number of enterprises participating	Form of ownership		Size of organization			Labour costs		Sector (in per cent)		HR strategy exists (per cent)	Place of HR (per cent-ban)		Usage (in per cent)	
		Domestic	Foreign	Large <1 bn HUF and 250 persons	Large medium	medium <50 persons and 100 million HUF	<30 per cent	>30 per cent	Industry	Other sectors		First management level	Second or level or lower level	Outside consultant	Existence of HRM software
2004	27	40.0	60.0	67.0	33.0	0.0	70.0	30.0	34.0	66.0	60.0	59.0	41.0	63.0	100.0
2002	112	35.0	65.0	45.0	47.0	8.0	0.0	0.0	38.0	62.0	68.0	63.0	37.0	0.0	0.0
2001	46	39.0	61.0	100.0	0.0	0.0	80.1	19.9	42.4	57.6	75.6	46.1	54.9	88.6	100.0
2000	54	34.0	76.0	98.0	2.0	0.0	86.9	13.1	56.1	43.9	89.5	61.1	38.9	87.0	85.0
1999	27	26.0	74.0	97.0	3.0	0.0	72.0	28.0	44.0	56.0	81.5	65.4	34.6	85.2	96.8
1998	71	25.6	74.5	87.0	13.0	0.0	90.0	10.0	60.0	40.0	62.0	49.3	51.7	63.4	84.3
1997	72	21.0	79.0	98.0	2.0	0.0	86.0	14.0	50.0	50.0	65.0	61.0	39.0	60.0	80.0
Average of 7 years	409	32	70	85	14	1	69	16	46	54	72	58	42	64	91
Weighted average of 7 years	58	31	70	75	20	2	61	12	47	53	70	58	42	53	64

Source: Pitti, 2007.

- in the majority of the organisations participating in our surveys wage costs amounted to less than 30 per cent of total turnover;
- in these seven surveys the proportion of manufacturing companies – compared to other sectors – was around 46 per cent; in recent years this number has decreased significantly, in line with the restructuring of the Hungarian economy.

The overall results from these seven years of research have produced a number of observations, and these are the noteworthy characteristics of management in Hungary in the middle of the first decade of the new millennium:

- *Private ownership:* since the change of regime, privatisation has come about and HR has developed significantly. Throughout the decade, for-profit organisations underwent several parallel change processes. These included changing mind-sets, restructuring critical core processes, and establishing core competence in disciplines previously lacking these – such as purchasing, finance, sales, marketing and human resource management itself. Current HRM practice in privately and publicly owned companies differs enormously from that of a decade ago.
- *Increased competition:* there has been much increased competition over the past decade, and with substantial foreign investment in Hungarian business, new competitive pressures have been brought to bear. Additionally, there has been increased competition among workers, and those individuals who perform well expect rewards for their work.
- *Improving economic performance:* despite the recent downturn in the economy, the overall economic trend over the past decade has been positive.
- *Integration with the global economy:* in the prevailing global economy, companies of every nation are affected, and Hungarian businesses are no exception. The interface of organisations in Hungary with the global marketplace has been facilitated by substantial foreign investment which has taken the form of wholly foreign-owned enterprises and joint ventures between foreign and domestic companies.
- *Dominance of foreign ownership:* consequent upon this last point, foreign investment has been very substantial.
- *EU membership:* Hungary became an EU member on 1 May 2004. EU membership has had a profound impact on the political and economic practices of the country.

Research project 2: HRM in major subsidiaries of multinational companies in Hungary (1988–2005)

In the this section we target our research on the HRM functions of multinational corporations (MNCs) operating through their subsidiaries in Hungary during the period 1988–2005. We wanted to learn by means of this research how these functions were executed and how practical applications were widely used during an era of major political turbulence and rapid economic change. Previous research suggests that modern management practices from the West cannot be adopted wholesale in emerging or transitional regions of the world. Both academics and practitioners suggest that HRM policies and practices need to be modified if they are to be relevant to these countries. However, there are others who contend that HRM functions can be moulded and changed rapidly and that convergence is close at hand (Brewster *et al.*, 2004)

The basic research items are framed around the five evolutionary stages of MNC subsidiaries in Hungary: privatisation (1988–1998), the arrival of MNCs by acquisition – either within or following privatisation, or by means of greenfield investment (1988–98), Transition & Learning and Development (1988–2001), 'Slowdown-Shakeout' (2001–3), 'Steady State' (2003 to date). Many of these stages may overlap, as has been experienced by individual companies. Dates are approximate and conform to general macro-environmental conditions as these conditions have changed in Hungary. The third research project aimed to analyse the changes within HRM in the sample research period.

The selection of the research method was determined by the fact that data for the five phases of the survey could be collected most effectively by the grounded theory development provided by personal interviews. We applied the 'sequential logic' of research planning (Hellriegel *et al.*, 1998: 623) and, in preparation for the interviews, studied the transformation of HR with respect to the development of the subsidiaries. In this stage of the research process we received feedback from several local HR professionals in the Budapest region. To facilitate the preparation phase for the respondents and the collection of the necessary data, an English-language survey form was developed. Researchers filled out some informational items from company websites, providing some background data which were verified with the respondents during the interviews.

The 42 companies participating in this interview-based research represent the type of key MNCs in the Hungarian economy:

- ninety per cent belong to the large enterprise category in terms of EU categorisation by headcount – that is, with 250+ employees;
- the foreign owners of a large percentage of these companies acquired majority control or started their greenfield investment between the end of the 1980s and the mid-1990s;
- of the foreign proprietors, 33 per cent arrived in the form of start-up-operations (green-field investment), whilst the remaining 67 per cent attained a majority holding or a controlling stake in the course of privatisation or by follow-up acquisition;
- most foreign owners of these companies acquired majority control or started their green-field investment between the end of the 1980s and the mid-1990s;
- participating companies originate from 11 countries, a considerable percentage coming from the United States, Germany and France.

Seven major conclusions emerged from the third research project:

- *Decreasing numbers of foreign expatriates:* in accordance with international trends (although less so in respect of Japanese companies) the number of foreign postings has fallen in recent years in the companies concerned. The number of these employing no foreign expats increased by 9 per cent, whilst the number of companies employing fewer foreign expats increased by 43 per cent. This regressive trend applies to members of the management board also. The number of staff and of expats show a positive correlation, which relates to longer periods of the 'Transition & Learning' phase than to today's 'Steady State'.
- *Increasing numbers of Hungarian expats and 'impatriates':* as a further sign of localisation, the number of Hungarian expats is gradually growing, a good number of whom are posted to the Central East European region or to a third country. The number of Hungarian 'impatriates' posted to headquarters also increased somewhat during the period under examination. Shorter foreign study tours and work-experience assignments for acquiring knowledge already existed when MNCs came on the scene, but longer-term foreign expatriate postings became more widespread during the transition period. The number of companies employing Hungarian expats has increased noticeably from 38.1 per cent to 75.6 per cent in comparison with earlier periods. Currently, almost two-thirds of the companies concerned (66 per cent) post Hungarian colleagues abroad.
- *Dominance of HQ in managerial HRM issues:* the centralisation of headquarters has increased due to the furtherance of global standardisation and to cost-cutting policies introduced during the recession. A limited degree of independence from HQ was experienced in the period in question by no more than one-quarter of the interviewees, and probably even this level of independence will be further reduced due to the expansion of MNC networks – particularly if MNC subsidiaries are be unable to function as sub-centres. Although the HQ impact on executive positions is significant, it would appear to be less relevant in relation to other employee-related HRM procedures.
- *Training and personnel development in focus:* in the three research periods the role of trade unions has significantly diminished. However, the importance of training and personnel development and the functions of remuneration have increased compared to the beginning. This can be regarded as a positive trend since these two functions can be identified as a base of innovation.
- *Cooperation and business partnership as key HRM competencies for success:* in all three periods cooperation and business partnership were important, as were HRM competencies, and in addition to these the respondents emphasised competence in change management, teamwork and rapid decision-making. It is surprising that in these companies a knowledge of foreign languages was not a key success factor. This could, perhaps, be attributed to the fact that a majority of the interviewees themselves had a good command of foreign languages.
- *Firms from low context cultures employ younger and more female HRM professionals:* the age and sex of respondents among HRM professionals within companies from low context business cultures (e.g. the USA and the UK) showed

a negative correlation compared with other companies. They were younger and most of them were woman.

● *Efficiency and globalisation as key future issues:* the research established certain principles to be borne in mind regarding any future changes to the HRM framework in local subsidiaries in our region. The companies participating considered efficiency improvement, adaptation to globalisation and the key issue of company development as the most important fields on similar scales. EU accession is regarded as less important by multinational companies, no doubt since the preparation period raised numerous issues continuously in those years.

Research project 3: CRANET research in Hungary (2005)

Our survey in 2005 was based on the questionnaire produced by the CRANET (Cranfield Network/European Human Resource Management Research Network) programme. This programme was started on the initiative of Cranfield Business School in 1992. Today there are 42 member countries with Hungary becoming a full member of the programme in 2004.

Eleven hundred organisations were randomly selected from the Top 100 list, from multinational companies, the directories of the Hungarian Chamber of Commerce and local authorities. By means of the standardised questionnaire the 2005 CRANET database received data and comments related to the policies and practices of organisations in the fields of staffing, employment and human resource management from 32 countries, including Hungary for the first time. Fifty-nine Hungarian organisations completed and returned their questionnaires before the database was closed. However, the data from a further 38 organisations which returned the completed questionnaires later were also processed and these are analysed in this study. Therefore, the total supplemented in this way included 97 from Hungary (Farkas *et al.*, 2007).

Research was undertaken into various HRM fields: Strategy and HRM Strategy, Staffing, People Development, Pay and Benefits, Industrial Relations and HRM Information Systems. The majority of companies responding were from the medium-sized and large company category. Among those taking part, foreign-owned companies formed the majority. In relation to the high proportion of foreign companies we should note that foreign capital plays a very significant role in the Hungarian economy (Farkas *et al.*, 2007).

More than half of the respondents completing the questionnaire worked as HR managers.

The great majority of these entities were companies in the manufacturing (46.2 per cent) and service (39.8 per cent) sectors, whilst the remainder (14 per cent) were from the public administration sector (see Table 7.3). The majority of participants – in terms of headcount – came from medium-sized enterprises and large corporations;

Table 7.3 Percentage distribution of organisations in the Hungarian ($n = 97$) samples of the research project

Sector	Per cent	Number of employees	Per cent
Agriculture	0.0	<250	38.5
Manufacturing	46.2	251–1,000	34.4
Services	39.8	1,001–5,000	20.8
Other	14.0	5,001+	6.3
Total	**100.0**	**Total**	**100.0**

38.5 per cent of the companies employ fewer than 100 people, whilst more than two-thirds employ fewer than 1,000.

One of the main indicators of the importance of the HR function within an organisation is the ratio of labour costs to total costs, that is, the labour cost ratio. The average labour cost ratio of the Hungarian companies examined was 28 per cent.

The position of the head of the HR department in the organisational hierarchy is clearly indicative of the importance and role of the HR department in the organisation. The data of the Hungarian sample are, in this respect, somewhat below the average value of the 32 countries. Whilst the head of the HR department is a member of the board of directors or the senior management team in more than half (55 per cent) of the responding organisations in all of the countries surveyed in the sample, the corresponding rate in the Hungarian sample is slightly lower at 47 per cent.

The Hungarian respondents recruited their most senior HR managers in almost equal proportions externally (49 per cent) and internally (51 per cent) (see Table 7.4). With regard to the involvement of the person responsible for HR in developing the business

Table 7.4 The position and role of the HR function and the HR department of Hungarian companies

Country(ies)	Labour costs (per cent)	Head of HR on Board of Directors (per cent)	Head of HR recruited		Involvement of head of HR in strategy development (per cent)	Existence of strategies (per cent)	
			outside (per cent)	within (per cent)		Business	HR
Hungary	28	47	49	51	58	76	60

strategy of the organisation, and the existence of an HRM strategy, Hungarian HR practice belonged to the upper third of the mid-range group of the 32 countries. The majority of Hungarian respondents do develop an HRM strategy and nearly 60 per cent of these organisations involve the person responsible for personnel in this process; 76 per cent of the companies have formal strategies, and more than half also have a written HRM strategy. In more than half of the companies the HRM manager was involved in the development of the business strategy from the very early stages. These data correspond with the figures produced by the two earlier surveys.

Of the companies surveyed 92.8 per cent have an HR department. Seven per cent of the Hungarian organisations have no HR organisation or independent HR job positions. The average number of employees in the HR departments of nearly half (44 per cent) of the Hungarian responding organisations is between one and five. This is almost the same percentage as that (44.54 per cent) found in the organisations surveyed in all the countries which we examined (Farkas et al., 2007). The second most significant size category of HR departments comprises six to ten employees in both the total sample and that of Hungary, whilst the percentage of organisations with large HR departments also shows similar figures (16–17 per cent) in both the total and the Hungarian samples. The number of those working in HR in these organisations exceeds 20.

It is clear from the data in Table 7.5 that female employees predominate in HR jobs in the Hungarian sample. Nearly 35 per cent of the Hungarian organisations examined have no men working in their HR departments. The Hungarian sample indicates that HR is much more of a female profession in Hungary than in other countries.

A 'hard' feature of the HR department and the work undertaken there is the type of information system used to support departmental processes. When the question was posed 37 per cent of the Hungarian organisations said that they did not have a computerised HR information system, whilst 43 per cent had independent (stand-alone) systems and the remaining 20 per cent used an HR information system integrated into a wider management information system.

The decision-making authority of the HRM department in various human resource policy issues is usually not exclusive, and decisions are mainly made in agreement with line managers. Local practice also follows the patterns described in other

Table 7.5 Gender distribution in HR departments of Hungarian companies

Country(ies)	Gender distribution in HR		
	Male (per cent)	Female (per cent)	Total (per cent)
Hungary	21.5	78.5	100.0

CRANET surveys – that is, HRM is not disappearing, although line management has a rather dominant role (Brewster *et al.*, 2004). In line with other international data, the most dominant role of HRM in this sample can be seen in the field of labour relations.

Nearly half (48.9 per cent) of the respondents in Hungary claimed that they had increased the use of external service providers in the field of training and development in the past three years. The importance of external consultants has increased in the fields of benefits, redundancy, workforce reduction and outplacement and HR information systems to a smaller extent than in those of training and development, although something in the region of one-quarter of the respondents indicated that the rates were similar. The survey, however, also revealed that more than half of the organisations did not use external specialists in fields outside training and HR information systems.

The samples studied show a great similarity in training and development in that this is the HR function where external professional service providers have a strong presence everywhere. More than 85 per cent of the responding organisations in the Hungarian sample stated that they used the specialist services of training companies. External providers are also used by organisations (at a rate of some 78 per cent) when HR information systems are configured and developed (see Table 7.6).

Nearly half of the Hungarian and other East European organisations turn to external providers when developing, running and managing pay and benefits systems. In the payroll area, the difference from or the lag behind the frequency of use in the total sample is not significant (merely 5 percentage points) but it is more remarkable in the area of benefits (nearly 15 percentage points).

It was also observed that, whilst the organisations which had a large HR department had decreased the use of external providers, those with a small department had increasingly turned to such specialists, although the smallest organisations rarely or never use external providers.

Table 7.6 Use of external professional providers in Hungary (percentage of organisations)

Country(ies)	Use of external professional providers (per cent)					
	Payroll	*Benefits*	*Pensions*	*Training and development*	*Workforce reduction, outplacement*	*Human resource information systems (HRIS)*
Hungary	45.2	48.4	37.0	86.2	45.2	78.7

Staffing

Over the past three years the total number of full-time employees has decreased in 42.3 per cent of the respondent companies. The most frequent reason for this is internal reorganisation, layoffs and a fixed headcount.

The most frequently used resources and practices in workforce expansion, recruitment and selection were investigated according to staff categories, and so we shall present the results likewise. First of all, we will analyse *recruitment*:

- The firms participating in the survey mostly rely on internal resources when filling management positions. They will also use the services of recruitment agencies and headhunters in this situation. In the total sample, internal recruitment and headhunters account for 40 per cent and 30 per cent of the cases respectively. The utilisation of job advertisements is also notable (1/5). Hungarian respondents revealed that the use of headhunters was quite popular, whereas job advertisements were placed only in 9 per cent of cases.
- When sourcing professional and clerical employees organisations in all three samples turned to job advertisements. The other methods frequently used by organisations in the total sample – recruitment agencies and internal resources – also feature in the Hungarian sample, but their ranking is the opposite. Although the use of electronic recruitment is low – it does not exceed 6 per cent in any of the samples – it is still regarded as a valid practice.
- Manual workers are most often recruited through advertisements and in Hungary this practice approaches 50 per cent. Word of mouth is another important way of sourcing employees and ranks as the second or the third most frequently used method.

An analysis of the methods and techniques used (or avoided) in the selection procedure generated some further characteristic features (see Table 7.7):

- All the data show that special attention is paid to the selection of managers. On the one hand, this is clear from the fact that certain methods (e.g. assessment centres) are only used when filling management positions; on the other hand, selection decisions are made following the simultaneous use of various techniques.
- The data also indicate that selection decisions regarding manual workers are located at the opposite end of the scale of importance: such employees are usually selected by means of more simple and inexpensive methods.
- A common feature of the samples studied is that one form of interview almost certainly has a role in selection, but it is, at the very least, the flagship method among the most frequently used techniques.
- Application forms rank as the second or the third most important method in almost all of the staff sub-categories covered by our sample, although in Hungary only some 20 per cent of the organisations reported using them, irrespective of staff category.

Table 7.7 Selection methods for managerial, professional and manual staff categories in Hungary (per cent of organisations)

Selection methods	Employee groups		
	Managerial	Professional	Manual
Interview panel	70	64	31
One-to-one interviews	52	41	38
Application forms	19	19	19
Psychometric test	25	20	8
Assessment centre	11	5	0
Graphology	14	6	1
References	42	29	8

● Hungarian respondents do rely on references when filling management positions (42 per cent), but they rarely use them when selecting manual workers (8 per cent).

Only an insignificant proportion of the organisations have detailed action plans on how to handle disabled employees. Companies increasingly utilise employment forms which differ from those applying to normal full-time employment: the role played by overtime, temporary employment, part-time employment and multi-shift employment is constantly increasing. The demand for flexibility in employment and the increasing cost of employment are two major reasons given for this situation.

Performance management

On the basis of the data in the completed Hungarian questionnaires it can be asserted that performance appraisal systems were quite widely used in the year of the survey. They are, in fact, used by 80 per cent of the organisations responding when evaluating employees in management and professional positions. Moreover, nearly three-quarters of the organisations use them in respect of clerical workers also. The role of performance appraisal is the least significant in the manual worker category, with scarcely more than half of the organisations responding assessing manual workers by means of a formal appraisal system (see Table 7.8).

One further aspect of performance appraisal systems was investigated: which other HR fields both rely on and use information derived from appraisals? The answers provided in the questionnaire consisted of a simple Yes or No, as appropriate.

According to the data, appraisal results are most frquently considered (86–7 per cent) when planning training and development needs. In the Hungarian sample this is

Table 7.8 Assessment by means of a formal appraisal systems in Hungarian companies (per cent)

Country	Percentage of use of formal appraisal systems			
	Management	Professional staff	Clerical staff	Manual staff
Hungary	80.0	80.0	71.0	52.5

followed by career and pay determination, which have the same level of importance (77 per cent). The corresponding values in the total sample are 78 per cent and 72 per cent, respectively. HR planning and work organisation make up the last two places in the ranking order.

Training and development

The importance of training and development in the life of the organisations can be demonstrated through an analysis of the proportion of an organisation's annual payroll cost which is spent on training. As Table 7.9 shows, the average of these training cost ratios in the sample amounts to 3.54 per cent.

The time spent in training is an indicator which can very effectively reflect the importance of training. When we examine the number of days spent in training by staff category, we note that, in Eastern Europe the training provided for managers and professional employees is longer than that given to manual workers. Managers spend the most time in training, followed by professional and clerical employees, and, finally, by manual workers (see Table 7.10).

Methods used in career development

In the Hungarian sample the methods most frequently used in managerial career development are participation in project team work, involvement in

Table 7.9 Proportion of annual payroll spent on training in Hungarian companies

Cost ratio (per cent)	Frequency
<1	24
1.01–2	30
2.01–4	28
4.01–6	11
6.01–	7

Table 7.10 Number of training days per year in Hungarian companies

Country	Number of training days per year			
	Management	*Professional staff*	*Clerical staff*	*Manual staff*
Hungary	5.9	6.2	3.7	4.3

cross-organisational tasks and other special tasks to stimulate learning. Two other methods (preparing formal career and succession plans) were marked in our sample, even if their importance is not especially significant (some 15 per cent). The three most commonly employed career development methods in non-managerial staff categories are the same as those in the managerial category, but they are used to a smaller extent.

Trade union and employee communication

Since 1989 the high numbers of union membership have declined by more than 50 per cent. In the Hungarian CRANET sample the level of employee involvement in trade unions is relatively high when compared to samples recorded earlier (1997–2001). This is partly due to the participation in our surveys of several large companies still in local ownership. Nearly 70 per cent of the employees of the companies participating in the survey are trade union members, and 87.5 per cent of the employers consider trade unions as a forum for negotiation.

Compared to international data we can see that the role of employee communication is increasing both in Hungary and abroad (Brewster *et al.*, 2004). A significant proportion of the companies inform all employee levels on job organisation issues, but formal communication on business strategy and financial performance is usually targeted only at managers. Both communication directed to employees and employee opinions provided in an electronic format show a growth trend.

THE FUTURE OF HRM IN HUNGARY

Change in Hungary has been rapid and remarkable. Within a relatively short period of time – slightly over a decade – the country has seen sweeping changes in the political, legal, social and economic systems. Accompanying those changes has been a surprisingly rapid development of the human resource infrastructure within those Hungarian businesses which were surveyed during this period. Policies and systems were developed and/or updated, and in many firms the human resource function evolved from an underdeveloped set of activities to the role of strategic player within an astonishingly short period of time.

The increasing focus on HR systems and strategy suggests a bright future for HR in Hungary in future years. Both past actions and future plans are generally consistent with sound HR practices, and, in fact, many of the practices reported mirror or even surpass those found in a number of Western companies. Undoubtedly, strategy-oriented HRM gained ground in Hungary.

What is not known from the existing data is the degree to which there is serious substance in Hungarian HR practices. Most of the basic HR systems (grading, performance evaluation, bonus, etc.) have been introduced by the companies operating in Hungary. The Hungarian motivation system moved in the direction of US practice, which tolerates greater differences in the competitive sphere. Specifically, the data show the presence of a variety of HR systems and activities, but they do not reveal the details of these HR components. Future research should focus on better documentation, on a better understanding of the details within these systems and on identifying areas for continued growth and continuous improvement.

HRM departments have not lost ground in Hungary, and line management has not taken over HR responsibilities. On the contrary, larger HR departments have rearranged and centralised decision-making and modification functions.

Observations are possible in respect of two areas of HR and provide an example of the previous point. Training and development in Hungarian companies appears to be quite insufficient to meet the demands of the competitive global marketplace. Additional investment in the knowledge and capabilities of employees is necessary and could be expected to yield improved business results.

Performance management appears to represent another area for improvement. Whilst many companies report that they have performance management systems, the small amount of money invested in training and development suggests that these performance management systems might not yet be complete. An effective performance management system depends on a great deal of expertise and business shrewdness by all managers and supervisors within the company, and such competency in performance management can be expected to require a substantial investment of time and money in training and developing these officials fully to assume their roles as performance managers. No set of policies – regardless of how well crafted – can obscure the need for well-trained, skilled managers to manage the performance of their employees.

Pay and benefits continue to lag behind Western counterparts. This practice could lead to a 'brain drain' if it persists. Particularly with regard to strategically vital employees (at all levels), pay must become competitive with rates offered in other European countries to avoid the loss of some key employees to organisations outside Hungary.

Consulting is widely used in this area. The reason for this is that, for several decades, this field was kept very much in the background, and today there is still a need for additional services in this profession (Gross *et al.*, 2003). Computer support and integration of Hungarian HRM is still lagging behind the practice of Western countries.

Outsourcing in Hungary is still in an immature phase, although it is making rapid progress.

HRM activities in an international brick manufacturer[2]

Wienerberger Bricks Plc (Wienerberger Téglaipari Rt) is the largest manufacturing company in the Hungarian building-materials industry and is the market leader in the field of brick manufacture. The firm achieved uninterrupted dynamic growth between 1990 and 2004, and in this case study we shall sum up the life-cycle stages which the company underwent – together with the development of its structure, HR management and the culture of the organisation based upon the business policy measures introduced. Wienerberger Bricks Plc was founded in 1990. The firm is the Hungarian subsidiary of the Wienerberger Group (Wienerberger AG), whose headquarters are in Vienna. The group has over 11,000 employees and 218 plants in 23 countries and ranks first in Europe in the production of bricks and clay pipes.

Wienerberger is the largest building-materials producing company in Hungary and market leader in the field of brick production. Its most important product is the 'Porotherm' Brick System and from the several elements of the system a complete house can be built. The company also produces the 'Profipanel' ceiling-panel system, and ceramics-coated beams. 'Terca' facing bricks are mostly imported into Hungary, but exports also play a fairly important role in the life of the firm. Besides the actual production, the company sells its products to distributors and provides its clients with technical support.

Its headquarters are in Budapest, and currently the company has 15 production sites in the country, covering the whole of Hungary.

Wienerberger Bricks has undergone clear life-cycle stages since its establishment, i.e. between 1990 and 2004, and in the following pages we shall describe the development path of the company based upon the changes in structural features, human resource management and organisational culture – starting with the business policy measures introduced.

Phase 1 (1990–9): establishment and consolidation of market foundations

Business policy and strategy

Wienerberger Bricks plc was founded in 1990 by the Wienerberger group of Vienna with the strategic objective of introducing its technology and products to the whole of Eastern Central Europe. The management principles and philosophy of the parent company were characterised by a strict formalisation of the business strategy of its subsidiary. By 1999, the company had acquired eight plants through privatisation and had built one as a further investment. Business strategy focused on investing in high-quality production, in the introduction of production as well as sales know-how and the rationalisation of the labour force. (See Table 7.11.)

continued

Table 7.11 The main development stages of Wienberger Bricks Plc, 1990–2004

Phase 1 (1990–9)	*Phase 2 (2000–3)*	*Phase 3 (today and the near future)*
Establishment of the Hungarian subsidiary	Dynamic growth	Exploitation of maturity
Consolidation of market foundations	Achievement and consolidation of market leader position	Initiation of new innovation cycle

Structural features

In this development stage, the primary division of labour was based upon the functional principle and the division of authority was characterised by a high degree of centralisation. Coordination was mainly achieved by technocratic means. The configuration of the company followed the structural principles of a functional organisation, and the organisation was led by a general manager appointed by the parent company. The main functional units consisted of production, sales and finance departments, which were managed by directors. Nationwide, the plants – as well as functions such as central IT, marketing, product development, quality management and procurement – were integrated into a functional hierarchy.

Human resource management

Personnel tasks mainly consisted of administrative duties connected to human resources, and certain elements of personnel management appeared merely as secondary features. The operative tasks related to these (recruitment, organising training and professional education and the establishment of labour relations) were carried out by the directors of the functional departments of the organisation on an ad hoc basis.

Organisational culture

After the change of regime, the process of adapting to the requirements of foreign capital investors and the new market conditions was supported by the development of a technocratic role culture. For the employees of the subsidiary, following the stringent rules of the parent company and abiding by precisely set, basic principles marked the path to follow, defined the framework of independence and provided the foundations of the sense of security connected to expected market success. At this stage, the management had a rule- and objective-oriented approach. The unique value-system of the company was gradually established in the organisation and market success increased the self-confidence of employees. For those working at the centre, favourable conditions for consolidating socialisation and loyalty to the organisation were created, a new head office for the company was built, a high-quality infrastructure was established, and regular skills development and team-building training was held.

Headcount

By end-1999 the staff at the eight plants and at central management headquarters totalled 356 (53 at head office and 303 working in the plants).

Phase 2 (2000–4): dynamic growth and consolidation of market leader position

Business policy and strategy

In 2000, a merger was carried out with Balaton Bricks Ltd and with Transdanubia Brick Factories Ltd, thus increasing the number of factories to 14. At this point the SAP management system was introduced on a group-wide basis, resulting in the overall restructuring of the IT systems. The significant enhancement of production capacity required the sales network to be developed, and this in turn led to the expansion and specialisation of customer service and technical support units. Further investment in expansion was made in the factories, and, as a result of greenfield investment, a ceiling-panel plant was built in Ócsa, and the company launched its new product. The product range was further extended with the importation of facing-bricks, whilst, at the same time, exports became more important, all of which made it necessary to establish a logistics base in the eastern region. In the production units themselves, quality management and environmental management systems were introduced. The company then founded Wienerberger Houses Ltd, which specialises in planning, building and selling complete houses made of bricks and clay-tile roofing. The activities of this unit were mainly focused on the Budapest agglomeration, and in 2004 this unit was absorbed into Wienerberger Bricks plc.

Structural features

The increasing volume and complexity of corporate activities were accompanied by the emergence of multidimensionality in the division of labour within the organisation, with reference to the functions, products and regions alike. The coordination tools became more specialised and, in addition to the technocratic methods, the establishment of horizontal relations also became important, although the vertical hierarchy still retained its dominant position. The configuration of the organisation also changed and, at the beginning, was rather unstable, owing to the rapid expansion of the labour force. Certain strategic groups became more specialised and started to grow, and their leaders were promoted to middle management in the company. Even though they were strictly controlled by senior management at the beginning, they continued to gain more and more independence over time. The basic structure of the company still bore the

continued

features of a functional organisation, but, in certain fields, a matrix structure appeared together as project teams were formed to perform periodic tasks.

Human resource management

The basic principle of Wienerberger group strategy is that central human resource management only involves the senior management and key experts of the companies within the group, and only their career management is affected. As a consequence, the subsidiaries manage their human resource activities at all other levels in a decentralised way, always taking their own regional peculiarities into consideration. The elaboration of these is delegated from group headquarters to the senior management of the subsidiaries, and so the human resource experts in the subsidiaries are not given senior management positions by the parent company. As a result of this, human policy cannot be directly linked to strategic planning, but is based upon the systematic management of operative tasks in a 'bottom-up' manner. At the end of 1999, when it was obvious that the business policy changes in the company also necessitated significant human resource development, the management decided to hire a human resource consultant to perform certain operational tasks. The HR consultant was integrated into the organisation as a member of staff, under the line-supervision of the finance director of the company. His authority mainly involved carrying out operational tasks related to employees belonging to head office and elaborating a structural framework for certain sub-systems of the human resource activities. The primary objective of this was to shift these activities (still firmly entrenched at the level of personnel administration towards personnel management. From then on, the management of the company's human resource activities involved two levels of management: human resource planning, job analysis, design and evaluation as well as management of the compensation system and industrial relations, which remained in the hands of senior management. The HR consultant, on the other hand, was authorised to elaborate sub-systems for recruitment, selection, performance evaluation and occupational health. In relation to training and development, career management and organisational communication development, the HR consultant was given an advisory role alongside senior management. At this stage, the consolidation of recruitment policy was of strategic importance, and by end-2002 61 new white-collar employees (mainly with a higher education background) were added to the Wienerberger head office staff of 53 (1999 figure). Human resource development on this scale can only be successful in any organisation provided that the recruitment policy is based upon mature consideration. In the Wienerberger case, the majority of successful candidates were recruited externally and not through internal staff transfers. Fluctuation has clearly remained low until now and the socialisation of most new employees has been both successful and rapid. The other subsystem elaborated by the HR consultant was performance evaluation. The establishment of theoretical foundations as well as a solid practice of performance evaluation was motivated, in the first place, by two urgent demands. On the one hand, the time had come to map and define the competency demands of the organisation, whilst, on the other hand, several phenomena indicated that internal communication, in particular the willingness to give feedback, was inadequate. The repertoire of competencies considered in the course of performance evaluation was established and defined by the HR consultant, and these were then both specifically detailed and weighted as individual jobs by management. Competencies were not differentiated as general and key competencies: their significance within the organisation (as well as in the individual functions) was expressed purely by their weighting. In the early days there was strong resistance to performance evaluation within the company, but this has, in fact, been used more extensively by the management since then.

The subsystems of recruitment and performance evaluation were then organised on a bottom-up basis with the competency approach being the link between the two, although the other subsystems of human resource management have not as yet been organised into a single system. The activities belonging to these fields are currently carried out as operational tasks.

Organisational culture

Owing to the rapid increase in employee numbers in the company, it was crucial to keep stable core values as well as to define and emphasise the identity and, above all, the strengths of the company. The socialisation of the successful candidates was limited, in the first place, to their functional departments, but their loyalty was also linked to their immediate surroundings, and so role culture was further reinforced. Horizontal relations remained loose, whilst task culture only emerged in those fields which required matrix relations. At first, the recruitment wave caused generational conflicts since the new employees had, for the most part, graduated only a few years earlier and had achieved middle-management positions after relatively brief periods of professional training. Senior management, therefore, controlled middle management quite strongly at first, but the latter became much more independent as time passed. The company consolidated its market leader position in its external environment, and, in parallel, the rule- and objective-oriented culture of the company gradually shifted towards a supportive culture with an internal focus. Extensive employee training acquired notable value and, although the compensation system was not formally transformed into a 'cafeteria plan', supportive tailor-made training was turned into an important motivational tool. Higher education and postgraduate training, language courses, IT and other specialised professional training, as well as skills development and training in sport and recreation were available regularly and were available for employees on a large scale. The management of the company hired an external public opinion pollster to carry out an annual internal satisfaction survey, and the results were then announced to the employees. An in-depth analysis of the findings of this research work goes beyond the framework of the present summary, but it must be said (as an indication of the level of acceptance of the survey) that the majority of employees participated in filling in the (anonymous) questionnaires. They clearly value the security of belonging to a market leader with a solid capital base – and this is a dominant

continued

factor in their lives amid the uncertain economic circumstances of our time. On the other hand, the information flow within the company and the immaturity of the efforts to improve it were strongly criticised. The shortcomings were, in fact, principally due to the wish to avoid possible conflicts and to postpone resolving problems that remained unresolved.

One of the main positive features of the organisational culture of Wienerberger Bricks Plc is that several events, formal and informal programmes, were integrated into the everyday life of the company and these contributed to relaxed, even friendly, relationships amongst employees.

Headcount

The staff of the fifteen production units and of central management totalled 760 at the end of 2003 (100 people at head office and 660 working in the plants).

Phase 3 (since 2004): exploitation of maturity and initiation of new innovation cycle

Business policy and strategy

The investors continue to invest in expansion of the production units and, as a further greenfield investment, the company has built a new brick factory in Tiszavasvári. The market progress of the ceiling-panel business and of Wienerberger Houses is the main focus of the company, and the infrastructure and sponsorship activities are being enhanced. One task of particular significance is the smooth introduction of the new rules and standards resulting from EU accession.

Structural changes

The division of labour will remain multi-dimensional, and the decision-making authority will become less centralised. Delegation will also come to dominate in the vertical hierarchy. The raison d'être of matrix structures and project teams will multiply within the organisation. Among coordination tools, monitoring, process regulation and person-oriented coordination instruments are the most important. The configuration of the company will basically retain its functional features, but, nonetheless, project teams are planned to gain further significance in the future.

Plans for human resource development and cultural change

The objective of human resource policy is to recruit, motivate, train and retain employees who have the capability and determination needed to sustain the market leader role of the company as well as innovative energy to search for new approaches. Senior management, therefore, now considers career management to be the HR sub-system of strategic importance. It has also become necessary to rethink the unique competency system of the company. In 2005, the competency repertoire for performance evaluation was modified and key competencies to be taken into account when evaluating the leader of any group were defined as follows: (1) ability to plan and think strategically, (2) decision-making skills, (3) organising talent, (4) leadership and motivation of subordinates, (5) creativity and innovation skills. A new competency vocabulary has also been compiled, since the understanding of certain terms has changed as circumstances have changed. Senior management will shortly select those talented and motivated employees (at head office as well as within the production units) who are to take part in the special training programme intended to give potentially key people of the future the appropriate management and professional schooling. The success of career management obviously postulates the rapid unification of the other human resource sub-systems into a single framework, the development of organic relations between them as well as an integrated human resource management system. The management of the company will concentrate on the creation of prerequisites for a future, innovation-oriented organisational culture, and it therefore took the first steps to reorganise training and development and labour relations as well as the compensation system in 2005.

NOTES

1   We would like to thank the following individuals for their valuable help and suggestions in the preparation of this chapter: Dr Ferenc Farkas, Dr Martonne Karoliny and C. S. Chadwick of the University of Pécs, Hungary; Norbert F. Elbert, Allen Engle and Mike Roberson of Eastern Kentucky University (USA); and Andrew Gross of Cleveland State University (USA).
2   Source: Takats, 2006.

REFERENCES AND FURTHER READING

Antal, L. (2004). *Can Growth Be Maintained?* (in Hungarian). Budapest: Economic Review Foundation.

Arva, L. and Dichazi, B. (2006). *Globalisation and Foreign Investment in Hungary* (in Hungarian). Budapest: Kariosz Publishing Co.

Bakacsi, Gy., Takács, S., Karácsony, A. and Imre, A. (2002). The East European Cluster: Tradition and Transition. *Journal of World Business*, 37: 69–80.

Bangert, D. and Poór, J. (1995). 'Human Resource Management under Change in Hungary'. In Shenkar, O. (ed.) *Global Aspect of Human Resource Management*. Boston: Irwin.

BBJ (2007). 'Economic Growth Slows to 11 Year Low of 1.4 per cent'. *Budapest Business Journal,* 14 August.

Berki, E. (2004). 'Pay, Compensation and Salary Convergence in Accession Countries' (in Hungarian). *Hungarian Labour Review*, 9: 23–29; 10: 28–32.

Brewster, C., Mayrhofer, W. and Morley, M. (eds) (2004). *Human Resource Management in Europe: Evidence of Convergence?* Oxford: Elsevier Butterworth-Heinemann Publishers.

Dowling, P. J. and Welch, D. E. (2004). *International Human Resource Management*. Mason: Thomson–South Western.

Farkas, F. (2005). *Change Management* (in Hungarian). Budapest: KJK-Kerszöv Publishing House.

Farkas, F., and Karoliny, Mné. and Poór, J. (2007). *Human Resource Management in Hungary in the Light of East European and Global Comparison*. Faculty of Economics and Business University Pécs, Working Paper Series.

Hellriegel, D., S., Locum, J. W. and Woodman, R. W. (1998). *Organisational Behaviour*. Cincinnati: Thomson–South Western.

Hethy, L. and Mako, Cs. (1972). *Labour Behaviours and Companies* (in Hungarian). Budapest: Academia Publishing.

Karoliny, Mné., Farkas, F., László, Gy. and Poór, J. (2003). *Human Resource Management* (in Hungarian). Budapest: Közgazdasági és Jogi Kerszöv Publishing.

Karoliny, Mné., Lévai, Z. and Poór, J. (2005). *HRM in the Public Sector* (in Hungarian). Budapest: Szokratesz Publishing.

Kornai, J. (1980). *Economics of Shortage*. Amsterdam: North Holland.

Kovari, Gy. (1995). *Development of Human Resources* (In Hungarian). Budapest: Szokratesz Publishing.

Laszlo, Gy. (1995). *Labour Market Handbook* (in Hungarian). Pécs: University Publishing.

Mercer (2005). *Compensation and Benefit Study*. Budapest: Mercer Human Resource Consulting.

OECD (2007). *Economic Survey of Hungary 2007*. Policy Brief, May.

Palánkai T. (2004). *Economics of the EU Economy* (in Hungarian). Budapest: Aula Publishing Co.

Pearce, J. L. (1991). 'From Socialism to Capitalism: The Effects of Hungarian Human Resource Practices'. *Academy of Management Executive*, 5: 75–88.

Peng, M. W. (2006). *Global Strategy*. Mason: Thomson–South Western.

Pitti, Z. (2007). *Foreign Investment from the EU and from Outside the EU* (in Hungarian) Budapest: Világgazdasági Kutatóintézet-CEUUNS.

Poór, J. and Engle, A. (2005). 'From Traditional Payroll to Modern Compensation Management: Findings From Central and Eastern Europe'. *International Compensation and Benefit*, December: 3–8.

Poór J. and Roberson, M. (2003). 'Global Development. Effectiveness of Human Resource Management in Hungarian Companies' (in Hungarian). *Hungarian Management Review*, 1: 13–19.

Szabó, J. (2005). 'HR in Local, Regional and Global Roles' (in Hungarian). National HR Conference, Balatonfüred (Hungary), 3–5 May.

Szegedi, E. (2007). Pensions in Transition in the Light of Local and Global Perspectives (consulting report). Budapest: Mercer.

Takats, J. (2006). 'HRM Activities at an International Brick Manufacturer'. In Poór, J. *HR in Transition – Internationalisation in HRM* (in Hungarian). Budapest: MMPC Publishing.

UNCTAD (2005). World Investment Report, 2005: Transnational Corporations and Export Competitiveness. Geneva: United Nations.

World Bank (2005). *Enhancing Job Opportunities in Eastern Europe and the Former Soviet Union*. Washington: World Bank.

8 Managing human resources in Slovenia

IVAN SVETLIK

INTRODUCTION

The character and development of HRM in Slovenia in some respects differs from those in the other new member states. This is primarily because of different starting points and different social and economic backgrounds in Slovenia at the beginning of the transition process in comparison to the other transition countries. In Slovenia, as one of the republics of the former Yugoslavia, the level of economic development was relatively high. The exchange of goods and other forms of cooperation with Western economies were better than with Eastern ones. The planned economy was complemented by market forces, including limited functioning of the labour market. The management of enterprises and other organisations was rather decentralised, with a significant proportion of employees self-managed. The interference of politics in organisations' management was relatively weak except for the strategic economic and personnel decisions of large and medium-sized enterprises. This is why the HRM function started to develop rather early. It helped restructure the economic and other organisations rather than being the result of restructuring. However, during the transition period further steps in its development have been made (Svetlik *et al.*, 2007). One could say that HRM has contributed to the soft and less painful transformation of Slovenian organisations and has preserved some of the achievements of self-management. In this activity it has often found itself on the side of relatively strong trade unions that could be considered the main force against radical change. We elaborate on this story in the following paragraphs.

THE TRANSITION PROCESS

Slovenia belonged to the multi-ethnic state of Yugoslavia, which was known for its refusal of the Eastern bloc type of communism. The regime declared itself socialist. It was characterised by decentralisation and self-management as two main principles of internal organisation, and by relatively high openness towards economic and political cooperation in international relations. It succeeded in industrialising the country and in generating a quick economic growth in the first three decades after World War II. However, it failed to manage a shift from extensive growth based on labour intensive production to development generated by the introduction of new technologies, utilisation of highly skilled labour, innovation and productivity. Therefore in the 1980s Yugoslavia started to sink in a deep economic crisis characterised by increasing foreign debt, losses in industry, redundancies, falling wages and unemployment. Economic growth was a strong integrative element, a kind of glue that kept the culturally, politically and economically highly diversified country together. When it ceased, political tensions occurred and got ever stronger (see, e.g., Phillips and Ferfila, 1992; Glenny, 1992; Zimmermann, 1996; Djokić, 2003).

Long-lasting political debates between the representatives of six Yugoslav republics, Bosnia and Herzegovina, Croatia, Macedonia, Montenegro, Serbia and Slovenia, and two autonomous regions, Kosovo and Vojvodina, which went on in the second half of the 1980s, did not lead to a viable compromise. To the contrary, they revealed increasing differences in views about the future. In Slovenia especially civil society movements exerted increasing pressure on the political elite to democratise social and political life and to rely less on central state regulation of the economy and more on market forces. Liberal Party leaders found no better option and a shift to democracy became only a question of time and method. Since Slovenian leaders could not convince the others in Yugoslavia to support these changes and to give up the idea of centralisation of the country, they decided to break away.

During 1990–1 preparatory activities, such as a referendum on independence, constitutional and legal provisions and free elections, were carried out. On 26 June 1991 independence was declared. A ten-day war with the Yugoslav army followed until the intervention of the EU calmed the conflict. The way to real independence was paved. However, because of the loss of Yugoslav markets, the crisis in the Eastern bloc and some reluctance in the international community to recognise a new country, the Slovenian economy sank into even deeper crisis than before. It reached the bottom in 1993 when the gross domestic product (GDP) fell by about one-quarter and in a labour force survey unemployment reached 10 per cent. In this period international recognition was also achieved (see, e.g., Fink-Hafner and Robbins, 1997; Ferfila and Phillips, 2000; Mrak et al., 2004).

The period between 1993 and 2004 was characterised by a stepwise reconstruction of social and political institutions. Among them a system of social partnership has been established. It provided for effective negotiation between strong trade unions and other partners and for social peace. It also prevented the radical transformation that was proposed by some International Monetary Fund (IMF) and World Bank advisors, such as Sachs, at the beginning of transition. Ineffective economic units were gradually closed down or modernised. New markets were found, predominantly in the EU, to which two-thirds of Slovenian exports now goes. Large enterprises from the socialist period have split into smaller ones, service units have been outsourced and new entrepreneurs have entered the scene. The number of economic units has increased from fewer than 20,000 before the transition to over 120,000. The economy has been increasingly privatised, with a significant share given to the citizens, which has also contributed to social peace. Steady economic growth of about 4.1 per cent has been achieved. In May 2004 Slovenia joined NATO and the EU, and in January 2007 it entered the euro. Its GDP per capita in 2006 was €14,811 and 56.4 per cent of GDP was exported (*Konjunkturna gibanja*, 2007). Slovenia has become known for its soft and successful model of transition.

In Autumn 2004 the domination of a centre-left political coalition of more than a decade ended. The new centre-right government started with radical criticism of a so-called gradualist approach. It prepared a reform programme strongly inspired by neo-liberal ideas. Its implementation started with the replacement of chief executive directors in all the public institutions and industrial organisations where the state had maintained a majority share. Social partners have been ignored whenever and wherever possible. This provoked a severe workers' protest in Autumn 2005 and more coordinated action by different trade unions. Developments in 2006 and 2007 showed a decreasing government enthusiasm for the proposed reforms. The idea of a uniform tax rate has been dropped. In the new labour legislation agreed upon between social partners the majority of existing workers' rights have been preserved. Social partners agreed on a new wage model allowing for the raising of wages depending on inflation and productivity.

THE CONTEXT OF HUMAN RESOURCE MANAGEMENT

The transition process brought about several changes in the economic, social and political systems that create the context in which HRM has been practised. However, in Slovenia the transformation of the main societal institutions has been gradual. This applies to stakeholders' organisations, labour market institutions and legislation.

The scene of trade unions has shifted from a monolith to a plural one. In the socialist period there was only one confederation of branch organised trade unions substantially influenced by the Communist Party. New trade union organisations appeared before the change of political institutions and were one of the important agents of opposition and transformation. Apart from some smaller ones, six main trade union confederations have been established. Among them the strongest is the old, but transformed, Association of Free Trade Unions of Slovenia (Stanojević, 2003). New trade unions started their activity by opposing the old ones. The political affiliation of both old and new was obvious at the beginning of transition. Gradually they started to cooperate, especially when some important workers' issues were on the agenda. Concerted action against radical neo-liberal reforms is only one of the recent cases. Apart from common interests, the democratisation of the old trade unions has also contributed to cooperation.

Unlike in the other post-communist countries trade unions in Slovenia have not lost much of their power. After the introduction of free membership the number of unionised workers is gradually falling. However, about 40 per cent still pay a membership fee. According to some research (CRANET, 2001, 2004) their influence is even increasing. There could be several explanations for this.

The most plausible is a historical or path-dependency one. In spite of the dismantling of the self-management system, the core of which was workers' participation in different forms, the positive valuation of workers' participation and expectations that organisations should enable employees to have a certain influence have not disappeared. Since several bodies of workers' representation in organisations have been removed, such as workers' assemblies, work councils, commissions for employment, remuneration, social standards, etc., employees turned to those which remained, i.e. to trade unions.

Second, the reintroduction of capitalism has been associated with increasing flexibility of employment and pressures to increase productivity. Several new entrepreneurs, being driven by the motive of 'primary accumulation', and having experiences with 'time-consuming and useless discussions of self-management bodies', use a rather authoritarian style of management. They often do not see the potential of participative management and deeper involvement of their employees in production and business issues. They prefer temporary employment and contractual work to permanent employment. In addition, small organisations are not obliged to put into practice as many participative forms as large ones are. Therefore employees seek ways to compensate for increasing insecurity and dependency.

Third, the position of trade unions has not been weakened by legislation. On the contrary, they have got more power through their representation in the central national bargaining body, the Socio-Economic Council. The law on workers' participation was accepted at the beginning of the 1990s. This was to compensate for the 'lost self-management'. In fact it gave more power to trade unions and made other workers' representative bodies weaker or optional.

In spite of the intention of the self-management system to promote the direct participation of workers, it remained undeveloped, especially in workplaces. The accent was on several representative bodies. When these bodies were removed indirect democracy via trade unions' representation strengthened, while direct participation remained undeveloped as it was before. In certain respects there has been not only a reintroduction of capitalism but also a retraditionalisation of industrial relations (Stanojević, 2002). This has been most visible in terms of traditional topics addressed by trade unions, such as wages and working conditions. Much less attention has been paid to modern development-focused issues, such as the introduction of new technologies, training, employability and competence development.

A shift from self-management to traditional industrial relations has diminished the participation and influence of employees in HRM. The issues of job analysis and job design, employment, remuneration, education and training, promotion, working conditions and so on, previously dealt with by workers' representative bodies, have only partially been put on the agenda of trade unions. HRM professionals and line managers have had to take greater responsibility for them. If this contributed to the higher professionalism of HRM, professionals and line managers lost an important partner, which makes change management more demanding.

Employers in Slovenia have been represented by various chambers, such as the Chamber of Economy, the Chamber of Crafts, the Agricultural Chamber and some professional ones. The model of chambers was a Central European one using compulsory membership and financial contributions (Pilgrim and Meier, 1995). However, in 2006 this model was changed by a new Law on the Chamber of Economy, where membership has been made optional. Some organisations left the Chamber of Economy and others formed new ones, e.g. the Chamber of Commerce. In spite of such a situation employers seem to be well represented by the chambers. Chief executives of the largest companies are on the managing boards. They have taken an active part in the nationwide negotiations with trade unions, especially in the Socio-Economic Council. They make official statements on national economic and social issues and openly demand changes, such as increasing flexibility of employment and labour relations, reduction of workers' rights on paid breaks during working time, on compensation of travelling costs to and from work and so on. This is perhaps the main reason why newly founded employers' organisations remain weak.

The other reason for weak employers' organisations could be gradual structural change and privatisation. In the first transition years employers had to seek new markets, new and better products and higher productivity. They needed social peace. Even more, due to the self-management heritage they could count on workers' loyalty and efforts to overcome the crisis years. This was demonstrated in several companies, where workers continued to work without protest even though they were not paid for several consecutive months. Perhaps the most important factor was privatisation carried out in a rather liberal way. Top managers were remunerated by and were buying shares of the managed companies. Some of them established their own off-shoot firms, which were selling and buying products for the main ones, or deliberately led firms into the red so that they would go bankrupt and could be bought back at a low price, etc. (Žnidaršič, 1994). For these operations, which in principle differ from one case to another, management needed social peace and individual ideas and action. Common management and employers' interests were of secondary importance.

Throughout the 1990s and up to 2004 the state was governed by more or less the same centre-left coalition. It deliberately refused a shock therapy for economic and social restructuring and adopted a gradualist approach. As a consequence the change in the economic, social and political institutions was stepwise, and government played a mediation role taking into account the interests and power of the other social partners. Consecutive social agreements provided for social peace in terms of a low strike rate (Stanojević and Vrhovec, 2001) and contributed to steady economic growth.

The change of government in 2004 caused a shift from centre-left to centre-right. The new government has addressed the criticism of gradualism, aiming at faster economic growth. It has been inspired by neo-liberal ideas including a weaker accent on social partnership and social issues. This has provoked a strong reaction by trade unions and several civil society groups and organisations. Therefore a quick introduction of a radical reform programme is less and less likely.

Stepwise privatisation leads to a rather slow withdrawal of the state from the business sector and lower professionalism than desired in the public sector (Kohont, 2006). As a consequence the influence of coalition parties on HRM in several public organisations and enterprises remains high. In spite of the declared professionalism the new government replaced the majority of chief executives in health, education, employment and other public organisations. Irrespective of the economic performance all chief executives of larger companies in which the state (via its funds) has the majority share have also been replaced. This sets certain limits to HRM professionalism and places these organisations behind the others in terms of an HRM strategic role and the implementation of its expertise.

In Slovenia a limited labour market existed before the transition. There was competition for jobs, which in reality were not guaranteed to everybody in spite of constitutionally guaranteed work. Therefore young school leavers increasingly registered with employment offices during the 1980s. However, when a person found a job they were not likely to lose it except for misbehaviour. The consequence was rather high hidden unemployment and low productivity (Svetlik, 1992). When new legislation enabled lay-offs for economic reasons the registered unemployment rate increased from 2.2 per cent in 1989 to 14.4 per cent in 1993. Along with economic growth since then, registered unemployment was falling slowly and reached 9.4 per cent in 2006 (ESS, 2006).

A specific feature of unemployment in Slovenia is a large difference between the registered and labour force survey unemployment rates. The latter has never exceeded 10 per cent and fell to 6 per cent in 2006 (ESS, 2006). This indicates that a significant share of the labour force has been active in the informal economy, which serves as a buffer against unemployment. For HRM a paradoxical situation has been created in terms of great difficulties in recruiting workers for less attractive jobs, for example, in the construction industry and public utilities, in spite of the fact that more than 40 per cent of the registered unemployed do not have vocational qualifications.

Various sources (Stare et al., 2006; ESS, 2006; Bevc et al., 2006) indicate that other structural inconsistencies also persist in the labour market. Newly created jobs demand at least vocational qualifications and increasingly also post-secondary education. While nearly 100 per cent of the younger generation have been enrolled in secondary education and more than 60 per cent continue to the post-secondary level (RNPVS, 2006), the education and training of the existing labour force is not satisfactory. Nearly 20 per cent of workers are without vocational qualifications, and since they are older it is difficult to retrain them. The number of experienced workers with post-secondary education is not sufficient either. Only about 18 per cent of the labour force has post-secondary education, while in the majority of EU countries this figure is above 25 per cent (Bevc et al., 2006). Although younger generations increasingly go to school it has been estimated that their interest in general programmes and studying social sciences is too high in comparison with vocational education and training and with science and technology programmes. This creates occupational inconsistencies irrespective of the expected further growth of the service sector, in which currently about 55 per cent of labour is employed (Stare *et al.*, 2004), and where more graduates with general and social competencies are needed. Regional inconsistencies also persist. They are associated with low propensity to be regionally mobile and with enormous differences in the price of housing.

Structural inconsistencies have been addressed mainly by labour market policy. If in the first phase of transition passive measures such as early retirement were used, later on increasing emphasis has been given to active measures, among which training has been paid special attention. In addition there has been a permanent plea for higher flexibility in the labour market. Flexibility increases steadily in the forms of self-employment, contract work, fixed-term work and part-time work (Kanjuo and Ignjatovič, 2006). Although there has been a criticism of legislation as too rigid, the fact is that several possibilities already given are not being used. This could be explained by historical factors. Workers who have experienced full-time jobs and have contracts of unlimited duration are not very keen on any form of numerical flexibility. For instance, it is difficult to expect full-time employees to start working part time and give up half of their income and social rights. As a consequence numerical labour market flexibility falls mainly on the shoulders of the younger generation (Svetlik and Ilič, 2006). Employers also do not offer part-time jobs because they do not have experience of them, except for workers with disabilities and health problems. Functional flexibility is increasing, however (Kopač and Trbanc, 2005).

At the beginning of transition a legislative framework for the functioning of the labour market was created. In addition to the then existing competition for new jobs to which first job seekers were exposed, redundancies and lay-offs of permanently employed workers have been introduced. The Law on Labour Relations and the Law on Employment and Unemployment Insurance have been amended several times and each amendment shifts some labour market risk from employers to employees. In other words employers are getting more freedom in hiring, managing and firing labour while workers are losing rights and benefits as unemployed and as employees, and feel increasing pressure to comply with employers' and labour offices' demands. One could say that labour legislation provides for increasing flexibility of employment and for tighter conditions for the registered unemployed. Recently this trend has been intensified by the so-called activation policy (Kopač, 2004), meaning that several measures have been used in order to make the registered unemployed actively seek jobs. Examples of such measures are employment plans specifically prepared for each unemployed person, an obligation for the registered unemployed to take less suitable jobs and to participate in various labour market programmes or to risk their unemployment benefits.

EU membership has not brought a radical change. Throughout the 1990s there was the accession period, which demanded change in social, political and economic institutions to fit in the '*acquis communautaire*'. The free flow of goods and capital accelerated structural and technological change. This is indicated by the increasing added value per employee, which went up from €21,300 in 2000 to €31,153 in 2006

(*Konjunkturna gibanja*, 2007). The free flow of services and labour has been postponed due to the restrictions set by the old EU member states, however. From the HRM perspective one could observe that EU membership and preparation for it have contributed to the new HRM practices brought into the country by foreign firms. As is shown later in Table 8.3, HRM services have been increasingly offered in the market either by the new private agencies or by foreign ones which have opened subsidiaries in Slovenia. There has been a visible change in the attractiveness of the job offers in the media. The inflow of labour to Slovenia is increasing. In 2006, 44,654 work permits were issued, which was 30 per cent more than in 2005. While migration from non-EU countries has been stable, additional workers are coming from the old and new member states. In 2006 there were 5,196 registered workers from the EU (ESS, 2006). International HRM has developed due to foreign firms coming to the country and Slovenian firms opening their units abroad (Svetlik and Alas, 2006).

TRENDS AND DEVELOPMENTS IN HUMAN RESOURCE MANAGEMENT PRACTICES

The nature of the HR function

At the beginning of transition HRM functions in Slovenian organisations were rather developed in comparative terms (Svetlik *et al.*, 2007). In all medium-sized and larger organisations one could find special personnel departments employing various kinds of professionals. They followed the practices of the developed world, introducing new methods of professional work. Special undergraduate and graduate programmes for the education of personnel professionals were in place at the universities, where research and publishing in this field was carried out. HR professionals had their nationwide professional association. However, HRM was adjusted to the planned economy and to more rigid and closed organisations.

In the late 1980s economic difficulties demanded that enterprises cut their costs. Many personnel activities were abolished or restricted (especially new jobs, in-company training and support for part-time study by employees). The personnel field remained highly regulated by legal norms that defined employment, redeployment, payment and training of employees. Neither the legal system nor personnel managers were prepared to face the redundancies that occurred in enterprises.

With independence and transition Slovenian enterprises had to restructure quickly and profoundly in order to find new and more demanding markets. Cost-efficiency in production had to be attained, the quality of products and services raised, old equipment sold, redundant workers laid-off, new technology introduced, etc. Enterprises started to outsource peripheral units and split into well-defined core business units. The role of personnel departments in this process was very demanding. First there were redundancies, including those in personnel departments.

Later on more attention was given to employee skills and competences. Personnel departments had to adapt to the new employment and social legislation and to the changing labour market. Special focus was put on the training and development of managers. According to CRANET (2001, 2004) the number of days spent on training was higher for managers than for any other group. Some larger organisations have established 'management academies' in order to select employees with the highest potential and to prepare them for managerial roles.

Zupan's research from that period showed that formal and informal personnel programmes and activities, such as the development of a personnel strategy, training and career planning, were working well. Major changes were seen in better defined and standardised processes of employee reduction, in the establishment of personnel information systems and in personnel strategy development (Zupan, 1999). It could be said that personnel strategy and the utilisation of professional personnel methods were developing the whole range of the personnel function.

In that period it would be difficult to find a general manager who would deny the importance of the personnel function. This was more difficult to demonstrate in practice, however. By the end of the 1990s the personnel management undergraduate programme at the Faculty of Social Sciences of Ljubljana University was complemented by a master's degree programme. Subjects in personnel management have been taught at several faculties of all universities and post-secondary private schools. New research in this field was undertaken and linked with international research networks, such as CRANET (2001, 2004). An increasing number of independent personnel management agencies offer a variety of services to other organisations. During the 1990s the Association for Personnel Management intensified its activities. For instance, two national HRM conferences have been organised every year. The field of personnel management has reached a high level of professionalism.

Since 1993 the Slovenian economy has been in the process of permanent restructuring characterised by labour saving measures and productivity growth, introduction of new technologies, penetration of global market niches, takeovers by foreign companies and by reorganisations in terms of outsourcing, slimming down organisations and making or joining bigger corporations' networks. Personnel management has followed the course of change and assisted it from its perspective. New professional methods have been introduced and professional managers have been involved in the internationalisation of business activities. In quite a few cases the number of employees in HRM departments has been reduced, some units such as training centres closed down and some HRM services outsourced. As shown in Table 8.3, this trend continues.

The CRANET data compiled in 2001 and 2004 and presented in Tables 8.1–8.3 indicate the devolution of personnel management (Brewster and Larsen, 1992; Mesner-Andolšek and Štebe, 2006) and its shift towards human resource management. This development has been characterised by the increasing strategic role of HRM in terms of the fact that the head of the HRM department has a place on the main board of directors and that he or she participating in the creation of the organisation's strategy from the outset, as well as that organisations create distinctive HRM strategies. It has also been observed that responsibility for HRM decisions and tasks has shifted from HR departments to line managers. In addition, the number of employees in HR departments is shrinking while organisations partially outsource their HRM services and increasingly utilise HRM market services provided by the newly established HRM, training, employment, IT and similar private agencies.

The devolution thesis has been confirmed except for two of the indicators used. There were slightly fewer organisations in 2004 where heads of HR departments were involved in the development of the strategies (see Table 8.1), and the responsibility for industrial relations shifted back to the HR professionals (see Table 8.2). The last exception could be explained by the increasing power of trade unions, which have rather centralised organisations and accept the main decisions on the branch or national levels.

Shifting responsibilities for HR issues from HR professionals to line managers has been part of the effort to reduce cost and increase productivity and efficiency. Top

Table 8.1 Changing strategic role of HRM in Slovenia

	2001 (per cent)	2004 (per cent)
Head of HRM has a place on the main board of directors	56.2	66.9
Head of HRM is involved in corporate strategy development from the outset	58.4	55.8
Organisation has an HRM strategy	53.8	62.7

Table 8.2 Sharing of responsibilities for HRM issues between line management and HRM professionals in Slovenian organisations

Primary responsibility	Line managers		HR professionals	
	2001 (per cent)	2004 (per cent)	2001 (per cent)	2004 (per cent)
Pay and benefits	68.3	72.8	31.7	27.2
Recruitment and selection	47.1	51.9	52.9	48.1
Training and development	45.1	49.4	54.9	50.6
Industrial relations	53.1	43.3	46.9	56.7
Workforce expansion/reduction	54.3	62.9	45.7	37.1

Table 8.3 Utilisation of selected external HR services and staffing of HR department in Slovenian organisations

	2001 (per cent)	*2004 (per cent)*
Pay and benefits	7.8	47.5
Training and development	62.3	92.8
Outplacement/reduction	4.7	51.6
Number of HR experts per 100 employees	1.1	0.9

management argues that it needs fewer but more highly qualified HR experts who understand HR issues and put them in a business context and who are good advisors to managers. For instance, it would be unreasonable to employ an expert to recruit managers if his or her expertise is needed only a few times per year. Cheaper and better services of this kind are available in the market. Top management also aims to redefine managerial roles, trying to make them more people focused. That is why a lot of 'soft' topics, such as communication, conflict resolution, motivation, interviewing techniques, etc., are included in the management training courses. It seems that top management sees the possibilities for productivity advancement in better people leadership and not just in task and technology management.

This trend is not without risks, however. In spite of training, line managers need time to change how they fulfil their roles. Some never change their behaviour although they recognise that they ought to. Under the conditions of increasing work intensity (Parent-Thirion *et al.*, 2007) such a change becomes even more difficult. In addition, if an organisation reduces the number of HR professionals below a certain level, the rest become overburdened by routine tasks and have no time and energy to deal with strategic issues. The possibilities for contributing to strategic and competitive advantages on the basis of excellent HR management are shrinking.

Recruitment and selection

Transition started with a deep economic crisis and institutional backing of market forces. In companies cost management dominated. Managers, who often came from outside the organisations, were 'cleaning' organisations in terms of closing down unprofitable production units, selling off unutilised equipment and premises, outsourcing peripheral production units, seeking new production programmes and new markets and so on. The main personnel issue in that period was the selection of workers to be made redundant. Several personnel managers commented that it was not as difficult to determine the number of surplus workers as it was to identify individuals to be laid off and to tell them and explain the decision. Many could not understand that after two or three decades of service in the company they had to leave involuntarily.

A fortunate circumstance for employees was that labour legislation was only gradually liberalised and that restructuring was assisted by labour market policy measures. In the first years of transition the government formed a task force to assist the organisations with the biggest redundancy problems. Several meetings with personnel managers from those organisations took place and individual advice and financial assistance also made available. The principle embedded in the legislation was that all other measures had to be applied before individuals were laid off. On that basis personnel departments, quite often in cooperation with workers' representatives, sought innovative solutions. If a person's job was not needed any more another job was sought. If another job in the organisation was available one could get training assistance to be able to perform it effectively. Employment in other organisations was also sought. Some workers were offered assistance by the organisation, or from the purse, public or both, in terms of money, training, advice, favourable cooperation contracts or means of production (premises, trucks, odd machinery, etc.) if they started their own business as self-employed. Individuals were encouraged to form internal semi-autonomous units offering services to the mother company in addition to the operations in the open market. Older workers were offered early retirement schemes. Workers who decided to leave voluntarily were given redundancy money if it was available. The last resort was to send them to the employment office.

The biggest redundancy wave ended around 1993 and the situation normalised. While there have been occasional crises in certain branches of industry, such as textiles and the shoe industry, many organisations are growing. However, those reducing the number of employees increased significantly also. According to CRANET 2001, only 4.2 per cent of organisations reported an increase in the number of employees, in 88.4 per cent there was no change and 7.4 per cent reduced the number of workers. In the CRANET 2004 survey the respective figures were 45.9 per cent, 18.9 per cent and 35.2 per cent. The methods of employee reduction are shown in Table 8.4.

Table 8.4 Percentage of Slovenian organisations which reduced the number of employees using specific methods

	2001 (per cent)	2004 (per cent)
Recruitment freeze	34.5	61.1
Early retirement	49.0	54.7
Voluntary redundancies	44.1	63.0
Compulsory redundancies	15.1	31.4
Redeployment	65.0	76.4
No renewal of fixed-term/temporary contracts	42.1	81.5
Outsourcing	37.8	47.2

Higher percentages in 2004 indicate the higher variety of methods used. In general Slovenian organisations prefer soft methods, such as redeployment, early retirement and voluntary redundancies, to hard ones, such as compulsory redundancies and outsourcing of labour. However, this also depends on environmental conditions. The rank order of methods used in 2001 and 2004 changed because early retirement has become much more expensive for employers and employees. On the other side the practice of temporary employment has become firmly rooted in organisations and supported by legislation. In 2006 among all the free posts in organisations, 75.3 per cent were for a limited period (ESS, 2006). Redundancy policies are becoming harder.

One of the most difficult problems related to redundancies was how to select individuals to be laid off. Few left organisations voluntarily because there were no good alternatives except early retirement for older workers. If there were other jobs the best employees would find them first, which was not favoured by the organisations' management. The main criterion set by legislation and agreed upon by social partners was job performance. However, the difficulty was that systematic and documented performance appraisal was rare at that time. Ex-post appraisal for redundancy purposes only was interpreted as illegal. Therefore laid-off workers often succeeded if they appealed to labour courts. Vulnerable groups of workers, such as the disabled, young mothers and workers in difficult social situations were especially protected. This caused quite a few problems in the industrial organisations with difficult working conditions, where disability and professional diseases occur. Disabled workers, for instance, could not lose their jobs except in the case of bankruptcy. When the number of employees was cut to the planned figure there were not many workers left who were able to carry out production effectively.

In recruitment and selection one can identify two typical practices. The older organisations that restructured have updated their professional approaches. In the case of recruitment there has been a visible improvement in the quality of job advertisements. While in the past advertisements were rather formal and unattractive they have now been given a marketing style in terms of their form and content. In the past advertisements focused primarily on employers' expectations, but recently employers' offers in terms of job content, career possibilities and remuneration have been added. Organisations increasingly use external HR services to recruit employees either in the case of there being demanding procedures to fill key posts or in the case of massive recruitment when new production units start to operate. Due to the improved supply of labour many organisations have ceased to practice long-term recruitment strategies, such as financial support to students and their occasional involvement in the process of work. However, the lack of key workers for specific jobs has recently strengthened this practice again.

The data presented in Table 8.5 do not allow for clear comparisons between the two periods. However, some conclusions about the recruitment practices in Slovenian organisations can be made. First, internal recruitment has been used for managers and

Table 8.5 Percentage of Slovenian organisations using various recruitment methods

	Management, 2001			All groups, 2004			
	Senior (per cent)	Middle (per cent)	Junior (per cent)	Manage- ment (per cent)	Profes- sionals/ techni- cians (per cent)	Clerical workers (per cent)	Manual workers (per cent)
Internal recruitment	64.3	79.8	77.2	66.0	22.9	33.8	17.0
Recruitment via agencies	9.8	13.0	13.5	9.6	12.7	5.5	17.0
Advertising in the media	38.5	49.7	43.1	15.4	45.9	35.2	38.2
Word of mouth	27.7	33.2	25.6	5.8	5.7	9.0	8.1

to a certain extent also for clerical workers, which is in line with the strong internal labour markets (Svetlik and Ilič, 2005). Second, the most important method is advertising in the media, which comes first for non-managerial groups. Informal methods such as 'word of mouth' seem to be less frequently used recently than in the past and recruitment via employment agencies is becoming more common.

Selection procedures are less clear. It seems that they haven't changed much in the older organisations. Because of the possibility of employing new employees for a limited period they have perhaps become more relaxed. The opposite trend towards more sophisticated methods has occurred in the case of key workers. Some organisations have shifted the responsibility for recruitment and selection to employment agencies. In short, practice has become more varied.

A detailed comparison of recruitment methods cannot be made. However, as shown in Table 8.6 interviews have undoubtedly been most frequently used. Among them panel interviews seem to have become more important, especially for more demanding jobs. This is also true for references, which some years earlier were not frequently reported. Testing has also been more frequently practised than before, while application forms have perhaps been abolished in some organisations.

New organisations led by new entrepreneurs do not always follow the patterns described. Because they are smaller they do not employ many personnel staff and the development of the personnel function does not seems to be a priority. Recruitment and selection are shared between the top management and specialist external agencies in the case of key posts and between middle management and employment services in the case of peripheral jobs. New entrepreneurs also use all forms of flexible arrangement for recruitment and selection purposes.

Table 8.6 Selection methods used in organisations

	2001		2004		
	All/most appoint-ments (per cent)	*Managers (per cent)*	*Professionals/ technicians (per cent)*	*Clerical workers (per cent)*	*Manual workers (per cent)*
Panel interview	36.4	59.6	55.3	27.3	21.1
One-to-one interview	83.3	71.4	70.2	68.9	61.5
Application form	70.4	37.3	46.9	47.8	44.7
Psychometric test	15.5	29.2	26.1	18.0	11.2
References	7.1	72.0	70.2	42.2	29.2

Reward and performance management

Before the transition, performance and reward systems could be characterised as rather bureaucratic and administrative. Performance appraisal was not used much except for production workers. Interviews with employees were not frequently practised since management was production rather than people oriented. Managers tended to set up certain formal procedures to be respected by employees and then minimised their personal leadership role (Svetlik, 1996). Performance-related variable pay was seldom used for workers outside the immediate production process. If it was used it was rather non-participative and tended to become egalitarian. Since managers did not have at hand good methods of performance appraisal and egalitarian value orientation was strong, they tended to distribute variable pay equally among the employees. In some cases everybody got the same money, which was in general a small amount, in other cases a circulation principle was applied, meaning that some group members were paid first and others were paid in subsequent months.

The payment systems were determined by law, with the focus on fixed wages, which were strongly related to the formal education demanded to fill certain jobs. Wages were modest, adjusted to the cost of living and quite often also to strike pressure. Workers were remunerated also by means of paid breaks, free meals, paid travel to work, subsidised holidays and utilisation of company holiday facilities, favourable loans for apartment purchase or house building, utilisation of company apartments, sports and recreation facilities, provision of days off for study and personal needs, provision of cheap foodstuffs, etc. In larger organisations there were usually two units within the personnel department, one dealing with wages and the other responsible for so-called social standards. Remuneration and social standards issues were the main concern of trade unions also.

The transition period started with a sharp decline in real wages. It was psychologically buffered by high inflation, which allowed for nominal raises in wages from month to month. This was interpreted as the cost of political independence, which should shortly bring improvements. Privatisation also played a critical role here. All the citizens received certificates, which were exchanged later on for shares. Many exchanged them for their companies' shares, which maintained the feeling of ownership created by self-management under the socialist regime. The shock of unemployment was an important factor also: it was better to have a badly paid job than no job at all. Later on, this turned out not to be always the case. Some organisations got into such a bad economic position that they had to reduce wages to the legal minimum and could not provide for regular payment for several consecutive months. Employees were better of if they were registered at the employment office and receiving unemployment benefits.

An important role in the reward system has been played by the social partnership established in the first years of transition in the early 1990s. Wages and salaries have been regulated by social agreements at the national and the branch of industry levels rather than by law. At the same time trade unions did not allow for the total dismantling of remuneration arrangements from the past. They accepted, for instance, that organisations had to sell their housing and holiday facilities to become more cost effective, but they kept paid breaks and subsidised meals during working time, as well as subsidised travel to work. They insisted on legislative backing for minimum wages and on the adjustment of wages according to living costs and productivity.

In the process of restructuring organisations had to sacrifice some of the social standards provisions in order to become more profitable. At the same time they were seeking new approaches to performance and remuneration management. On this basis there has been an increasing focus given to the development and application of performance appraisal in all the organisations, including those in the public sector and public administration, where it has been introduced by law. CRANET data presented in Table 8.7 show that performance appraisal was used in most of organisations as early as the turn of the century. It's level of use varied from 76.3 per cent for clerical workers to 83.2 per cent for manual workers, with other groups in between. In 2004 these figures went up slightly, varying between 82.8 per cent for clerical workers and 86.1 per cent for professionals and technicians; managers and manual workers fell in between.

The data from the two observed years are not strictly comparable. They indicate, however, that organisations increasingly utilise performance appraisal for different purposes. Performance-related pay remains at the top. The biggest increases in the utilisation of performance appraisal results were made in training needs analyses and improvements in work organisation.

Recently there has been much debate about new remuneration possibilities, such as profit sharing, company retirement schemes, additional health insurance, etc. In Table 8.8 the increased utilisation of employee shares and, even more, profit sharing is presented. This is the case not only for management but also for other

Table 8.7 Percentage of Slovenian organisations using performance appraisal for different purposes

	2001 (per cent)	2004 (per cent)
Personnel planning	–	50.0
Training needs	34.6	58.0
Career and promotion	34.6–62.0	58.3
Performance-related pay	76.1	87.5
Organisation of work	26.3	49.3

Table 8.8 Percentage of Slovenian organisations using financial participation schemes

	Employee shares		Profit sharing	
	2001 (per cent)	2004 (per cent)	2001 (per cent)	2004 (per cent)
Managers	6.8	16.1	26.3	28.0
Professionals/technicians	3.9	11.8	9.8	18.0
Clerical workers	3.9	9.3	7.3	14.9
Manual workers	3.9	8.1	7.3	14.3

groups of workers. New legislation for the regulation of workers' financial participation in organisations is being prepared.

Training and development

In the old socialist regime training was considered to be one of the workers' rights. Employees had a right to part-time education and companies had to offer them some days off to attend courses and examinations. Special education and training funds were used to subsidise or even fully cover the cost of formal education if it was considered to be in accordance with the company's needs. Young students were offered financial support for their studies as a part of long-term recruitment schemes or simply as part of companies' social programmes. Larger organisations had their own education and training departments and in some cases their own training centres. These departments dealt with all the education and training issues, with the aim of adapting workers' skills to changing needs. A kind of internal training market was established in companies. Demand was expressed in terms of individuals' or their managers' desire for certain training and education programmes, and supply in terms of training offered by external schools and agencies or directly by the organisations' training departments. Training departments had the role of mediators and organisers of training, using internal and external experts as trainers. Anticipatory training needs analysis was not practised frequently.

Due to the strong accent on internal labour and training markets, one might have expected a dynamic promotion and development in organisations. This unfortunately was not the case. In one of our analyses (Svetlik *et al.*, 1997) we found out that employees were promoted every seven years on average and that nearly 40 per cent were never promoted. Career development was seldom practised in an organised way.

The crisis period before and in the first years of transition affected the training function significantly. It was one of the first to be downsized since its effects are long term. Some companies closed down their training centres and made experts from this field redundant. Company education and training funds were significantly reduced. It would be wrong to speak of career development at that time. However, organisations that restructured made a selection among their employees and tried to retain key ones. This was made possible because they often laid off a certain number of employees, raised productivity and started to pay those who remained better.

The restructuring of organisations involved the replacement of less demanding production in textile, shoe, metal and similar industries by more sophisticated production. Large numbers of employees needed retraining. Organisations were often assisted in this by labour market policy measures. At the same time they started to build their new internal markets composed of highly qualified key workers.
This brought back the need for training experts, training programmes and career development. According to CRANET data Slovenian organisations spent 2.3 per cent of the wage bill on education and training in 2001 and 2.8 per cent in 2004. In the same period the share of employees on training fell from 49 per cent to 46.2 per cent. Managers, professionals and technicians led with respect to days of training in comparison with clerical and manual workers. While in the observed period the number of days of training for managers and clerical workers fell from 7.3 to 6.3 and from 3.4 to 2.7, respectively, the number of training days for professionals and technicians and for manual workers went up from 6.3 to 6.5 and from 2.4 to 2.8, respectively. It seems that since the managerial and administrative restructuring finished, the need to give additional training to those directly involved in production has been recognised.

Although in the first years of transition management got the impression that there was a large choice of labour in the pool of the unemployed, organisations soon realized that there was a lack of experts specific knowledge and competencies. In addition, it has been increasingly difficult to find experts with the organisations' specific knowledge and skills, which in principle must be developed internally. Therefore in the last few years one can observe increasing competence management practices in Slovenian companies. According to CRANET data, planned job rotation has been used most, followed by succession and formal career plans.

THE FUTURE OF HRM IN SLOVENIA

Tables 8.1–8.3 clearly confirm the devolution theses in the case of Slovenian HRM. One can expect smaller HRM departments which are oriented towards top management and strategic issues, on the one hand, and towards line managers assisting them to carry out classic personnel tasks, on the other. In addition, some HRM expertise will be outsourced or/and purchased in the market. At first sight this might look as though HRM will be contracting. We think, however, that it will expand in terms of specialist expertise offered by HRM market agencies and especially in terms of a line management shift from technical tasks to people management and leadership. Line managers will have to be trained particularly in dealing with personnel issues. In addition, close cooperation of the head of HRM with top management and the assistance of line management by HRM experts will increase HRM's status inside organisations.

Judging by the frequency of topics dealt with at national HRM conferences since 1999 (see Kadri, 1999–2006) the most discussed issues have been the emerging knowledge-based economy and the role of HRM in this process. This issue has been addressed by the concept of the knowledge cycle, composed of the creation, transfer and utilisation of knowledge (OECD, 2000), and its organisational and HRM correlates: innovation, detection and development of talents, learning, education and training, competence development, competence management and vocational qualifications. Other topics have occurred less often. In addition the following should be mentioned:

- organisational culture, values and climate and various aspects of employees satisfaction;
- industrial relations, employment, workers participation and related legal provisions;
- labour market situation, demographic changes and mobility of labour;
- health and safety at work, work accidents and disability issues;
- globalisation, intercultural management, international HRM and benchmarking.

These topics indicate very few narrowly focused HRM issues, such as health and safety. All the other most discussed ones are equally of concern to general management as to HRM. It is to be expected that HRM will bring the right issues to the attention of top management and will take part in finding adequate solutions. It will strengthen its role as strategic partner and agent/facilitator of change (Ulrich, 1996).

Changes that have not been sufficiently observed in Slovenia and might have an impact on HRM are:

- intellectualisation of work and a shift towards knowledge-based organisations, in which HRM will have to come close to or even merge with the knowledge management;

- internationalisation of economic activities that increasingly push home-based organisations to establish their subsidiaries abroad and bring foreign companies and labour to Slovenia, which brings HRM closer to intercultural management;
- ageing of the home population, which will change the age of employees with different abilities, flexibility and expectations than today's ones and will demand that HRM to develop new professional approaches.

In the following paragraphs we present the case of Gorenje. It belongs to the core of modernised industrial organisations in Slovenia. Although it went through a difficult restructuring process it has found a remarkable place among European small producers of home appliances. Its HRM has also been in the process of modernisation and has assisted the transformation of production. It is representative of the transforming HRM scene in Slovenian organisations. Furthermore, Gorenje demonstrates how some of the beneficial aspects of HRM self-management practices could be preserved and upgraded.

Gorenje

Case study

With almost 10,000 employees Gorenje Group is the largest company in Slovenia. We started our business in 1950 with the production of cookers, which we soon started to export to Germany. We expanded our product range in the 1970s to refrigerators and washing machines. In the 1970s we established a network of subsidiaries in Western Europe. Today Gorenje exports 93 per cent of its products abroad and its net income amounts to €1 billion.

Gorenje had to tackle the greatest crisis in the 1990s when Yugoslavia was broken up. We lost a great deal of the domestic market but succeeded in entering foreign markets, which helped us increase our sales. This was enabled by improved cost effectiveness and investment in new technology. The accent has been on the implementation of higher technological and ecological standards and on design. New subsidiaries have been established or acquired, especially in Eastern Europe and former Yugoslavia. Before the crisis Gorenje had 20,000 employees and this number has halved in the last 15 years.

Before the crisis the Gorenje Group was rather loosely linked with subsidiaries, which had a high level of autonomy. This is also true of the HR function, which lacked a strategic role. Most of the Gorenje companies opted for self-sufficiency in the field of human resources management. However, the restructuring process of the 1990s characterised by the integration of companies into a tightly knit Gorenje Group, has led to the adoption of better defined corporate policies. This is reflected in the centralisation of certain functions, mainly those requiring concentration of skills and expertise. In the HRM field these are, in particular, HR development, the assessment centre, organisational climate research, personnel counselling, education and training and HR information systems. Several changes in HRM have been introduced on this basis.

In the past every employee was responsible for a small number of tasks and we could easily replace him or her. Labour turnover was high. We realised that each employee should be able to perform various tasks and become more flexible. Therefore we put a greater emphasis on training and became more people oriented by increasing opportunities for personnel development. Even though we reduced the number of employees our sales increased.

We have realised that our competitive edge lies not only in technology, but also in investing in people. Every year we allocate €260 per person for training. At least once every two years each employee attends a training programme. We organise a wide range of training programmes, such as:

- periodic training in the quality and safety at work required by law;
- language and computer training;
- continuing professional training in various fields;
- management training.

In the recruitment process it is impossible to check for all the required skills and competencies. Some are revealed only when one is working. Therefore the main requirement is that the candidate is willing to learn and develop professional and personal skills. In matching the right person with the most suitable position we use the following practice:

- determine the field in which the person would like to develop;
- determine the knowledge and skills in which he or she excels;
- determine the knowledge and skills, which he or she should enhance;
- match the needs of the individual with the company's needs;
- on this basis plan his or her career.

With these activities we enhance career development and retain individuals in the company. The company's main concern is to help employees know themselves better, to discover their outstanding skills and limits and to make sure that the company's goals are also the goals they are eager to achieve.

HRM has become increasingly a line management concern. Employees feel a positive atmosphere in the workplace through their relationship with their managers and co-workers. The main task of managers is to know how to take advantage of the human assets available so that each individual in the group has the opportunity to develop the practical knowledge and skills needed to effectively perform his or her duties and to achieve the overall objective of the group. In order to guide the employees, managers

continued

must know how to guide, delegate responsibility, lead conversations with co-workers as well as properly assess them.

For better HR management we introduced the following instruments:

- Job satisfaction questionnaire, by which we try to get information on employees' aspirations, job satisfaction, motivation, interests for continual education, job mobility and commitments.
- Annual performance appraisal interview and annual employee development plan, which are among the most effective means to create an atmosphere of trust between the manger and the individual. We aim to encourage employees to consider their career goals and professional ambitions. A manager and an employee elaborate the career plan and describe the steps to be made, including training required and change of job.
- Management training programme, which is offered to managers of various ranks and covers topics such as negotiations, interpersonal communication, motivation, teamwork, project management. We introduced this programme 15 years ago, and it has become an important tool which helps identify and enhance the outstanding abilities of the employees and improve communication between various departments.
- Assessment procedure, which aims at systematical assessment of individuals' potential on the basis of their intellectual abilities, personality, creativity and skills. The aim is to assist employees in setting their work goals as well as in making decisions about their career development.

Our remuneration system is based on collective agreements. However, it has been augmented with personal performance-based bonuses and a promotion system. As a result, the payment of workers performing the same jobs can vary significantly. In addition, our company traditionally pays high attention to the services offered to employees, such as promotion of health care, cultural, sport and leisure activities, and sponsoring of local communities, where the employees come from.

REFERENCES AND FURTHER READING

Bevc, M., Svetlik, I. and Pavlin, S. (2006). *Indikatorji za merjenje prenosa znanja – nabori, opis in uporaba* [Indicators for knowledge transfer measurement – sets, description and utilisation]. Ljubljana, Institute for Economic Research.

Brewster, C. and Larsen, H. H. (1992). 'Human Resource Management in Europe: Evidence from the Countries'. *The International Journal of Human Resource Management*, 3, 3: 409–34.

CRANET (2001, 2004). *The Cranfield Network for the Study of Human Resource Management in Europe*. Cranfield: Cranfield University, School of Management.

Djokič, D. (2003). *Yugoslavism: histories of a failed idea 1918–1992*. London, Hurst.

ESS (2006). *Employment Service of Slovenia: 2006 Overview*. ESS.

Ferfila, B. and Phillips, P. (2000). *Slovenia: On the Edge of the European Union*. New York and Oxford: University Press of America.

Fink-Hafner, D. and Robbins, J. (eds) (1997). *Making a New Nation: The Formation of Slovenia*. Aldershot: Dartmouth.

Glenny, M. (1992). *The Fall of Yugoslavia: The Third Balkan War*. London: Penguin Books.

Kadri (1999–2006). *Strokovno informativna revija Zveze društev za kadrovsko dejavnost Slovenije* [Cadres 1999–2006, review of the Slovenian HRM Association].

Kanjuo, M. A. and Ignjatović, M. (2006). 'Unfriendly Flexibilisation of Work and Employment – the Need for Flexicurity'. In Svetlik, I. and Ilič, B. (eds) *HRM's Contribution to Hard Work*. Bern, Berlin and Brussels: Peter Lang, pp. 315–50.

Kohont, A. (2006). 'Shallow Policy without an HRM Strategy in the Government Administration'. In Svetlik, I. and Ilič, B. (eds) *HRM's Contribution to Hard Work*. Bern, Berlin, Brussels: Peter Lang, pp. 381–404.

Konjunkturna gibanja (2007). 'Ocena in analiza tekočih gospodarskih gibanj' [Estimates and analysis of the current economic flows], *Konjunkturna gibanja* 2, XV. Ljubljana: Gospodarska zbornica Slovenije.

Kopač, A. (2004). *Aktivacija – obrat v socialni politiki* [Activation – a turning point in social policy]. Ljubljana: Faculty of Social Sciences, University of Ljubljana.

Kopač, A. and Trbanc, M. (2005). 'Razvoj zaposlenih' [Employees' development]. In Sadar, Č. N. *et al.*, *Upravljanje človeških virov 2004, tabelarni pregled* [Human resource management, tables review]. Ljubljana: Faculty of Social Sciences, University of Ljubljana.

Mesner-Andolšek, D. and Štebe, J. (2006). 'The HRM Function and Line Management in European Organisations: How Far Has Devolution Gone?' In Svetlik, I. and Ilič, B. (eds) *HRM's Contribution to Hard Work*. Bern, Berlin and Brussels: Peter Lang, pp. 59–96.

Mrak, M., Rojec, M. and Silva-Jauregui, C. (eds) (2004). *Slovenia: From Yugoslavia to the European Union*. Washington, DC: World Bank.

OECD (2000). 'The Production, Mediation and Use of Knowledge in Different Sectors'. In Knowledge Management in the Learning Society. Paris: OECD, pp. 37–66.

Parent-Thirion, A., Fernandez Macias, E., Hurley, J. and Vermeylen, G. (2007) *Fourth European Working Conditions Survey*. Dublin: European Foundation for the Improvement of Living and Working Conditions.

Phillips, P. and Ferfila, B. (1992). *The Rise and Fall of the Third Way: Yugoslavia 1945–1991*. Halifax: Fernwood.

Pilgrim, M. and Meier, R. (1995). *National Chambers of Commerce: A Primer on the Organisation and Role of the Chamber Systems*. Bonn and Washington, DC: Centre for International Private Enterprise (CIPE).

RNPVS (2006). 'Resolucija o nacionalnem programu visokega šolstva' [Resolution on the National Programme of Higher Education 2006–2010]. Available at: www.mvzt.si/fileadm/mvzt.gov.si/pageuploads/pdf/visoko_solstvo/RNPVS.pdf (accessed 15 May 2006).

Stanojević, M. (2002). 'EU Enlargement and Employee Participation: New Functions of an Inherited Pattern within Slovenian Organisations'. In Biagi, M. (ed.) *Quality of Work and Employee Involvement in Europe*. The Netherlands: Kluwer Law International, pp. 279–93.

Stanojević, M. (2003). 'Workers' Power in Transition Economies: The Cases of Serbia and Slovenia'. *European Journal of Industrial Relations*, 9, 33: pp. 283–301.

Stanojević, M. and Vrhovec, P. (2001). 'Industrial Conflict in Slovenia'. *SEER, South-East Europe Review of Labour and Social Affairs*, 4, 1: 29–37.

Stare, M., Kmet, R. and Bučar, M. (2004). 'Slovenia on the Road to Information Society'. Available at: www.gov.si/zmar/projekti/iceg.php (accessed 15 May 2006).

Svetlik, I. (1992). 'Changing Labour Market and Employment Policies'. In Svetlik, I. (ed.) *Social Policy in Slovenia: Between Tradition and Innovation*. Aldershot: Avebury, pp. 55–65.

Svetlik, I. (1996). 'Quality of Working Life'. *Družboslovne razprave*, 12, 22/23: 15–27.

Svetlik, I. and Alas, R. (2006). 'The European Union and HRM: Impact on Present and Future Members'. In Larsen, H. H. and Mayrhofer, W. (eds) *Managing Human Resources in Europe*. London and New York: Routledge, pp. 21–44.

Svetlik, I. and Ilič, B. (2005). *HRM's Contribution to Hard Work*. Bern, Berlin and Brussels: Peter Lang.

Svetlik, I., Gnidovec, M. and Ilič, B. (1997). *Status and Job Mobility of Labour in Slovenia*. Working paper No. 49, Faculty of Economics, University of Ljubljana.

Svetlik, I., Kaarelson, T., Alas, R. and Kohont, A. (2007). 'The Development of the Personnel Function in Transition Countries: Slovenian and Estonian Experience'. *TRAMES Journal of the Humanities and Social Sciences*, 11, 1: 35–53.

Ulrich, D. (1996). *Human Resource Champions: The Agenda for Adding Value and Delivering Results*. Boston, MA: Harvard Business School Press.

Zimmermann, W. (1996). *Origins of the Catastrophe: Yugoslavia and Its Destroyers*. New York: Random House–Times Books.

Žnidaršič, K.A. (1994). *Privatizacija ali zakonita kraja: divja privatizacija, načrtovana kraja, neznanje ali slovenska nevoščjivost?* [Privatisation or Legal Theft: wild privatisation, planned theft, ignorance or Slovenian envy?] Postojna: Dej.

Zupan, N. (1999). 'Ravnanje s človeškimi viri v slovenskih podjetjih' [Human resource management in Slovene enterprises]. Doctor's dissertation, Faculty of Economics, Ljubljana University.

9 Managing human resources in Bulgaria

ELIZABETH VATCHKOVA

INTRODUCTION

The management of people at work in Bulgaria has been an area of significant, fast and controversial changes for the last fifteen years. These changes can be categorized as contextual, institutional, theoretical and practical ones.

From a contextual point of view, they have affected the very understanding of human resource management (HRM) in its political, social and economic aspects as a result of the transitional process from centralized planning to a market economy. The socialist state, which guaranteed full employment, a high level of social security, mass access to free education, and health care, collapsed. As a result, the model of managing people at work has altered – the roles of all stakeholders have been rearranged, the span and type of their responsibilities have become different. People management strategies and policies, formerly elaborated, implemented and strictly controlled by the state and the ruling Communist Party, the only party in existence, started to be developed by the companies themselves. Initially businesses, especially those which were privately owned, tried to minimize the social and labor costs, additionally pressed by illegal companies as the shadow economy grew. There was a lack of HRM professionals and their dominating competence covered administrative and pay and compensation functions. In general, external and internal conditions for HRM were unfavorable.

The transition to a market economy in Bulgaria was taking place under conditions of continuous economic, political and social crisis. Its sharpening in 1997, when the country entered an inflationary spiral (700 percent inflation), resulted in the decision to introduce a currency board as a tool to limit and neutralize the destructive tendencies in the economy. The standard of living of the population fell sharply and Bulgarian citizens' quality of life worsened. The real income per capita decreased by 65.6 percent for the 1990–6 period. According to information from the Institute for Social Research, 21 percent of households were below the 1992 social minimum, compared to 85 percent in the middle of 1997. In June 1997 the cost of living was 4.5 times higher than the minimum wage (Vatchkova, 2000).

Along with the transition to a market economy a new institutional structure has been developing to replace the state monopoly of HRM. Lots of new laws and regulations have been adopted, and the Labor Code has been revised. Due to the development of democratization processes the constituents of civil society have come to the fore, starting to create their own contributory image.

Theoretical research and sociological studies have been encouraged by the still slow but stable demand by institutions, companies and practitioners in the field of HRM. Western HRM concepts and theories have been transferred and promoted since 1990. In 1996, Bulgaria became a member of the CRANET Network and in the last decade three national surveys have been undertaken (1996, 1999, 2003). Bulgarian membership of CRANET gave an opportunity to become acquainted with European HRM practices and facilitated the transfer of the best ones to Bulgarian companies.

From a practical point of view several factors have significantly influenced HRM activities in contemporary Bulgarian organizations since 1990. The increased transfer of advanced HRM practices from multinational companies to Bulgarian ones is a stable trend. The increased competition pressed companies to go beyond the paradigm, formerly followed by the socialist state, of 'Higher employment – lower level of productivity', and to explore the one relevant to new market realities of 'Lower employment – higher productivity'. Practically, this has accelerated the introduction of new HRM approaches, methods and techniques. The harmonization of the Bulgarian legal framework for the labor market with the European legislation is another factor underlying the positive changes.

All the above-mentioned processes took place under very dynamic and complicated external and organizational environmental conditions.

The transition which began on 11 November 1989 radically changed the political climate in the country: the one-party system was replaced by a multi-party system. Some of the emerging parties had unclear political platforms and unidentified voters. The only trade union that existed previously was replaced by a number of new trade unions, which made tripartite negotiations particularly difficult. For example, during a brief period of time in the early stages of the transition, before legislation was updated, the management of some companies in structurally important industries had to make decisions regarding personnel taking into account the standpoints of as many as seven trade unions. During the first years of the transition period the macro-environment was characterized by political instability, chaos and significant social tension.

The restructuring of the economy led to the loss of the country's traditional markets and to the closure of a number of successful and effective enterprises, some of which were very large. Privatization and changes of ownership, along with unemployment, which had been unknown to Bulgaria for fifty years, forced the managers of companies in the process of reform to manage permanent crises, conflicts and non-compliance with the outdated and inadequate legislation.

The stabilization of the political system and of the economy after 2000 gave a new impulse to positive changes in all spheres of social life and speeded up improvements in opportunities for professional people management in the reformed companies.

An additional energizer to this rush ahead was the need to meet the requirements of the European Union after Bulgaria joined the Union in January 2007.

Two important approaches will be used to describe and analyze the transitional developments of Bulgarian HRM: the European integration process and the creation of a knowledge-based economy. The main focus will be on the contributory role of contemporary and future Bulgarian HRM to support the establishment of a competitive economy based on knowledge.

THE TRANSITION PROCESS

The years of the transition to a market economy are too few to draw any general conclusions, although the European Commission has already recognized that Bulgaria has a functioning market economy. The initial years of the transformation process were characterized by strong recession. Official statistical information did not always reflect properly the ongoing changes due to its instability and the methodological discrepancies in calculating the economic indicators in individual countries. In this sense, a proper understanding of the main features of the transition period can be derived from the trends taking shape rather than the existing levels of specific indicators.

Gross domestic product (GDP)

After the initial years of volatility, the currency board arrangements were introduced in the country in 1997. That stabilized the economy and created opportunities for maintaining GDP growth rates of about 5 percent. Nevertheless, it was not until 2003 that the GDP level of US$16.8 bn in 1990 was exceeded, reaching US$19.9 bn. The per capita GDP reveals a clear upward trend, doubling in the period under review to reach US$4,089 in 2006 (Figure 9.1).

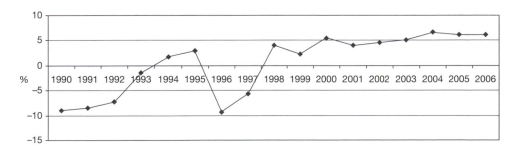

Figure 9.1 GDP growth rates, Bulgaria, 1990–2006

Source: National Statistical Institute (NSI), www.nsi.bg.

The GDP sectoral structure

This has stabilized in a 10:30:60 ratio of agriculture, manufacturing, and services over recent years. No comparable information is available for the beginning of the transition process but then the economy was defined as industrial and agrarian in a ratio of 80–85 percent to 15–20 percent (National Statistical Institute, www.nsi.bg).

Current account of the balance of payments

The current account of the balance of payments has been negative almost throughout the whole period 1989–97, following a distinct downward trend in the wake of the financial stabilization of the economy in 1997. Prior to economic stabilization the negative levels of the current account resulted from the crisis in all spheres of the national economy, whereas after the stabilization the reason was the accelerated importation of capital goods. The need for technological improvement of the national economy underpinned the faster growth of imports than of exports. The traditionally positive effects of services are still insufficient to set off the adverse effects of the negative foreign trade balance but capital goods are expected to start 'working' to the benefit of exports in the years to come, starting a period of gradual reduction of the negative trade balance and improvement of the current account.

Foreign direct investments (FDI)

The instability of the Bulgarian economy in the early 1990s was accompanied by weak investment activity. The interest of foreign investors increased as the economy stabilized and the country's credit rating gradually improved. The legislative changes in that sphere also contributed to that effect because they created favorable investment conditions. As a result, investment levels exceeded US$18 bn in 2006 (Figure 9.2).

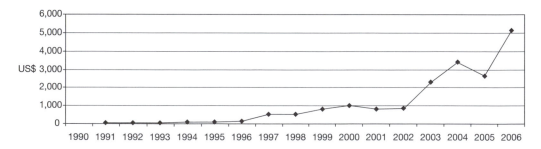

Figure 9.2 Foreign direct investment in Bulgaria, 1991–2006

Source: Bulgarian National Bank, www.bnb.bg.

Over the last decade FDI has focused primarily on processing (25 percent), trade (19 percent), financial intermediation (17 percent), transportation (12 percent), and real estate (10 percent). The countries which have the largest investments in Bulgaria are Austria, Greece, Italy, Germany, the Netherlands, Belgium, Cyprus and the United States.

Interest rates

The base interest rate is a function of the supply of and demand for money and it is also a tool for government regulation of investment activities. The levels of 40–50 percent in the early 1990s were followed by the peak levels of up to 300 percent during the second half of 1996 and the first half of 1997. The base interest rate level returned to normal after the introduction of the currency board arrangements and after inflation processes came under control. It was around 4 percent until 2002 and since then it has been slightly over 2 percent. This trend encourages investment and contributes to attracting the necessary foreign capital.

Inflation rates

The most notable feature of inflationary processes in Bulgaria during the transition period was their sudden escalation in 1996 and 1997. The three- and four-digit inflation rates registered at that time destabilized the financial sector and the whole economy. The year 1997 saw the introduction of the currency board arrangements and, as a result, inflation rates came under control. Since 1998 they have moved around 5–6 percent and have been influenced mainly by international prices of basic commodities, as well as the process of adjustment to the excise tax rates applicable in the EU. Analysts believe that it is appropriate for the currency board arrangements to be preserved until accession to the eurozone.

Foreign exchange rate

As in the case of the other macroeconomic indicators, the dynamic pattern of the foreign exchange rate can be divided into two periods before and after the currency board arrangements. The Bulgarian Government re-denominated the national currency in July 1999 when BGL 1,000 was re-denominated into BGN 1. The financial and economic stability which has followed over the last ten years has enabled the foreign exchange rate to stabilize within the range of BGN 1.5–2 to US$1 and peg the exchange rate to the euro in a ratio of BGN 1.95583 to €1.

Unemployment rates

The collapse of the integration within the former socialist system was followed by an active privatization process. It could be seen in the bankruptcy of many enterprises, the loss of positions in international markets for goods, rapid growth of inventory levels, and increasing unemployment rates. All these processes were particularly pronounced in the first half of the period 1995–2006, but afterwards they were overcome and since 2000 there has been a lasting trend of reducing unemployment in absolute terms and as a percentage of the active population.

The year 2006 saw the most significant increase in employed persons in the last five years while the employment rate increased twice as fast as in 2005. In June 2007 the Employment Agency registered record low unemployment – 7.42 percent on average for the country. Statistics show that during the same month the unemployed in Sofia made up only 1.81 percent of the active population, in Bourgas 3.02 percent, in Gabrovo 3.85 percent. Formally speaking, there is no unemployment in these towns and nationwide the level is below the critical 10 percent. In June 2007 there were 17,900 vacancies in the Agency, 2,692 of which were in Sofia. The variation range between the minimum and the maximum level of unemployment in the country continues to decrease.

This situation is due to the overall economic state of affairs, which affects the labor market positively through:

● sustainable economic growth;
● rising trend of the Estat index of the business climate;
● establishing industry as the most dynamically developing sector;
● increased domestic consumption;
● widened scope of information and communication technologies;
● significant contribution of services to increased gross domestic product;
● opening of new jobs by private entrepreneurs; and
● decreasing social insurance burden for employers.

In conclusion, the post-1989 period was characterized by strong recession in the beginning, destabilization of all spheres of economic life, changes of ownership, and adjustment to the new market conditions. In 1993, Bulgaria signed the Europe Agreement for accession to the EU, underpinning the economic reform process. Many bilateral agreements were signed to facilitate the access of Bulgarian exports to external markets. The country joined the World Trade Organization (1996) and the Central European Free Trade Agreement (CEFTA/EFTA) in 1998. Since the introduction of the currency board arrangements the economy has stabilized and positive trends have taken shape in the development of macroeconomic indicators; domestic demand andlending have been fostered; the openness of the economy has been preserved; and the major trade partners are the EU member states (60–65 percent). In 2002, the European Commission recognized Bulgaria as a functioning market economy. International rating agencies are gradually improving the country's credit rating.

Since 1 January 2007 Bulgaria has been a full-fledged EU member. The potential for faster adaptation of the Bulgarian economy to the requirements of the common European market and for speeding up economic growth is already being utilized. During the first six months of 2007 GDP increased by 6.4 percent, while in EU-27 average growth was 3 percent. The inflation rate for the same period was 2 percent, while the unemployment rate in June was as low as 7.4 percent. The current account deficit during the first six months was 10.6 percent of GDP, the main reason for this being the foreign trade deficit (12.3 percent of GDP), but it is mainly due to the dynamic economic development. Trade remains oriented towards Europe – the EU accounts for 65 percent of all exports and 53 percent of all imports. The growth of direct foreign investments continues. By the end of June they amounted to 7.9 percent of GDP and covered 75 percent of the current account deficit. The total government and government-guaranteed debt at the end of June 2007 was 21.6 percent of the GDP forecast for 2007. Thus Bulgaria remains in compliance with the Maastricht criterion, which is 60 percent. All these factors make it possible to sustain the positive trends in the development of our country and form the basis for effective use of financing from the EU structural funds during the 2007–13 period.

THE CONTEXT FOR HUMAN RESOURCE MANAGEMENT

Main Stakeholders

Labor relations between employers and employees and the interaction between their representative organizations and the government are part and parcel of the socio-economic system in Bulgaria. They ensure the balance between economic and social relations and they are objectively necessary to overcome social conflicts.

Small business predominates in Bulgaria (Table 9.1). The number of small employers in the private sector tends to grow in a sustainable manner in the market economy context. The number of foreign investors is increasing in Bulgaria with the improvement of the investment climate; 500 new foreign companies or international organizations were registered on an annual basis over the period from 2001 to 2004. The number of medium-sized and large organizations tends to remain stable. There is a reduction, although insignificant, in the number of companies in the public sector. The largest employers in the country have state or municipal interest in them.

Employers are associated in sectoral organizations and they are members of some representative organizations like the Bulgarian Chamber of Commerce and Industry (BCCI) and the Bulgarian Industrial Association (BIA). They, in turn, are

Table 9.1 Number of employees by the size of business in Bulgaria, 2004

Number of employees	Number of businesses in 2004	Percentage
1–10	119,069	81
11–50	19,859	14
51–100	3,904	3
101–500	3,172	2
501–1,000	334	0.2
1,000+	136	0.1
Total	**146,474**	

Source: National Statistical Institute, 2005.

members of the Association of Bulgarian Employers, together with some similar organizations.

Trade unions are a major participant in the collective bargaining process. The Bulgarian representative trade union organizations which are members of the European Trade Union Confederation and the International Confederation of Free Trade Unions are the Confederation of Independent Trade Unions in Bulgaria (CITUB) and Podkrepa Labor Confederation. Both organizations were founded in the period 1989–90, immediately after the changes began.

CITUB is the largest and most influential representative trade union organization in the country. It comprises 34 federations, syndicates and unions, among which are the Syndicate of Bulgarian Teachers, the Federation of Independent Syndicate Organizations from Light Industry, the Federation of Independent Construction Syndicates, the Syndicate of Railway Workers in Bulgaria, and the Federation of Independent Syndicates of Bulgarian Miners. It covers 7,500 primary trade union organizations and has 3,500 members.

The Podkrepa Labor Confederation comprises 36 regional syndicate unions, 30 federations and national syndicates and four associated organizations. It has 150,000 members, among which are the following federations: the Radio and Television National Syndicate, the Light Industry Federation, the Metallurgy Federation, etc.

Trade unions are considered to be a traditional communication channel between employers and employees in most countries. The survey reviews their role in the development of a democratic model of organizational communications in Bulgaria. In 2003, in 73.3 percent of Bulgarian organizations most of the employees declared that they were trade union members (Table 9.2). Notwithstanding the lack of long trade union traditions, employees in the Bulgarian organizations involved in the survey were trade union members more frequently than their peers in Central and Eastern Europe.

Many Bulgarian companies stated that the influence of trade union organizations was reduced or not felt at all in work processes for the period 1999–2003. Trade union influence increased in only 10.2 percent of the respondents and remained unchanged in another one-third of the companies. Nevertheless, the unionization of Bulgarian companies compared to other European countries was relatively high. In 15 percent of the companies it ranged from 1 percent to 25 percent, and in another 15 percent it ranged between 76 percent and 100 percent. The most likely reason is that the newly established organizations in the private sector have not adopted this form of association of employees to protect their collective interests yet, while trade union membership is very common in big companies with long traditions.

At the same time, fewer organizations recognize trade unions as parties to the collective bargaining process (Figure 9.3); their share dropped from 75 percent in 1996 to 49.7 percent in 2003. One of the reasons is probably decentralization and the tendency to apply individual negotiations between employers and employees.

Table 9.2 Approximate percentage of employees who are members of a trade union

Country	Percentage					
	0	*1–10*	*11–25*	*26–50*	*51–75*	*76–100*
Estonia	65.2	13.9	7.8	4.3	2.6	0.9
Slovakia	41.6	5.5	6.3	14.1	14.1	7.8
Greece	32.4	13.3	8.1	11.6	10.4	21.4
Hungary	32.2	8.5	11.9	18.6	18.6	3.4
Cyprus	13.1	2.4	2.4	4.8	6	70.2
Finland	0.3	0.3	1.4	5.2	18.3	67.6
Sweden	0	0.8	2.6	6.1	19.5	66.1
Denmark	0	2.5	4.9	10.7	23.3	53.9
EU average	15.5	12.5	10.8	13.4	14.7	20.7
Turkey	49.4	1.3	3.1	5.6	16.9	20.6
Bulgaria	26.7	6.7	8	10.7	18.7	15.3
USA	57	8.2	11.7	9.4	6.6	5.5
Philippines	71.4	10.2	2	8.2	4.1	4.1

Source: CRANET Survey, 2003.

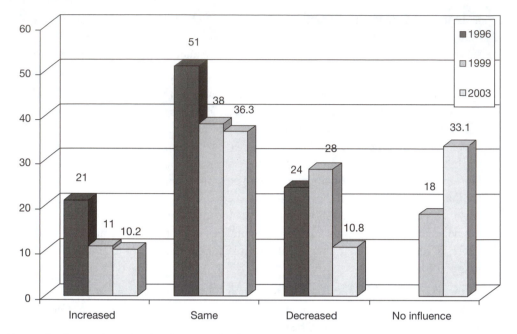

Figure 9.3 Proportion of Bulgarian organizations where the influence of trade unions has changed, 1999–2003

In comparison to all information exchange forms surveyed, the most substantial decline was observed in communication through trade unions, which was largely due to the weakening of their role and the fact that Bulgarian employees hardly recognized them as a way to protect their interests. Public opinion polls reveal that trade union organizations do not enjoy great credibility among Bulgarian citizens. This is another reason for the weakened role of trade unions. The reduced influence of trade unions can be explained also by the fact that the share of state-owned companies has decreased in Bulgaria and it is precisely in the public sector that trade unions hold the strongest positions.

Industrial relations are regulated in the Constitution of the Republic of Bulgaria and the Labor Code. The Constitution envisages two major rights: the right to association of employees in trade unions for the protection of their labor interests and of employers in organizations for the protection of their business interests; and the right of employees to go on strike. The Labor Code (LC) provides for tripartite cooperation as the fundamental principle underlying labor relations. The Labor Code is a pivotal law regulating employment relations in the Republic of Bulgaria. The aim of the Code is to ensure the freedom and protection of labor, equitable and dignified working conditions, as well as the conduct of social dialogue between the state, employees, employers, and their organizations for the purpose of settlement of labor relations and other immediately related relations.

Key labor market developments

The labor market system covers the population of the country, employees, unemployed people, people outside the workforce, jobs, employers, the price of manpower, the institutional structure, and the infrastructure. The regulation of economic relations generated by the supply of and demand for manpower is institutionalized in the Labor Code, the secondary legislation adopted by the government, the European Employment Strategy, and the Employment Promotion Act.

The major labor market institution is the Ministry of Labor and Social Policy, which drafts, coordinates, and implements government policy with regard to unemployment benefits, employment promotion measures, the training and retraining of the unemployed, and the protection of the national labor market. The Executive Agency for Employment, together with its regional and local subdivisions, carries out government policy in the field of employment. Social partners play an important role in the regulation of social relations in the labor market at the national and regional level. These are trade unions and employers, which are the major social agents in the labor market, and non-governmental organizations. As well as the government institutions operating in the labor market, there are 115 private labor exchanges for intermediation within the country, 57 private exchanges for jobs abroad, and 17 specialist agencies for hiring sailors.

In 2005, the labor market was characterized by the following parameters:

- the economic activity rate[1] was 62.1 percent, compared to approximately 70.4 percent in EU-25;[2]
- the number of employed people was 2,945,200 on average and some 75 percent worked in the private sector;
- the employment rate[3] was 55.8 percent, compared to 64.1 percent in EU-25;
- the unemployment rate[4] was 10.2 percent, compared to 8.9 percent in EU-25;
- the unemployment level[5] was 11.46 percent in terms of the number of unemployed people registered with labor offices;
- unemployment was strongly polarized in regional terms (Figure 9.4).

The comparative analysis shows that in 2006 the average annual unemployment levels in the euro-zone and the EU-27, according to Eurostat data, were, respectively, 7.8 percent and 7.9 percent, while in Bulgaria the level was 8.9 percent. In this respect Bulgaria is in a better position than Poland (14 percent) and Slovakia (13.3 percent) and ranks similar to Greece and France (9 percent), but is far behind from the achievements of Ireland and Cyprus, which sustained low-level unemployment, 4.4 percent and 4.9 percent respectively, during the same year (Employment Agency, 07).

In 2006, labor offices announced 280,000 vacancies, 80 percent of which were from private employers in the real sector (primary labor market); the rest were under employment programmes.

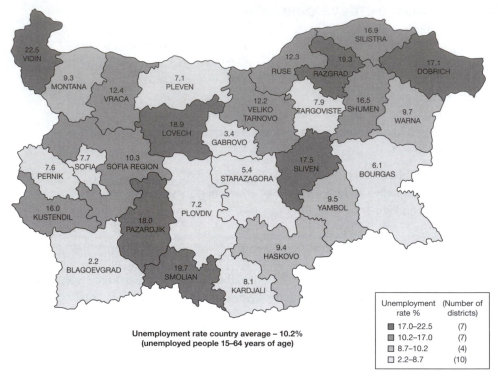

Figure 9.4 Territorial unemployment rates in Bulgaria, 2005

Source: Employment Agency, 2006.

The average annual number of unemployed people in Bulgaria in 2006 was estimated at 356,000 or 9.61 percent of the active population (Figure 9.5). This was the lowest level since the beginning of the transition period, resulting from the implementation of numerous government programs for the promotion of employment, and effective intermediation in the labor market. Other factors contributing to the rise in employment include the heightened economic activity of the population, the new jobs created by private entrepreneurs and, to a great degree, the lighter social insurance burden imposed on employers, which created conditions for legalizing some of the 'hidden' employment.

We must point out that during the same year the growth in work productivity was lower than the growth in employment, which means that the economy is developing to a greater extent due to higher employment, not due to the more efficient work of the employed. The economy is still unable to abandon the 'high employment – low efficiency' model. The pace of growth in tourism, a structurally important industry, is slower; agriculture is not sufficiently lively. From a social perspective, a worrisome trend is the increasing number of unemployed single mothers and mothers with children aged three and below, while the combination of these factors with the low birth-rate will have an increasingly negative economic impact. Another serious

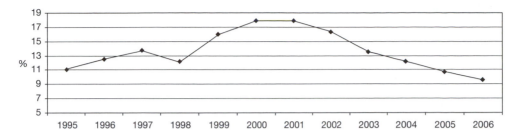

Figure 9.5 Bulgarian unemployment rates, 1995–2006
Source: Employment Agency, 2006.

social and economic problem is the high unemployment rate among young people, which has been high for several years.

There are significant regional disparities in unemployment. The disparity between demand and supply of workers is deepening, particularly at municipal level, where the labor market reflects to a greater degree the impact of natural factors, demographic processes, socio-economic factors, and the professional and educational structure of the work force[6] (Figure 9.4).

The demand for manpower depends on the overall economic situation, seasonal factors and the development of subsidized employment. The disparities observed in the supply of and demand for manpower largely depend on the education and qualifications of job seekers and, last but not least, on the mobility of manpower. In 2006, a representative survey was conducted to identify the needs of employers for people with specific qualifications (Balkan Institute, 06). The survey revealed that the occupations in the greatest demand in terms of both quantity and geographical outreach were those in construction, the textile industry, metal working, trade and services (especially tourism, hotels, and restaurants), and food industries. Further down on the list were qualifications related to high-tech industries. In those areas, however, "applied specialists" were the most preferred and one might expect higher requirements of employers in hiring people with adequate qualifications, experience, and motivation for the job.

Labor offices hold vocational training courses geared to the requirements of the labor market in order to reduce those discrepancies. Almost 31,000 unemployed people were involved in training in 2006 (Employment Agency, 07).

Key legislative provisions

The recent changes in Bulgarian labor legislation are aimed primarily at harmonization with the EC Directives, the ILO Conventions and the European Social Charter (revised) as ratified by Bulgaria in 2000. The entry into force of the Amending Act to the Labor Code on 31 March 2001 resolved a number of important issues concerning social dialogue, tripartite cooperation, the introduction of new forms of flexible working hours, a reduction of the opportunities for signing a series of fixed-term labor contracts, the right of employees to information in the case of collective redundancies, the introduction of new grounds for termination of labor contracts in exchange for severance compensation, etc.

The Labor Code was amended and many accompanying labor laws were passed, such as:

- the Collective Labor Disputes Act, passed in 1990 (last amended in 2001);
- the Employment Promotion Act, passed in 1998 (last amended in 2006);
- the Healthy and Safe Conditions at Work Act, passed in 1997 (last amended in 2006);
- the Guaranteed Pay Act in Cases of Employer's Bankruptcy, passed in 2004 (last amended in 2006).

Many of the outstanding issues which occurred subsequently were resolved through secondary legislation related to the enforcement of the Labor Code. That was a way to develop the achievements of labor legislation, to adjust it to international labor standards to a greater extent, to adapt to the *acquis communautaire*, and to expand the freedom of bargaining. The most essential feature of the period under review was the regulation of the rights and obligations of stakeholders by establishing minimum standards, while the collective and individual bargaining process could lead to more favorable terms of employment.

Until the early 1980s, Bulgaria was among the countries which had ratified and incorporated into their domestic legislation the greatest number of ILO Conventions. In 1997 alone over twenty-five labor conventions with regard to working hours were ratified, the protection of maternity, night-shift work, the right to association, compensation for accidents at work, weekly rest, paid annual leaves, trade union freedoms, and the protection of the right to trade union association, the protection of wages and salaries, the right to organization and collective bargaining, equal pay, discrimination in the field of labor and professions, etc.

TRENDS AND DEVELOPMENTS IN HRM PRACTICE

Over the fifteen years of Bulgaria's transition to a market economy, significant changes have been observed in the approaches to and methods of managing people at work. In this section, we examine the most important changes which took place during the period 1996–2003, when three CRANET surveys were carried out, in 1996, 1999, and 2003. The analysis is based on the following perspectives:

- the need to create conditions for a fast and successful integration of Bulgarian companies in the European business and social environment through testing HR practices in their relation to the convergent HRM processes;

- the need to accelerate the contribution of HRM to the development of a knowledge-based economy through testing its role in the creation of learning organizations.

The survey covers companies with over 200 employees. The sample universe in Bulgaria consists of approximately 848 companies, which accounted for 0.3 percent of the total number of enterprises in Bulgaria in 2003 (the total number of enterprises in 2003 was 218,136). The survey covers large production enterprises and companies operating in construction, the banking and financial sector, and transport. Small sectors of the national economy, such as agriculture, health, and organizations in public administration, are also involved (Table 9.3).

The survey includes 65.6 percent private, 23.4 percent state-owned, and 7.1 percent mixed companies. According to the regular report on small and medium-sized enterprises, the share of private companies in the category of large companies (over 250 employees) is 20 percent. Insofar as there is a slight increase of the share of

Table 9.3 Percentage of organizations involved in the survey by activity

Sphere of activity	Share (per cent)
Manufacturing (including food, beverages, tobacco, textiles, garments, printing industries, processing of rubber and plastics, etc.)	22.2
Production of metals; mechanical and electric engineering, tools manufacturing; office equipment	13.7
Energy and water	12.4
Chemical and mining industries; processing of non-energy minerals	7.8
Trade and distribution; hotels and restaurants; repair and maintenance works	7.8
Building and civil engineering	7.2
Banking, finance, insurance, business services (including consultancy, public relations, and advertising, legal services, etc.)	6.5
Transport and communications (railways, postal services, telecommunications, etc.)	5.9
Healthcare	2.6
Agriculture, hunting, forestry, fisheries	2.0
Services (radio and television, research, charities, etc.)	1.3
Public administration	1.3
Others	9.2

public enterprises, this is due to the objective of the survey to involve as many of the largest companies in terms of the number of employees as possible.

According to the National Statistical Institute (NSI, 2004) employees in the public sector accounted for 24 percent of all employees in 2003. At the same time, public enterprises accounted for only 0.5 percent of all enterprises. Therefore the orientation of the survey to this group of companies and even the slight over-emphasis on this group are fully justified from the perspective of the subject-matter and objectives of the survey.

The nature of the HR function

The results of the survey indicate that for the period 1996–2003 the position of Bulgarian HRM strengthened and its overall significance to organizations increased. The formal proofs of this conclusion are as follows: the inclusion of HR professions in the National Classifier of Professions and Positions, the increased number of companies having HR departments, and the enhanced involvement of HR managers in the top management bodies.

In EU countries more than 90 percent of companies have HR bodies and their heads tend to participate in the main boards in a percentage ranging from 40 percent to 70 percent (Vatchkova, 2007: 10). Although the three surveys show a delay in the constitution of HRM departments in Bulgarian organizations compared to the EU countries, the general trend is positive. It is proved by an 11 percent increase in companies with such bodies in 2003. Since 1999 there have been changes in the number of HR directors who sit on the main board – the registered increase is more than 7 percent. However, if we look further back to the findings in 1996 it seems that there was a small decline in board level HR involvement. Organizations with no participation of HR heads in the top management bodies predominate in Bulgaria. A regional trend is observed: the country is among the southern Balkan group, together with Turkey, Greece, the Turkish Cypriot community and Cyprus, where this participation is less common than in the EU member countries (Vatchkova, 2007: 10). Still very often the HR function is represented by directors who have other responsibilities in addition to that of HRM. In 1999, among those not represented at board level 65 percent of the respondents represented the function through the CEO, 14 percent through the administrative director and 6 percent through the finance director (Vatchkova, 2007: 25). Representation on the main board by those with different portfolios could be seen as the sign of an increasing integration between HR and other roles.

Early in 1996 and 1999 senior HR positions in the company were most often occupied by HR specialists from outside the organization. Later on this practice changed. According to 2003 data, Bulgarian HR directors were typically recruited from within the personnel department, which offered a good opportunity for HR managers to make a career in their own organizations. Today an increasing number of companies foster the career development of HR specialists. The number of participants in different qualification programs, including the Chartered Institute of Personnel and Development (CIPD) in the UK, is increasing. With the support of far-sighted managers, more and more personnel managers are certified according to the professional standards of CIPD and the Bulgarian Association for HRM and Development.

The participation of HR managers in the elaboration and implementation of corporate strategies is another indicator of their role in the overall strategic process. The main point of interest is whether HR is becoming a strategic partner and whether the function turns into a core one or whether its administrative character predominates. One important circumstance favorably influenced the change in the HR function – the stronger strategic orientation of Bulgarian companies observed during the survey period. From 1999 to 2003, the number of organizations which had corporate strategies doubled, while the popularity of unwritten ones showed slow progress from 22 percent to 32 percent[7] of the companies.

The level of involvement of the HR department in the strategic management process significantly increased during the period under review, which is evidenced by the increased number of organizations, in which HR managers participated in the elaboration of the business strategy at all three stages – from the outset (30 percent), through subsequent consultation, and mostly on its implementation (38 percent). In contrast to the other EU member states, where most respondents proactively contribute to the design of business strategies, Bulgarian HR managers are more often strategy implementers.

Bulgaria definitely lags behind nearly all surveyed countries in terms of having written mission statements and written value statements. For example, in the Czech Republic about 75 percent of the companies reported that they had corporate value statements, whereas only 34 percent of Bulgarian companies had such documents. The reasons for this situation can be seen partly in the fact that the market economy did not have long traditions in Bulgaria and therefore those corporate instruments and their importance for the competitiveness of the organization were still less known and even underestimated. Another reason for the weak popularity of mission and value statements is the fact that the development of projects in the field of corporate culture, codes of conduct, and corporate social responsibility programs has evolved only over recent years. In line with the convergent European trends, more Bulgarian companies have elaborated written HR strategies. Their number increased from 34 percent in 1999 to 44 percent in 2003, while unwritten HR strategies remained less popular.

The survey examines the changed responsibility of various elements of the HR function. In compliance with the prevailing EU trends, it is common in Bulgaria for HR and line managers to share responsibility for recruitment and selection. In training and development of employees the shared responsibility is dominated by HR. This creates opportunities for applying a systematic approach to training and for initiating the creation of a learning organization. External consultants are most actively involved in this function (in 53 percent of the surveyed companies), supporting the efforts of HR departments to improve the process of learning. Still weak is the role of the HR body in the decision-making process concerning pay and benefits and industrial relations, where the leading role is played by line managers. The activity of both managers is relatively balanced in the decisions affecting workforce expansion/reduction.

The computerization of HR activities and the introduction of information systems are important factors in the improved effectiveness of managing people at work. External HR information systems providers are used extensively; moreover, Bulgaria is within the group of countries showing the greatest increase in their implementation. More than a half of the surveyed companies (58 percent) reported that they used primarily independent HR systems; 18 percent utilized primarily systems integrated into wider management information systems. As in most countries, e-HR allowed mainly one-way communication, giving employees access to some personal information. Two-way communication, where the employee is able to
update simple personal information, was applied in nearly 10 percent of the responding companies.

The discussion about the nature of the HRM function is acquiring new dimensions for both employees and employers in Bulgaria today. Now the main focus is not only on whether the administrative function should be replaced by the strategic one and how to approve it. More companies, having already understood and accepted the HR manager as a strategic partner, face a new conflict – misunderstanding the real span of his or her duties and responsibilities, sometimes either having too high expectations, without providing the necessary resources, or overloading the HR body with unspecific responsibilities.

The profession of HR manager is relatively new to Bulgaria, but it is more and more consciously needed and in demand both because of the sharp deficit in a number of professions in the labour market and because of ever-stricter monitoring for compliance with European requirements in people management. Many companies hire people for this job without having a clear definition of its functions and responsibilities. In interviews conducted during the survey qualified HR specialists mentioned instances where the senior management declined responsibility for occupational accidents, failed to comply with their obligations pursuant to the organization's internal rules, and attempted to make the personnel manager responsible for the consequences.

Increasingly, the resolution of all conflicts, be they industrial, employee-related, or other, is being pushed in the direction of HR managers, with executive management stepping away from their responsibilities as prime conflict handlers. This is contributing to increased levels of stress and falling job satisfaction among HR managers, who feel that they are being handed all the political "hot potatoes" of the firm. This causes disputes, conflicts, and tension in people management and partly explains the recent increased turnover of HR managers observed in Bulgaria.

Recruitment and selection

In the context of continued economic growth, the employment activity of Bulgarian organizations increases every year. The vast scale of emigration of highly qualified personnel and the shortage of specialists in many professions compel HR bodies and recruiting companies to work more intensively to improve their recruitment and selection practices, and to develop strategies for winning the war for talent. The tendency observed since 1999 of predominantly internal management recruitment continues, but, at the same time, recruitment agencies/consultancies are becoming more active participants in company recruitment and selection processes. This has become possible because of the more intensive offering of such services, the greater competition, and hence the improvement in their quality.

The most common recruitment method among Bulgarian companies is the individual interview, which has replaced application forms at the top of the list (1996–9 surveys). Thus a more convergent area of recruitment practices with EU member states has been identified. Individual interviewing is preferred in 64 percent of companies for managerial positions and clerical staff and in 76 percent of them for technical personnel. References have been required in one out of four companies on average, the use of psychometric tests for different positions varies from 17 percent (managerial staff) to 14 percent (technical), 12 percent (clerical), and 7 percent (manual). Graphology and assessment centres are still seldom used in the recruitment practices of Bulgarian companies. Since 1999 most Bulgarian organizations have had difficulties in the recruitment of managerial staff (32 percent), IT specialists (23 percent), and other specialists. Half as many again companies have had difficulties in the recruitment and retention of manual workers, while the recruitment of administrative personnel appears to have caused problems in only 7 percent of organizations (1999 data).

Flexible working practices

Since 1990 flexible working arrangements (FWAs) in Bulgaria have been an area of very active research, discussion, and debate at the nationwide and organizational level from the legal, social, and managerial perspective. Official statistics (NSI, 2002) indicate that 97.2 percent of the people employed in 2002 worked on the basis of full-time contracts. Although the analysis based on the three CRANET surveys shows a stable upward tendency in flexible working practices, there are various types of difficulties which still hinder their development. In this section we explore the typology, studying the following types of FWAs (Vatchkova, 2007):

- working time (part-time work, weekend work, overtime, shift work, compressed working week, annualized hours, flexitime);
- contractual (job sharing, temporary/casual work, fixed-term employment);
- externalized (home-based work, teleworking)

Over the whole period surveyed, time flexibility prevailed (Figure 9.6). Shift work remained the most common FWA, used in 69.4 percent of organizations. Nearly half of all companies reported the use of overtime; part-time work was used in 36.7 percent, followed by annual hours contracts (32.5 percent), and flexi-time (24 percent). This may be explained by the fast growth in service industries, particularly tourism.

Bulgaria scored high in terms of fixed-term contracts (55.5 percent) and temporary/casual contracts (42.7 percent). More than 50 percent of companies reported that they did not use job sharing. Externalized flexible arrangements – home-based work and teleworking – are becoming more common, but very slowly. Convergence trends are valid for fixed-term contracts, shift working and annual hours contracts. It seems that the potential of part-time work and teleworking will not be tapped in the near future.

Compared to other European countries, Bulgaria has a dynamic pattern of flexible employment with the following characteristics:

- slower expansion of the range of these contracts;
- massive introduction of types of flexible employment which cause social problems, or which are beneficial to the employer rather than the employees;
- slower implementation of the various forms of flexible employment, allowing the rationalization of working time and achieving a better work life balance.

Reward and performance management

Reward, compensation, and motivation invariably attract the greatest interest from both employees and employers. They always rank among the top three main

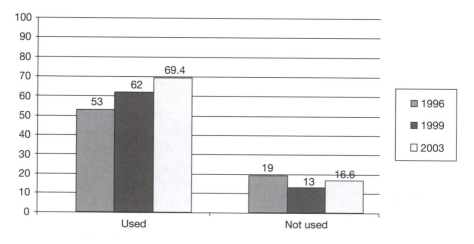

Figure 9.6 Percentage of organizations using shift work in Bulgaria

challenges for HR managers and specialists in Bulgaria, where they have undergone many different changes. Before analyzing them, it is necessary to consider some important facts related to the current price of labor.

1 While in most of the countries participating in the CRANET project labor costs account for 25–50 percent of the total operating costs, they have the lowest impact on the total operating costs in former communist countries: Hungary (27 percent), the Czech Republic (26 percent), Bulgaria (25 percent), and Slovakia (19 percent) (Horten, 2002: 8).
2 In 2005, the average monthly salary in Bulgaria was lowest in the fast growing tourist industry and highest in the financial sector, followed by the energy sector.
3 The average annual income per capita in Bulgaria was one of the lowest in Europe, lagging behind Slovenia, Hungary, the Czech Republic, and Poland.
4 According to the National Social Security Institute, the average salary in Bulgarian organizations was BGN 320 (about €163) in 2006 (NSI, 2006). The upward trend in the price of labor since 2005 continues – the salary increase in the 350 'best social security payers' in Bulgaria (the biggest companies) is 7–12 percent.

Empirical results from all three Bulgarian CRANET surveys show that pay and compensation policies have been elaborated in almost all surveyed organizations, the most popular being HR policies in Bulgarian organizations. Line managers participate very actively in their elaboration and implementation. There is evidence that in nearly every other organization they have the main responsibility for pay and compensation policies. We have grounds to claim that there is no balance of power in the decision-making process for this highly sensitive issue. Undoubtedly, line managers have the most complete and accurate picture of the performance of their subordinates and it is logical for them to be involved actively in determining remuneration. At the same time decisions made by only one person presuppose a high degree of subjectivity. Another negative aspect of this practice is the fact that line managers usually have a significant workload related to production process issues for which they are largely responsible. Due to lack of time and professional skills in the field of HRM, as a rule, line managers are unable to use accurate remuneration techniques and methods or update existing ones. The use of established stereotypes and egalitarian solutions is still widespread, which is demotivating for good employees and for people. A concerted effort should be made in the future with a view to sharing responsibilities for determining remuneration policies and methods with the HRM department.

The survey shows a major trend towards decentralization of pay to lower levels, from national/industry-wide to company and individual level (Vatchkova, 2007). The majority of organizations indicate that they determine basic pay at the individual level. For managerial staff the figure is 50.3 percent of companies, for professionals 31.2 percent, for clerical staff 28.7 percent and for manual workers 26.1 percent. Pay determination at establishment/site level is most popular for manual workers (in 39.5 percent of cases) and least popular for managers (in 19.7 percent of the companies surveyed).

Performance-related pay has shown great dynamism since 1996, when 67 percent of the respondents declared an increased use of variable pay. In 1999, it held true for 46 percent of companies. The latest survey showed the following proportion of organizations in the private sector using different types of financial participation and performance-related pay:

- shareplan – 9 percent;
- profit sharing – 14 percent;
- options – 14 percent;
- team performance-related pay – 10 percent;
- individual performance-related pay – 28 percent;
- collective/organization performance-related pay – 20 percent.

In general, the use of these schemes is more common for management and professional staff and less widespread among clerical staff and manual workers (Vatchkova, 2007).

In state-owned organizations the application of these schemes is not popular, although some pilot projects experimented with individual and team performance-related pay. For example, in the past few years there have been several unsuccessful attempts to introduce performance-based remuneration for civil servants. In places where it was experimented with, it did not contribute to improving the quality of administrative services and stultified the efforts and costs for the experiment. Differentiated payment for teachers in state-owned schools, proposed by the Ministry of Education in 2007, was met with resistance both by teachers and school managers and is unlikely to be implemented in the near future. This can be explained by the egalitarian attitudes propagated widely during the socialist regime, which have not yet been overcome.

Fringe benefits and non-financial incentives have lost their great popularity of communist times and now some new models are appearing, mainly in multinational companies.

Since the beginning of our performance appraisal studies (1996) a phenomenon has been observed in Bulgaria, which is not typical of EU member countries. This is the prevalence of formal appraisal systems for manual staff rather than for managerial staff, which is the common European practice.

Special attention should be given to the evaluation of managers at all levels in Bulgarian organizations. Interviews with HR managers and HR specialists conducted during the 2003 CRANET survey create the impression that the prevailing management style in Bulgarian organizations is authoritarianism. This is also evidenced by the analysis of results from the survey in the Business Communications section, which examines the dynamics of horizontal and vertical oral and written communications between managers and their staff. Decreasing use of upward communication channels is observed. This indicates a return to authoritarian management, the scope of which had decreased according to the 1999 survey. This management style, which is typical of centralized planned economies, presupposes the managers' "untouchablity" and a lack of interest in evaluations and self-evaluation. Another feature which is still typical of Bulgarian business – the fact that management is underestimated as a factor in the organization's performance and prosperity. Such attitudes are remnants of the producer-based economy which Bulgaria had until 1989. Nevertheless, positive changes have been taking place towards increased use of management appraisal (Figure 9.7)

Immediate superiors were involved most actively in the process of performance appraisal, as was the case in 67.3 percent of organizations in 1999 (in later surveys that question was not asked at all). Next-level superiors were subject to performance appraisal in 47 percent of companies. Customer appraisal scores high in Bulgaria compared to other EU countries, being used in one out of four organizations. The results from the appraisals were used mainly for the purposes of determining individual performance-related pay and the organization of work. Information from those systems was still ineffectively used in the decision-making process concerning career development, as well as in individual and organizational training needs analysis.

Training and development

By the beginning of the new millennium, all European economies were experiencing growing pressure caused by globalization, increased competition, and fast technological changes. The advanced countries responded to these forces by creating a new socio-economic environment – that of the knowledge-based economy. This

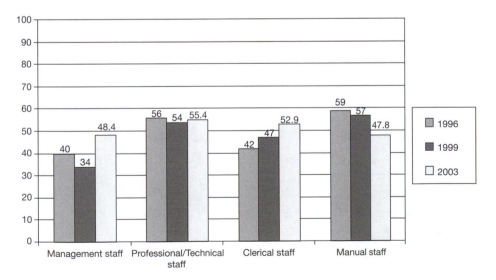

Figure 9.7 Percentage of organizations in Bulgaria with formal appraisal systems

fostered efforts to improve the standards and performance of the educational system (Pilbeam and Corbridge, 2002), which was seen as an important instrument to meet the changing needs of the labor market for a more flexible and adaptable workforce.

Growing efforts to improve the level of training in the workplace also came in response to the new demands. The knowledge-based economy calls for new HRM functions as a subject governing organizational knowledge. These new functions deserve special attention if we share the understanding of De Geus that 'the greatest competitive advantage of the contemporary company is its ability to learn'. A hypothesis could be launched that the HR managers' involvement in corporate training is increasing. This assumption is supported by the results of the three last CRANET surveys, which show (Table 9.4) that the primary responsibility of the HRM department in Bulgaria for major policy decisions on training and development has significantly increased. This process suggests an equivalent decrease in line managers' accountability for this function. Shared responsibility has become more relevant.

During the last ten years the idea of training and development as a major competitive advantage has been gaining ground in all countries in transition. There has been a tendency to increase investment in training, to develop new personnel qualification methods and techniques, and to improve the efficiency of these activities. The effectiveness of training and development is closely evaluated in all the countries studied by the CRANET survey. This is reflected in increased systematic training needs analysis as well as in measuring training outcomes. The last three CRANET surveys show that more money and time are invested in corporate training, in spite of the still relatively low investment capacity of Bulgarian business during the fourteen years of transitional, compared to other European countries.

Table 9.4 Primary responsibility for major policy decisions in Bulgaria compared with EU average (percent of organizations)

Primary responsibility for training and development policy decisions	Bulgaria			EU+ countries not in EU (extremes 1998–9)		EU+ average
	1996	1999	2003		Minimum	
Line management (LM)	40	27	22	41 (N)	3 (I)	15
LM in consultancy with HRD	27	37	29	53 (CH)	22 (P)	36
HRD in consultancy with LM	15	16	28	55 (F)	9 (N)	35
HR department (HRD)	9	12	16	27 (I)	3 (S)	10

Note: N = Norway, CH = Switzerland, F = France, I = Italy, P = Portugal, S = Sweden

Correspondingly, the requirements for more effective use of these investments are obvious. The share of companies measuring the effectiveness of training increased from 53 percent in 1996 to 60 percent in 1999. Another positive fact is that more companies started to systematically observe training needs – their number increased by two percentage points for the same period.

This typically convergent tendency could be explained by a number of factors – the increase in investment in training, the enhanced requirements for professionals on the staff where international collaboration is required by the management of multinational companies, and the sudden reduction of the modern professions' life-cycle.

The analysis of the data on investment in training shows a positive tendency. Organizations' expenditure on training and development is located within a band between 2 percent and 4 percent of annual payroll costs in most of the countries in the survey (Vatchkova, 2007: 53). In Bulgaria the number of organizations allocating less than 1 percent of the salary and wage bill to training and development fell sharply during the period 1996–2003. Over the same period, the share of organizations spending from 5 percent to 9.9 percent for the same purposes increased. In Bulgaria the greatest increase in investment in training was achieved by the group of companies allocating more than 10 percent – their share increased by twenty-three percentage points. Thus, in 1999 the proportion of Bulgarian companies having similar (relatively) training budgets came close to that of Portugal, which recorded the highest value for this indicator, and exceeded the average European level. This positive trend is observed in the results of the last survey. In 2003, the group of companies whose annual training budgets exceeded 4 percent, had more than doubled since 1996. Bulgaria reported the highest value of the indicator "money spent on training as percentage of annual payroll costs" – 6.32.

Most Bulgarian organizations recognize the importance of training and development for the success of their business but they face problems in funding these activities. Managers often set other investment priorities (e.g. new technology) rather than investing in people. There is still a belief that it is the employees' responsibility to achieve, and subsequently improve, their competence. Employers often overestimate the role of university and college education in providing relevant qualifications to graduates and meeting specific corporate expectations. This standpoint holds back the rapid modernization of corporate training and development systems and partially explains the relatively low level of investment in these activities compared to the average for EU countries. Here the level of investment is assessed as "low" if we consider it in absolute figures, not as a share of the annual payroll costs, because currently the remuneration level in Bulgaria is relatively low.

Another indicator of corporate training and development in Bulgaria is the number of training days per year and per employee. A significant correlation between money spent and training days used is observed. The values of these two indicators are rather higher in Bulgarian organizations than the EU average values. Managerial and clerical staff in Bulgaria received more training in 1999, which corresponded to the need for improving the qualifications of these staff categories and meeting current European criteria. Organizations spent more days on training managerial and professional or technical staff than the EU average. As far as clerical and manual staff are concerned, Bulgaria spent much more time on their training than EU countries on average. It seems that Bulgarian organizations emphasize the training and development of managers and specialists as the key people, and they, in turn, become informal trainers of other categories of employees. There is a remarkable change in the dissemination of clerical staff training, which is quite reasonable under the pressure of new information technologies and the sharp need to strengthen the administrative capacity of Bulgarian employees in all industries.

The average training days per year for different staff categories in 2003 were as follows:

- management – 10.65;
- professional/technical – 9.93;
- manual – 9.66;
- clerical – 6.39.

The analysis of investment in people places Bulgaria in a special "leading" position, but this situation deserves a more detailed and profound analysis to identify the real drivers and reasons for this situation. One possible explanation is the increasing gap between the demand for and supply of labor force profile and quality. New information technologies and the requirements they impose, the shortened life-cycle of professions, increasing personnel turnover, the greater mobility of labour, and above all the "Europeanization" of the business environment in Bulgaria are natural incentives for increasing the volume of company training and investment in such training.

The hypothesis about the recognition of the pivotal role of employee training in a successful transition to a more effective HRM is supported by the data about the proportion of organizations systematically analyzing employee training needs. During the period 1996–9 the share of Bulgarian organizations performing such analysis grew from 42 percent only to 44 percent. Thus the level of this indicator still remained significantly lower than the minimum identified in EU countries. There was a remarkable increase in the percentage of organizations monitoring the effectiveness of their training. The last survey when this indicator been monitored (in 1999) showed that in Bulgaria the indicator reached the EU average. Understandably, with their inadequate financial resources Bulgarian organizations are particularly concerned about the effective allocation and utilization of their training and development investments.

The CRANET survey systematically studies the dynamics of training areas, considered by HR managers as a major issue in the next three-year period. Compared to the previous two studies, where computers and new technologies, marketing, and people management retained the top three positions, the latest survey shows an obvious move towards professional and/or vocational skills development (7 percent), information technology (6.4 percent), and teamwork building (5.1 percent). After the fifteen-year-long transition to a market economy, the primary challenges for the personnel function ranked by HR managers categorically shifted the focus of attention from restructuring (4.7 percent) and staff reduction (3.3 percent) in 1999 to competence development (5.9 percent) in 2003. This data prove once again the concept of the key role of training and development as a competitive accelerator.

THE FUTURE OF HRM IN BULGARIA

Bulgaria's EU membership is the greatest catalyst of reforms and changes in the social and labor environment. Observing the new rules and regulations can significantly increase the price of labor. Mergers and acquisitions are intensifying. Bankruptcies of small companies and local producers can be expected, causing a new wave of unemployment. On the other hand, the labor market is nearly exhausted; many sectors and activities suffer from lack of a labor force. The emigration process, which affects mainly highly qualified and young people, could prove difficult to stop. Stricter control over employment law should decrease informal (unregistered) employment and improve labor conditions in many small companies.

Comparison of the state and development of Bulgarian human resource management and development on the basis of CRANET surveys for the period 1996–2003 shows that Bulgaria is keeping up with EU countries in some important areas. Two of the most significant areas of backwardness – the low popularity and the unstable position of the HRM department, as well as the low strategic orientation of Bulgarian companies – are in a process of considerable change. In 2003, the number of Bulgarian companies with an HRM department increased and their position and functions strengthened. HR became more strategically oriented. There are sufficient reasons to conclude that Bulgarian HRM is on its way to converging with positive European trends and it really needs a qualitatively new type of training support. A novel approach has to be found to allow adequate, effective, relatively inexpensive, quick, and strongly targeted human resource management and development (HRMD) training and development in order to approach the best European practices and to facilitate the process of labor integration of Bulgarian companies. This can be achieved only by ensuring synergy between the combined efforts of various subjects, overcoming their institutional boundaries and utilizing the advantages of information technologies. The joint efforts of educational and research institutions, businesses, civil society organizations, and the state administration could contribute to filling in the gap between modern-day requirements of the HR profession and its present capacity (Vatchkova, 2004).

Recognizing the importance of this task, the Bulgarian Human Resource Management and Development Association initiated the establishment of an informal (for the time being) National Social Network for Vocational Training in the Field of HRMD. All training activities are based on the professional competence standards. The Bulgarian Human Resource Management and Development

Association (BHRMDA) operates as its intermediary, integrator, and main sponsor.

The establishment of this network builds on the main principles of:

● network organization of work;
● virtual organization;
● learning organization.

The network organization is one of the essential changes that shape the character of modern HRMD systems and help overcome national boundaries and differences. It is accomplished through the construction and integration of informal, flexible, open nets, including partners from different territories and organizations performing various activities which can contribute to the improvement of professional competence in the field of HRM. This dynamic network reflects the new social relationships between professional organizations, groups, and individual professionals. Every partner produces an impact with his or her distinctive competencies so that, if successfully constructed, the network could increase the level of specialization, market adaptation, and flexibility of all participants. This dynamic network is an extremely flexible structure, capable of combining high complexity and maximum specialist competency. The network process is not managed by any organization on its own, since the network can survive only if it constantly alters and modifies the relationships between partners. But it could be performed within the framework of one organization as a process parallel to its official structure.

The virtual organization is a model of the future, which assumes a constant unification process of small organizations and people, administering more than just their own resources, sharing their costs, relying on internal and external collaboration between the partners. A wide range of temporary contracts is explored to utilize the specific opportunities of its members' competence portfolios.

The learning organization, i.e. an organization "skilled at creating, acquiring and transferring knowledge and at modifying its behaviour to reflect new knowledge and insights" enhances the learning process when it:

● comprises a change in the organizational knowledge base;
● happens in an interplay of individual and organization;
● takes place through interaction with the internal and/or external environment;
● leads to an adaptation of the system to the environment;
● helps in gaining a higher level of problem-solving capacity.

Taking into account the above-mentioned concepts and principles and translating them into practice, the Bulgarian network is being constructed as an open system, with the following main participants: BHRMDA and its professional clubs, the Institute of Certified HRMD Professionals, the Bulgarian Chamber of Commerce, New Bulgarian University, Bulgarian Business Leaders Forum, and TechnoLogika (core members), attracting on a temporary basis universities, consultancy companies, high schools, and other institutions (flexible partners).

Summarizing the results of the CRANET surveys and taking into account the new requirements of globalization under the conditions of the knowledge-based economy, the successful development of the HR function in Bulgaria will meet the following challenges:

- increasing professionalism in the field of HRM services, doing away with the lay performance of this function;
- introducing systems for HRM in large companies;
- best HRM practices to become more popular in small and medium-sized enterprises;
- higher control over the level of performance quality of all HRM activity.

These challenges, in their turn, will raise the following expectations:

- increased future demand for outsourced HRM services to small and medium-sized because of the predominant number of them;
- enhanced implementation of the professional standards for HRM specialists, which have already been introduced;
- further computerization of HRM activities;
- mass introduction of HRM audits and corporate social responsibility audits.

The operational programme 'Human Resource Development' was launched in Bulgaria in 2007. Its budget consists of €1,213,869,575 from the EU and BGN182,080,436 – from national co-financing. The budget will be used to improve labor force quality and management. This is Bulgaria's first real opportunity to obtain financing for the training which is equally needed by employers and by employees. This training will improve the balance of demand and supply of labor in terms of quality and quantity and will facilitate Bulgaria's successful integration into the European labor market.

The performance-related bonus system in Schneider Electric, Perushtitsa[8]

Case study

Perushtitsa is a small town at the foot of the Rhodope mountains with a population of 5,513. It has a rich history dating back to the Second Bulgarian Kingdom and the period of struggle for liberation from Turkish occupation. Today Perushtitsa is a popular tourist destination. The food and beverage industry is the most widely developed industry in the region. During the years of transition to a market economy the town suffered very high unemployment rates, as a number of industrial plants were shut down. Subsequent foreign investment helped revive the industry.

continued

On 8 February 1999 Schneider Electric Bulgaria purchased a portion of the company EAZ in the town of Perushtitsa. Pursuant to the acquisition agreement the existing employees were rehired in the new company. The company started operating with 100 employees. Following the acquisition, the building was refurbished in order to be made suitable for new production. Significant investments were made in the overall initial refurbishment, for which the company received the 2000 award for best foreign investor of the "Made in Bulgaria" Union.

Schneider Electric is a world leader in the field of power distribution and industrial control, with three major brands: Merlin Gerin, Square D and Telemecanique. Schneider Electric Bulgaria EOOD was established in 1998. It has 320 employees in total working in Sofia, Varna and Perushtitsa. The factory in Perushtitsa employs 250 people manufacturing electrical engineering products.

Discussions about alternative remuneration systems and their implementation in Bulgaria began in the 1990s. The subjective determination of remuneration is still dominant in Bulgarian companies, as is evident from the results of the CRANET survey on the role of line managers in this process. In this context the management of Schneider Electric are among the leaders working towards a switch from fixed to flexible remuneration, a switch from a bonus awarded by the management to a bonus determined on the basis of precise criteria.

New forms of remuneration, including performance-based remuneration, are gaining popularity among private companies in Bulgaria. One of the conductors of ideas and practices for flexible remuneration is multinational companies operating in the country. In the last ten years these companies have had a significant impact on the methods of people management in Bulgarian companies. A typical example of this is the new remuneration system introduced in Schneider Electric Bulgaria.

In the last three years (2005/6/7) the Bulgarian economy has been developing at a fast pace. Analysts point out the potential risks of overheating in the economies of the new EU member states. Lack of sufficient workforce is a typical phenomenon in overheated economies. According to a survey conducted by *Manpower Bulgaria* (Markova, 2007) almost 90 percent of the companies operating in different industries, both in Sofia and other large towns, stated that they find it difficult to recruit suitable personnel. The management of the company introduced a differentiated bonus system with the objective of long-term motivation and retention of good employees, who are difficult to recruit in smaller towns located far from the capital Sofia. The type, structure, and amount of the employees' remuneration result from a series of managerial decisions aimed at achieving as much employee satisfaction as possible within the framework of the financial capabilities of the organization and high economic performance levels.

Schneider Electric Bulgaria has internal rules which define the technologies and procedures with regard to:

- the calculation, distribution, and regulation of the wage bill;
- the calculation of individual salaries under the labor contracts;
- the calculation of additional remuneration;
- the calculation of the actual amount of salaries.

Salaries include a basic component and additional remuneration. The amount of the basic salary is defined in the labor contract and depends on the position and on performance. It is then used to calculate the additional remuneration.

Characteristic features of the bonus system

A special bonus to the salary is intended to promote the commitment of staff and to enhance labor productivity. The criteria for calculating bonuses are specific to each professional category. They may be changed at any point in time by the managing director, depending on circumstances. The monthly bonus is paid when the planned targets are attained or exceeded. It is expressed as a percentage of the basic salary and updated on an annual basis depending on the objectives of the company. The bonus system includes general bonuses applicable to the whole staff and specific bonuses intended for certain categories of employees. The employees are grouped into a number of categories. The criterion for grouping is the contribution of the position to the manufacturing process.

The bonus system is made up of three elements applicable to the whole staff:

- collective bonus;
- attendance component;
- individual bonus.

The collective bonus is applicable to the whole staff. There are three criteria for its calculation: Q/TT, QS, and IQ.

1 Q/TT – Productivity

This criterion can be defined as follows:

- Q = Quantity of output;
- TT = Technological Time for the assembly works in the workshop.

It includes the working time of operators, distributors, quality inspectors, warehouse workers, and adjusters.

Productivity accounts for 80 percent of the collective bonus.

2 QS – Quality of Service

This criterion reflects delays in the fulfillment of orders. It is based on the sequence of the orders placed with the manufacturing department. The criterion is calculated as the

continued

total number of delayed orders as a percentage of the total number of orders for the period.

The quality of service accounts for 10 percent of the collective bonus.

3 IQ – Index of Quality

This criterion is based on the day-to-day quality control in manufacturing. The index depends on the monthly results of quality assurance expressed on the basis of the number and gravity of errors.

Quality accounts for 10 percent of the collective bonus.

Calculation of the bonus

Targets are planned for each element:

- Productivity – X low-voltage switches per hour;
- Index of Quality – Y percent low-voltage switches of poor quality;
- Quality of Service – Z percent

(See Figure 9.8.)

Q/TT = 18 poles per hour – bonus 80 percent

IQ = rate of 6.5 – bonus 10 percent

QS = 95 percent – bonus 10 percent

In February, the indicators were quantified as follows:

Q/TT = 18 poles – bonus 80 percent

IQ = rate of 3.85 – bonus 11.8 percent

QS = 94.5 percent – bonus 9.5 percent

Aggregate bonus for that department – 101.3 percent

Distribution of the bonus by categories of staff:

Category I – 100 percent = 101.3 percent

Category II – 50 percent = 50.6 percent

Category III – 25 percent = 25.3 percent

Category IV – 15 percent= 15.2 percent

Figure 9.8 Plan for the low-voltage manufacturing department of Schneider Electric during the first half of 2005

The specific bonus for each employee is calculated in terms of the basic salary of each employee.

Attendance bonus

One major disadvantage of the workforce in Bulgaria, compared to Poland and Hungary, is the poor discipline of staff employed in the industry. This is a result of the relatively weaker industrial traditions of Bulgaria's economy which went through a process of rapid industrialization in the years following World War II. In rural areas and in smaller towns people still combine work on their small family farms with work in industrial plants. They frequently take a leave of absence during the grape-picking season, while livestock care distracts and burdens people employed in industrial plants. In order to limit unwanted leaves of absence, the company introduced special incentives for attendance aiming both to improve work discipline and to increase productivity.

This bonus is intended to provide a fair and comprehensive mechanism encouraging the regular attendance of employees. It contributes to the better balance in protecting the health of employees on the one hand and the interests of the factory on the other. The goal is to reduce absences due to frequent sickness down to 4 percent. Three attendance levels have been selected:

- Level 1 – if absences exceed 9 days per 12 months, the collective bonus is reduced by 30 percent;
- Level 2 – if absences exceed 18 days per 12 months, the collective bonus is reduced by 50 percent;
- Level 3 – if absences exceed 27 days per 12 months, the collective bonus is reduced by 80 percent.

There is a special net bonus for regular attendance:

- BGN 50 – for 12 months with up to three days of absence;
- BGN 100 – for 12 months with no absences.

The bonus is calculated every end of the year.

Individual bonus

The third element of the bonus system is specific to workmanship and it is intended for:

- workers in the manufacturing process;
- assembly workers;
- adjusters.

continued

As is evident from Table 9.5, the ratio between the basic salary and additional remuneration is approximately 50:50. Initially employees were skeptical about the innovation, but then they adapted quickly to the new remuneration system. Consequently, the management achieved its objectives: decreased staff turnover, improved work discipline, and better performance. The system is being continuously improved. They are working for more efficient communication of work results, for popularization of good performance, and for further implementation of non-cash incentives as part of an overall system of staff remuneration and motivation.

Table 9.5 Bonus calculation system at Schneider Electric

Components	Performance (percent)	Adjustment (percent)	Adjustment (BGN)	Remuneration (BGN)
Basic salary				250
Collective bonus	101.3	101.3	253.25	
Individual performance	6	4.47	11.18	
Attendance	100	0	0	
Total			**264.43**	**514.43**

Note: In December, the worker will receive a regular attendance bonus of BGN 100.

NOTES

1 The economic activity rate is calculated as the ratio between the labor force and the population in the 15–64 age bracket.
2 EUROSTAT, 3rd quarter 2005.
3 The employment rate is calculated as the ratio between the number of employed people and the population in the 15–64 age bracket.
4 The unemployment rate is calculated as the ratio between the number of unemployed people and the workforce in the 15–64 age bracket.
5 Calculated as the ratio between the number of unemployed people registered with labor offices and the active population. Source: Employment Agency.
6 Source: Labor Market 06 Annual Survey, Employment Agency, 06.
7 Valid percentage.
8 The information for this case study was provided by Mariya Nikovska, an employee in the HR department in Schneider Electric, Perushtitsa. The full text of the case study was written and edited by Elizabeth Vatchkova.

REFERENCES AND FURTHER READING

BILSP (2006). *Methods for Research, Identification and Observation of the Vocational Training of the Employers, Workers and Employees in Bulgaria*. Sofia: Balkan Institute for Labor and Social Policy.

Horton, S. (2002). "Competencies in People Resourcing". In Pilbeam, S. and Corbridge, M. (eds) *People Resourcing. HRM in Practice*. Prentice Hall.

Koubek, J. and Vatchkova, E. (2004). "Bulgaria and Czech Republic: Countries in Transition. In Brewster, C., Mayrhofer, W. and Morley, M. (ed.). *Human Resource Management in Europe: Evidence of Convergence?* Amsterdam: Elsevier; Oxford and Burlington, MA: Butterworth-Heinemann.

Labor Market 2006 Annual Survey, Employment Agency, 06.

Markova, Z. (2007). "The luck of specialists Outside Sofia is Sharpening." *Dnevnik*, 26 September. Sofia.

NSI (2004). *National Statistical Institute Year Book*. Sofia: NSI.

Papalexandris, N., Rassmussen, E., Stavrou-Costea, E., Tyson, S., Gooderman, P., Poutsma, E., Mayerhofer, W., Dany, F., Hatt, F. (2006). *CRANET Survey on Comparative Human Resource Management – International Report 2005*. Cranfield: Cranfield University.

Pilbeam, S. and Corbridge, M. (eds) (2002). *People Resourcing. HRM in Practice*. Prentice Hall.

Vatchkova, E. (1997). *Human Resource Management in Bulgarian Organizations – Results from the Sociological Survey*. Sofia: International Business School Transbusiness-E.

Vatchkova, E. (2000). *Human Resource Management in Bulgarian Organizations – Results from the Sociological Survey*. Sofia: International Business School Transbusiness-E.

Vatchkova, E. (2000). "Human Resource Management in Bulgaria – Hot Problems of the Transition to Market Economy". In Brewster, C. J., Mayrhofer, W. and Morley, M. (eds) *New Challenges for European Human Resource Management*. London: Macmillan.

Vatchkova, E. (2001). "The Speed of Changes – The Bulgarian Way to the Integrated European HRM". In *Personalmanagement im Transformationsprozess*. Munich: Rainer Hampp Verlag; Mering: Hampp.

Vatchkova, E. (2004). "Competence-Based Approach to Training". Report at the International Conference on HRM in a Knowledge-Based Economy, Ljubljana, 2–4 June 2004.

Vatchkova, E. (2004). *Human Resource Management in Bulgarian Organizations – Results from the Sociological Survey*. International Business School Transbusiness-E.

Vatchkova, E. (2007). *Survey on Competitive Human Resource Management. National Report for Bulgaria, CRANET*, 2006. Sofia: IBS Transbusiness-E.

WEBSITES

www.az.government.bg
www.knsb-bg.org
www.podkrepa.org
www.mlsp.government.bg

10 Managing human resources in Russia

IGOR GURKOV AND OLGA ZELENOVA[1]

INTRODUCTION

This chapter outlines the recent trends, the current situation, and the likely development of Human Resource Management in the Russian Federation. The chapter is organized as follows: we briefly introduce the past experience of the Russian economy, describe the societal and institutional context of HRM, give details of the essential legislation and primarily pay attention to the essence of the HRM function – its place in company management, recruitment, selection, performance appraisal and remuneration practices, training and development. An illustrative case study presents all these points in their "natural" setting.

To move our chapter from anecdotal to more systemic evidence, we largely use the results of our own studies in HRM practices. In particular, we refer to the surveys administered at the end of 2003 and the end of 2004. Each survey covered 1,700 CEOs and 2400 managers of companies of all industries, sizes, and forms of ownership. We also used various Russian references. Extracts from official statistics are presented in an Appendix.

THE TRANSFORMATION PROCESS

Although similar sections in other chapters of this book are entitled "The transition process," we have several reasons for using the term "The transformation process." Indeed, there are a number of key differences between the changes in Russia and similar events in Central and East European countries.

First, for most Central and East European countries, despite the differences in the point of departure, there was an identified *point of destination* – to rejoin the wider Europe, to re-establish "normal" economic and social relations, to reach the European level of economic and social welfare. For Eastern Germany such a "leap backward" happened virtually overnight, with the reunification of Germany; other Central and East European countries have traced and are still tracing their own trajectories in joining the European Union, but the target itself is clearly visible. For Russia there was never a clear point of destination, neither in the economic nor in the societal aspects of transformation. Today Russia continues her search for identity, with little reference to a particular national or regional model. This means that there is no notion of an "ideal" society as well as no clear benchmarks for management models and processes.

Second (fortunately for them), none of the Central and East European countries have experienced such well-targeted genocide of their own people. Whole cohorts of the most energetic groups of the population (city entrepreneurs and wealthy peasants in the late 1920s, industrial engineers in early 1930s, Red Army officers in the late 1930s) were totally annihilated. Millions more spent the greater part of their life (on average 20 years) as state slaves in the Gulag in 1937–56. Peasants received the right to move from their villages only in the 1960s, graduating students were offered the right to select their places of employment only in 1990. This brutal tradition of forced labor is still visible. Today more than 10 million Russian citizens bear the experiences of labor camps (as detention places are officially called).[2]

Third, the communist experiment in Russia lasted for 70 years (almost three generations), that is, a generation longer than in any Central and East European country. This excludes the possibility of passing on as family memories any habits and know-how regarding private enterprise and self-employment. As a result, the acquisition of such habits and skills was made at enormous costs and at great personal risk to the individual.

All the abovementioned causes force us not only to call the process that has taken place in Russia over the past 20 years "transformational," but also to pay more attention to the particular stages of the process.

The first stage of the transformational process was 1986–9. Three subsequent laws ("Law on Individual Working Activities" (1986), which officially permitted for the first time since 1929 any entrepreneurial activities and self-employment; "Law on Enterprise" (1987), which stipulated the election of general directors of enterprises by the employees; and "Law on Cooperatives" (1988), which de facto made legal the existence of the capitalist firm) created a short "golden age." Millions of people rushed to form cooperatives. Some of them quickly occupied the missing niches in production of consumer goods or in private services,[3] while many other "cooperatives" simply channeled funds from state enterprises into private pockets by overpricing subcontracting and intermediary services. Such a system could not last for long. Additional income without additional production of goods coupled with frozen prices of state-supplied goods and services created from autumn 1990 a situation of total shortages of basic goods and foodstuffs. This made the end of the Soviet Union inevitable.

The second stage of the transformation process has exact start and end dates. It started on 1 January 1992 with the liberalization of prices and ended on 22 August 1998 with the banking crisis and fourfold devaluation of the ruble. The very essence of this period is convulsions in the economic and societal systems to adapt themselves to the break-up of the Soviet Union and the destruction of the system of central planning. Galloping inflation, annihilation of savings frozen in the state savings bank, barter exchanges between enterprises, and large wage arrears were among the main features of the period. Among others we should distinguish the sharp fall in industrial production that was not accompanied by a similar fall in employment. Gross domestic product (GDP) fell in 1990–8 by 42.5 percent, while the number of those employed decreased from 75.3 to 63.6 million persons, i.e. by 15.3 percent. The absolute maximum of registered unemployment was reached in April 1996 – 2.8 million people, or 3.8 percent of the economically active population.

The greatest decline of employment was in industry – 8.6 million people. Industrial employment as a share of total employment shrank over the 1990s from 30.3 percent to 22.2 percent. Many engineers and qualified workers (by some estimates, up to eight million) became so-called "shuttles," regularly traveling to Poland, Turkey, and China and bringing back portmanteaus of cheap garments, footwear, and electrical appliances for retail "bazaars."

However, this period was not totally dark. Russian enterprises have learned the basics of marketing and financial management. At the same time, new private sectors (including banking) have emerged. Last but not least, this period was characterized by the expansion of higher education – newly created and old universities alike feverishly educated marketers, financiers, economists, and lawyers for a new economy. The share of university graduates in the total labor force grew from 17.6 percent in 1992 to 25.2 percent in 2001.

At the beginning of 1999 the current stage of the transformational process started. The sharp devaluation of the national currency eliminated foreign competition and provoked industrial revival. This trend was strengthened by the very favorable prices on world markets for most types of raw materials, especially oil, gas, and ferrous and non-ferrous metals. The "golden rain" of petrodollars enabled the state to have a significant budget surplus and to assume once again a "patronage" role in society, launching pension and social welfare reforms.[4] Over the last two or three years there have also been persistent and more efficient attempts to re-establish state control over the most lucrative sectors of the national economy. Today large Russian corporations are under direct or indirect state control does not prevent them selling shares on international stock exchanges and pursuing aggressive overseas expansion. Simultaneously the state takes a more "dirigist" approach in stricter regulation of all other segments of economic activities.

THE CONTEXT FOR HUMAN RESOURCE MANAGEMENT

Industrial relations context

The current context for industrial relations is predetermined by the growing force and involvement of the state in the economy and the clearly visible desire "to maintain peace and tranquility" in political as well as in social spheres. The dejure ruling party "United Russia" (which has a majority in both chambers of the Parliament and supports (and is supported) by the President) proclaims in its Program Declaration that "clusters of social tensions still remain" and postulates "the effective social policy" that should protect disabled persons and promote self-employment and entrepreneurship.[5]

On a more practical level this means that the state takes the role of the supreme arbiter in labor disputes. Such a role is enhanced because the major trade unions united in the Russian Confederation of Independent Trade Unions are "tame" and do not present any real pressure. Needless to say, they do not dare to organize large-scale actions. The recent fierce labor disputes, for example the strike at the Ford Motors' plant near St. Petersburg, were organized by alternative trade unions. Various associations of employers (including the Russian Association of Employers, Russian Union of Industrialists [association of large businesses] and "OPORA" (association of medium-sized and small businesses) do not hesitate to express their adherence to "civilized social partnership."

The main form of social partnership in Russia today is the so-called "collective agreement." The collective agreement is a contract between employer and employees. The parties to the contract are the general director and the local unit of a trade union. If there are no trade unions in the company, employees may elect their representative. The major clauses of the collective agreement are:

- forms, systems, and levels of wages and salaries;
- other types of compensation;
- employment levels, retraining, and firing;
- working time, including leave and holidays;
- work safety;
- interests of employees in the privatization of a company, including privatization of dwellings in company ownership.

There is also a special article that stipulates that strikes are not allowed unless the major clauses of the contract are violated. In general, the government favors collective agreements and promotes their wider use in large companies.

When we look at small and medium-sized businesses, the situation is much different. There are no active trade unions in small businesses, and workers are usually totally powerless against the arbitrary rule of an employer as local controlling bodies (trade inspections) rarely interfere. However, when an employee brings the case to court, Russian courts are inclined to take the side of an employee as a "presumed victim".[6] Thus, the very threat of bringing the case to court serves in many cases as a very good argument in individual labor disputes.

Key labor market developments

The best Russian expert in labor issues named his monograph on the Russian labor market development "Adaptation without Restructuring" (see Kapelushnikov, 2001). At first glance, this seems exaggerated. The Russian statistics present the common trends of a post-industrial society – decline of employment in industry and agriculture, and the sharp rise of services (see Appendix, Table A10.1). The economy also absorbed the additional entrants to the labor force – the number of the population of working age experienced stable growth 83.7 million in 1993 to 87.3 million in 2001, while unemployment remained low. In 2000–5 the total number of unemployed stood at the level of 2 million (2.8 percent of the active population). The number of unemployed calculated according to the methodology of the International Labor Office was in April 2005 around 5.8 million, or 7.9 percent of the economically active population.[7] This figure remained stable in the second half of 2005 and the first half of 2006.

Low unemployment in many aspects is due to the expansion of the "informal" sector – unregistered employment that is free from income and social taxation as well as from any legal regulation of working conditions, payment systems, etc. The major spheres of unregistered employment are construction, the retail trade and catering, agriculture, and different types of private services. On some estimates, the size of the informal sector is 12 million people (16–18 percent of total employment); for 7–8 million unregistered employment provides the sole source of income. The informal sector is also a primary destination of migrants from other countries of the former Soviet Union (especially Moldova, Ukraine, and Azerbajan).

Low unemployment figures disguise the ineffective functioning of the labor market. First, there is low adjustment of employment regarding the fluctuation of production levels. Small business, presumably more vibrant, still occupies a modest place in the Russian economy, providing jobs to 12.8 percent of all employees in 2006.[8] In large enterprises, complicated legal procedures of mass lay-offs coupled with low salary levels encourage the maintenance of an excessive labor force even when there are no chances of keeping it occupied it in the future (see Gurkov, 2006).

Second, there is low cross-sectional and especially territorial mobility within Russia. While in the first half of 1990s the level of internal migrants (persons who moved to other administrative units within Russia) was around 600,000 per year, in 2001–4 this number was around 100,000.[9] Low territorial mobility creates two types of problems. The first problem is the excessive labor force in several regions with high birth rates. For example, in North Caucasian republics the real unemployment rate among men is more than 30 percent, while married women are largely excluded from the active working population. The second problem is the fragile existence of so-called "single-factory towns" – communities built around a single plant (mine). The very existence of such communities totally depends on the performance of such industrial establishments. The total population of such single-factory towns is 24 million.

Low mobility of the workforce also puts clear boundaries on the location of new production facilities. Everywhere in Russia (except the Moscow region) commuting is possible only via railroads and major motorways (local roads are usually awful), thus new production sites are typically in existing towns or villages. This lesson was well learned by foreign companies. Nowadays foreign investments in production facilities (automotive plants etc.) look for medium-sized old industrial towns as their destination.

In coming years the Russian labor market will be characterized by a gradual decline of the working population (as the generation born in 1989–92, the years of the lowest birth rates, reaches an economically active age), reduction of migration from the former Soviet republics due to tightened immigration policies, and growing shortages of particular professional groups (especially industrial labor force, workers and engineers alike). The abovementioned inefficiencies of the labor market are unlikely to be eliminated.

Key legislative provisions

Two major laws that set the current framework for labor relations in Russian are the Labor Code and the Taxation Code. The Taxation Code set the uniform rate for taxation of personal income from any source – 13 percent. This helped to move "out of shadow" a significant proportion of jobs in the informal sector and removed psychological barriers for wage rises. In addition, since 1 January 2005, the maximum rate of the Uniform Social Tax (a tax paid by employers) was decreased from 35.6 to 26 percent. This difference was split between employers and employees and contributed to significant increase in wages in 2005.

The Labor Code, in effect since 1 February 2002, that replaced the old Labor Code of 1971, targets all organizations in the Russian Federation, regardless of ownership, size, and legal status. There are four major areas of innovation in the new Labor Code:

1 The primacy of law in labor relations. Thus, all clauses in individual labor contracts, even if a contract is voluntarily signed by an employee, that reduce the conditions of employment regarding existing legislation are illegal.
2 The rights of trade unions are seriously limited. For example, the approval of a trade union in mass lay-offs is not required any more, trade union activists may be easily fired, and the employer is not obliged to provide the necessary conditions for trade union daily activities.
3 A special chapter was devoted to the contracts of executives, thus enabling owners stricter control of top managers in their companies.
4 Dismissal of employees became easier. An employee may be fired:
    ● after a single serious violation of his or her job duties (previously a series of violations was required);
    ● if an employee refuses to continue work after a change in ownership;
    ● if an employee refuses to move to another workplace for medical reasons.

In addition, the Code contains an inclusive set of reasons for temporary work contracts.

In general, Russian labor legislation became more flexible. However, some innovations have met with fierce resistance; some have proved to be ineffective. In June 2006, more than 300 amendments to the Labor Code were proposed by the Duma (Parliament). Most of these amendments were included in Federal Law No. 90 and came into force in October 2006.

TRENDS AND DEVELOPMENTS IN HRM PRACTICE

The place of the HR function in Russian enterprises – zenith, fall and gradual revival

In Soviet times, under conditions of chronic labor shortages, non-existent marketing and rudimentary finances, the HR function occupied a very strong position among all functions, just after production. However, the HR function was largely decentralized. In any large enterprise there were five units responsible for personnel issues. The local Communist Party committee supervised the general social atmosphere and had the final say in all promotions.[10] The personnel department dealt with routine legal paperwork in hiring, firing, and performance assessment. The local trade union was responsible for social life, including holiday camps, kindergartens, sport and social events, and – the most important issue – allocation of housing among employees. The salary department was responsible for salary administration. Finally, a special unit under the direct supervision of the chief engineer dealt with issues of job design and work safety. Such decentralization meant that there has never been a clearly articulated HR strategy at enterprise level. Even when such programs were designed as part of "complex enterprise development plans," they were mostly a mechanical combination of particular measures and initiatives. Only under extraordinary circumstances (the appointment of a new general director, massive expansion of production facilities, etc.) was the old Stalinist slogan "The cadres decide everything" re-used to adjust the system of HR policies to new conditions. Even in such situations the emphasis was given to *resources*: to arrange with the industrial ministry higher rates for particular works, to "squeeze" from the local authorities production facilities for housing construction, and to set low performance targets to have more reasons for quarterly and annual premiums and bonuses – these three tricks were largely considered as the key to all problems in HRM in the Soviet Union.

The destruction of central planning, elimination of the Communist Party, and the fall in trade union activism in 1991 created a vacuum. Among the various units which dealt with HR issues, only the personnel department survived, as the amount of legal paperwork related to employment issues has not changed. Salary administration was transferred to accounting departments, and the motto of any real accountant – "small (checks) are beautiful" – is largely applied nowadays to paychecks too.[11] Designing new safety measures became "a luxury" not only for top management, but even for workers affected by such measures.[12] Fifteen years after the end of central planning, despite new tasks and challenges in HRM, personnel departments are still unable to fill the vacuum and to assume the pivotal role in HRM processes (see Table 10.1).

We may see that in most cases personnel departments are separated from strategic decisions. Two-thirds of the surveyed personnel departments also cannot advise executives on issues that are vital when qualified personnel are in extremely short supply – analysis of the job market and assessment of the psychological climate. Therefore, it is not surprising that the HR function occupies the lowest rank among all functions in company management. We also should mention the "personnel

Table 10.1 Functions of personnel departments in Russia (percent of organizations)

Function	Percentage of personnel departments that assume this function
Registration of hiring and firing	92
Staffing	90
Discipline measures	72
Participation in conflict resolution	67
Training	56
Performance assessment of workers	56
Performance assessment of specialists	54
Planning the level of employment	51
Informing personnel about company performance	46
Sociological studies of employees	41
Design of corporate culture	38
Workplace design and assessment	38
Design of wage and benefit systems	36
Analysis of local job markets	36
Performance assessment of managers	31
Assessment of moral and psychological climate	28

Source: Bizukov, 2005.

problem of personnel departments." Traditionally, heads of personnel departments were of two types. In heavy industries they were usually retired officers of the KGB, Interior Ministry, and similar services. In less sensitive industries (e.g. textiles, food processing) the position was usually occupied by women in their late forties, who had passed through all ranks in the personnel department, starting as receptionists and administrators. Both categories are still clearly visible, especially in "old" privatized and state-owned companies. However, their successors are different. Taking into account the very limited offer of special programs in HRM,[13] nowadays the vacancies for heads of personnel are filled by persons of diverse backgrounds in the humanities and social services – former school teachers, psychologists, sociologists, lawyers, experienced "personal assistants to the general director," and so on. In addition, a recent study of the executive job market in Russia confirmed that jobs in the personnel function are a "dead-end" in an executive career – there are almost no cases of HR executives who are promoted to the top and occupy a position as CEO (Solntsev, 2006). We should stress that subsidiaries of foreign companies in Russia share such attitudes towards the HR function with their local colleagues. Although the HR departments of foreign subsidiaries pay more attention to training, analysis of the job market, and evaluation of the psychological climate, HR heads still struggle to enter the inner circle of strategic decision-makers.

However, in the past five years the industrial revival has created a new situation for most Russian companies that may be characterized as an extreme shortage of a "qualified labor force." Today top Russian managers rank HR issues as their third major preoccupantion, after finances and marketing. When we look at businesses that are really expanding, the situation is even more alarming. The share of Russian CEOs who believe that "staffing of a new project by a qualified labor force is an extremely difficult task" is 45.5 percent. This situation does not depend on a company's size, current performance, or even type of activity. For example, in metallurgy, one of the most prosperous Russian sectors, 57 percent of CEOs see staffing as an extremely serious problem.

Table 10.2 The scale of innovations in HRM implemented over the past few years in Russian organizations (percent of CEOs)

Existence/scale	New methods of staffing	New methods of performance appraisal	New remuneration systems
No innovations	26.3	28.6	15.3
To a minimal extent	33.7	29.3	27
To some extent	28.5	27	33.7
To a great extent	11.5	15.1	24

Source: Survey of 1,740 CEOs at the end of 2004, our calculations.

Such a situation forces the majority of Russian companies to embark on experiments in staffing, performance assessment, and remuneration (see Table 10.2). This happens in all sectors of economic activity. There is a visible trend – the better the current performance of a company is, the greater the changes in HRM practices that have taken place over recent years.

The data presented in Table 10.2 show that more than half of the surveyed companies have embarked on experiments in new remuneration systems, and more than one-third on a search for new methods in staffing and performance appraisal. The reader should bear such figures in mind as we proceed to describe each process in detail.

RECRUITMENT AND SELECTION

Recruitment

The insufficient assistance most Russian companies may get from their HR departments in qualitative issues of recruitment and selection makes such functions quite challenging. Recruitment is especially tricky as Russian managers prefer to deal with employees who do not need special training before occupying the position and also require a minimal adjustment period (see Table 10.3). Besides proven qualifications and work experience, Russian CEOs respect education, not only for managers, but also for workers. We should also stress that "personal connections" are a great advantage in Russia, where most businesses depend on the favorable attitudes of local authorities and tolerance of competitors and business partners. Of course, to get such an "ideal" workforce is difficult, so companies use a whole battery of methods to reach promising candidates (see Table 10.4).

Table 10.3 Requirements to the recruited personnel in Russian organizations (percentage of CEOs)

Qualities	Percent of CEOs who consider such qualities "extremely important"	
	For managers	For workers
Qualification	97.8	95.3
Sufficient level of education	90.8	70.7
Work experience	82.8	80.8
Personal connections	61	14.5
Recommendations	41	33.3

Source: Survey of 1,740 CEOs at the end of 2004, our calculations.

Table 10.4 Recruitment methods in various Russian industries (percentages of CEO who confirmed the use of the method in their companies)

Sphere of activity	Methods						
	State employment centers	*Personal connections*	*Search for announcements in the press*	*Publication of announcements in the press*	*Via the internet*	*Via colleges and universities*	*Via professional associations*
Extraction of raw materials	18.8	72.7	13.3	38.9	13.3	63.2	29.4
Energy	23.5	74.0	43.2	50.0	43.2	51.2	56.0
Timber	18.8	76.9	26.3	52.2	33.3	68.2	72.0
Chemicals	10.5	66.7	30	37.5	23.8	59.4	71.8
Pharmaceuticals	23.8	70.6	54.2	59.9	38.1	37.5	64.5
Metallurgy	8.3	76.2	44.4	57.1	27.4	69.6	55.0
Machine building	20.7	77.9	44.9	52.3	55.6	62.2	66.3
Electronics	32.5	80.0	40.0	58.2	40.3	68.5	68.0
Food industry	19	83.9	35.8	51.3	36.7	48.5	60.7
Textiles	24.1	53.1	44.8	51.3	31.6	46.9	67.3
Construction	25.6	79.7	34.9	47.5	34.8	48.4	70.2
Agriculture	26.9	81	26.1	50	34.5	67.6	60.6
Retail and catering	14.7	79	31.8	50.4	38.4	53.7	72.0
Wholesale	12.6	74.4	35.4	53.6	45.1	51.7	74.7
Information technology	13.1	79	29.2	53.3	40.4	44.2	72.3
Consulting	5.8	76.5	25.9	52.4	29.4	45.0	75.6
Education, science, and culture	25	78.8	16.7	40.9	26.5	60.0	64.3
Housing services	16.7	66.3	25.0	37.1	40.0	40.0	60.0
Finance and insurance	7.1	74.1	40.0	52.0	27.3	38.9	74.1

Source: Survey of 1,700 CEOs in 2003, our calculations; published in Klyachko and Krasnova, 2006.

Personal connections of managers and participation in professional associations (another form of personal connections) are still the main ways of obtaining promising candidates in all sectors. However, despite their desire to find a workforce with practical experience, nowadays Russian companies should look towards graduates of colleges and universities. This trend is especially visible in machine building, electronics, and pharmaceuticals. However, in the timber industry and agriculture, which were neglected for 15 years as desirable sectors for employment, the shortage of young professionals is especially acute.

The internet also became an important source of information for both employees and employers. However, in the popular perception the internet is still separated from other sources of mass communication.

Although there are visible differences in the use of recruitment methods at industry levels, there are no significant differences between various forms of ownership, with one important exception – state-owned companies more often use state employment centers (see Table 10.5).

Selection procedures

If there is a great variety of recruitment methods, selections methods in most Russian companies are limited just to two forms – interviews and a probation period.[14] Other forms of selection are not significant in Russia. Written letters of recommendation are not popular due to the prevailing attitudes of employers in seeing those who leave the

Table 10.5 Recruitment methods in Russian companies by type of ownership (percentage of organizations)

| Form | Type of ownership | | | |
	State	Individual	Limited partnership	Joint-stock company
State employment centers	27.4	9.4	16.9	18.5
Personal connections	74.8	72.4	75.3	77.7
Publications in the mass media	27.8	35	33.8	33.3
Placement of publications in the mass media	39.6	51	51.6	52.3
Via the internet	25	31.6	40	35.2
From universities	55.2	48.8	47.9	52.8
Via headhunting and recruitment agencies	46.5	63	71.7	73.7
Via professional associations	44	31.4	43.3	53.8
Via databases	25.9	15.2	11	19.2

Source: Klyachko and Krasnova, 2006.

company as "traitors."[15] Thus Russian employees prefer to find a new job, pass the selection procedures, and negotiate job conditions before leaving their current employer. Different tests are not popular in most Russian companies as selection tools either. Professional tests are difficult to develop, as many jobs are believed to be unique and tailored to the specific needs of a particular company. Psychological tests were very popular in the 1990s, but have lost their appeal as the tests themselves became well known and standard. In addition, managers and production engineers have accused psychologists in selection units of putting too much weight on the personal characteristics of candidates and failing to capture "real professionals," who may be too arrogant or too diffident.

As a result, interviews and probation periods remained two methods that are considered reliable and efficient. Interviews "Russian style" are usually carried out in two or three stages. The first interview is carried out by a person from the personnel department. This interview is often very formal and helps to fill the "job card" with a candidate's personal data. No serious decisions are made at this stage. However, if a person from the HRM department discovers some strange facts in the biography of a candidate, she or he must share the suspicions with the head of company security.[16] The second interview is with the future direct supervisor. This interview is carried out in most cases in a very informal way. For a person entering the labor market for the first time, the main goal of the interview is to demonstrate the qualities Russian supervisors appreciate most – reliability, trustworthiness, obedience, modesty, and willingness to work hard (see Gurkov and Maital, 2001). For a more experienced person the best tactic in such interviews is to mention "reference points." For each job and specialty the reference points may be different – for a qualified worker this may be technical characteristics and "tricks" of equipment he or she has worked with; for a manager or an engineer this may be the name of a respectable "patriarch" of the field she/he knows personally, etc. Almost 80 percent of jobs are found through "personal connections," common ground is established before the interview. Once common ground is established and the reference points are found, the candidate is considered as having successfully passed the "friend-or-foe reconnaissance system." For low-ranking positions this puts an end to the selection process. For top positions a third meeting may be necessary. For this meeting the future supervisor takes the likely candidate to his/her own boss. During this meeting the supervisor ascertains whether the person he/she is bringing is the right one. The candidate usually remains silent most of the time, politely replying to some routine questions. If the big boss puts tough questions and shows hesitation, this means that "the meeting was badly prepared." This is considered as the fault of the supervisor, not of the candidate.

After the positive approval of the big boss, the real bargaining on job conditions, especially on salary level, may start. Experienced candidates try to move the agreement on payment conditions towards the very end of the selection processes, where the "extras" demanded are counterbalanced by the cost and time of the repeating the process all over again. Bringing the agreement to the very end of negotiations is simplified by the fact that there are still no standards for remuneration for managerial positions, and the take-home sum may differ by 50–60 percent for similar positions in similar companies.

Once all interviews have been passed and negotiations on payment conditions have reached a mutually acceptable agreement, real employment or the probation period may start. The probation period is still considered in Russia not as the beginning of real employment, but as an employer's trick to save on salary and benefits. Indeed, Russian employers nowadays often prefer not to make "normal work contracts" with a special probation period, which cannot last more than three (for managers, six) months and should have clear criteria for success or failure. Instead they force employees to make special temporary contracts separately for the probation period. In such contracts salaries usually are minimal. Temporary workers are also excluded from all social benefits offered to "normal fellow-workers." Such contracts may be terminated at any time without any explanation from the employer. Therefore, a probation period is accepted only by persons who have no other place to go.

REWARD AND PERFORMANCE MANAGEMENT

As in most other countries, the labor market in Russia is divided into three largely separate groups:

- industrial workers and front-line employees in services;
- managers (including foremen or women and supervisors) and qualified "specialists" with a university education;
- executives.

It would be better to describe reward and performance management for these groups separately, as they largely differ in salary level and performance criteria. However, we should first present the legal provisions associated with reward and performance management in all categories of employees.

The official system of reward management is based on two pillars – a minimum wage and a tariff system. According to Item 133 of the Labor Code the minimum wage is set at the same level in all the territory of the Russian Federation by a federal law. No full-time salary may be lower than the minimum wage. On 1 May 2006 the minimum wage in Russia was 1,100 rubles (around €32) per month. On 1 May 2007 the minimum wage was set at 1,400 rubles and since 1 September 2007 it has been 2,300 rubles (€66). Needless to say, the subsistence level is much higher. For example, in Moscow city the minimum subsistence level for a working person (without dependent) in the second quarter of 2007 was somewhere around 5,800 rubles per month.

The wage scale is set according to a tariff system. The tariff system determines the complexity of particular work and the relative level of payment for particular jobs of various complexity. The Russian tariff system includes:

- tariff rates (a fixed hourly rate for work of a given complexity);
- tariff grid (allocation of all jobs to particular tariff rates);
- tariff coefficients (the difference between the particular tariff rate and the level of the lowest rate (or for the most simple work).

On 1 September 2007 the tariff rates were separated from the minimum wage, and regional authorities were able to set tariff rates higher or lower than the minimum wage. Salary taxes were lowered in 2006 making up 47.2 percent of the total wage bill, compared with 64.5 percent in 2002 (see Table 10.6).

Official provisions also stipulate that jobs with special conditions (very unhealthy work, work in the Far East or in the Northern territories) are paid higher rates. The law also stipulates that two major salary systems – time-based payment and piecework – may be combined in various ways. There are no legal limitations on additional payments and benefits from net profit, and no limits on social benefits to employees (although some benefits are accounted for as a salary and have double taxation – profit tax for companies and income tax for employees).

It is important to note that the Russian legal system does not allow any fines of employees. In piecework payment systems work of inferior quality may not be accepted and, subsequently, not paid for. In hourly payment systems, it is the duty of the supervisor to ensure the proper quality. Only the additional bonus for employees may be decreased or not paid, but the basic hourly rate cannot be touched.

Practices of reward and performance management for workers and front-line employees

As the officially set tariff system and official rates secure only subsistence, most reward systems for workers and front-line employees are based on two parts of salary. The basic salary, sometimes set according to the official tariff system (in privatized and state-owned companies the tariff system is used more often), is the first part and may make up between 10 and 60 percent of take-home pay. The second part is called a "premium," but is usually considered as automatically given. Besides the salary system, nowadays Russian companies are rebuilding the social benefit system, both in monetary and non-monetary forms (see Table 10.7).

Among the most popular benefits are additional health insurance, which enables employees to use private clinics and hospitals, meal and transport allowances and special holiday allowances. We should also stress the wider use of the educational allowance. The popularity of the educational allowance is partly explained by the fact that the Labor Code treats this allowance as a credit to the employee that may be totally or partly repaid to the employer when the employee leaves the company. So, the educational allowance is considered a good "anchor" to keep valuable, educated employees. The levels of social benefits are usually based on seniority principles – the greater the overall time an employee has spent in the company, the greater the

Table 10.6 Taxation of salary in Russia; taxes paid by employer and employee, 2006 versus 2003

Period effective	Taxes on employer								Tax on employee (percentage)	Remaining after all taxes (percentage)
	United social tax (percentage)					*Insurance (percentage)*		*Total after taxes on employer*		
	Tax base	*Federal tax*	*Social insurance tax*	*Medical insurance tax*		*Financing the insurance part of pensions*	*Financing the accumulated part of pensions*			
				Federal	*Local*					
Since 1 January 2006	100	20	2.9	1.1	2	10	4	60	13	**52.8**
1 January 2002– 31 December 2004	100	28	4	0.20	3.40	11	3	50.40	30	**35.28**

Note: The maximum personal income tax rate, applicable after 60,000 rubles ($2,000) per annum.

"pie." In practice most full-time employees are entitled to all forms of benefits, only the share of their direct contribution varies. For example, sophomores must pay 50–60 percent of the total value of additional health insurance; after five years of service this option is given free of charge, etc. In addition to all wages and social benefits Russian workers expect a special Christmas bonus – "the thirteenth salary", which indeed is roughly equal to the monthly take-home pay.

As most reward systems are composed of small salaries and solid "premiums," to ensure the proper performance of any worker is not a problem – it is sufficient to deprive a worker of a monthly premium to make him or her obedient and compliant. The performance management of workers and front-line employees is based on direct observations and registration of quantity and quality of their work by a supervisor (foreman). Usually a single complaint about the quality of work may result in the loss of part or all of the monthly "premium," so the direct supervisor usually has total command over the "life and death" of subordinates. In principle, a worker may appeal about his/her direct supervisor to higher positioned managers, but few workers dare to do so, as many firms make a list of all situations that will cause premiums to be derived.[17] Workers with piecework, who are directly paid for the quantity of operations of acceptable quality, may also be asked to compensate the firm for the whole value of a detail (item) lost for further utilization by the inaccuracy (negligence) of the worker.

Having a whole battery of punishment measures for every worker, Russian companies nowadays are trying to avoid peer-based systems of performance appraisal (popular in 1980s), as such systems promote co-operation and unity among workers in their resistance to supervisors.

Table 10.7 Percentage of Russian companies that finance particular social benefits for their employees (partially or completely)

Type of benefit	*Percentage*
Additional medical insurance	55.7
Additional training	39.7
Transport allowance	34.4
Lunch allowance	34.3
Additional holiday allowance	32.1
Additional medical treatment allowance	26.8
Pension supplement	9.2
Kindergarten allowance	7.8
Allowance for education of children	6.3
Other types	5.4

Source: Survey of 1,700 CEOs in December 2004, our calculations.

In general, the reward and performance systems for workers implemented in Russian companies may look old-fashioned, but they are consistent and efficient. If the company allocates sufficient resources for direct supervision and social benefits, the systems ensure compliance with work rules and provide possibilities for productivity improvement.

Practices of reward and performance management for managers and qualified "specialists"

If we have assessed positively the prevailing Russian systems of reward and performance appraisal for workers, the systems for managers may be described as "chaotic" and arbitrary. At first glance, the reward system for managers is very similar to that for workers – there is the same two-tier system of basic salary[18] and premium, as well as a developed system of social benefits (which may include many additional perks such as "allowance for mobile phone," "allowance for education of children," "special mortgage from the company," etc.). The difference here is the stability of the salary. If workers expect a stable salary for routine work of satisfactory quality, the take-home wage of managers is never secure. It consists of a permanent part (not related to performance) and a variable part, depending on performance appraisal. For production units, engineering, IT, or HR functions the variable part is usually set at 20–40 percent of take-home pay. For the sales (installation) department the variable part may be 50–70 percent of take-home pay. The real problem here is not the relative size of the variable part, but the performance measures that determine it. For traditional functions, like production and engineering, fulfillment of a monthly plan or timely delivery of an order is usually the sole measure of performance. Thus the plans themselves are set as low as possible; orders are scheduled for the last acceptable period. In addition, the direct costs of achievement are rarely taken into consideration, as production and engineering are kept as far as possible from finance and "real money."

For relatively new functions (sales, marketing) the situation is even worse. There is neither an established tradition of performance measures, nor good "cookbooks" for performance design for such specialists. As a result, the simplest observable parameters, which may be beyond the control of particular managers, became the criteria for their success or failure. For example, a head of sales who (usually) has no direct authority over the advertising budget, no power to make alterations to prices, and no ability to prioritize deliveries, is assessed by the dynamics of company sales.

When Russian companies are trying to implement newly imported managerial "fads," like Balanced Scorecard (BSC), the situation becomes totally absurd. BSC schemes are introduced in a top-down manner, so middle managers are made responsible not for a single measure, but for a battery of measures, all of them beyond their direct influence.

This state of affairs in the performance appraisal of company managers is not new – it reflects the established Russian tradition of "delegating responsibility" to lower levels of the managerial hierarchy while keeping the real power and resources at the top.[19]

The system also in many cases creates situations where newly appointed managers receive much higher salaries than the people who have worked in the company for a long time, as new appointees start bargaining at the higher level. The wide dispersion of practices for setting very different pay levels for the same jobs causes many Russian companies to force employees to sign special documents that prohibit them from revealing their real income to anyone outside and especially inside the company.

An additional consequence of this situation is the clearly superior attractiveness of jobs in foreign subsidiaries over their Russian competitors for experienced middle managers and specialists. Foreign subsidiaries of multinational corporations (MNCs) usually offer more modest career opportunities (as top positions are often retained for expatriate managers) and (nowadays) lower salaries, but self-respecting Russian middle managers value orderly and consistent performance appraisal, which makes them masters of their own destiny.

Practices of reward and performance management for executives

Executives are heads of companies (general directors and, for joint-stock companies, chairmen of the board of directors)[20] and their direct subordinates (vice-presidents, chief accountants, and, in some cases, trusted personal assistants). In Russia, there is a clear divergence between reward and performance management for executives of the largest open joint-stock companies and for those in smaller companies.

Large Russian open joint-stock companies have successfully implemented over the past five or six years all the "tricks" in executive compensation developed in large American corporations over the past 30–40 years. For example, the Russian oil giant LUKOil models its executive compensation scheme on Chevron. There are three parts to the reward system for executives – basic annual salary, bonus related to financial performance of the corporation (around 100–150 percent of the annual salary, paid as a lump sum at the end of the year), and stock-related rewards. Although different option plans and "phantom shares" are nowadays widely used in large Russian corporations, top executives still prefer real stock. For example, in AFK Sistema, the largest high-tech Russian conglomerate, at the end of 2005 the controlling owner made a Christmas present to several executives of a direct transfer of shares (valued at that time at several million US dollars).

In Russian companies not listed on stock exchanges, the prevailing form of executive compensation is profit-sharing schemes. It is widely believed that allocation of net profit solves the "principal–agent" problem. In addition, setting a uniform measure for all top managers in the company increases the coherence of the management team.

TRAINING AND DEVELOPMENT

We have seen that Russian managers value education as a selection criterion even for workers. The respect for education in Russian society has contributed to the rapid expansion in the past 15 years of various forms of professional and business education. Nowadays all kinds of retraining program are available to any Russian company that is ready to pay for it – from one-day "update" seminars to internationally recognized programs of Doctor of Business Administration. The Russian Association for Business Education (RABE) now comprises more than 140 respectable business schools and retraining centers from 33 regions. Russian business schools have recently started to be accredited by the Association of Masters of Business Administration (AMBA) and have even appeared in the list of top 100 European MBAs.

The government pays serious attention to the promotion of business and management education. In 1998, under the auspices of the President of Russia, a large-scale program targeting managers of small and medium-sized companies was launched. This program combines intensive theory classes (up to 500 contact hours) with a prolonged period (up to six months) of work in another company, including foreign ones. Every year since 1998 more than 2,600 managers have passed through this program annually, so the total pool of alumni is now more than 20,000.

Although this program is in many ways unique, the data received from its alumni show the consequences of a well-designed management retraining program (see Table 10.8).

Table 10.8 Consequences of participation in retraining program for Russian companies

Consequence	Percentage
Expansion of power	54
Salary increase	47
New job offers from other Russian companies	42
Job promotion	27
Starting own business	12
Joining the managing board	10
Job offer from state authorities	9
Job offer from foreign-owned company	8

Source: Survey of 2,600 participants of the President Program for Retraining of Management Cadres in December 2004, our calculations.

We can see that time and money spent on managerial retraining is a very effective investment – more than half of all alumni immediately received job offers from other companies. Salary rises and job promotions are also likely outcomes of the retraining program.

If we look in more detail at the impact of the acquisition of new knowledge and skills (see Table 10.9), we will see the ingredients that contribute to the career and business advancement of alumni – raised self-respect, better understanding of the company's business, better vision of overall perspectives of an industry or particular sectors of the national economy.

Although individual participation in retraining programs has a clear positive impact, nowadays Russian companies prefer to order special company-tailored programs. Such programs usually embrace all managers at a particular level in the company. In some cases, the whole managing board (10–12 executives) is enrolled in an MBA program.[21] Some estimates put the overall demand for MBA programs in Russia at 100,000 (Kuzminov and Filonovich, 2005).

As business and management education prospers and expands, professional retraining for workers is still struggling with the consequences of its total neglect in the 1990s.

Table 10.9 Impact of the retraining program

Impact on ...	Assessment of the impact				
	Very negative (percent)	Negative (percent)	No impact (percent)	Positive (percent)	Very positive (percent)
Self-respect	0.35	0.96	8.64	35.17	54.88
Understanding of company's problems	0.27	1.12	6.88	40.19	51.55
Vision of perspectives	0.31	1.24	7.34	42.60	48.51
Improvement in company's management	0.90	2.39	18.43	44.05	34.23
Efficiency of my own work	1.18	3.25	21.40	45.20	28.97
Relations with subordinates	1.36	2.91	25.64	43.98	26.11
Relations with superiors	3.39	3.31	32.51	36.86	23.93
Relations with colleagues	0.97	3.15	30.29	41.86	23.73
Career growth	6.63	4.69	36.26	29.27	23.15
Relations with business partners	12.57	5.59	50.11	19.65	12.08

Source: Survey of 2,600 participants of the President Program for Retraining of Management Cadres in December 2004, our calculations.

Most professional staff of vocational schools and technical colleges have left the public educational establishments for managerial positions in business; experienced workers and technicians with pedagogical skills are not willing to occupy poorly paid jobs in the public sector. The temporary solution many Russian industrial companies see as an effective tool to overcome the shortage of qualified younger workers is to rebuild the in-company mentoring system. Unskilled staff may be taken on with a special "apprenticeship" contract, which sets the obligations of the company to train a person towards a particular specialty and level of qualification. More importantly, instructors who provide such on-the-job training (presumably, the most experienced and patient workers and technicians) usually receive significant additional payment for such duties.

THE FUTURE OF HRM IN RUSSIA

We have retraced the development of the main features of HRM in Russia. Some of them are deeply rooted in the previous historical and social development of the country; some are more volatile and are subject to alteration and change.

The Russian economy (and politics) is largely dependent on oil prices, and, naturally, the future of HRM is also determined by them. The crucial assumption for all our predictions is that the current high prices for oil, gas, and energy-related products (fertilizers etc.) will last for the next three or four years. In such a situation the following developments are highly likely:

- The energy sector in Russia will prosper, accumulating more financial resources in the large state-controlled companies.
- Two sectors that directly depend on the energy sector – the financial sector and the Russian government – will also experience "good times."
- In all three sectors salaries and incomes will grow quickly, thus widening the existing large gap between those sectors and the rest of the economy (see Appendix, Table A10.5). Job attractiveness in those sectors will also be high. Moreover, more and more families with high incomes earned from "petrodollars" will be able to afford personal servants.
- With plenty in its coffers the government will embark on large infrastructure projects, thus creating more demand in construction.[22] The expansion of the energy sectors will also necessitate more construction.
- Last but not least, as Russia currently "flexes its muscles" with a sharp increase in its defense budget, money will also be poured into the production of armaments. A renaissance of the Russian industrial military sector, largely neglected for a decade, will depend on the creation of a new generation of scientists, engineers and qualified workers.

In general, six sectors will expand quickly in the next two to four years – energy, financial services, government service, heavy industry, construction and household services. The first four sectors will create demand for a highly educated and qualified workforce; the two last sectors will absorb less qualified personnel. These six sectors will be also the primary directions for young people. The job attractiveness in other sectors will be much lower. Taking into account the demographic "pause" in 2006–8, the shortage of labor, especially in sectors with no direct links to petrodollars, will become critical in 2008.[23]

Companies in those not-so-lucky sectors, limited in financial resources, will be unable to raise labor expenses as a proportion of total costs. The only solution will be greater attention to productivity improvement and better utilization of the labor force. Thus, we expect (as an optimistic scenario) that unprivileged sectors of the Russian economy will give an impetus to accelerated changes in HRM. These changes are likely to proceed in several directions.

First, recruitment will still be largely based on "personal connections," but selection procedures will become tighter. Already in 2005–6 the demand for "working tests" and "qualification assessments" for workers, engineers and managers alike was booming. In addition, in searching for personnel, companies will look deeper. Already in 2006–7 companies have started early recruiting campaigns in universities, attracting second- and third-year students as part-time or even full-time employees for shop-floor supervising and other lower managerial positions.

Second, performance assessment will become tighter but more variable, reflecting the demand for greater labor productivity. In addition, some forms of peer assessment will be reintroduced, especially with possibilities of retaining and reallocating the salary of the dismissed co-workers to their more productive colleagues.

Third, in reward systems more attention will be given to social benefits, which will be considered a good device both to attract new employees and to increase the costs of leaving the company for existing ones. Thus, more types of benefits will be offered not just to the employee, but to the whole family (as we have seen in the case of Yakutskenergo).

Fourth, more attention will be devoted to training and development. They will increasingly be considered not as perks, but as joint investments by employee and employer in human capital. Thus, a greater return on such investments will be expected both by employees (promotions and salary increases) and employers (loyalty and productivity). In training and development greater co-operation between employers, including the establishment of joint training centers, will become widespread.

Fifth, the greater use of flexible working is also likely, especially for engineers and other specialists. This will include flexible working time, and more use of part-time employment and teleworking. Russian employers will also use sub-contractors for particular works rather then employing their own permanent personnel.

All the abovementioned developments will put stronger demands on the HRM function, which should take the lead in such changes. This demand will be met by quick dissemination of best practice via professional associations, informal communications of HR managers, and wider use of external trainers and consultants.[24] In the most optimistic case, somewhere around 2008–9 there will be a new set of MBA-like programs in HRM that will combine international standards of the profession with proper attention to and knowledge of the local specifics.[25]

However, some features of HRM will not be altered. In our opinion, the position of HRM executives in the management hierarchy will not improve much, the HRM function will still be a "dead-end" in an executive career; and organized labor will still be an exception, especially in small business.

JSC AC Yakutskenergo – warm hands in the freezing lands

Case study

How should we measure the size of an energy company? We may talk about energy output in MegaWatts, sales, profit before or after taxes, market capitalization, or the number of employees. But for integrated electricity suppliers, which combine production, transmission, distribution and marketing of electrical energy, the size of the serviced territory is significant. On the basis of the latter, Yakutskenergo – an electricity company in the far north-east of the Russian Federation – is the largest company in the world. It serves the territory of the autonomous republic Sakha-Yakutia, which occupies 3,100,000 km^2 – bigger than the European Union with all its old and new members.

Although only 910,000 people live in that territory, to serve their needs 20,000 km of power lines, a cascade of hydrolytic power stations, three gas/coal power stations, and 164 small diesel oil generators are used. To maintain all this infrastructure 8,211 people are employed in the company.

For the territory, where the usual winter temperature is –50°C, a break in the electricity supply of 40 minutes means that nobody will see the light again. In addition, tough guys who service diesel oil generators are usually the only persons with technical skills in a radius of 100 km. So the company provides not just electricity, but the life and civilization in this immense territory.

The company itself is a subsidiary of the RAO United Electrical Systems of Russia, but it enjoys complete independence in all questions of management, including HRM policies. Unfortunately, this independence also includes financial independence. Being physically isolated from the main energy markets, with high operating expenses, the current financial situation of Yakutskenergo is not bright, and profitability of sales was in 2005 just 3 percent (profitability of assets was 1.5 percent). The company must subsidize customers in rural areas; overall demand for electricity decreased in 2005. In addition, there is a permanent deficit in the investment budget, as reliability standards are high and the maintenance costs of the dispersed infrastructure are immense. And

continued

there are good opportunities to begin exploration of large local oil and gas reserves, with the ultimate consequent loss of mechanics, compressor operators, builders, etc. The top management clearly sees that an effective HRM policy is crucial to the very existence of the company.

The mission statement of the company is written according to best practice and reads as follows:

We see our destiny in improving the quality of life of the people and creating conditions for the economic development of the Far East of Russia. We reach this goal by offering quality services in electricity supply in inclement climate conditions. By quality we mean reliability and non-interruption of energy supply while maintaining technical standards. The base for our efficiency is the employees. We value them for their high professionalism, teamwork and results orientation. We provide employees with deserved remuneration and opportunities for development.

Translating such grandiloquent words into plain English, we may see that the company is desperately looking for a means of preventing personnel, especially "open-air workers" (electricians, constructors) and engineers from moving to other territories or sectors. As a result, HRM policy indeed occupies an important place in corporate management. The current strategic program of Yakutskenergo contains an extended description of measures in HRM. Four areas are considered the most essential in HRM policies:

- development of an efficient performance management system;
- extension of social benefits;
- training;
- maintaining good moral climate.

Development of a performance management system was considered as a priority for 2005. The system was built using external consultants. A very simple scheme was proposed for each functional department as well as operating divisions – one negative and two positive parameters in quarterly performance assessment determine the level of the quarterly and annual bonus. The negative parameter is the events (variable) that must be 100 percent avoided (minimized). The positive parameters are the variables that should be maximized. All negative parameters are specific and reflect the responsibility areas of departments (units). One of positive parameters is specific for each department (unit), the second is the same for all departments, thus creating uniform attitudes towards company performance.

Extension of social benefits at aimed to systemizing all the forms used in the company. The total list of benefits is as follows:

1 Health:
   - allowance for holiday travel expenses for employees and their children;

- subsidies for health spas;
- organization of sport events.

2 Support for families:
- present after birth of a child;
- stipend to single mothers;
- 100 percent subsidy for children's summer camps for single mothers and families with 3 or more children;
- 100 percent subsidy for kindergarten.

3 Support for low-paid employees:
- additional holiday allowance;
- 100 percent subsidy for electricity and heat.

4 Support for retired employees:
- additional pension scheme;
- 100 percent subsidy for electricity and heat;
- present at retirement.

5 Additional benefits:
- compensation for rent;
- credits for house purchase;
- participation of the company in investment projects for apartment blocks;
- special credits and grants in extreme family situations (death of a family member etc.).

Training was considered a necessary part of professional development. The chief executive officer and chief financial officer themselves passed in 2003–4 through the extensive MBA-like program at the Academy of the National Economy in Moscow. For middle managers and engineers two educational programs offered by Canadian energy companies were organized in 2004. In the same year the company's training center was set up. It provides training for 105 working specialties. In 2004, almost 1,000 workers passed through retraining programs. In 2005, the proportion of managers with university and college degrees was 91 percent, for workers 29 percent.

Maintaining a good moral climate was prioritized according to the American-inspired model "Great place to work." A special survey that covered 30 percent of all employees was administered in 2004. It demonstrated sufficient job satisfaction in corporate headquarters and in units for energy transmission. To improve job satisfaction in production units various new forms were developed. For example, the best personnel in the cascade of hydrolytic stations is offered the title "Knight of the Cascade" or "Lady of the Cascade." There is also an objective to promote so-called "working dynasties," when several generations work for the company. In 2005, there were 228 "working dynasties."

continued

So far, the effects of HRM policies seem positive:

- almost all positions were filled – the number of unfilled vacancies was just 2.2 percent of the total workforce in 2006;
- young professionals stay longer in the company – in 2006 more than 80 percent of young specialist stayed while in 2005 the figure was 67 percent;
- various retraining programs trained 2,100 employees, i.e. 27 percent of the total labor force;
- job evaluation (assessment) was performed to assess the performance of 400 employees.

At the same time, the company was under constant organizational restructuring. More than 3,000 employees were transformed to other legal entities. On the one hand, this allowed some "rejuvenation" of the workforce – the average age of the workforce was around 43 years in 2005, and just 38 years in 2006. On the other hand, reorganizations were accompanied by high personnel turnover. In 2005 the personnel turnover rate was less than 8 percent; in 2006 it increased by two-thirds and reached 13.8 percent (http://www.yakutskenergo.ru/social/empl/).

APPENDIX: SELECTED SOCIO-ECONOMIC INDICATORS FOR 1990–2006

Table A10.1 Russian employment statistics, 1990–2006

	1990	1995	1996	1997	1998	1999	2000	2001	2002	2003	2004	2005	2006
Number of enterprises and organizations*	288,423	224,9531	250,4518	2,727,146	2,901,237	3,106,350	3,346,483	3,593,837	3,845,278	4,149,815	4,417,074	4,767,300	4,506,600
Average monthly salary (until 1998, thousand rubles)**	0.303	472.4	790.2	950.2	1,051.5	1,522.6	2,223.4	3,240.4	4,360.3	5,498.5	6,739.5	8,554.9	10,727.7
Average number of employed (thousands)***	75,324.7	66,409	65,950	64,692.5	63,812	63,963.4	64,327.3	64,709.5	65,359.3	65,666	66,407.2	66,792	6,7017
Average number of employed (percentage of the previous year)	No data	No data	99.3	98.1	98.6	100.2	100.6	100.6	101	100.5	101.1	100.6	100.3
Number of small enterprises (thousands)	No data	No data	No data	861.1	868	890.6	879.3	843	882.3	893	953.1	979.3	1,032.8
Number of employed at small enterprises****	No data	No data	No data	6,514.8	6,207.8	6,485.8	6,596.8	6,483.5	7,220.3	7,458.9	7,815.1	No data	8,582.8

Source: *Regions of Russia. Socio-economic indicators. 2005 – M.: Rosstat, 2006: 384–5; Russian figures. 2007: Short Statistics Handbook. – M.: Rosstat, 2007: 176.

**Ibid.: 140–1; Federal State Statistics Service of Russian Federation, http://www.gks.ru/free_doc/2007/b07_11/07–07.htm.

***Ibid.: 80–3; Federal State Statistics of Russian Federation, http://www.gks.ru/free_doc/2007/b07_11/06–03.htm.

****Ibid.: 394–5; Russian figures. 2007: Short Statistics Handbook. – M.: Rosstat, 2007: 178.

Table A10.2 Number of personnel employed in Russian companies and organizations by type of ownership

	1995						2006					
	Total employed	Ownership form					Totally employed	Ownership form				
		State and municipal	Private	Public and religious	Mixed Russian	Foreign and join		State and municipal	Private	Public and religious	Mixed Russian	Foreign and join
Thousands of persons												
	66,409	27,938.9	22,837.7	474.1	14,732.6	425.7	6,7017	22,148	37,145	352	4,758	2,614
Percent												
	100	42.1	34.4	0.7	22.2	0.6	100	33.0	55.4	0.5	7.1	3.9

Source: Federal State Statistics Service of Russian Federation, http://www.gks.ru/free_doc/2007/b07_11/06-02.htm.

Table A10.3 Employment in various sectors in Russia (1000s of persons)

Year	Industry	Agriculture	Forestry	Construction	Transport	Communications	Trade and catering	Housing	Health and social services	Education	Culture	Science	Other sectors
1995	17,160.8	9,744	258.6	6,207.8	4,374.6	874.6	6,675.8	2,979.1	4,442.7	6,179.5	1,136.5	1,688.4	4,686.6
2004	14,301.5	6,891.1	276.5	5,215.8	4,404.5	919.5	11,431	3,182.8	4,698.1	5,958	1,273.7	1,165	6,689.8

Source: Ibid.: 84–91.

Table A10.4 Employment in various industries in Russia (1000s of persons)

Year	Total	Industries														
		Agriculture and hunting	Fishing	Extraction of raw materials	Manufacturing	Energy, gas, and water production and distribution	Construction	Trade and repair services	Hotels and restaurants	Transport and communications	Finances	Realty services	State services, including military and security	Education	Health	Other personal services
2004	66,407	7,430	113	1,088	11,787	1,900	4,743	10,843	1,152	5,293	835	4,825	3,447	6,125	4,488	2,330
2005	66,792	7,381	138	1,051	11,506	1,912	4,916	11,088	1,163	5,369	858	4,879	3,458	6,039	4,548	2,460
2006	67,017	7,106	133	1,036	11,255	1,917	5,075	11,315	1,183	5,423	928	4,936	3,579	6,014	4,603	2,492

Source: Federal State Statistics Service of Russian Federation, http://www.gks.ru/free_doc/2007/b07_11/06–03.htm.

Table A10.5 Average monthly salary in Russia by year (1000s of rubles)

1990	1995	1996	1997	1998	1999	2000	2001	2002	2003	2004	2005	2006
0.303	472.4	790.2	950.2	1,051.5	1,522.6	2,223.4	3,240.4	4,360.3	5,498.5	6,739.5	8,554.9	10,727.7

Table A10.6 Average monthly salary in Russia by sector, 2006 (rubles)

Total	Industries														
	Agriculture and hunting	Fishing	Extraction of raw materials	Manufacturing	Energy, gas, and water production and distribution	Construction	Trade and repair services	Hotels and restaurants	Transport and communications	Finances	Realty services including	State services, military and security	Education services	Health	Other personal
10,727.7	4,577.7	12,205.9	23,234.0	10,250.9	12,863.3	11,252.9	8,309.2	7,267.1	13,310.9	27,794.9	12,836.8	13,237.8	6,984.3	8,092.0	7,940.0

Source: Federal State Statistics Service of Russian Federation, http://www.gks.ru/free_doc/2007/b07_11/07–07.htm.

NOTES

1 This work was undertaken with support of the research grant No. 06–04–0010 of the State University – Higher School of Economics. The authors acknowledge the valuable technical assistance of Alexander Mutovin during preparation of the paper.

2 According to official data, the average number of prisoners in 1995–2000 was around one million persons, including 107,000 persons sentenced for murder. In 2003–6, due to the liberalization of the criminal law, the number of prisoners decreased to 870,000 (see http://www.rol.ru/news/misc/crime/03/06/02_008.htm; http://www.estvse.ru/stat/vse/1080/vse/882/vse/; www.newsru.com/crime/07may2004/killers.html).

3 One of the authors worked in 1988–9 as a trainer for high school students aiming to take the entrance exams to the Moscow State University in one of the newly created "tutor cooperatives." The purpose of that cooperative was to provide private lessons for 16–17-year-olds in addition to their high-school classes.

4 To date, neither of them has proved successful by any means.

5 See http://www.edinros.ru/news.html?rid=3125.

6 See, for example, Mironov, V. I. (2006). *Praktika noveyshego trudovogo zakonodatelstva: enziklopedia pravoprimenenia v zaklucheniakh experta NEPS*. Moscow: Delo Publishers.

7 The economically active population was around 73.4 million persons in April 2005, or 51 percent of the total population of the Russian Federation.

8 We should remember here that Russian small businesses are the largest small businesses in the world in terms of number of employees. The legally set upper limit for small business in many industries in 100 full-time employees.

9 One of the reasons for lower in-country mobility is soaring prices for housing in large Russian cities, maintained by high incomes in the oil and gas sectors. Today the price for a modest family apartment in an apartment block in any large Russian city is equal to 20–30 times the average annual salary. Rent follows this trend. Mortgage financing is still in its infancy.

10 Before having any chance of taking up a managerial position, candidates would have to join the Communist Party. A person who received a "severe reprimand" from the local Party committee had no chance of promotion for the rest of his or her life; a person excluded from the Communist Party could occupy only worker positions in the least prestigious segments of the Soviet economy.

11 There are many industries in Russia (for example in retail) where competition is based mostly on minimization of labor expenses as a share of total sales.

12 The investigation into one of the recent catastrophes in Russian coal mines revealed that the newly installed automatic safety equipment, which stopped the work when the level of methane in the mine reached a critical level, had been intentionally reset by miners concerned with shift productivity and daily earnings.

13 There are only a dozen master programs in HRM in Russia; the number of bachelor-level programs is also limited.

14 Foreign companies operating in Russia, for example Arthur Andersen, use their standard procedures for selection, applicable to all countries of operation.

15 As the Russian Labor Code postulates the primacy of law, all clauses in individual labor contracts that prohibit immediate transfer of an employee to the direct competitor of the previous employer are worthless, as they contradict the law on freedom of employment.

16 The male co-author remembers a thrilling story, told to him by one HRM head during an executive seminar: "I ran a routine interview with a person who applied for a position as a truck driver in our company. I was sitting at my desk, filling in the 'job card' and even not looking at the man, in his late 40s, who was sitting just opposite me. When I reached the point 'marital status' and received the answer 'unmarried,' Without thinking I asked another question: 'Why?' The answer I received immediately was: 'I killed her'."

17 Such lists usually include detailed descriptions of case of "work rules violations" or "improper behavior." The later is mostly applicable in service industries. For example, a single guest's complain about a waiter may cost the waiter a monthly premium.

18 If the tariff system is used, the tariff (basic) part usually makes up between 5 and 20 percent of take-home pay.

19 Thus for any failure the boss has every possibility of blaming "irresponsible and incapable" subordinates and remaining personally innocent.

20 The Russian law on joint-stock companies stipulates the separation of these two positions.

21 The male co-author served in 2003–4 as academic director of a corporate-tailored MBA program for one telecommunication company. The general director and all her direct subordinates (14 persons) successfully passed the two-year program.

22 The success of Sochi in the context of hosting the Winter Olympic in 2014 refocuses these construction projects on a small strip on the Black Sea.

23 For example, in Zelenograd, a satellite city of Moscow with 47,000 persons currently employed in industry and services, in September 2007 there were 6,500 unfilled vacancies.

24 Already we may see in Russia the establishment of "communities of learning" within the HRM function. For example, the web portal www.hrm.ru includes the professional monthly journal *Personnel Management* (with a circulation of 40,000), the "Cadre Club" (a think-tank and a platform for conferences), links to trainers, consultants, etc.

25 The only MBA-like program known to the authors that combined international standards with the proper attention to the local specifics was started in Moscow School of Economic and Social Sciences in 2004 and was closed after two semesters due to insufficient demand and promotion.

REFERENCES AND FURTHER READING

Ardichvili, A. (2001). "Leadership Styles and Work-related Values of Managers and Employees of Manufacturing Enterprises in Post-communist Countries", *Human Resource Development Quarterly* (San Francisco), 12, 4: 363–73.

Ardichvili, A., Cardozo, R. N. and Gasparishvili, A. (1998). "Leadership Styles and Management Practices of Russian Entrepreneurs: Implications for Transferability of Western HRD Interventions". *Human Resource Development Quarterly* (San Francisco) (Summer), 9, 2: 145–55.

Bizukov, P. (2005). "Personnel Departments – the Managerial Periphery". In Kabalina, V. (ed.) *Practices of Personnel Management in Russian Enerprises* (Moscow) ISITO: 62–3.

Borisov, V., Clarke, S. and Fairbrother, P. (1994). "Does Trade Unionism Have a Future in Russia?" *Industrial Relations Journal* (Oxford) (March), 25, 1: 15–25.

Clark, A. (2003). "Returns to Human Capital Investment in a Transition Economy: The Case of Russia, 1994–1998". *International Journal of Manpower* (Bradford), 24, 1: 11–31.

Clarke, S. and Kabalina, V. (2000). "The New Private Sector in the Russian Labour Market". *Europe–Asia Studies* (Abingdon) (January), 52, 1: 7–32.

Clarke, S. and Donova, I. (1999). "Internal Mobility and Labour Market Flexibility in Russia". *Europe–Asia Studies* (Abingdon) (March), 51, 2: 213–43.

Clarke, S. (2005). "Post-Socialist Trade Unions: China and Russia". *Industrial Relations Journal* (Oxford) (January), 36, 1: 2.

Clarke, S. (2002). "Market and Institutional Determinants of Wage Differentiation in Russia". *Industrial and Labor Relations Review* (Ithaca) (July), 55, 4: 628.

Clarke, S. (1998). "Hot Coal, Cold Steel: Russian and Ukrainian Workers from the End of the Soviet Union to the Post-Communist Transformations". *Europe–Asia Studies* (Abingdon) (June), 50, 4: 721–4.

Clarke, S. (1998). "Trade Unions and the Non-payment of Wages in Russia". *International Journal of Manpower* (Bradford), 19, 1/2: 68.

Earle, J. S. and Sabirianova, K. Z. (2002). "How Late to Pay? Understanding Wage Arrears in Russia". *Journal of Labor Economics* (Chicago) (July), 20, 3: 661–70.

Fey, C. E., Pavlovskaya, A. and Ningyu Tang (2004). "Does One Shoe Fit Everyone? A Comparison of Human Resource Management in Russia, China, and Finland". *Organizational Dynamics* (New York) (February), 33, 1: 79.

Fey, C. E. and Bjorkman, I. (2001). "The Effect of Human Resource Management Practices on MNC Subsidiary Performance in Russia". *Journal of International Business Studies* (Washington), 32, 1: 59–75.

Fey, C. E., Engstrom, P. and Bjorkman, I. (1999). "Doing business in Russia: Effective Human Resource Management Practices for Foreign Firms in Russia". *Organizational Dynamics* (New York) (Autumn), 28, 2: 69–81.

Gauzner, N. (1994). "The Current Situation in the Russian Labor Market and Employment Policy". *Problems of Economic Transition* (Armonk) (January), 36, 9: 23–38.

Gimpelson, V., Gorbacheva, T. and Lippoldt, D. (1997). "Labor Force Movement". *Problems of Economic Transition* (Armonk) (June), 40, 2: 51–61.

Gurkov, I. (2006). "Strategic Genotype of the Russian Corporation". *The World of Russia*, 3 (in Russian).

Gurkov, I. (2002). "Innovations and Legacies in Russian Human Resource Management Practices: Surveys of 700 Chief Executive Officers". *Post-Communist Economies* (Abingdon) (March), 14, 1: 137.

Gurkov, I. and Maital, S. (2001). "How Will Future Russian CEOs Manage? *Journal for East European Management Studies*, 2.

Gurkov, I. (1999). "Training Needs in Russian Industrial Companies: Assessment by CEOs". *Post-Communist Economies* (Abingdon) (December), 11, 4: 541–9.

Hermann, E. (1994). "Post-Soviet HR Reforms". *Personnel Journal*. (April), 73, 4: 41.

Hutchings, K. and Michailova, S. (2004). "Facilitating Knowledge Sharing in Russian and Chinese Subsidiaries: The Role of Personal Networks and Group Membership". *Journal of Knowledge Management* 8, 2: 84.

Jack, A. (2001). "Labour Shortages Start to Tell in Russia: The Booming Economy is Forcing Companies to Look Abroad to Fill Vacancies, Reports Andrew Jack." *Financial Times* (London), 4 September: 3.

Kabalina, V. (ed.) (2005). *Practices of HRM in Russian Enterprises*. Moscow: ISITO (in Russian).

Kabalina, V. (2003). "Trends and Efficiency in Vocational Training and Retraining the Unemployed". *Problems of Economic Transition* (Armonk) (September), 46, 5: 31.

Kabalina, V. and Nazimova, A. (1993). "Privatization through Labour Conflicts: The Case of Russia". *Economic and Industrial Democracy* (London) (November), 14: 9–28.

Kabalina, V. and Nazimova, A. K. (1992) "Labor Conflict Today: Features and Dynamics". *Russian Social Science Review* (Armonk) (May), 33, 3: 17.

Kamen, K. (2005). "Change and Continuity – the Experience of Trade Unions in the Cultural Sector of the Former Soviet Union". *Employee Relations* (Bradford), 27, 6: 613–23.

Kapelushnikov, R. I. (2001). *The Russian Labor Market: Adaptation without Restructuring*. Moscow: HSE (in Russian).

Klyachko, T. and Krasnova, G. (eds) (2006). *Requirements of Employers to the System of Professional Education*. M.: MAHK Press.

Kuzminov, Y. and Filonovich, R. (2004). "Business Education in Russia". *Problems of Economics*, 1.

Lawrence, P. and Vlachoutsicos, C. (1993). "Joint Ventures in Russia: Put the Locals in charge". *Harvard Business Review* (Boston) (January/February), 71, 1: 44–51.

Linz, S. J. (2003). "Job Satisfaction among Russian Workers". *International Journal of Manpower* (Bradford), 24, 6: 626–54.

Magun, V. and Gimpelson, V. (1993). "Russian Workers" Strategies in Adjusting to Unfavorable Changes in Employment". *Economic and Industrial Democracy* (London) (November), 14: 95–107.

May, R., Young, C. B. and Ledgerwood, D. (1998). "Lessons from Russian Human Resource Management Experience". *European Management Journal* (London) (August), 16, 4: 447–59.

Mironov, V. I. (2006). *The Newest Practices of the Labor Legislation: Encyclopedia of Court Decisions in Statements of NEPS" Expert*. Moscow: Delo Publishers (in Russian).

Nivorozhkin, A. (2005). "An Evaluation of Government-sponsored Vocational Training Programmes for the Unemployed in Urban Russia". *Cambridge Journal of Economics* (Oxford) (November), 29, 6: 1053.

Puffer, S., McCarthy, D. J. and Naumov, A. I. (1997). "Russian Managers" Beliefs About Work: Beyond the Stereotypes". *Journal of World Business* (Greenwich) (Fall), 32, 3: 258–76.

Puffer, S. and Shekshnia, S. V. (1994). "Compensating Local Employees in Post-Communist Russia: In Search of Talent or Just Looking for a Bargain?" *Compensation and Benefits Review* (Saranac Lake) (September–October), 26, 5: 35–43.

Puffer, S. (1993). "A Riddle Wrapped in an Enigma: Demystifying Russian Managerial Motivation". *European Management Journal* (London) (December), 11, 4: 473–80.

Ralston, D. A., Holt, D. H., Terpstra, R. H. and Yu Kai-Cheng. (1997). "The Impact of National Culture and Economic Ideology on Managerial Work Values: A Study of the United States, Russia, Japan, and China". *Journal of International Business Studies* (Washington), 28, 1: 177–207.

Schramm, J. (2004). "Global Challenges". *HRMagazine* (Alexandria) (December), 49, 12: 128.

Shkaratan, O. I. and Galchin, A. V. (1994). "Human Resources, The Military-Industrial Complex and the Possibilities for Technological Innovation in Russia". *International Journal of Technology Management* (Geneva), 9, 3/4: 464–80.

Solntsev, Sergey (2006). "The Labor Market for Executives in Russia". Unpublished Ph.D. dissertation. Lomonossov Moscow State University (in Russian).

Vlachoutsicos, C. A. and Lawrence, P. R. (1996). "How Managerial Learning Can Assist Economic Transformation in Russia". *Organization Studies* (Berlin), 17, 2: 311–25.

Index

Note: Page references in *italics* refer to Figures; those in **bold** refer to Tables